George Herbert Hill was born in I
he spent in France during the Gr
Belfast Telegraph. After the pu
worked successively with the sc
producer Brian Desmond Hurst. In 1939 he returned
Telegraph as a war correspondent and after the war joined the Daily
Mail until his retirement. He died in 1969.

Richard Holmes is Professor of Military and Security Studies at
Cranfield University. He has presented seven BBC documentary
series, and has written nearly twenty books on military subjects,
most recently the bestselling *Tommy: The British Soldier on the
Western Front 1914–18.*

Tauris Parke Paperbacks is an imprint of I.B.Tauris. It is dedicated to publishing books in accessible paperback editions for the serious general reader within a wide range of categories, including biography, history, travel, art and the ancient world. The list includes select, critically acclaimed works of top quality writing by distinguished authors that continue to challenge, to inform and to inspire, These are books that possess those subtle but intrinsic elements that mark them out as something exceptional.

The colophon of Tauris Parke Paperbacks is a representation of the ancient Egyptian ibis, sacred to the god Thoth, who was himself often depicted in the form of this most elegant of birds. Thoth was credited in antiquity as the scribe of the ancient Egyptian gods and as the inventor of writing and was associated with many aspects of wisdom and learning.

RETREAT FROM DEATH

A Soldier on the Somme

GEORGE HERBERT HILL

FOREWORD BY
RICHARD HOLMES

TPP
TAURIS PARKE
PAPERBACKS

Published in 2005 by Tauris Parke Paperbacks
An imprint of I.B.Tauris and Co Ltd
6 Salem Road, London W2 4BU
175 Fifth Avenue, New York NY 10010
www.ibtauris.com

In the United States of America and Canada distributed by
Palgrave Macmillan a division of St. Martin's Press
175 Fifth Avenue, New York NY 10010

First published in 1936 by Hutchinson and Co.
Cover image: British troops near the Western Front during World War I
Hulton-Deutsch Collection/CORBIS

ISBN 1 85043 754 8
EAN 978 1 85043 754 3

A full CIP record for this book is available from the British Library
A full CIP record is available from the Library of Congress

Library of Congress Catalog Card Number: available

Printed and bound in Great Britain by TJ International Ltd, Padstow, Cornwall

CONTENTS

CONTENTS

BOOK II

FOREWORD

The First World War stands like a set of iron gates in British history, shutting off the old world from the new. Of course the Second World War was a much larger world event, involving far more people, servicemen as well as civilians, causing far more casualties, and spreading its devastation across a wider area. But it was the First World War that saw the biggest army in British history—over three and a half million men were serving in November 1918—and this army lost over 700,000 men, compared with the 264,000 killed in the Second World War. One cannot quantify human suffering, and the scale of the First World War ought not to blind us to the fact that some of the fighting in 1939–45 was every bit as dreadful as what went on in 1914–18. Yet many factors—the sheer number of casualties; the attritional nature of the struggle on the Western Front and the fact that a combination of volunteering on an unprecedented scale coupled with the first use of conscription made this a genuinely national army—all combined to give the First World War its own distinctive place in British history.

Most of us come to the war through literature before we encounter it as history. We will perhaps have studied war poetry at school, read the novels of Pat Barker and Sebastian Faulks, or maybe seen the extraordinarily powerful 1930 film of Erich Maria Remarque's *All Quiet on the Western Front*. Several historians have suggested that this process has obscured the 'real' historical war.

Some of the war's survivors also felt that the war they knew was being fictionalised. Charles Carrington, a decorated veteran who had fought on the Somme and at Passchendaele, complained that as the memory of the 'real' war receded, so: "dirt about the war was in demand... Every battle a defeat, every officer a nincompoop, every soldier a coward." Cyril Falls, another veteran, lamented literature in which: "The soldier is represented as a depressed and mournful spectre wandering about until death brought his miseries to an end."

There is no doubt that many of the men who served in the war did indeed remember it in terms of unrelieved horror and misery, and that for them the bitterness which characterised so much of the literature of the 1930s was wholly authentic. But, equally, it is evident that this was not a universal view. What soldiers wrote during the war, when they were linked by a sense of common purpose and bound together by the bonds of mateship, was often a good deal less gloomy. One twice-wounded infantry officer wrote that: "One of the curious things about a nation at war—and one of the tragedies too—is that life is intensified. There is much happiness in wartime, much that is admirable, much that is just jolly..." For so many combatants, the real bitterness came after 11 November 1918, not before it. They had 'done their bit' to the best of their abilities, and many would have agreed with C. E. Montague, who volunteered, over-age, for the infantry, that:

> The war had to be won: that was flat. It was like putting out houses on fire, or not letting children be killed; it did not even need to be proved; that we had got to win was now the one quite certain thing left in a world of shaken certainties.

But too many of them went home to unemployment, not to the jobs they felt their endurance had earned them, and in the 1930s far too many of them looked back on the war through the prism of the Depression. It was difficult for them to see that the struggle had had any point at all, and the myriad of irritations, injustices and uncertainties that had formed part of their time in the army now had no emotional counterweight: so the gloomiest views of the war emerged from the late 1920s onwards.

George Herbert Hill's *Retreat from Death* is a classic of its genre. First published in 1936, it emerged at a time when the tide of anti-war literature of the sort described by Charles Carrington was running very strongly indeed. It is a part-fictionalised account of Hill's service in the infantry, and concentrates heavily on his experiences in First Royal Irish Rifles, under the flail of the great German offensive that rolled out astride the Somme on 21 March 1918. Hill was a clerk in a Belfast office, "a small firm, in a small street", who volunteered for the army in July 1915 after two "flashily-dressed girls with rouged cheeks" presented him with a white feather. He spent most of the war in Ireland, where he was involved in the suppression of the Easter Rising, though the chapter dealing with this was so sharply critical of British conduct that it was omitted from the book.

It was not until early 1918, by then an acting corporal, that he was sent to France, travelling from Southampton to Le Havre, a short voyage on which "my comrades were transformed into drunken oafs and made wet, swinish noises." After a brief stay at Etaples he was posted 'up the line', and one of his comrades was not pleased that they were destined for a Regular battalion: "a lot of bloody toughs and jailbirds...The Regulars are all the same. And the officers are duds." Hill himself found it "more soldierly and romantic" to belong to the First Battalion of his regiment than a wartime-raised battalion, but the pleasure did not last.

His initiation into trench warfare was harsh: a German raid left him the sole survivor of his section, and a fellow NCO who lied to the subsequent enquiry was recommended for a decoration. A German killed in the attack lay in No Man's Land, blackening visage snarling in defiance: Hill thought that he still looked "virile and dangerous". He found his second stripe a burden, because he knew far less than the seasoned trench-fighters, and out there a man earned his rank "by right of conquest, as it were," and so he reverted to the rank of lance-corporal and joined his battalion's signallers.

The shocking bombardment that accompanied the German offensive on 21 March 1918 left him "alone in a world gone mad". He admired the "cynical calm" of a trench-mortar crew who stood fast as the wreckage of defeat swirled past them, and then found himself carrying back some survivors of his battalion. "Ostensibly we belonged to a battalion, a brigade, a division," he wrote. "In retreating an infantry unit was a company and the rest abstractions." Hill sketches out a series of vignettes: an officer threatening a staff-colonel with his revolver, a tough captain going mad, and a contemptuously cursed general giving a pep talk. Once the front had stabilised he visited an estaminet where a girl gave herself to him 'pour l'amour', but this was a scant ray of sunshine in a gloomy world, and he soon lost his remaining stripe, after a manifestly unfair 'trial' for inattention to duty.

The army offered him nothing that he wanted. He thought that it was "run on the caste system," and he admired the Australians and Canadians who were not ground down by "a cast-iron discipline that killed initiative." His own comrades were, he thought, "slave men, without sufficient courage to break the bonds." Gassed in the summer of 1918, he spent some time in hospital and then at a convalescent camp before being posted to a holding unit deep in the rear: he was there when the Armistice was signed. "The false comradeship of war would be a thing of the past," he wrote, "to be forgotten as soon as possible—to be ashamed of, even." On Armistice night he reflected on what he had seen, and concluded: "I had never fired a shot. I had never wanted to fire a shot. I had never been a soldier."

Hill's service record shows that he was discharged from the army in July 1919, on the grounds that his gas injuries left him unfit for further service. He got a job as a reporter on the *Belfast Telegraph,* and then, after the publication of his book, worked as a scriptwriter for Alexander Korda and the British producer Brian Desmond Hurst. He returned to the *Belfast Telegraph* as a war correspondent in 1939, and joined the *Daily Mail* after the war, working as a news journalist and then as assistant to the news editor. He was a committed trade unionist and 'father of the chapel' who retired in 1963 and died five years later.

It is impossible to be sure how much of Hill's account accurately portrayed what happened at the time, and how much reflected the passage of nearly twenty years in which anti-war opinion had hardened and he had honed his considerable skills as a writer. There are sufficient minor factual slips to suggest that at least part of the work was emotion inaccurately recollected in tranquility. For instance, German officers generally carried automatic pistols rather than the revolvers he describes; staff officers' red tabs actually covered the whole of the front collar and were anything but 'little', and twice a day infantry carried out an alert procedure called stand to, not, as he has it, stand on. It is hard to find any cliché of the genre not repeated here, from the girls with their white feathers at the start of the book to the unhelpful military policemen at its close. This is not to say that

Hill's tale is largely a fabrication, or that the incidents recounted in it could not have happened. But it comes swinging in hard from one flank of the debate, which is precisely what its author intended. It is concerned neither with balance nor objectivity. It is one man's view of a life-changing experience, and no reader who seeks to understand the war in its myriad faces can afford to ignore it.

Richard Holmes

BOOK I

RETREAT FROM DEATH

THE START

IT happened like this.

My brother, who was nearly two years older, had joined up, and I left school to take over his job as a junior clerk. Everything was steadily getting dearer and scarcer, so that the loss of his small pay would have been severely felt at home. His employers, after some hanging back, agreed to give me a trial, and a new suit of clothes, with long trousers, was hastily got for me so that they would not think me too young and offer only office boy's wages. The job was mainly writing out invoices from an order-book (which my brother had left about six months in arrears), and the idea was that I should carry on until he came back from the war and then hand the job back to him.

It was a small firm, in a small street, but it was a good business street and they did a steady trade in spite of the drab shop window in front, with its fly-specked pyramids of once-garish tins and odds and ends of merchandise. With the exception of an old doddering book-keeper with shaky, bloodless hands in an office by himself upstairs I was the only clerk, with a desk in a poky office at the back of the shop.

The two brothers who managed the business, and apparently owned it, although their name was different to the style of the firm, were keen, active men. The younger sported a pointed black beard—an odd thing in our town of clean-shaven men. They were both married. They were very religious. They kept household account-books, and compared notes regularly.

The first week I was there, when Saturday came, and the workmen were all paid, Mr. Samuel, the younger brother, selected a clean £1 note from the safe. He folded it carefully, in front of me, before putting it away in his purse.

" This is for my collection at church to-morrow morning," he said softly ; " Mr. Silas and I make a habit of giving a pound note each as a thanks-offering to God every week. It used to be a golden sovereign. But this terrible war . . ."

I lowered my eyes and said nothing. My brother had received 12s. a week and after some persuasion they had agreed to give me 9s., making it clear that they were actuated by patriotism, though I flattered myself I could write invoices as well as he could. The black, smooth-flowing ink and the glazed invoice forms, with their imposing printed top, and red ruled lines, fascinated me as I filled in the name and address of the customer and the details of his purchases—shellac, timber, hardware, oils, bevelled glass. Everything I wrote seemed beautiful and perfect until one day Mr. Silas told me gruffly to make my g's and y's in the ordinary way with a loop instead of with the corkscrew I had invented.

" It's an old-fashioned house, ours," he said.

The business, for all its air of quiet prosperity, seemed at first to fluctuate greatly. Customers would come in from the country and be met with stories of ever-rising prices by one of the brothers, or both if the customer was an important one, and the utter impossibility of getting goods of the quality they had been used to. Mr. Silas always spoke bluntly as one man to another. Mr. Samuel rolled his eyes and his black beard jerked excitedly as he explained the disastrous position the war had placed them in. Sometimes they shook their heads despondently, and spoke of the day when they would be compelled to give up the struggle and

close down altogether. Eventually the impressed customer—
a retailer—would take what was offered, after beating down
the price until he was satisfied he had got the better of the
two good men, and depart amid a doleful shaking of heads
and hands, well primed with a tale for his own humble
customers should they in turn complain of high prices and
second-rate goods.

At the end of the day when the shop was closed, and the
brothers were busily engaged balancing the cash and discussing the day's doings, they appeared quite cheerful and
optimistic about the future. The bearded one would crack
little harmless jokes, his eyes glistening as the silver and
pennies formed neat columns on the desk in front of him,
and the notes rustled through his fingers. Sometimes, when
things had gone especially well, the stern face of the elder
would relax too. His harsh voice, trying vainly to sound
playful, creaked and broke like an old machine that had
long been disused.

The weeks, and then the months, followed each other
monotonously. When my brother came home on leave I
listened eagerly to his tales of camp life. Surreptitiously I
tried on his khaki tunic. How dull the office and the brothers
were.

Nearly every day when I returned from my dinner Mr.
Samuel was deep in a whispered conversation over the
phone. A glass partition, raised a couple of feet above the
desk, divided the office into two tiny compartments, and
for a long time I took no particular notice, but once, coming
in a little earlier than usual, I saw him go over to the phone,
turn the handle and start the usual low-voiced conversation
without asking for a number.

The talk would go on for about half an hour, and often
Mr. Samuel's black eyes would glisten, as if he were counting
the cash, and little suggestive pauses were followed by
throaty chuckles. When Mr. Silas, returning from lunch,

raised the counter flap, or his gruff voice bidding a customer in the shop good-day was heard, the receiver was replaced, and when he entered the office Mr. Samuel was writing industriously. If it became necessary for Mr. Samuel to ring up a customer a few minutes later he would ask the operator for the number in a curt, businesslike voice.

As time went on he ignored me, or took me tacitly into his confidence. His voice sounded openly amorous as he talked into the mouthpiece, and he wetted his lips with a pink tongue, his long legs crossing and uncrossing jerkily as if independent of the rest of his body, hunched over the telephone.

Sometimes he spoke a kind of lisping baby talk, which sounded strange coming from a man with a beard, and the conversation on his part ended with a muttered " To-night, then."

With this exception everything connected with the business was done decorously. Bills were met punctually on the date they fell due. Defaulting debtors were made bankrupt. The last penny that the concern could be made to yield was squeezed into the brothers' pockets.

Even the ragged, boozy looking workmen tried to assume a respectable air when they came shuffling up to the office on Saturdays, and waited in a group until their names were called by Mr. Samuel, and Mr. Silas handed over their wages, both blandly ignoring the fact that the men's sodden faces showed only too clearly which way most of the money went. Possibly the drink made them more easily satisfied with their lot, or more easily cowed.

A slow aversion to religious business men grew up inside me. I determined to get a substantial rise or look round for another place, preferably one with a less godly atmosphere. One where the boss would give me a little more on Saturdays and put a little less in the plate on Sundays.

Although a suit with long trousers had been bought for

me, I had continued to wear my school cap with the school initials on the front. One day, working on the same principle as the long trousers, I bought a cheap soft hat. I was tall for my age, about five feet nine, with fairly good shoulders but thin, with long, skinny legs, and small-boned wrists.

Looking at myself in the glass with my new hat on I thought that at a pinch I could pass for eighteen or nineteen. My hopes ran high. But I was destined never to ask for an increase of pay.

I was walking along the main street of the town that evening, very self-conscious of my new purchase, which everybody appeared to stare at rudely, as if aware it was my very first hat, and why I had bought it, when the thing happened. I had just passed two flashily-dressed girls with rouged cheeks and an impudent, questing air—quite imposing-looking to my unsophisticated eyes—when I heard one of them calling out behind me. I paid no attention, but her voice came louder:

" Slacker."

" Big coward."

" Here's a white feather."

Looking round to see who the offender might be—glad that the passers-by had something to stare at besides my new hat—I found the girls' eyes fixed on me. Some people, men and women, also attracted by the shouts, stopped to see the fun, smiling maliciously. I looked about and then over my shoulder to see where the slacker was. One of the girls settled the matter by advancing towards me purposefully, a little white feather in her outstretched hand. I stood stupidly, my head in a whirl, until she was barely a yard away. I saw her contemptuous eyes fixed on the lapel of my jacket. Then scarlet with shame, and with the titters of the knot of onlookers in my ears, I turned and hurried away, followed by the scornful laughter and taunts of the girls.

That night I didn't sleep well. The scene on the street

kept forcing its way into my memory. I writhed in the warm bed.

In the morning I made some excuse to Mr. Silas and got permission to go out for half an hour. The recruiting office was barely ten minutes' walk away. I went towards it doggedly. On the way I sucked in great mouthfuls of air in a last-minute attempt to increase my chest measurement.

A few loafers hung about the big red-brick building, yawning. A fat recruiting-sergeant with a ribbon in his cap teetered against the wall. The first careless rapture of the war had disappeared. Business was slack. The front of the building was plastered with gaudy posters bearing familiar slogans, " Remember Belgium," " Your King and Country Need You," and, below an Army cap, the advice " If the cap fits you put it on." The loungers, however, had apparently forgotten all about Belgium, or else its plight left them cold. None of them showed any inclination to rush to the aid of either King or Country. They seemed well content, too, with their own dirty headgear.

My ardour somewhat cooled, I pushed open a swing-door and went hesitatingly up to a desk, at which sat a red-faced Sergeant with a pile of buff forms before him. He was very proud and military-looking.

" Well, my lad. Want to do your bit ? " he said jovially, looking up.

Not knowing just how to explain the distinction between wanting to get into a uniform and wanting to do my bit, I coughed, and didn't answer.

" Age ? "

" Nineteen."

" That's the proper spirit," said the Sergeant heartily, but with sly, appraising stare.

" And what regiment do you want to join ? "

" The lancers, sir—the cavalry, y'know," I blurted out. " I—I think I would like them."

The Sergeant vetoed this suggestion immediately.

" Closed, my lad. Closed for recruiting altogether. Couldn't take a bleeding jockey even, let alone a smart young fellow like you. But any other regiment——"

" Well, what about the Army Service Corps. They would do ? "

" That's not a regiment," retorted the Sergeant with a grimace. " Besides there hasn't been a vacancy in that bleeding crowd since 1914, and not likely to be either, the way things are shaping, unless a few of them get kicked by the mules." Then, with a change of voice, and sticking out his chest : " But what about the infantry ? What's the matter with them, my lad ? The finest branch of the service. Heh ? "

I was silent, not knowing exactly what was the matter with the infantry, but with a suspicion there was something. A fond dream of natty riding-trousers, chesty bandolier and jingling spurs faded into thin air. Cavalry looked more like real soldiers to my mind than the infantry. They walked with a swing, and always seemed to take more pride in their appearance than their humbler brothers.

The Sergeant followed up his advantage by mentioning the names of the local regiments. He launched into a ready patter of their fame and history. There was something faintly ominous about the sound of those sonorous names. I felt a little sinking sensation. The Sergeant's bold eyes were on me, waiting impatiently. I had gone too far to retire. At random I selected a regiment. The Sergeant smiled and rubbed his hands.

He had got another mug.

In a surprisingly short time I found myself out on the street again, my head in a whirl. The loafers still hung about, still in the same attitudes. I stared at them for a moment. It seemed odd that they should act as if nothing had happened. And then a nervous exultation seized me as I felt the King's shilling in my pocket, and thought of the medical examination—the doctor who had taken no notice of my thin legs in his anxiety to sound my chest and heart and test my eyes. The mumbled rigmarole oath, hand upraised.

Hurrying back to the office I came on Mr. Samuel and told him what I had done. He stared at me unbelievingly at first, and then was annoyed.

" You are putting the firm to a lot of trouble, you know," he said peevishly. " However, it's done now and can't be helped, but you are very foolish."

Mr. Silas heard the news frowningly.

" You shouldn't have been accepted. You are far too young," he said.

" Oh, I just said nineteen, and they believed it straight away," I said, simply enough.

" But that was an untruth," put in Mr. Samuel. " You know the good Book says you should never tell or act a lie under any circumstances."

" Oh, well——" I said lamely, and stopped, taken aback by this statement, and the cold reception where I had expected smiles and compliments.

There were more complaints when they heard I had to go to camp next day, but I didn't care, and said it would be necessary for me to leave at dinner-time to get my things together.

" Might as well have a half-holiday out of them as not," I thought. Mr. Silas carefully computed what was due to me up to dinner-time and I departed, glad to be rid of them at any price. I had expected to get a full week's pay.

At home the news was greeted more as a joke than anything else. My father was proud that I had been passed fit by the doctor. Mother, proud too, laughed resignedly. The war would be over and done with, she said, by the time I was old enough to go to France.

Next day I set off for a reserve battalion about a dozen miles away.

THE CAMP

EVERYTHING was strange about the camp, but the strangest part was that I was treated exactly like a man. I received the same rations as big, broad-shouldered countrymen, and the same number of blankets, and the same kit, including a razor, which I didn't yet need but nevertheless treasured. I even got the same pay, but as it was more like a boy's—three and sixpence—that wasn't quite so odd. Still, I had never before had so much pocket money, and felt very rich for a week or two. I couldn't eat all my rations. The tea, served up in bowls, was too strong, and the bread was cut too thick. The huge dixies of stew and meat, and the sight of men ladling it out roughly, compared oddly with our frugal meals at home and mother's housewifely care. But the days out drilling and doubling about soon broke me in. The camp was in a wooded demesne, and I enjoyed myself. It was summer-time and we slept in bell-tents. The office and its smug owners seemed very drab and far away, and soon I forgot them completely. Physical jerks and the awkward squad, roll calls, the formula of parading, learning to salute, cleaning buttons.

The instructor was a stocky, red-nosed Sergeant who, on acquaintance, turned out to be decent enough. At first he cursed, mocked and threatened, but later on, when he had us whipped into some kind of shape, he would take us off into a corner and give us lectures, if the day was hot, and try half-heartedly to instil into us a proper appreciation of our luck in being privileged to serve in such a regiment as ours. In return the squad clubbed up and presented him before falling out with three or four shillings as a reward for not being too hard on them.

The summer passed quickly. We were moved into newly-erected huts. These were warm and comfortable, but I didn't like them so well. There wasn't the same carefree gipsyness about them. We had to be tidier and more bound by rules and regulations. The Sergeant in charge of our hut was a stranger. He had the filthiest tongue I ever heard of in a man, and was constitutionally incapable, even in friendly conversation, of speaking without coming out with fearful oaths. One word, starting with an f, did duty as noun, adjective, verb and adverb, as occasion arose. He was a great burly man with many ribbons on his chest, red-faced, black-haired and with a neck that bulged over the collar of his tunic. His voice, from long years of roaring on barrack squares, was husky, and he was reputed to be a heavy drinker. At first I was terrified of him. Whether under his influence or not, I could not say, but the language of the rest of the men in the hut got rapidly worse, with the result that the Sergeant's language seemed to become less pronounced as time went on. We soon found out, too, that he was a kindly man, who only exercised his authority when necessary, and sometimes not then.

He had a weakness for mushrooms. When he took us out in the morning for a run round before breakfast he sent us in among the trees to look for his favourite delicacy, and himself acted as look-out in case the C.S.M. or an officer should take it into his head to come along. Nearly every morning he had the full of his big bandana handkerchief to feast on for breakfast, and was grateful accordingly.

The second-in-command of the hut was a Lance-Corporal. He was at once admired and detested by us recruits, especially the younger ones like myself. He was not a bully in the ordinary sense of the word. He would have been highly indignant if anyone had called him one. His fetish was physical strength. His favourite pastime was to match himself with one or other of us, or several at a time, in boxing, wrestling or rough-and-tumble, at all of which he was adept.

When he couldn't get anyone to join him voluntarily he would select one of the young fellows—the married men objected—and after a wild chase over the bed-boards and round the stove catch his victim and subject him to a process known as " sighting."

Shy at the best of times, when this game was afoot I always sat quiet, hoping to escape his attention, and dreading the ordeal. It was no use attempting to slip out. One or two had tried to do that and had been seized on immediately by the Corporal as easy marks.

My turn came one wet afternoon. Two or three fellows had struggled gamely and been overcome. The Corporal, flushed with excitement and looking for fresh victims, caught sight of me as I shrank back in a corner.

" Hey, you. It's your turn," he shouted, and the chase was on.

Like a hare with the hounds in full cry I dashed madly round the hut. Time after time eager hands stretched out. I eluded them miraculously. Others joined in, and in a moment the hut was in an uproar. The blood pounded in my ears as I darted and twisted, filled with blind, unreasoning terror of what was before me, until, tripping over a bed-board, I fell headlong. Many hands grasped me, but I struggled on, biting and kicking like a maniac. The Corporal's sweaty, triumphant face appeared above me, filled with the ardour of the chase. Reaching up, I clawed at his eyes. He drew back just in time. The grin vanished.

" Hold the bastard down, or I'll break his jaw."

The others obeyed, holding my arms and legs tightly. I was helpless now, but still strove vainly to break free, almost crying with rage and despair. Only my voice was left.

" All right, all right, I give in. But as sure as God I'll go

straight to the Sergeant-Major and report you. You'll be
stripped for this."

There was a pause. The Corporal stopped his groping,
sensing for once that he had gone too far—suddenly fearful
for the stripe he was so proud of. Curiously enough, there
appeared to be no doubt in his mind but that I would do as
I had said.

"Let him go, or he'll go off into a fit or something,"
he said lamely and stood up, knocking the dust off his
clothes.

The others obeyed unwillingly. Getting shakily to my feet
I went out of the hut. It was still raining. After wandering
about the camp for a while I went into the lavatory. To
my excited imagination it seemed that as a result of my
resistance I would be looked on as queer, and become
the butt of the hut. The Corporal would have his knife in
me, and I would lead a dog's life. I quailed at the prospect.
I felt a sudden, strong desire for a life with more privacy to it.

But I needn't have worried. That particular practice
stopped, and the Corporal was transferred to the Machine-
Gun Corps shortly afterwards. The rest seemed relieved at
getting a bit of peace from his restless energy.

There was really some excuse for the Corporal's love of
muscular display and feats of strength. He was as strong
as any two men in the hut, and had a magnificent body. His
skin was white and fine, and sleek-swelling muscles rippled
when he moved.

At night in the hut, before "Lights out," he would
perform all sorts of acrobatics and go through exercises.
Afterwards he would rub himself down with a rough
towel until his body glowed. Sometimes, standing naked,
he would ask us to admire his body.

On Friday afternoons we paraded for pay and afterwards
played "banker."

Each hut had its own " school," and the cards were nearly always marked, sometimes twice over. When shuffled and cut the banker laid the pack face downwards on the table, dividing it into as many hands as there were players, but always taking care to overlap the bottom card in each hand as much as possible. When all bets were laid and covered the hand left to the banker was turned up and its value ruled the board. From being the simplest game for quick gambling it thus became a game of skill, the one trying as best he could to cover the bottom card in each hand, and the rest trying to spot its value, and at the same time give the impression that their choice was guided purely by luck. The players watched each other like hawks, and disputes were frequent.

Several times I tried my luck, but I soon discovered that I was a bad gambler, and wisely stopped. A sentence in a book I had read not long before served to educate me—" It takes a good gambler to lose and a better one to win," or something to that effect it had run. I hadn't understood the meaning behind it when I came across it first.

When I won I became excited, reckless and jubilant, and forgot that the others had lost. When I lost I sat raging at my stupidity and looking dismally to a long week without money to buy cigarettes or tea and cakes in the dry canteen. I had got over my objection to Army food. The difficulty now was how to get enough of it. At home on week-end leave the tea tasted watery and the food insipid.

The camp held for me a far greater attraction than cards. Over in the Y.M.C.A. hut was a well-stocked little library, and I read omnivorously. Before joining up I had been bitten with the desire to learn foreign languages, and had taught myself, with the aid of text-books out of the town's public library, to read French and Spanish, with frequent recourse to the dictionary and intuition. I had brought a paper-backed book in Spanish, bought in a second-hand bookstall, from home and read it too. It was *Gil Blas*, and

I loved and understood most of it—the robbers' cave, Dr. Sangrado, Escipion, and all the funny people.

The Y.M. man got for me a book by Anatole France, which I loved, too, but didn't understand at all. Long afterwards it struck me that he hadn't understood it either, or he wouldn't have lent it to me.

At the beginning of November the recruits fired their musketry course, which occupied an exciting two or three days. It was hardly over when rumours of a big draft being wanted for France began to circulate in the camp. One day I woke up to find the rumour was true. My name was down for it.

We paraded—the draft—a couple of hundred strong, and learned we were bound for the pioneer battalion of the Division, for which our lot was a feeder. Also, that our leave was cancelled and we would depart in three days. It was all very startling and earnest after our easy life, and the men groused incessantly at not getting leave. But they got no satisfaction. The draft was needed in a hurry, it appeared. When, on inquiry, I discovered that a pioneer battalion was another name for a navvy battalion, whose job it was to dig trenches, make roads and latrines, and generally do the dirty work, any glamour there was in going out to France faded as far as I was concerned. I had become stronger with the healthy life of the camp, but I was no navvy.

Thinking the matter over, I sat down and composed a colourless letter home, saying baldly that I was going to France in three days and would get no leave as we were needed urgently. For a PS. I put : " They say we're going out to a navvy battalion," knowing that " pioneer " would be as Greek to them as it had been to me.

The next few days were spent in parading here and there, and at all hours of the day, getting new uniforms, boots and underclothing, falling in for this and that, and falling out again without getting anything but abuse for not having it already. It was " The draft. The draft. Fall in the draft " all day long.

The fateful morning dawned, cold and wet, without any word from home. I resigned myself to going. We had hardly got our breakfast when we fell in for a kind of leave-taking inspection down at the battalion orderly room. It was the first draft to leave since the battalion was formed, and therefore an event. The fat old militia Colonel was to make a speech. He had recently returned from a tour of the trenches, and had delivered a lecture to the men entitled " How I shot half a German," a glowing account of how he and a sniper had fired simultaneously at a German and killed him between them. Like the rest of the recruits, I had swallowed it all, open-mouthed, filled with admiration for the Colonel's bravery and sang-froid, vaguely comforted at the idea of shooting Germans being so easy. The lecture had been quite a humorous affair.

After the lecture was over I heard two returned B.E.F. men, now convalescent, discussing the Colonel—two or three hundred of them had arrived lately in the camp, and were housed in a separate wing—morose fellows who kept to themselves and looked with veiled contempt on the rest of us who had not been to France.

" It's all bunkum," said one disgustedly. " Lord God, ain't he a hell of a liar ? "

The other profanely agreed. " He'll get a medal for it too, wait to y'see," he prophesied gloomily.

Before the Colonel made his appearance the second-in-command came round the ranks of the draft. He was the sergeant-major-promoted type of officer usually found in training battalions—full to the neck with pride and exuding discipline at every pore. He was big-bellied, and had a dewlap neck like an old washerwoman, and spiky, greying hair. Everybody trembled before his fierceness and irascibility. Followed by two or three respectful officers he strutted along the double line of men, stopping here and there to damn a soldier's eyes for not looking to his front, or his soul for not having his buttons properly cleaned.

When he came to the rear rank where I was, he looked at me and was about to pass on when one of the attendant officers reached forward and whispered something. It was my company officer, an old schoolmaster, who went under the name of " Rubbermouth " on account of the way his lips kept twitching to one side, as if sucking at a hollow tooth.

The Major stopped, and stared me up and down.

" What's the matter now," I thought, wondering which button I had forgotten.

" What's your name ? " he demanded harshly, and peered short-sightedly at a limp telegraph form between his fingers.

" Yes. I think you are the fellow," and then, encouragingly, " Well, my man, and what age are you ? "

There was a suggestive emphasis about the " my man " which I did not fail to notice.

I cleared my throat, and stammered irresolutely. Then the dreary prospect of digging endless lines of trenches and messing about latrines appeared before my mind's eye, startlingly close. I plucked up courage.

" Seventeen this month, sir."

There was a shocked silence. The Major stared at me for a long moment as if his ears had deceived him. Purpling with anger, he stepped back a pace.

" Seventeen this month ! " he repeated loudly and sneeringly. " Are you quite certain it's not thirteen or fourteen ? "

His escort looked at me with cold, hostile eyes. The men on either side sniggered and craned their necks, sensing that for once no reprimand would be forthcoming for their breach of discipline.

" Fall out. Get to blazes out of this back to your company," shouted the Major.

I obeyed woodenly, burning inwardly with shame, and with hanging head went back to the huts and dumped my equipment on my bed-boards.

Half an hour later the draft departed. The battalion band played stirring music at its head. The men in the ranks exchanged jokes and handshakes with their cheering comrades lined along the camp road to see them off.

From the back of the crowd I looked on, thrilled by the music, but ready to duck if any of the draft who had been standing near when I was dismissed should recognise me and call out. The draft passed out of sight. Downcast and sad I returned to the lonely hut, pursued by the lessening, poignant strains of " Tipperary." How bright and cheerful they had all seemed.

By and by I recovered. Already the draft was a thing of the past. There was a half-read book in my kitbag. It struck me, too, that for all their contemptuous laughter the men on either side had looked envious as I left the ranks.

Life went on as usual until Christmas, when we got eight days' leave. At home I amused myself trying on " civvy " clothes, but they were too small for me, and I had to go about in my uniform.

My father said nothing when I pulled out a packet of cigarettes and smoked, but for all that I was more at ease in the camp. Home life was cramped and strange, in spite of its quiet charm. The rooms were very small compared with the big bare hut. I had to keep a guard on my tongue in case I should come out with soldier-talk. House furniture looked cluttery compared with rude forms and trestle-tables, cups and saucers instead of bowls.

Mother had a habit, too, of treating me as a schoolboy, or as if I had never left home, which nonplussed me. In the camp instructors ranted and cursed, but as soon as their back was turned we could curse them to our heart's content.

The leave was soon over, and I was no sooner back than a notice appeared in battalion orders that men were wanted to form a signal section. " Must be intelligent and able to read and write," it said. My intelligence, such as it was, had grown weary of the eternal unchanging details of squad drill. The fact that applicants had to have some rudiments of education was an inducement in itself. Accordingly I presented myself to the Company Sergeant-Major at the first opportunity and asked permission to enrol. He took my name unwillingly, as if he disliked the idea of anyone passing out of his control.

" It's all a lot of damned silly nonsense, this signal stunt," he grumbled.

He was a curious-looking man, the C.S.M. He had small, muddy-brown eyes set in a yellowish-brown face. A long, wispy black moustache hung down on either side of his mouth, like a stage Chinaman's. He chewed tobacco continually, and his decayed teeth were the same colour as his complexion. He had been a sailor before being a soldier, it was said, and strange rumours were current about him and his partiality for certain young men.

When I understood I looked at the Sergeant-Major in much the same way that I would have looked at some strange beast of the jungle. He seemed all the more strange for being in human shape.

A couple of days later I became an embryo signaller, and departed for another hut. The work, for me, was intensely interesting. I took to it like a duck to water. Learning the Morse Code was the hardest part of it, but I worked overtime at it and made such rapid progress that I was rewarded by being promoted Lance-Corporal. It was fun adapting the Morse to flags, flappers, phones, buzzers, electric signal-lamps, heliographs, learning semaphore, and

setting up practice stations in the pleasant woods and fields
The signal officer was a nice young fellow, fair-haired and
blue-eyed. He was in love with his job. He often bought
equipment out of his own pocket rather than wait for the
slow process of Ordnance issues. He acted more like an
enthusiastic scoutmaster than an Army officer. Soon after
getting my stripe he sent me off on a course, and I became
an instructor. They were all youngsters in the squad, having
mostly been weeded out of the companies because of their
age, and we were a happy family. I acted as assistant to the
elderly, malarial Signal Sergeant in teaching them, and,
rather to my surprise, got on all right. So long as they didn't
let me down when the officer was about I was satisfied.

When I got promoted to full Corporal it was just the same.
I was of the type of N.C.O. whom the privates persisted in
calling by their christian name.

Then the inevitable changes came. In the summer the
young officer was packed off to France, and the section was
transferred to a newly-formed Army Signal School three or
four miles away, where signal squads from seven or eight
reserve battalions in the area were to be trained together.
Luckily for me, our section, being the nearest, was the first
to arrive at the school, and I was made orderly room clerk.
It was a soft job with nothing much to do after the initial
month's rush of getting the school going smoothly. In the
mornings a return of strength—men were soon constantly
coming and going—had to be made out from the reports
of the officers in charge of the various sections, along with
indents for equipment, and so on. In the afternoons the
School Commandant, a handsome, Regular Army Captain,
with a penchant for Scotch whisky, went off with his Adjutant to the parade-ground, and I was left in charge, with little
to do but read such literature as I could lay hands on,
including my beloved French and Spanish.

We shared the camp with another battalion, at whose mess

the signal officers dined, leading, the rumour went, to some friction. There was an empty officers' block in our half of the camp, and by and by our officers used it as a kind of annexe, or club, only visiting the battalion mess for meals.

Just after Christmas I took up my quarters in it with a lance-jack, who was given the job of wine waiter and general factotum. Being an Old Contemptible he knew when he was on a good thing, and soon initiated me. He developed a system of giving the officers bad measure in the whisky and, being a confirmed beer drinker himself, exchanged the surplus thus gained with the school butcher and baker, who drank anything they could lay their hands on, for steak and bread. The result was that every night we had such gargantuan feeds of fried steak and dipped bread that as a rule we were unable to take any breakfast.

THE GIRL

THERE was a small factory town a couple of miles away from the camp. The cobbled streets were narrow and dirty and lined with small, grimy houses. Here and there the slender factory chimneys reached into the sky, belching black smoke, which hung like a pall over the town, shutting out the sunlight. It was a drab, slumlike place, its only redeeming feature for me being a small picture house. For others it must have had other attractions, because in school orders there would appear from time to time a solemn warning to the effect that such and such a house was out of bounds to the troops. It was not uncommon either for a girl from the town to appear at the camp with a complaint. The unfortunate soldier concerned was generally forced or cajoled into premature wedlock.

" It's easy money for them," the soldiers said. " They get the separation allowance, and if anything happens to you they get a pension for life. They can't lose anything but their modesty."

One night at the pictures someone stumbled over my feet in the darkness and sat down in a vacant seat beside me. Towards the end of the picture—it was the " Birth of a Nation," with panic-stricken negroes running wild and vengeful white-robed horsemen in pursuit—I noticed it was a girl sitting beside me. Every little while she glanced round provocatively. Just before the picture came to an end she rose and went out, and partly out of sudden impulse and partly to avoid standing at attention while the pianist hacked out " God Save The King," I followed her out on to the street. It was later than usual owing to the length of the picture, and the girl started off at a brisk pace in the moonlight. I was about to give up my half-formed intention of stopping her—there had been something fetching about her—when she looked back over her shoulder invitingly. Encouraged, I followed quickly and caught up on her just as she turned the corner of a gloomy street.

" Good night," I began tentatively.

" Good night," she echoed, looking up with a surprised air.

" Are you just getting home ? " I asked stupidly.

She made no reply and edged a little away, and I went on blunderingly, more to break the silence than to get information.

" How did you like the picture ? Wasn't it good ? "

She agreed without any show of interest that it had been " All right." I searched frantically for something to say, but without success.

" Where's your girl to-night ? " she asked pertly, taking charge of the conversation.

I didn't answer, but took in her poor dress and white cheeks. It struck me that she was a mere kid and I drew back disappointed. She seemed to divine my thoughts and I caught a flash of stormy black eyes, set in a pale oval face, and a small mouth, half parted, red and enticing.

" Haven't got such a thing ; wish I had," I answered eagerly and truthfully, suddenly aware that the last part of the answer was as true as the first. She was very young, but there was a curious challenging air about her as if she knew herself secretly to be a woman and wished to be taken at her own valuation. Some obscure instinct in me thrilled in response. I lost my gaucherie in a voluble effort to convince her, before she should run off home, leaving me standing like a fool.

" Honest to goodness, I've never been out with a girl before, never, and that's the truth," I finished up.

The girl laughed, showing her even white teeth. The ice

was broken, as probably she had intended it to be with her question.

" Go on, stop telling the tale," she said illogically.

Nevertheless she was half inclined to believe me. I persevered, with such success that before I left her I had made an appointment to see her in three days' time, wet or dry. I had tried to make it for the next night, but she was wiser than I, and refused. If I couldn't wait three days to see her again it didn't matter. All the next day I kept asking myself what had possessed me to pick up a girl. Afterwards I wondered if she would turn up at the meeting-place or pick up another lad in the meantime. There were plenty of troops for her to choose from, older, smarter, more knowing fellows than I.

I was ill at ease and backward before strangers and the actual, concrete idea of going with a girl hadn't occurred to me until recently, and then in a subconscious way. The healthy, active life of the camp had taken up all my energy, and my body had only recently caught up on my height, as it were. Latterly desire had begun to trouble my dreams—maybe sitting at a desk most of the day and the steak suppers had something to do with it.

Oddly enough, the stupid obscene stories told in the huts at night had so far hardly affected me. When the others laughed at dirty yarns or told tales of easy conquests I paid no particular heed, perhaps because the stories were generally coupled with bouts of drinking. I had escaped these recitals since taking up residence in the officers' mess, except on the infrequent occasions I visited members of my old section in the huts.

The very last time I had gone one of the older men had related to a little audience crouched round the stove how he received a letter from his wife wanting him home for the week-end. This in itself had caused much winking and jogging of elbows. After getting half drunk in the canteen he had started to walk the distance—seven or eight miles. On the way he had fallen in with a woman tramp. He gave a lurid description of his experience.

When he had finished the story, his eyes heavy with recollection, the others—mostly youngsters—hid their disgust and laughed, capping it with other cleaner tales of their own amorous doings.

I had laughed with the rest, feeling rather foolish because I had nothing to tell. It was the custom to sit round the stove and swop yarns in the long winter evenings, and the talk always turned to women. Very few of the men read books, and they had to pass the time somehow, like old women knitting. They were being sociable and meant no harm.

The bodies of some of the old soldiers employed as storemen, batmen and so on, back in the battalion, were covered with tattoo marks, particularly if they had served in India. Naked figures which made obscene movements when muscles were expanded or relaxed, or which came together realistically, pregnant women, great scaly snakes which coiled round the neck and ended in the backside.

The old sweats took delight in exhibiting their " decorations " to the recruits and in telling of the pain they had suffered in getting them.

Afterwards they would touch the impressed rookies for the price of a drink.

Only an elusive memory of a pale oval face, flashing black eyes, and slim body remained with me when I set off for the meeting-place. For the life of me I couldn't remember her features and what she actually looked like. I racked my brains in despair. And if it was doubtful whether I would recognise her, how much more doubtful was it that she would recognise me ? Men in uniform were much the same.

But when I went to the place, taking care to be punctual,

the girl was standing waiting for me. After an initial shyness, due more this time to having had her so much in my thoughts than to her actual presence, I found myself talking away at a great rate and asking all kinds of questions, some of which she answered and others parried.

It was as easy to see that she was as poor as a church mouse. Her dress, all too thin and clinging for January, was sufficient proof of that. She worked in one of the mills dotting the town, and was practically uneducated. Withal she had a wary, agile mind and was not in the least dull.

She held certain very strongly-engrained ideas, I soon discovered, the principal one being that no man would be intimate with her until she was well and truly married to him. She enlarged on this topic in a way which sounded ridiculous in so young a girl. It was as if she had estimated her own chances and attractions to a fraction and, with so many bad examples among the girls in the town before her, was determined not to be caught napping.

In spite of all this, however—which rather damped me— she gave a curious impression of being at bottom only half-civilised, an impression which for some reason I liked immensely.

We went to the pictures again. There was a different picture, fortunately, though I wasted no time looking at it, being too busy trying to get acquainted and break down her rather childish suspicions. The first was easy enough, but the second was difficult.

I persevered, and when leaving her at the same dark street corner, she held up her mouth to be kissed—by way of encouragement.

I had now not the slightest doubt whether I wanted to see more of her and let slide a week-end at home to suit her convenience and meet her on the following Sunday night. She had to mind her sister's baby, it seemed, two or three nights a week.

It didn't occur to me to question this story. There was something offhand about the way she mentioned the baby, and the sister who went out to work in the mill, which made me think that perhaps it had something to do with her own fierce determination to be lawfully wedded before such a thing happened to her.

Sunday came, dry and cold, and as soon as we met I proposed a walk in case she should propose going to church. There was a church in the town very popular with the troops—a free tea was provided for them afterwards as a reward for going—but I suffered from a different hunger.

She had no notion of going to church. Her Sunday best was hardly good enough for church-going, though she tried to hide the fact and I pretended not to notice. What did I care about such things !

We walked out of the town and along a deserted country road. After half an hour's slow progress we came to an old shed a few yards off the road. The road, grey with frost, stretched ahead, cold and lonely. We went into the shed talking disjointedly for a while in the darkness, until, lighting a cigarette, I espied a big packing-case in a corner against the wall. I edged over to it, and by and by we sat down, side by side. Putting my arm round her waist I drew her clumsily closer.

For a while I sat in vast, satisfying silence, and then throwing the half-smoked cigarette away, I bent my head and stole hasty kisses. In a little while she was sitting on my knee, but that seemed the utmost of her concessions. Her old wariness asserted itself and she warded off my embraces. After some ineffectual wrestling I gave it up and sat in sulky silence, supporting her loosely with one arm and letting the other fall away.

We didn't speak and there seemed nothing to do except hold her supple young body, with its slightly animal smell.

I wondered dismally where the joy of being with a woman

came from—and if it was not greatly over-rated. I tried to imagine what some of the men back in the camp, who boasted of their easy conquests, would do in my place. None of their stories seemed to fit in, somehow.

It was cold in the shed. I got angry, and then restless, and then bored. It would soon be time to take her into the town again. I would be rid of her for good and all. My free hand, moving at random, touched a slim, coarsely-stockinged ankle, and I stroked it absent-mindedly for a time, obsessed with sad thoughts.

Imperceptibly, almost of its own volition, my hand strayed upwards to her knee, and rested there awhile. The girl took no notice, except to turn her face farther away.

Talking rapidly to distract her attention, using the first thing that entered my head as a topic, I poured out a stream of words without having the least idea of what I was talking about. A warm cheek brushed against mine. There was no need for talk now. Bending down I found her lips in the darkness.

We sat motionless, lost in a rosy glow of vague enchantment. The first pulsating desire of youth possessed me, firing my blood. But still I sat on, hardly able to breathe, not daring to break the sweet spell.

We were silent at first on the way back. The girl clung confidingly to my arm as we picked our way on the rutty road. Once she gave a startled cry as some beast moved suddenly on the other side of the hedge, and pressed close in alarm. Putting a protecting arm round her I reached down and stole a kiss. We went on, laughing. Her usual pert self-confidence had deserted her however. She seemed uneasily afraid that she had let me go too far for future safety on our very first walk out the road. I was, for the first time almost, completely at ease and natural in her company.

" You won't try to do me any harm, will you ? " Her voice trailed off.

" You needn't be a bit afraid of me," I answered stoutly, and meant it.

" You know, if I got into any trouble I'd be put out of the house. My father's terribly strict that way."

We took longer over our leave-taking this time. I went back to the camp walking on air, feeling curiously alive and big. The only fly in the ointment was that a long four days must elapse before she could get out again to see me. After that she would be able to see me oftener, and, after all, what were four days !

I was young, and had a girl.

THE DRAFT

WORKING at my table facing the wall in the orderly room, I heard the Commandant, busy at the morning's mail, reading a communication aloud. I paid no attention, although it was an unusual thing for him to do, until I heard my own name mentioned. There was nothing unusual for that matter in hearing my name called, but this time it was not called, but read out, number, rank, name.

I was sitting making out the usual daily return of strength —not so much dealing with the work in hand as in a brown study over the events of the previous night.

How sweet she was, and how enticing. But she was straight as well. I started, and looked round wonderingly.

The Commandant stopped reading. Without looking at me he went on in a slightly less formal voice. I heard him quite distinctly now.

" We shall be very sorry to lose his services, but everybody's turn must come some time. He has been a very good man, and I wish him the best of luck."

I froze, and stared stupidly, but with a faint premonition now of what was coming.

" Well, I'm afraid you'll have to leave us, Corporal," he said kindly, catching my eye. " There is an order here from your battalion to return to join a draft."

My lips shaped into the semblance of a respectful smile.

" Yes, sir. When shall I go ? "

" At once, it says," replied the Commandant, looking at the paper in his hand. " Yes, at once, I'm afraid," he added, and went on with his correspondence.

I sat looking at the half-filled form in front of me. Dipping

37

my pen into the inkpot mechanically, I started to complete it. The " at once " echoed in my ears. I replaced the pen carefully on the little rack in front of me. But who would complete the form ?

There was silence in the room—the Commandant, the Adjutant and the Sergeant-Major intent on their work. Familiar work. Familiar room. Familiar, friendly people— who had suddenly become strangers. The form lying before me on the desk seemed all at once very trivial. I no longer thought of completing it.

The silence grew in the room. It seemed as if those in it, the furniture and the air I breathed, were waiting. Rising stiffly from my chair I clicked my heels smartly in front of the Commandant.

" Yes, sir. It's about time I went," I said with dry lips, and felt his eyes upon me approvingly. Reaching forward he held out his hand in comradely fashion and smiled.

" Good luck, Corporal."

Turning on my heel I went out of the room.

Back at the battalion I found myself involved in a whirl of activity—parades without end, kit inspections, gas-masks on in a hut filled with prickly tear gas, bayonet drill, wild charges at the bags under the menacing eye of a red-haired physical jerks Sergeant-Major, who sported a silver skull and cross-bones for a cap badge, and yet belonged to a funny corps of his own—a terrible fellow who cursed and fumed and exhorted, and who, it was whispered, had never been in France in his life. Practice-trenches, where each man pulled the pin out of a Mills bomb, threw blindly and ducked down. Doing this once apparently qualified me for France, although I couldn't for the life of me understand why.

The girl in the town became a memory only to be conjured up in idle moments away from the draft, generally in the privacy of the latrine, or after lights out, when the sweetness of my last night with her crept over me and made me writhe.

The draft numbered around fifty. Without exception the rest of the men were returning to France. I was unable to share their outlook, for all their rough good fellowship. There was a gap, deep, broad and unbridgable between the men who had been in France and the men who hadn't. It was as if they spoke a different language and had different modes of thought. I could never be at ease with them. France, I thought, is an old story to them, who know all about shells and bullets, gas and bombs, while I knew absolutely nothing. A longing to get to France and become initiated seized me. It was the only way to meeting and mixing with them on equal terms. But along with that a slow revolt grew in me that I should be shoved off to the front just when life had taken on a fresh significance. The life of the signal school was already a thing of the past, like the girl, but, surprisingly, the girl came first although she was almost a stranger.

She was pretty, too, with her black hair curling round her face. And young and intelligent. The last time I had been with her I had noticed how she had tried to put a good face on what she didn't know, to be more careful with her grammar and how she expressed herself. With a little coaching and better clothing she would pass muster anywhere, for hadn't she youth on her side. Warm, boyish visions of getting her interested in some of the good books I had read, and then—when I was a little better at it myself— some French or Spanish. A lovely girl that a chap could take anywhere without being ashamed. I dreamed on. And when that stage was reached we could be married. The war would be over. I would work and study. Perhaps there would be a tiny baby.

Harsh reality obtruded. I hadn't known her long enough

to make any real impression. Not one that a successor couldn't wipe out in a week or two when I went on the draft. She was too pretty and avid for life, for all her funny notions, to go about alone in a town full of young men in uniform. They would have no scruples about supplying all the knowledge of life that mattered to a girl if they got the ghost of a chance, a chance such as I had had that last night—and hadn't taken.

The sense of what I had missed grew in me and made me reckless.

" Maybe I can still get down to the town, and then things can take their course," I thought. Once with her it wouldn't be I who called the tune, but the draft.

" Fall in the draft."

Another day passed in a scurry of parades. Drafts were precious nowadays, and required watching, so we were confined to camp.

" You'd think we were looking for a chance to clear off," my new comrades grumbled discontentedly.

" They're bloody good judges, too," said one, bringing a laugh.

Monday, Tuesday and then Wednesday passed. Thursday commenced with the same rigmarole, but after dinner we fell in and found ourselves due for four days' draft leave.

By the time we were paid and received our railway warrants it was tea-time. The rest of the draft left at once, anxious to spend every possible minute at home. I fell in as usual when the " Cookhouse Door " blew. Afterwards I went through the routine of a soldier getting ready for short leave, until, freshly shaved, with gleaming buttons, shining cap-badge, highly polished belt and boots and—the young war-time infantryman's most treasured possession— a highly unregulation pair of riding breeches, I was ready. In the signal camp the town had been a bare half-hour's walk away. Now it was two hours' steady going. Even so I was too early.

It was the girl's turn to be confused when I took her arm possessively and started off in the same direction as before. We left the dimly lit streets behind, where soldiers paraded in pairs, smacking their legs with their canes as they ogled the girls, also in pairs.

It was silent and deserted outside the town, but the girl chatted away merrily, hugging my arm.

The old shed stood empty and inviting as before. She hesitated and then went on under my compelling arm.

" Would it not be nicer in there ? " she whispered uncertainly, looking up with a little, secret smile.

When we came to a narrow lane off the road a faint question formed in her eyes, but I didn't answer it. The lane had gentle rising banks, grass-covered and smooth. I drew her down.

We sat, talking low, and in between I stole kisses.

The air was cold and I pressed closer, one hand caressing her breasts through the opening of her coat—" to keep it warm," I lied.

The minutes fled, and I had a train to catch. The luminous dial of my watch warned me to be quick. My free hand caressed the soft lines of her body. Desire, immeasurably stronger now that it had a goal in view, made my throat dry.

Lying back on the bank, I drew her down with me. Her breath, hot and odorous with the mystery of her body, drugged my senses.

" Remember, you promised faithfully to be good," she murmured almost inaudible.

Again the whisper came, with an urgent note, but I paid no attention and drew her closer to me. Desire blinded me and drummed in my ears. With its coming the girl's personality was lost.

For a moment she lay pressing against me, soft and receptive. Then, in an instant she was fighting like a wild-cat to escape my embrace, twisting, rolling and scratching on the grassy bank. The feel of her warm flesh maddened me, but always she just managed to elude me. We rolled off the bank on to the laneway. A despairing cry came as I bore down her resistance. I was the stronger.

Suddenly she gave in and lay passive in my arms, almost fainting. Her eyes were closed and her lips parted.

Reaction came. I looked at her in disgust as presently she recovered and sat up.

" I knew fine well you'd try to play a dirty, mean trick on me," she burst out. " You're all the same, you soldiers, a pack of dirty beasts."

" Little devil," I thought sullenly, and kept silent.

" I'll never go out a step with you again—never, never, never. I'm a decent working girl. Yes. Not like some of the rest that trollop about the streets at night. You can go with them if you like, but you won't get me to go out with you again," she went on.

" You're right there," I thought, " only you didn't know it before." Feeling suddenly cold, I got to my feet. Lighting a cigarette, I stood looking down at her, anger fading. Going to France without having been with a woman didn't seem a very important thing after all, and anyway, she wasn't to blame for her part in the fiasco.

I had just muddled it, though how or why, I didn't know. She seemed very young and forlorn, too, as she crouched on the bank, trying to repair the work of my clumsy hands.

" Well, you needn't be so cross about it. After all, there's no harm done, is there ? " I said.

" It's not your fault there isn't. You soldiers think you can play about whatever nasty way you like. Then off you go to France or some other outlandish place and the girl never hears from you again. She's left to put up with what happens to her and what the neighbours say. If she has a baby, she's ruined for life. And I thought you were such a nice, quiet boy, so different to the others that——"

" You'll never see me again, so you needn't worry. I am going off to France on a draft," I broke in hurriedly as she started to cry. " That's just why I did it, you know—or tried to, rather—so you are quite safe now. Besides, I didn't really want to do you any harm. I only wanted something to remember." A thought struck me. I looked at my watch.

" Come on, for God's sake," I cried in a panic. " I have a train to catch to-night, no matter a damn what happens."

Silent and constrained, we hurried along towards the dark town, walking well apart. At first the road was deserted except for our two selves. When people began to pass us I made a pretence of casual conversation in case they would notice there was something the matter. The girl kept her head averted. Back at the corner of her street I stopped for a moment to say good-bye.

" You'll never see me again, so good night, and you needn't bear me any hard feelings," I said, and, snatching a surprise kiss, ran for my train.

Just before turning the corner out of sight, I glanced back, and saw her looking after me doubtfully.

The leave fled swiftly. We were no sooner back in camp than we were warned to be ready to depart. At home they had wanted to send another telegram.

" You are still too young," mother pointed out. " It's just a case of some of the soldier clerks having made a mistake and put your name in with the others. We can easily send them word."

But I would have none of it. " If I don't go this time everyone will laugh at me. I am going to go, no matter whether you send a telegram or not. I'll swear I'm the right age and they'll be only too glad to take my word."

We were all weighed and ready to fall in when the post Corporal came round with a first delivery. I didn't expect anything, for our route lay through my home town where we had to change trains. I was to see father and mother there for the leave-taking. But I got a soiled letter with a badly spelled, almost illegible address. I tore it open, but the bugles were blowing for the fall in, and I had to defer reading it until we were in the train.

It was from the girl in the town. I read it slowly, like a man deciphering a musty record that had long since lost its significance.

" I'm sorry I was so cross with you that last night, I was sorry afterwards. But come and meet me on Sunday night again and I'll let you do anything. Don't be cross with me because I love you. I'll be waiting for you at the same place, so be sure and come."

There was no signature, only many shakily made crosses and many blotches.

And Sunday was already gone.

I read and re-read the scrawl, and then folded it carefully and unbuttoned the flap of my breast pocket, the left one, over the heart.

" Last letter from the intended, Corporal ? " laughed the Sergeant of the draft, a lean, brown-faced fellow with kindly eyes.

I looked at him dumbly for a moment and then shrugged. Crumpling the letter in my fist, I threw it out of the open carriage window.

" Wait till you have a wife and a couple of kids to say good-bye to and you'll know something," said the Sergeant with a strained grin.

Pulling out his water-bottle, he held it over invitingly.

" Here, take a slug of this. It's the real root for a time like this."

The bottle was full of whisky, and I choked as the fiery

stuff burned my throat, causing the Sergeant to laugh again, heartier this time.

I got my breath back and turned to the window, avoiding his eyes.

The country-side flew past, with its old familiar tale of neatly hedged fields, rounded hills and patches of trees in the curving bottom lands.

" The intended. The intended," rumbled the wheels underneath.

THE ARRIVAL

WE had a wild night for the crossing to France and a good many were seasick. Our crowd were nearly all drunk, anyway, and not a few of the other " passengers " were in the same case. The officers on board kept discreetly out of the way. They were probably drunk, too.

Once out of Southampton the boat began to rock violently, and I gave myself up for lost. It seemed inevitable that something terrible should happen as she reeled under the heavy seas. It was my first journey away from home, and, oddly enough, I wasn't seasick, but the men's drunken indifference to the danger of sinking seemed to make the danger more acute. The others rolled helplessly with the motion of the ship, spewing and retching in the crowded hold.

I sat braced against a pillar and looked about me fearfully for the first signs of panic. Every time the boat plunged a sickening fear possessed me that she would never come up. I kept my eyes down and strove to hide my feeling by looking vacantly at the heaving floor.

But nothing happened, except that the smell became a stench that could be tasted. From being smart, well-disciplined soldiers, my comrades were transformed into drunken oafs and made wet, swinish noises. The more sober amongst them sat in huddled groups and sang or quarrelled over cards.

They were a wild lot, and I wondered doubtfully would I ever lose my timidity and self-consciousness sufficiently to be able to mix with them on a common footing. Behind them again was the unknown, the question mark that represented the front line.

Early in the morning the ship berthed, but we were kept on board for a couple of long hours while, to the tune of much trampling and shouting, other drafts landed. Then, pale and woe-begone, we lined up on the quay and set off, stumbling along until we regained our shore legs and cringing under our heavy packs.

Along the road old, blear-eyed, walrus-moustached French soldiers were engaged in scavenging. I looked at them in astonishment and disappointment, the idea strong in my mind that men in uniform were bound to be real soldiers, although these were more like old roadsweepers at home than anything else. I had thought, too, that all Frenchmen would be very civilised, rather foppish-looking individuals.

When we reached the town, slatternly women passed us indifferently, not even bothering to look up. Their mouths and ears were covered with dirty cloths as a protection against the raw morning air—which struck me as odd, too. Where we came from, people accepted nipped ears and frosty air stoically, as a matter of course, and would never have dreamt of coddling themselves in this fashion. It seemed almost indecent—as if they had reached the stage when they no longer cared what their neighbours or the people they met on the street thought about their excessive fear of a touch of frost. At home one would have thought that there was an epidemic of mumps or toothache.

The women, besides being slatternly, were almost without exception, worn-looking creatures, who made no attempt to even ordinary good looks or appearance. And I had thought that Frenchwomen, without exception, were lovely.

Yet, it occurred to me that this muffling up of the ears and mouth on a winter's morning was a simple, logical way of avoiding the cold, and a good part of my surprise was due to the fact that these people should seize on such a sensible, direct, to-hell-with-appearances method of keeping themselves warm.

A little squad of boys appeared from nowhere and ran alongside us, begging in shrill, mechanical voices for pennies and bully-beef.

None of the others paid much attention to them, except to tell them to go to blazes, or to go and do something to themselves which would have required them to be grown-up contortionists to even attempt to comply. They had thin, bony faces and pipe-stem legs. They resembled most what I had expected the French to be like. Almost out of gratitude I threw a few coppers amongst them, and laughed with the other men at the wild dive they made.

Their blue army caps, shaped like Glengarries, but without the accompanying ribbons, and pallid faces, gave them a proper foreign air which their shrill, broken English, plentifully sprinkled with oaths in imitation of their teachers, only enhanced.

We left the town behind and trudged along, the road getting steeper and steeper. My comrades cursed Le Havre viciously and changed their rifles frequently from one shoulder to the other without getting any relief. None of us was in much condition for route marching that morning, especially up-hill, and we sweated, knees bent. Thin wintry sunshine dazzled our eyes.

By and by we passed isolated huts to the left of the road, and then turned in thankfully to the great Base. I thought naturally the march was at an end, but we went on steadily past compact blocks of huts and tents with big dining-halls and marquees marking the boundaries between the lines. The place had a harsh, serviceable appearance and a shiver of anticipation went through me. The trenches loomed nearer.

Whitewashed stones edged the paths running between the huts and tents, but instead of being decorative they had a done-as-punishment look. Groups of soldiers hung about the paths or sat at the roadside. Some of them glanced up casually as we passed by. Others who happened to be standing with their backs to us didn't bother to look round. They were cavalry and gave an impression that they had been there a long time, and were in no particular danger of moving. There was no sign of horses. Yet there was a glamour about them that ordinary foot soldiers lacked. They were fine-looking fellows, their neat riding breeches and waisted tunics setting off their slim hips and straight backs.

The cavalry gave place to artillery and still we marched on, groaning inwardly as we forced ourselves to step out and appear at ease in front of so many strange units.

When we came to the infantry lines I was tired out and hadn't sweated so much for a year. The others were feeling the strain too. The men we passed now were of a different stamp. They were mostly smaller and not nearly so smart or well set up. They hadn't the bored superciliousness of the cavalry, and eyed us in friendly fashion, taking care to look at our cap badges to see if we were bound for their particular regiment before turning away. I noticed, how-ever, that as well as being friendly, there was something slightly questioning in the looks they threw at us which puzzled me at first.

" Can you stick it, mates ? " cried one impudently from the midst of a lounging group.

" We were sticking it before your number was dry," came the quick retort from one of the draft, and we walked on smiling. If the draft had been composed of newcomers like myself there would probably have been quite a lot of " old soldier " humour expended on us, and I was corre-spondingly glad I was in such good company. Most of the draft sported gold bars on their sleeves. It was an old story to them.

D

We arrived at last at our own divisional lines and were distributed amongst tents. The others knew the ropes and were soon at home after a fashion, but I was at a loose end. I knew nobody, and my cursed shyness made it difficult for me to make friends easily. Besides, I had two stripes up, which made it harder. Though decent enough, I had noted the quizzical way the others accepted my corporalship, thought I had never dared to give one of them an order or trade on it.

For that matter I was really only a Lance-Corporal. At the last roll-call before we left the battalion I had found myself reduced to the rank of Lance-Corporal, this, it seemed, being my substantive rank, but as nobody had bothered on the journey out to see that I took the second stripe down, I had let it remain, strong in the idea that a full Corporal would be better off in France than a mere Lance-Jack. " It might be safer and, anyway, the food might be better," I had thought, forgetting what the B.E.F. men would think of it.

Parades came our way thick and heavy. Rifle inspections, medical inspections, kit inspections followed each and were succeeded by journeys up the hill past the horse hospital, to the gas huts, where gas-masks were fitted and tested. After tea I wandered about by myself or lay in the tent, a prey to loneliness.

The weather was cold and the food served up in the dining-hall very skimped. " Working the double " was a common practise at meal-times. This was done by hanging about the dining-hall before the bugle went and, when it had sounded, rushing into the top of the queue. Then a hurried meal, out by the rear door and back to the tail-end of the queue again, ready for another.

Even then I was hungry and spent money every night in the dry canteen, eating tinned rabbit and other funny things.

The N.C.O.'s on the Base Staff did their best to stop the

practice, but without success. They stood at the door glaring suspiciously at each man and challenged one now and then, to meet with an indignant denial. From the waiting line there would come anonymous grousings.

" Aren't we going up the line ? "

" Base wallahs can't do anything to us."

" Aren't we entitled to our grub ? "

" They never saw the sky over the lines and never will."

Fortunately they didn't challenge me, thinking, no doubt, that Corporals were above such practices, or I might easily have given myself away. As it was they looked threatening, affected not to hear, and let us past.

I received a visit from my brother, who had received a transfer from the infantry to the Royal Engineers. Before the war he had been an apprentice draughtsman and had only taken on the clerk job for the sake of the extra pay. Now he had turned his knowledge to good account and was in some R.E. unit in Le Havre, down at the docks. I got a pass out one night and went down with him to the town. He was full of his new job and I listened patiently, almost absentmindedly, as he went into details and technicalities. Our ways lay different.

I felt lonelier than ever going back to the camp. The tram was packed with troops, some of them drunk, who were everywhere except on the roof. A woman drove and a woman acted as conductor, two things which gave me a better idea of France than anything I had yet seen. Both were chic in their mannish uniform and, more important, both were highly efficient. The conductress collected fares far better than a man could have hoped to do, especially a civilian, and the driver sending the rackety, double-compartment vehicle clanging along at a great pace.

Rumour ruled us, for we knew it was bound to be right some time. During the day we never dared stray far from our lines in case the word would come for us to move.

When we were at breakfast the yarn went that we were going up immediately it was over. When dinner came the rumour came too, and the same at tea. " Up the line and the best of luck," the stock phrase of the Base, echoed in our ears.

The Staff N.C.O.'s and orderlies were officious fellows, who only spoke to us in the way of business. There was no love lost on either side. We looked on them with scarcely veiled contempt—my comrades did, that is—and I copied their viewpoint as much as possible. " Lousy Base-wallahs."

There were only two classes at the Base and between them all ranks from Colonels down to Privates were divided—the men who were there permanently, and the men who weren't. The slipshod orderly man in the dining-hall was immeasurably above the bronzed Sergeant of the draft with fifty men under him, and both knew it.

But, to my mind, a man who stood out by himself was the Quartermaster-Sergeant. His kindness and liberality were something to wonder about. There was something ominous indeed in the fatherly interest he took in seeing that we had everything in the line of kit we required. Nothing was too good for us. Did our boots hurt us ? Pick another pair. New uniforms ? Well, they're there for the taking. A new cap ? Certainly, take your choice. Warm gloves that turned our hands into paws—they had only one place for fingers and were connected by a string that went round our necks, so that they were always at hand when wanted. New shirts and drawers, thick socks, flannel body-belts, iron rations, heavy leather jerkin lined with wool.

" Anything else now, boys ? "

" Why, you would nearly think we were going on an expedition to the North Pole," I laughed gleefully to the man beside me in the store, with a lively remembrance of the parsimonious quarter blokes I had encountered at home.

" Just wait till you are up the line a week or two and you'll wish to Christ you were at the North Pole or any other pole," he replied sourly, not a whit impressed with the lavishness shown us.

My enthusiasm cooled.

The order came, but before we departed we paid another visit to the stores and waited while sombre colours were stitched on to our tunics just below the shoulder-straps, the colours of the First Battalion of the Regiment.

The men of the draft were all Kitchener's Army, and didn't take kindly to the idea. They had belonged to service battalions and didn't relish joining a Regular unit.

" We're for it now," they agreed ruefully, and cursed their luck as visions of rejoining their own crowds disappeared into thin air.

" Too much spit and polish," they said when I asked what was the matter. " You see, we won't know any of the lads either."

" And very likely they'll be a rotten crowd, a lot of bloody toughs and jailbirds from Christ knows where. The Regulars are all the same. And the officers are duds."

" Ay, and our own mobs'll be filled up with a lot of dirty conscripts instead."

I listened, but personally I was rather pleased at the prospect. To my mind it sounded much better to belong to the First Battalion than to the 12th or 20th Service Battalion. It was more soldierly and romantic. I felt proud of the colours on my shoulders.

It was interesting sitting in the train watching the country-side pass slowly in review, but as the hours passed the spectacle became monotonous. I was left with the novelty of travelling in a horsebox. The only food was hard tack and bully, with a tin of Maconachie stew once a day. The last was excellent, the only drawback being that it was never meant to go round three men.

The train trundled along at about five or six miles an hour·
At first, for fun, we would slide down on to the permanent
way, urinate, and scamper back laughing, to sit uncomfortably in the dark interior of the wagon, littered with
rifles and equipment, or dangle our legs in the open doorway.
When the continual jolting of the train set our bowels
rumbling we scrambled out in real earnest, ran quickly for
a hundred yards in the same direction as the train to gain an
extra minute, and squatted down hurriedly.

Sometimes the train stopped for no apparent reason, and
there would be a rush to the engine for hot water to make
tea. Unfortunately our wagon was away behind and more
often than not the supply was finished by the time the hundreds of men in front had got their canteens filled. The oil
driver would shrug his shoulders and wave his hands
excitedly.

" Fini ! L'eau fini ! "

The stops always occurred in deserted country, but on the
second day, by some mischance, a long halt was made at a
tiny village. A wild stampede ensued for the estaminet,
which in a twinkling was packed with eager men, crowding
round a wrinkled, querulous old woman and quarrelling
over precedence.

Madame, however, was equal to the occasion, and made
sure she was paid for one drink before doling out another
from a long, slender bottle labelled " Cognac," which was
easily the favourite drink. I joined in, too, and in exchange
for a franc bill got a thimbleful of the stuff. It didn't seem
worth all the excitement, and I went back to the train
disappointed. When a warning whistle came from the
engine, the rest came running back, three or four in our
wagon having obviously had more than one go at the
bottle. They loaded their rifles and started a shooting
competition at nothing in particular.

This ended abruptly when one took aim and shot a cow

grazing peacefully in a field. Sobering up, they cleaned their rifles hastily, swearing the rest of us to secrecy, but the train trundled on without any alarm being raised.

We were nearly ready to shoot the engine-driver when on the third day our journey came to an end. Instead, with the inconsistency of children, we forgot all about him as soon as we were out of sight of the railway. Before it even, for a gang of Chinese caught our attention as they went leisurely about the business of unloading coal in a siding.

They were dressed in blue dungarees and wore dirty towels round their necks and they smiled and chattered amongst themselves in high bird-like voices. They were big, hefty fellows with broad shoulders and bulging muscles. The amazing thing about them was that they were no more yellow than we were, but had healthy brown faces with broad cheekbones tinged with red. They were slow-moving and lazy-looking. Their smiling content made us smile in response. Many loud jokes were cracked at their expense, but the Chinks only smiled benignly and begged for bully-beef.

" They know damn well who the mugs are," said one of the draft.

We found ourselves in a small town with shuttered houses and empty streets. A quiet, almost solemn air pervaded the place, and I wondered how near we were to the front. We were billeted in tall, empty houses, and after dumping our equipment went out to explore.

The Sergeant of the draft, the same who had offered me the whisky in the train, went with me when night fell. When we came on a broader window in a narrow street, through which a dim light came, we went in and found ourselves in a little café. The Sergeant fished out a pocket-book and bought a bottle of champagne.

" Drink up, Corp," he said, " for you mightn't get a chance for a long time again."

We divided the bottle between us, and although I hadn't very much money, and the Sergeant wanted to pay again, I insisted on buying the second bottle. It cost ten francs, but it was worth it, if only for the sake of sitting in a real French café. Almost without my knowledge the stuff mounted to my brain, and I felt curiously alive and virile. In between my companion's talk I thought of the girl's letter and wished I had another chance with her. There vere no girls in the café.

The Sergeant got on to the subject of the war and of July, 1916, when he had been badly wounded, but the war didn't seem such a terrible thing after all. He was still alive, and hadn't I as good a chance as he—better, indeed, for I had all my chances to come, and some of his were already gone. It couldn't be so very bad. The Sergeant bought a third bottle and the café became slightly unreal.

I hadn't a very clear impression of getting to bed that night—some difficulty about getting my puttees and boots off—good-humoured difficulty, with no unpleasantness. In the morning it occurred to me with something of a shock that I must have been drunk. All that I had heard at school and in church about the terrible after-effects of drink occurred to me, and I was surprised that none of them troubled me.

"I've made a friend, too," I thought, with a hazy recollection of the Sergeant's confidences.

Next day we paraded in full marching order and set off to join the battalion. It was a stiff enough march, but I felt in better form for it. Twenty kilometres, the others said, but as I didn't know what a kilometre amounted to, I was none the wiser, and didn't like to ask. On the way we passed half-ruined, deserted villages, and once a working company of small, dark men.

"Italians or Pork-and-beaners," a man told me, looking at them contemptuously.

The journey ended in an even more dilapidated village than those we had passed on the road. Mounds of old bricks represented where houses had been. Here and there walls rose for a few feet into the air, An officer came along and we were split up into four, each group bound for a different company. For a while we sat in the street, resting but ill at ease, and then a Sergeant led us out of the village, along the road for three or four hundred yards, and off it along a narrow, slippery path to where a broad staircase led into the ground. Along with a dozen others, I found myself in " A " Company, and learned that the Battalion was going into the line that night.

In a way I was glad. The crowd of strange faces, the sharp N.C.O.'s and the impersonal officers made me feel very much alone. It was pitch dark down the steps and up above was cold and inhospitable. The fellows who had been with me disappeared and I found myself attached to a platoon of strangers. Everything was done in a hurry, and everybody bustled about getting ready. After tea, which was served up on top, there was more shouting and running, which purport I didn't understand. I kept trying not to look surprised or even interested at all, but when at last we fell in and answered our names, I had a premonition that the war wasn't such a simple thing as I had thought. There would be the same difficulty about getting to know people, and the ropes would be much harder to learn. I had always thought of war as such a simple, elementary thing, with none of the ordinary little human complications. I spoke casually to one or two, but they answered shortly and turned away to discuss questions I didn't know anything about and therefore couldn't talk about.

It got rapidly colder. Flurries of snow fell.

THE HERO

WE marched up a straight, smooth road with only a shallow ditch on either side separating it from the fields.

The men around me became more and more taciturn as we moved along until each was buried in some all-engrossing thought which forbade conversation. The gloomy earth had a desolate air as if it shared the secret thoughts of the tramping men, and sympathised. Every step carried me farther into a stark, elemental world where the pretty graces of civilisation were unknown, and unwanted.

I tried to imagine a little girl playing a childish game of make-believe, or a pair of young lovers walking hand in hand, but my mind boggled at such grotesque fancies. For no particular reason I became silent and preoccupied like the rest. We went on for what seemed a long time, our footsteps echoing on the metalled road, and then an order came down the ranks to form two-deep.

There was a long wait. We shuffled about, stamping our feet in an effort to keep warm. After one or two false starts we moved slowly forward and in turn groped our way into a deep, narrow trench at the right of the road. The trench was ankle-deep in pale mud, which clung to our boots, making every step an effort. I kept stumbling against the man in front and bumping into the trench wall, causing driblets of chalky earth to fall. My chief concern, being still very much the recruit, was for my beautiful, brand-new rifle.

The night was quiet. Only at rare intervals a dull boom, softened by distance, crept into the stillness like the noise of a distant sea breaking on a rocky coast. I listened eagerly,

and each time it came a little tremor of anticipation ran
through me. The sound conveyed nothing as yet of such
strange, far-off things as mutilation and death.

After about an hour's slow progress we were greeted
cautiously by the troops we were relieving and found
ourselves in a slightly broader trench. We stood pressing
into the side of it to allow them to squeeze past. Everybody
seemed nervous and apprehensive, but nothing happened,
and they disappeared the way we had come. Apparently
they had a quiet time. Their curt, earnest answers to the
muttered questions put to them were at once comforting
and friendly.

" Soft enough, mates."

" Not much doing."

" Good luck."

Nevertheless, they seemed glad to get away.

The Sergeant of my platoon—tall, raw-boned and dark,
with a long, stubborn jaw—had everything at his finger-tips,
and soon completed the job of putting our stretch of trench
into order. We dumped our packs into a deep dug-out with
a slimy sandbag stretched over the entrance.

I hadn't the slightest idea of what there was to do, but
everything worked smoothly. First the Sergeant brought
me round a couple of bays to where a trench went off at a
right angle to the front. A few yards up it a Lewis-gun team
stood peering over a rough breastwork.

" This used to be part of the old German line," he
whispered, " and this sap was once a communication
trench. It runs right into their front line."

I stared for a moment at the silent gunners, and then
retreated thankfully and followed my guide round a couple
more bays to where a narrow platform had been scooped
out of the parapet. A small group of men stood about
waiting. A man with hunched shoulders stood on the step
staring into the blackness of No Man's Land.

" This is your section, Corporal. Warn off your sentries and see to the relief every hour. Those not on can slide into the dug-out."

The Sergeant disappeared.

I looked at the men, nonplussed, and counted eight of them, not one of whom I would have recognised five minutes after. There was a little silence. A Verey light went up somewhere near. The squad remained shadowy with white blobs for faces.

" It's all right, Corp," said one, " Smith and Patterson here are going on first and they'll know who to waken."

The others murmured agreement. I found myself alone with two men, one on the fire-step and one sitting at his feet.

Impelled by curiosity, I clambered up and stared over the parapet, but there was nothing to be seen except a yard or two away a few stakes threaded with wire. Beyond that was patchy darkness. After a minute or two another light went up, but whose it was I didn't know. It hung for a second high up in the air and then came slowly earthwards. The ground in front reflected its pale light, but remained mysterious, empty and broken, with old craters and humps, and dark hollows which might have been creeping men.

My unaccustomed eyes tired of staring at nothing. I sat down beside the second man. He leant back, silently fondling his rifle. The fire-step made a cold seat. In a little while I got up and went slowly towards the dug-out, without speaking.

Round the first bay I stood for a while, communing with myself. The deep trench was full of mystery. The stillness and queerness of it all whispered of strange things. My thoughts went out to the men who had been here before me, and I wondered what their fate had been. It was very solemn standing there. It was almost like being in church. Instinctively I knew that that dim stretch of quiet trench had witnessed violence and bloodshed. The British, it seemed, had only recently taken over this part of the front, and the knowledge seemed to increase its mystery. It had drank deep of the blood of Frenchmen. In imagination I heard their quick, strange accents, and glimpsed the hopes and fears of old-time residents of the spot where I stood dreaming. Where were they now ?

The silence settled around me like a sweet spell. It seemed so strange, and yet natural, that men had died where I stood, perhaps—and the war went on, while they, and the obscure fates, were forgotten so completely that they might never have been. Had one of them appeared at my elbow in the flesh and spoken, the illusion would have vanished, for I could not have understood a word he said. And yet I knew them, and the dark trench remembered too.

I shivered, and was about to turn back to the two silent men on the fire-step for company's sake when I remembered the dug-out, and went on round the deserted bays, to where the remainder of the section was.

They lay, huddled together for warmth, at the foot of the steps leading up to the trench. Threading my way carefully, I sat down a little farther back. Pulling out a cigarette, I lit it with cupped hands. It was too cold, and anyway I was too impressed with the novelty of the situation to think of sleep. The dug-out was strong and deep, like the trench.

A pleasant sense of security came over me. They were good fellows enough in the section. When I got to know them better they would be all right. I was in the front line now. Even if I was wounded to-morrow I would be a front-line soldier ever afterwards. I felt comforted. There seemed little danger of a wound.

The cigarette went out. Putting the butt away, I snuggled closer to the earthen wall.

I must have fallen into a doze. I was brought to my feet by a wild clamour in the trench above. Heavy thuds shook the ground, and bits of earth fell from the dug-out roof. The men beside me shrank close to the ground as fitful flashes, penetrating down the steps, lit up their ghastly faces.

Explosion after explosion sounded and the unforgettable tang of high explosive, with its strong suggestion of hot, freshly spilt blood, came drifting down to us. Half-stupefied, I peered about me, not knowing what it was all about. The cowering men showed that here was something unexpected and terrible.

Suddenly the flap at the entrance was pulled aside. The voice of the Platoon Sergeant came harshly.

" Come up. Up quick, you bastards. A raid. A raid."

There was a panicky scramble for rifles and jerking on of equipment. Along with the others I blundered up the steps to the trench, where, a short time before, I had stood lost in reverie. Now it was bedlam of crashing explosions and drifting smoke, lit with gun flashes whose flickering, ghostly radiance, silently illumining the trench walls in the midst of so much noise, terrified me more than anything else. There was something uncanny in their white intensity, as of fitful moonlight magnified many times. In between the quivering flashes was utter darkness. Vicious red spurts came and went on the ground immediately behind the parados. Fumes caught at our throats.

We ran along a little way, bent double, and then stopped, stupidly enough, at a place where the trench walls rose like the side of a house. The others must have thought it was the safest place, and it didn't occur to me to do anything else but halt too. Without a word we crouched down in a row against the base of the parapet, awaiting I knew not what.

The idea of our repelling an attack, or even defending our-selves was absurd. Besides, there didn't seem to be anybody for us to fight. We were only a little squad of men hugging the earth to escape the shells, each praying that somebody else would be taken. I could see only the dark form of the man in front of me and a patch of flickering night sky, when I dared look up. We pressed close to the side, our heads down between our knees, each trying instinctively to use the man in front as a shield.

The explosions seemed to draw off somewhat, but the encircling uproar went on unabated. We remained in our uncomfortable crouch, pressing against the side of the trench and against each other. My legs began to feel numb.

We shrank lower still, holding our breath, as from the rim of the trench above our heads a voice shouted something indistinguishable. Nobody answered, and again the voice came, filled with menace.

There was a flash and a shattering roar in the narrow confines of the trench. The man in front of me shuddered and tumbled over on his face, but I remained motionless as before, my mind a blank.

A curious stillness followed. Then cries and groans rose about me. Shapes showed dimly against the chalky mud. Behind me a man started to laugh crazily. Still crouched double, I tried to see what had happened, strained my ears for the sound of the mysterious voice, but without success.

" What should I do ? What shall I do ? " I asked myself distractedly.

There was a rush. I was sent sprawling into the mud, but in a moment was on my feet following hard on the heels of those in front as they ran for their lives to the dug-out. Tumbling down the steps, we lay panting for breath as if we had run for a mile. The guns kept up their clamour outside, but I paid no attention. I was alive, and apparently that was the main thing.

There were other men crouching in the dug-out as well as my depleted section, but I was too bewildered to be curious. We lay higgledy-piggledy at the foot of the steps, without speaking. A burning sensation asserted itself in one of my fingers. Putting my hand to my mouth, I found it covered with sticky blood from a puncture in the tip of my finger.

I froze with the others as the sandbag flap at the dug-out entrance was pulled aside. A guttural voice called down, followed by a few random revolver shots.

We lay awaiting another bomb, but none came.

Gradually the firing slackened. We stirred cautiously and started taking stock. Cigarettes were lit with hands that shook. Some men were wounded. The rest looked at each other furtively by the light of a candle and cursed obscenely.

Presently I found myself one of a circle, staring down at a wounded man. One of his hips was a mass of mangled flesh. The blood gleamed blackly as it flowed to the dug-out floor. A couple of men with Red Cross armlets knelt beside him and applied bandages. The wound was so big that they had to borrow emergency dressings to cover it. As the iodine stung his raw flesh the man screamed and had to be held down. His eyes roved over the men looking down at him. Something in their expression frightened him.

" Christ, am I done for, boys ?—will I ever get over this one ? " he pleaded as if they held the power of life and death. His face was grey and drawn in startling contrast to his bloody flesh. His eyes beseeched each man in turn. We shuffled uneasily.

" You're all right, mate. You're right for Blighty," said one of the stretcher-bearers half-heartedly. But the wounded man was not to be comforted. Again and again his despairing cry came, his voice getting weaker each time until it was a mere whisper.

As he was being lifted on to the stretcher another stream of blood was noticed coming from his side. More first-aid bandages were requisitioned. I turned away, sickened at the long-drawn-out agony. The muddy rags of his uniform, soaked with blood, seemed to proclaim that mud and blood were akin, and would very soon be indistinguishable the one from the other.

I found that, barring the two men I had left on the fire-step, whose fate I didn't know, I was the sole survivor of the section. One had gone off his head and the rest had been wounded by bomb splinters and gone off to the dressing-station somewhere behind. The Lewis-gun post was no more. Two of the crew were killed and a third was missing, along with the gun.

I examined my finger, and extracted a splinter. Unfortunately it was too small a thing to go to the dressing-station with.

The man who had " gone off his nut," was the chief topic of discussion, the fate of the others being accepted as a matter of course, to be forgotten as soon as possible. Going mad was more original. There were many cynical conjectures as to how long the alleged madman could keep up the deception, and exactly what form it would take.

" He always was cute," said one enviously. " No matter how mad he is he's a sight wiser than the mugs he left behind," said another.

The stunt, if it was a stunt, must have worked, for the lunatic didn't return.

Next morning, when " stand on " arrived—which meant all hands lining the fire-step for some unknown reason— dixies of tea arrived from the support line and we had breakfast. Afterwards we discovered a message scrawled in red chalk on the cross beam of our dug-out entrance. It read : " Prussian Guard. Gott strafe English bastards."

" No wonder we got our backsides warmed if the Prussian Guards were up against us," the men commented, half-admiringly, and let the message remain.

I was to go down to Battalion headquarters to give evidence about the raid.

E

" There's an inquiry being held into it, or an inquest, whichever you like to call it. It's a bad business, but say as little as you can and you'll be all right," the Sergeant advised.

A stout, black-haired Corporal came up—he was to be questioned, too—and the pair of us set off. It was snowing again, but the effort of drawing our feet out of the thick chalky mud kept us warm. We kept along the front line trench for a couple of hundred yards. I was struck by the deserted appearance of the dug-outs and by the complete absence of troops. We turned down the communication trench, deserted too, and ploughed on.

" Each company has to hold a battalion front," my companion answered when I sought for an explanation.

" And were we all on our own last night when the raid was on ? " I asked, trying to digest this curious statement. Another thought struck me as the Corporal muttered an affirmative.

" Even so, but where was the rest of the company ?

" It just wasn't there. Don't you see, if companies take the place of battalions, platoons have to act as companies. It was our platoon that the raid was on, nothing else."

" We hadn't the ghost of a chance ; not an earthly," went on the Corporal. " Once they got the Lewis-gun in the sap the rest was easy, and well they know it."

" What's the inquiry for, then ? "

" Search me."

We passed the second line, which seemed to be deserted too, with the exception of a couple of men busy over a small oil stove at a dug-out entrance. Batmen, by the look of them.

The front was as quiet as the grave. When my companion proposed getting up on top to escape the mud I agreed with alacrity, eager to see what the place looked like. There was nothing to be seen. The falling snow seemed part of the greasy, chalky soil underfoot. Fifty paces away it was impossible to tell where the one ended and the other began.

I was vaguely alarmed about the coming questioning. Visions of a court martial for not doing something to repel the raiders, and perhaps a firing squad to end up with, came to me as we plodded on. The Corporal, burly and phlegmatic, seemed to have no such qualms.

" I can only say I was in the dug-out when it started and how we rushed out into the trench and got bombed. Will that do them ? " I asked him.

" Yes, that'll do them fine."

" I could tell them that the Germans were the Prussian Guards and what they wrote on the door of the dug-out," I added. " They might want to know that, eh ? Then they would know who was in front of us ! Don't they always like to know that sort of thing ? "

The Corporal grasped my arm. " For the Lord's sake don't say a word about that, man, or you'll get your head in our hands. Are you mad ? Just tell them the first part, about the bomb, and stop dead. If you give a whimper about the other, some crusty old Brass Hat as like as not will feel all insulted and send us over on a raid to-night to wipe the insult out in blood—our blood, you can bet your life."

" You were a mug to leave the dug-out at all—I didn't," he added calmly after we had progressed a few dozen yards in silence.

I stopped short, and stared at him, hardly able to believe my ears.

" But, but—what'll you say to the officers ? "

" Oh, you leave that to me, chum. I'll swing the hammer all right. What will they know about it, anyway ? If they're so all-fired anxious to know what happens in the front line they should come up and see for themselves. Admission's free."

We came to a steep incline and, sliding and tumbling, arrived at the bottom. A few yards round the side of the hill was a big sandbagged hut, with officers and N.C.O.s standing about outside. We reported. After a long, nervous wait I found myself in the presence of an immaculate officer with the little red tabs of the Staff on his collar. A number of other officers stood about. I related my simple story, putting the best face on it I could, and taking care to say as little as possible. Everyone listened attentively. When I had finished, the Staff Officer asked me about the Lewis-gunners. I denied all knowledge of them, and was dismissed to make room for the other fellow, who marched in quite at ease.

He was kept longer than I had been. I was beginning to think he had made a slip, or had been tripped up, but he came out smiling, and told me off-handedly that he had carried it off all right. I didn't ask for any particulars. Later, the Corporal's name appeared in battalion orders. He had been recommended for the Military Medal " for conspicuous bravery in organising resistance and repelling raiders."

THE REST

THE rest of the " tour " in the trenches was so quiet and uneventful that sometimes I rubbed my eyes and thought my imagination had played me a trick. It was bitterly cold. Not a shot was fired either by day or night, and more than once I boldly raised my head above the parapet and stared at No Man's Land, and away to where the Jerry line was, hundreds of yards away. In particular, I stared, along with other curious ones, at a gigantic dead Hun, who lay just outside our wire. He had been killed by a shell in the raid. His blackened lips were drawn back in a snarl of defiance. One of the men who seemed familiar with the German system of decorations said the dead man had been out since 1914 and was a Sergeant-Major. Even in death he looked virile and dangerous.

" What a loss he must be to them," I thought treasonably, eyeing his massive limbs.

I discovered that I had a curious disinclination to visit the latrine in the front line. I went along to it two or three times, but each time on reaching it stifled the body impulse and came away. It was a bare place raised well above the trench floor and a notice said " Beware of sniper." But it wasn't the idea of the sniper that held me back. I was too inexperienced to be afraid of invisible snipers. It was just the thought of a shell coming when I was partly naked that deterred me, and, although I knew it was silly, the feeling was so strong that I didn't attempt to overcome it. I found that a good many soldiers had the same idea.

The relief came. We went to the reserve line and then back to the underground barracks where I had first joined the battalion. It was a big place, capable of holding the whole battalion. Three main entrances led off into numerous narrow tunnels lined three deep on either side with roughly built mesh-wire bunks, which resembled scaffolding. Candles were at a premium. Without them I found it a hard job finding the way to my particular bunk in a pitch black tunnel which was a replica of a dozen other tunnels. I had no sense of direction and was continually taking the wrong turning and even entering the place by a wrong opening. It had a heavy, dank smell and water trickled down the grey, slimy walls. It was known as the Chalkpits.

Try as I would, I was always losing my way and wandered along looking anxiously for the unfamiliar features of my nearest neighbours, painfully shy and unsure of myself.

The others seemed to sense my timidity. When I passed a gossiping group gathered round a flickering candle I felt their eyes boring into my back. Once I heard a muttered voice inquire, good-naturedly enough, who the rookie Corporal was, followed by a smothered laugh. I hurried on, terrifically aware that I was being referred to.

I knew now that I had made a great mistake in not taking down the corporal's stripe before joining the battalion. N.C.O.s at home were different from those in France. Here a man was a sergeant, corporal or even lance-corporal by right of conquest, as it were. He was bigger, stronger, more energetic, or more experienced, and because of that was obeyed unquestioningly by the men, rather than by virtue of having one, two or three stripes up. The original regulars who remained with the battalion were almost without exception N.C.O.s, which made my newness and incompetence more pronounced. But it would have looked queer if I had reduced myself, without a word, to lance-corporal or private.

I didn't know what to do, but the first thing was to get a bit of candle. It was a mystery to me where candles came from. In desperation, I asked an oldish man, absorbed in writing a letter, for a little piece.

" I've only the one myself," he replied shortly without looking up.

" Where do you get them, are they an issue ? " I asked, determined to solve the puzzle.

" Why, in the canteen down in the village ; where do you think you would get them ? " he replied testily. I retired not much the wiser.

Sitting on my bunk, I pondered the matter over. It hadn't struck me that there would be such things as canteens up the line. It was a bit of an anti-climax that there should be white-overalled men serving candles and cigarettes and chocolate over a counter somewhere near, with a war on a mile or so away. And where was the village ?

That night I noticed a general exodus from the Chalkpits and decided to follow the crowd. The men all carried their dixies and I brought mine along too. Luckily they all went the same way—down a narrow, slippery path, which turned and twisted to keep some kind of gradient, and then turned right on to a broad road. It was too dark for me to recognise the road, but when I came to the " village " I recognised the mouldering heaps on either side.

The canteen was in what had once been somebody's backyard. Crowds of men stood about or sat on stools made up of loose bricks, drinking beer and gossiping. The talk was all about this or that battle, and the names Ypres, the Somme, Messines and Passchendaele were bandied about freely. Over in a corner an indistinct group was gathered around a crown-and-anchor board, the banker's chant rising above the hum of voices as he shouted the usual patter. I listened for a mention of the raid, but it had already faded into oblivion, if it had ever come out of it. After all, only one platoon had been concerned, so that fifteen-sixteenths of the battalion knew about it only at second-hand. Even in my own mind, with every passing hour, it assumed less and less importance—not worth remembering in the rush of unfamiliar happenings. I realised afresh that the principal thing for me about the episode, far outreaching the shells, the bomb, and the terror and confusion, was the fact that I had survived. The question whether I would survive similar episodes was only beginning to occur to me. Even so, it was fairly engrossing and left little room for memories.

I shook my thoughts away. Stepping carefully among the throng of men in the darkness, I went up to the counter and had my dixie filled with beer, and retraced my steps to the edge of the crowd. Not knowing any of them made me feel raw and out of place. I had never tasted beer in my life before. In the camps at home I had felt no desire to taste it, but I knew already that what I had done at home would have very little bearing on what I would do here. In the bitter cold dawns in the line I had taken my tot of rum with the rest and went off to sleep, warm and stupid as the strong, treacly stuff coursed through me.

The beer was cold stuff, and bitter as well. After trying to get it down in sips and then gulps I gave it up in disgust, and emptying my mess-tin on to the ground, turned away disconsolately. Having no liking for what the men about me were lapping up accentuated my apartness.

Another and greater disappointment awaited me when I went to the dry canteen, which was housed in an old shack. The supply of candles had run out. I cursed myself for not making for it first.

I followed the same plan to get back to the Chalkpits as I had used in getting to the canteen. Selecting a homeward-bound group, I walked along behind, dispirited and sad, railing at the cursed sensitiveness which kept me from knowing people. Unthinkingly, I followed my unconscious guides into the Chalkpits, only to find that I had come in by the wrong entrance. Along the narrow corridors, some in pitch darkness, others lit here and there with guttering candles, I wandered along, past card schools which made way grumblingly, laborious letter-writers, men asleep, drunk, or staring fixedly at nothing.

Up one dark tunnel and down another I went until I was hopelessly astray, wandering along stupidly, afraid to admit that I was lost, afraid to ask, staring into strange faces, examining empty bunks, trying to remember what mine had been like and not succeeding, wishing myself safe in the signal camp, or at home free from war altogether.

When I had almost given up hope I found my bunk. Rifle and pack, showing up dully in the light of a nearby candle, were old familiar friends, and I fondled them lovingly. The darkly shining rifle seemed different to all other rifles. My pack, with its meagre, intimate belongings, had a personality of its own.

Climbing up beside them, I lay with closed eyes, glad that I could so simply shut out the ugly man-made present. Only voices, pitched in a minor key, the chink of money and occasional abrupt oaths of the gamblers obtruded themselves into my consciousness. In an effort to reach complete detachment from my surroundings, I pulled my greatcoat closer round my ears, at the expense of my feet, and fell to musing.

Softly the quiet atmosphere of home came stealing over me. I lay motionless. My father, hale and hearty after sixty years, reading his newspaper through spectacles which he did not need, and innocently believing everything he read. Long, happy nights when I lay stretched before a cosy fire, my nose in a glittering tale of the Spanish Main, stumbling over the sonorous tongue of Cervantes, or wondering how French boys remembered all the different uses of *faire*—converting everything, English included, to my own, private pronunciation.

I tried to bring my mother into the picture—her greying hair, always slightly untidy, her pleasant, healthy face and trim figure, always on the go, but she persisted in appearing as I had last glimpsed her in the vulgar, echoing railway station, a pathetic, grieving woman reaching blindly through the iron grille of the platform barrier and smiling—the tears for herself and the smile for me.

I found myself involved in a fresh difficulty. I had been a signaller almost since joining the Army and remembered only the rudiments of how to drill ordinary squads. On parade after breakfast the platoon officer called me over and told me to put the platoon through squad drill. What I didn't know about drilling troops would almost have filled the manual of infantry training. What was far worse was the idea of me, only a few days at the front, shouting orders at men who had been there for months and years—the very men, perhaps, who had sat drinking their beer the night before, swopping yarns of Ypres and the Somme.

Under the critical eyes of the officer and sergeant I made an attempt at putting squad through their paces. It was no good. With Boy Scouts as material I might have made a brilliant success, but as it was, I was a failure, and knew it. I had had no confidence in myself to start with. The men knew it too. Seeing a chance to get their own back on authority, they added to the confusion by ill-timed movements and ragged dressing.

" Is that the best you can do, Corporal ? " asked the officer angrily, calling upon the squad to halt.

I was silent.

" But, my God, Corporal, that's hopeless. You are in a Regular battalion now, no matter what kind of a lot you belonged to before."

I was also in a false position, and saw my opportunity.

" I'm a signaller, sir, and don't know very much about ordinary drill. I would like to see at once about getting back into the ranks."

The officer relented.

" Oh, is that the way of it. Well, I will see that you get plenty of practice," he promised, and dismissed me.

" Why wasn't I wounded or killed in the raid," I thought as I rejoined the grinning platoon. Nothing would have mattered then.

The afternoon was taken up by a pay parade, and next morning, rather than face another ordeal, I went sick and had the satisfaction of seeing the platoon go out to their drill without me. I didn't know what to go sick with, and nearly made myself ill worrying about what the doctor would say when he found I was malingering. I needn't have worried. Reasonably enough the doctor took me for an old member of the battalion and accepted a lame yarn of a sore throat. The tip of my finger was suppurating where the splinter had torn it, and though I had forgotten about it, he noticed the dirty rag I had round it and supplied a clean bandage after cleaning out the puncture, and inquiring, incidentally, how I got it.

" Take the day off, Corporal," he said kindly, and I went away comforted.

When I went out again with the squad the platoon officer called me over. I obeyed with much the same trepidation as I had gone to the doctor in, but my fears were as quickly dispelled.

" I've been making inquiries on your behalf, Corporal, and I find there's a vacancy in the signal section. I don't think you could go as a full corporal, not straight away, anyhow, but you can go along and see the Signal Officer down in the village. Of course, if you'd prefer to stop with the company——"

" Thanks very much, sir. I'll go along straight away. Very much obliged, sir," I stammered.

" That's all right, Corporal. Let me know what he says."

My parting salute was not very smart, but the officer made no remark. Perhaps he guessed that it was heartfelt. A

sudden enticing vision of doing things I knew something
about appeared before me, and I found myself whistling as
I went along.

It struck me that the officer was not quite so disinterested
as he appeared, and for a moment I was obsessed with the
old sense of failure. Then I banished the idea lightheartedly.
What did I care what his motives were so long as I got away.
The prospect, too, of losing one stripe, or both, pleased me
immensely. I had no false notions on that score now.
Privates were better off than Corporals, and Corporals than
Sergeants. Platoon Sergeants were at once sheep and sheep-
dogs, and there was truth in the old saying that Lance-
Corporals were the Privates' batmen.

My naïve idea that the higher a man's rank the safer he
was was logical enough. Company Sergeant-Majors had a
better time, probably, than Sergeants, and very likely the
R.S.Ms.', was quite cushy, and so on up to Staff Officers; but
otherwise I had been wrong. I knew in my heart it would
take me all my time being a success as a full-blown Private.

The Signal Officer was a small man with a pink and white
complexion, the inevitable toothbrush moustache and a
rounded, girlish-looking chin. When I told him I held an
instructor's certificate he was quite agreeable to having me
transferred, provided I reduced to Lance-Corporal. As
that was all I really was I agreed gladly and was told the
transfer would be fixed up that very day. I saluted smartly
and went back for my kit. The sun shone warmly and life
was good. Before I reached the Chalkpits I took off my
tunic and solemnly reduced myself with the aid of my jack-
knife. As a non-com. I had been a washout. I longed for
insignificance.

The change over from the cold, impersonal company to
the comparatively small signal section acted as a tonic. I
made a mental resolve to make friends as quickly as I could
with my new mates. There was an easy-going, grey-faced

Regular Sergeant who gave the impression that long ago he had lost interest in the war and all connected with it, but carried on automatically from force of habit. Like the Corporal of the section, a big taciturn fellow with raven-black hair, he was a Mons man.

The first day out with the signal squad I made the acquaintance of what was—derisively, it seemed to me—called the Haig Line, an enormous system of half-dug trenches which stretched for miles between the village and the support trenches of the line proper. In no place were the trenches more than three feet deep and often only half that.

"Why is it they haven't every man digging away at it," I thought, "instead of doing stupid drill." Not that I wanted to dig, of course, but it seemed the sensible thing to do.

Under the eye of the officer we laid wires here and there and connected up the field telephones in readiness for practice messages. I was in charge of one phone, with three men with me, and everything went well for a time. The first message I took nearly proved to be the last. I was still far from being at home in trenches, even half-made ones, and my long period of office work had left me a bit rusty at the Morse. To make matters worse it was the officer himself at the other end giving some instructions. I missed a letter or two and got flurried, and ended up by making a mess of the message. No matter how keen a man's hearing may be it takes practice to hear over the telephone.

The Signal Officer, quite properly, ended up by telling me to get to hell out of the way. "For heaven's sake get Murphy on," he ordered, and putting down the headpiece I relayed the message.

An undersized, badly-made fellow with a soft brogue and a slum face rushed over and took my place at the instrument.

A minute later he turned with a half-concealed grin and informed me that he had been put in charge of the station for the remainder of the practice. The other two looked on non-committally, but with an expression that showed plainly that they only needed an opportunity to say what they thought of me as a signaller. I sat a little apart and they began chatting among themselves as if I wasn't there.

Black despair seized me, and I made no attempt to fight it off. Back I would go to the company—a double failure. The platoon officer would say I had made a fool of him, and would have his knife in me. The Sergeant and the men of the platoon would take their cue from him. It would make me clumsier and more backward than ever. Back to the Chalkpits, instead of the signal section's snug billet in the cellar. Wandering about the pitch-dark tunnels at night.

The battalion was a machine, cold and heartless, and I wasn't even a cog. A cog was useful, and I was no good. The machine didn't want me, but there was no escaping it. Up the line with the company I would only be in the way until such time as I got killed by a shell, or a bomb, or a bullet. The sooner the better.

I knew nothing about killing Germans, and did not want to learn.

The thought that it would be better to have done with it all straight away sprang full-fledged into my brain. I put a hand over my mouth to stop my lips trembling.

No! No! Not that!

But the idea persisted. It took possession of me. At home they would grieve, but the chances were they would never know. Probably they would get word, "killed in action," and would console themselves with that as well as they could.

After a long moment my hand came down to my side. My mouth set firmly. Lighting a cigarette I drew the smoke in, almost unconsciously, yet savouring its fragrance. My

eyes roamed over my companions, and away to the grey
landscape. I was no longer afraid of their veiled contempt.
What were they but cannon fodder, hoping against hope
that they would survive the war, suffering all the more
because of the little secret uncertainty that haunted them.
They were bloody fools and hadn't the wit to realise it.
Blast them all.

The face of the man who had been hit by the bomb on the
night of the raid came to me clearly. Again I stood in the
little circle looking down at him as he writhed on the dug-
out floor, at his frenzied, despairing eyes under the rough
ministrations of his fellows.

He was an old friend.

The mask which he had worn all his life, concealing his
innermost thoughts, had come away with his life blood,
leaving him revealed—facing death properly afraid, moaning
over his pain—grasping pitiably at the straws thrown to
him of Blighty and rejecting them—but human, natural,
stripped of pretence, and, therefore, a friend.

And the way he had gone I could go too, only easier—
away by myself, with nobody by me but a rifle, my beautiful
rifle, which had yet to fire its first shot.

I was aroused to present reality by my three companions
making ready to leave the raw trench which stretched like a
wound over the chalky ground. After helping mechanically
to pack the instrument I lagged behind as we wended our
way to the village. And with every step resolution grew in
me. I would never go back to the company.

We had been the farthest out and the rest of the section
was drawn up waiting for us. The officer looked us over,
his eyes resting angrily on me.

" All correct, sir," said the Sergeant, calling us to attention.

" Dismiss," came the order, and we turned right.

" The officer wants you," said the Sergeant as I broke
ranks with the others.

I went up and saluted.

"What the hell was the matter with you, Corporal. My God, man, are you stupid or what, that you can't take a simple message. You should have heard me quite plainly, it was a perfect line."

I stood woodenly, disdaining this time to make any excuse. The officer paused to clear his throat.

"Now for it," I thought, and steadied myself.

"You'll have to do better than that, or back you go to the company," he concluded pettishly, "so don't let it occur again."

I felt giddy as I walked towards the billet. The little Dubliner was standing at the cellar door and I nodded to him in friendly fashion as I went down.

My old skill at phones and flags and lines came back to me. I ate voraciously the tasty, skimpy rissoles the headquarter cook prepared out of bully beef. My only trouble was a splitting headache which grew worse and worse.

"I haven't been to the latrine since we were in the line," I confided to the big Corporal one evening just before tea.

"That's easy fixed, chum. Come along to the doctor's orderly and I'll get you a No. 9 or a dose of castor oil. You'll be right as a trivet in a couple of hours. What about lowering a couple of dixies of beer to-night."

"Right you are."

I enjoyed the beer fairly well.

One afternoon, instead of going out for flag drill, we marched up the broad St. Quentin road to be shown our "battle positions." Rumours of a German offensive were in the air, and had been for days past, but nobody got excited over them. For the men they were no longer rumours, but accepted fact. Here and there little groups would shake their heads over the half-deserted front line, where platoons took the place of companies and companies of battalions.

Their chief concern was that they should not be " in " when Jerry came over.

Jesting references were made of what they would do if they were. Some wag with half-arms half-raised above his head would mutter : " Kamerad, Kamerad," and there would be a general laugh.

I listened eagerly to such talk, not so much interested in the expected " do " as in the cynical comments. " What do the dodgers down the line care about us, so why should we care about them," was the way they put it.

Or again : " Of course, we'll stop them. Old Jerry'll drop dead with amazement when he sees all he has to beat."

I made no attempt to imagine what a big push would be like, and for that matter neither, apparently, did the others. " They know already, seeing they have experience," I thought. " They're disgruntled because nobody believes it's coming off but themselves, and they think they'll be left in the lurch. But they're not frightened."

I plucked up courage. There had been no shelling since the night of the raid, and I was content. The thrill of being near the line, of being in a Regular battalion, and of always having my rifle over my shoulder whether on duty or not—the ruined village and the billet in the cellar. These were enough for me.

" Why is everybody so sure there is really going to be an attack ? " I asked the Corporal rather sceptically.

" Why, everybody knows it," he said in surprise. " Up the line for weeks past you could hear the rumble of Jerry guns coming up. Didn't you hear it yourself ? "

An elusive memory came to me of a low monotonous noise which had seemed part of the night, and which I had thought nothing of at the time. I was silent. The steady rumble might have been hundreds and thousands of wheels moving up the Jerry line.

The section marched up the road in broad daylight as if

F

the war was a hundred miles away instead of a few kilometres.

I stared about me with interest, but the ground was like a desert. There were no trees and no grass, nothing but the grey chalk. It was an ugly, cheerless place, with something bleakly menacing about it which got stronger as we went on.

We marched steadily for an hour or more along the straight, level road. The men were uneasy, but I thought it was because the Jerry artillery might spot us. The squad was the only moving thing in the stark landscape.

Presently we halted. Three or four men were called out by the Sergeant and conducted across the field to the right to their battle position—a half-dug trench. The officer went over and explained what was to be done, pointing here and there with his stick. The men stood to attention, and saluted sharply when the officer turned to rejoin us on the road, leaving them behind.

I was hazy about the whole affair. Would the signallers be there by themselves ? If an attack came what good would they be ?

Turning to my neighbour I asked for enlightenment, but his reply was not very encouraging.

" It's all a lot of tripe from start to finish," he growled in an undertone. " If old Jerry comes over he'll knock hell out of us before you can say Jack Robinson. Who's to stop him ? "

" But what's the idea ? " I persisted. " What are we supposed to do ? "

" Christ only knows what you're supposed to do," he said, placing great emphasis on the supposed, " but I know what I'm going to do if I get a chance."

A third time we halted and another little squad left the depleted section.

My turn came. With three others, one of whom was the little Dubliner, we branched off the road for a hundred yards to where a small corrugated iron hut stood, its roof a bare three feet above ground. Inside it the earth had been excavated to a depth of about four feet, and set in a round hole in the centre of the floor was a telephone switchboard with half a dozen insulated wires rising from it, each a different colour.

After consulting a note-book the officer carefully selected a bright yellow wire, and proceeded to explain.

" This is a field exchange and test-box belonging to the R.E.s, and you fellows are damned lucky having some protection for your station. On no account whatever are you to touch any wire but this one. D'ye hear, Corporal ? "

" Yes, sir."

" This one leads back to battalion headquarters, and you'll hardly have any trouble repairing breaks, as it is underground the whole way. This is company headquarters, just along in the trench, that is, and you're to keep in touch all the time. On no account, remember, are you to meddle with the sappers in any way."

We returned to the road and started back to the billet, picking up the other stations on the way.

" It's all very simple," I thought, confident that I could do my share.

After tea we paraded again and were informed that we were to join our companies that night and proceed to the battle positions in the morning on our own. No one was quite sure when the show was due to start, not the exact hour, but it appeared to be an open secret that it would come off in the morning.

We were in battle order, which meant that we left our packs behind. Our iron rations were inspected for the last time, and in addition to full pouches we strung flimsy cotton bandoliers stuffed with ammunition around our necks. Then the field-telephones were served out—four of them, one to each company. The little Dubliner came over to me with the other members of the quartet, a morose fellow with a long, stubborn, backward-slanting chin, and a fair-haired, apple-cheeked boy with laughing grey eyes, who carried the phone slung over his shoulder.

We talked casually for a moment or two.

They belonged to a different company, I found, and the Dubliner explained that they would make for the hut separately, and I could join them there. Probably I would meet them on the road up. I agreed, paying little attention to what they said, and we went our different ways. I never saw them again.

A vague feeling of anticipation possessed me. I felt a bit nervous and wondered what the next day would really be like, but no premonition of actual personal danger troubled me. There might be a lot of men killed, but it was hardly likely that I would be one of them. I felt too new to it all for that to happen. Spring was in the crisp air, and war gave an added zest. I lit a cigarette and was only satisfied when the blue smoke went deep into my lungs, so that it needed two or three breaths to get rid of it all. Not a single gun broke the evening stillness. I enjoyed breathing even without the smoke, I found, when the cigarette was finished.

Shouldering my rifle I rejoined my company in their old quarters in the Chalkpits. Everything there was bustle and orderly confusion. Officers shouted instructions to their N.C.O.s or to their batmen. Lewis-gun teams oiled their pieces and bombing squads carelessly broke open boxes labelled " Mills." N.C.O.s were everywhere issuing, direct-ing, urging, cursing.

The men were excited and swore savagely at the least provocation, but their grousing was about little things ; stubborn rifle magazines that refused to fit, bayonets that resisted being bolted, buckles that refused to buckle and bandoliers that got in the way every time they stooped.

The whispered threats of " Kamerad " were forgotten

in the stress of getting ready. It made no difference now whether their numbers were many or few. They had rifles, machine-guns, bombs, and they had each other. The death of a trusted mate would affect them more than the loss of the battle. What did they care about the battle, anyway. It was none of their business.

A little thought came, and grew until it distracted my attention. To-morrow I would be alone until I found the hut—such a little hut. And when I found it I would still be alone, I knew, as I remembered my companions to be— except for the fair-haired fellow, perhaps. I had liked the look of him.

Things quietened down in the dug-out. A few older men wrote letters that would never be delivered. Some discussed their chance of leave that they would never live to enjoy. For some a last game of pontoon for money they would never spend.

Once more the hateful sense of apartness enfolded me. I lay down by myself near the door separating the officers quarters from the men's. On the other side of the door glasses clinked and mess orderlies kept coming and going. Each time the door opened a stream of yellow light escaped, and with it the strong odour of liquor and cigars. A gramophone played to the accompaniment of noisy laughter and snatches of song.

A quiet apprehension made my mouth dry, like the uncertainty of a boy who next day was to sit for an important examination, or who was about to start work for the first time.

Gradually the noise ceased in the dug-out. The orderlies stopped pattering to and fro. Leaning back against the earthen wall I drew my long legs close to my body for warmth and went to sleep with my formless fears.

THE ROAD

THE Company Sergeant-Major was nudging my backside with his boot.

Looking up, cold and stupid from heavy, comfortless sleep on the damp floor, I tried sluggishly to get out of his reach. His lips moved, and I recognised familiar oaths forming themselves.

But the words were lost.

A tremendous, roaring cataract of noise made the solid dug-out shake. . . . Bits of earth rained down from the roof, particles getting into my eyes. The air screamed as if in pain, or on the point of reaching some wild transport of sound beyond human comprehension.

I scrambled dazedly to my feet.

The Sergeant-Major put his face close to mine, his under-jaw thrust out threateningly, and shouted again, but again the words were lost. He motioned towards the steps, and I understood.

Up the steps !

Fumbling with the straps of my equipment, which seemed to have become inextricably mixed, I tried to listen, but gargantuan sound pounded me—exciting, stupefying, wildly inhuman.

A few men, their faces drawn with fear, ghastly in a strange, almost continuous glow which lit them eerily, came out of one of the tunnels, shepherded by a Sergeant.

They stopped beside me and huddled together, making a poor pretence.

One twisted his shoulders to reach a particular buckle.

Another looked to his rifle and bayonet.

A third bent over his puttees.

The Sergeant-Major came again, and they went slowly up the steps, crouching and looking fearfully about, overwhelmed by the stupendous, all-pervading roar of the guns.

As there was nothing else for it I followed, stupid like the rest.

Outside ghostly fire crowded across the sky. Great arcs quivered, shedding pale radiance, stabbing, jostling and colliding in some unearthly pageantry that suggested etheric silence and void in the midst of roaring and eruption.

And yet it was curiously dark. The sky was livid, but the earth remained lost in dense shadows which swirled and moved under the impact of mighty shells and yet clung close, holding us in a dank embrace.

Dimly from where I crouched at the dug-out mouth I made out, a few yards away, two ragged lines of men drawn up, men who performed a grotesque dance like so many marionettes as their bodies showed up darkly against a background of flame and sulphurous smoke. Fierce red glares, springing from the ground near at hand, told of shells bursting dangerously close, but their explosions were lost in the gigantic clamour. A thousand railway engines roaring and screaming over a thousand girder bridges might have equalled the noise—or passed unnoticed.

A late-comer blundered past me at an unsteady run, making for the platoons. I started to follow in his wake— and stopped. There had been something odd-looking about him, about the silhouette of his figure. Something faintly familiar. Something urgent.

" What's this ? " I asked myself, with a strong foreboding that if I did not find out at once I would pay dearly.

My numb brain awoke. Memory flooded it to the exclusion of all else. Dropping my rifle in panic-haste I clawed at my gas-mask and put it on, feeling that I had escaped a frightful death by a hair's breadth.

Picking up my rifle I took one last look at the yawning entrance to the dug-out. Safety was there, a yard or two away.

Stepping gingerly I made my way along the narrow, slippy path, a zigzag of insecure footholds, and reached the road. Down the road to the right was the canteen in the village. In front and all around was the rain of shells. Turning to the left I went up the road leading to St. Quentin.

With the putting on of the mask a terrible feeling of being blinded came over me. Peering through the filmy goggles I made out a bare yard or two of road, and beyond that nothing. I was enclosed in a world of my own, a blind defenceless world composed of soft flesh and rushing, roaring steel. Terror of death, sickening, horrible death, seized me, but I went on cringingly, a single question forming. If a shell burst beside me would I see it in time, sense it, with my face lost in the gas-mask, and my useless eyes ?

I went forward hesitatingly on the bare road—a blind man in the midst of falls.

Coming to a halt I raised my arms to pull the mask away. Anything was better than being taken unawares, being torn apart, without a second's warning of what was in store, and strewed in smoking, bloody shreds over the road.

The shells swooped down, relentlessly, majestically, unendingly, a vast screaming cascade of steel, filling the air with fiendish sound, gouging the earth.

And yet the mask was comforting, and I paused. Didn't it shut out some of the horror and keep from me the thick, acrid fumes of the high explosive ? And keep me from breathing poison-gas ?

For a moment I stood in miserable uncertainty. Dropping my arms to my side I shuffled on, head bent to save my face, shoulders rounded and stooped to shield my heart, elbows close and arms crossed to guard my stomach.

I was alone in a world gone mad.

Strange disconnected thoughts came to me, flitting in and out of semi-consciousness like moths round a glittering candle, thoughts which came quickly and disappeared as if striving to have a brief existence before it was too late. Death was all around. It might come before my advancing foot reached the ground, before I drew the next breath. Useless, filthy death. Like an ant crossing a road thronged with people, sensing danger with its tiny ant brain, but unaware that a thoughtless foot was about to crush it, I went forward. And through it all some impersonal part of me looked down, filled with pity and understanding and keeping pace with my halting steps. A part of me. The best part of me, perhaps—kindly, mocking, slightly inhuman. Or a hallucination born of the roaring guns. At first I tried to banish that other self, but without success. It was unnatural that some part of me should be calm and gently cynical about it all. Suddenly a terrible fear came to me. Fear of myself.

I thought of myself wandering about gibbering and clawing, no longer human.

The idea of offering up a prayer took root in my mind and grew. God would look after me—there on the road. And with it came, incongruously, the remembrance of pious boyhood problems. A fleeting memory of another walk. A quiet Sunday afternoon with a forgotten chum, a path of firm, brown earth and leafy trees bending and rustling overhead to let dancing sunbeams form a fairy carpet—a short walk with Sunday tea and cake and currant bread to follow, and in the morning back to school.

It was a sin to take the name of the Lord in vain. A senseless, ugly sin which we would never by any chance be guilty of. It would be a sin, too, to take the name of Moses in vain. And Heaven, for Heaven was the Lord's footstool. We had been boys then.

" But you are only a boy yet," said that other self, gently mocking.

A stupid question at best, so let it go. But the idea remained. I murmured an ancient prayer : " Our father which art in Heaven. Hallowed be thy name. Thy kingdom come. Thy will be done on earth as it is——"

I stopped. The rubber mouthpiece of the mask was dripping with slimy spittle, which clogged the air-tube and flowed coldly down my chin. What bloody, futile nonsense was this, anyway ? What was I praying for ?

I crouched, and the bellowing, tumultuous guns answered. Life.

No God. No kingdom here or hereafter. Only life.

Sweat broke out on me, and I broke into a lurching run to make up for that moment's pause. A shell might light on top of me—and I should have been a dozen paces farther along. A dreadful premonition of death—death before the end of the road—pursued me. What did it matter to God whether I came safely through or not ?

" Does it really matter to you ? " the aloof voice chided.

" Could God stop the shell already on its way ? If He saved me He would have to sacrifice someone else, and there was nothing very godlike about that. The other man might have been praying too. God Himself could not save all of us, and one man was as good as another while he was alive. Or the shells were blind and took the good and left the bad. One was taken and the other left, but the shells, and not God, decided.

Blind Luck was the soldier's god of battles, and whoever prayed to Luck ?

Almost reverently, and quite sensibly and finally, I gave up the idea of God doing anything for me. If Jesus of Galilee walked at my side, and a shell burst at our feet, there could be no resurrection either for Him or for me—not in the flesh.

A little obscure courage came to me and gave me peace.

I who in life had been lonely and useless would go west with a great multitude. The guns assured me of that, and it was somehow comforting. Men who knew all about life and what it had to offer were dying near me like flies, men who had known women and men who had children—real men.

A glow, at once comforting and sad, warmed me. What was I, a stripling youth, to cavil at Fate, when alongside me marched a legion, a ghostly, friendly legion, whose ranks extended to infinity.

Plucking up heart I mumbled curses on the clumsy mouthpiece of the mask which kept my tongue from performing its normal functions of gathering and swallowing spittle. It grew lighter, but a thick white mist, cold and clammy, covered the tortured earth. For a scant twenty or thirty yards I could see after a fashion. Beyond that a seemingly solid wall of mist blotted everything out, everything but the sound of the guns.

Sometimes I fancied I could distinguish a small movement, too quick to be registered before it disappeared, at either side of the road or a little in front. It was a simple, rather innocent occurrence in the surrounding uproar, and I paid little attention.

They were the duds, perhaps, of which I had already heard marvellous stories. Or some smaller shells with gas in them.

Still, I distrusted them.

Suddenly out to the left, right at the limit of my vision, there was a lurid flash and a great column of black smoke sprang billowing into the mist. Falling to my knees, and still watching, I put my hands up to shield my face. The pillar hung motionless, wavered, and was slowly swallowed up.

Rising to my feet I went on. I had seen my first actual shellburst of the war.

But my mask was awry as a result of the sudden movement, and in my blindness I tripped and fell headlong just as another great shell burst nearer the road. I hugged the ground, trying madly to claw into its hard surface as clods of earth rained down, striking my body dully. Something heavier struck my helmet and I lost consciousness.

I lay for a moment wondering what had happened. My head was sore and I was half covered with loose earth. Then I remembered the shell and put my hand shakily to my head. There was a dent in the helmet, but no blood flowed.

Getting to my feet I went on.

When I had put a hundred yards between me and where I had lain I whispered through trembling lips, " By God, I was near myself that time," as if the danger was safely behind me, instead of all around as before.

My confidence was shaken. I went along gingerly, peering into the blanket of mist. Every little while the little spasmodic movements came and went, as if invisible sparrows were having dust baths. The movements continually caught my eye, but always when I stared at the spot there was nothing there.

I didn't know how long I had lain unconscious on the road, and shivered when I thought of it. It must have been a long time, for I could see farther into the mist, almost twice as far, perhaps, though it was hard to tell. Still it was lighter, and I was able to walk a bit quicker. I hadn't gone far when, on the road ahead, I noticed something stationary. Coming nearer I made out a motor ambulance tilted drunkenly as if in the act of falling over on to its side. When I arrived abreast of it I looked curiously to see what the matter was. There was no one in the driver's seat. At the rear the splintered ends of a stretcher protruded through a big hole. One of the wheels was buckled. On the ground was a dark pool.

Something terrible had happened there, and some instinct impelled me to hurry on.

Hurry. And yet, for all its forlorn air, the ambulance was the first sign of life I had met with since starting off along the road. There was something comforting about the sight of it. For all its speed it had come to grief, while I, groping along like a blind man, was still alive.

At the end of a few dozen paces I glanced back over my shoulder, but the mist had already closed in behind and only a dim, drunken shape remained.

For the first time since I had started out I began to keep a lookout for the signal hut, but the mist and the gas mask limited me to a circle of grey road in front and the grey earth on either side, where the shells swooped down— primeval monsters determined, if baulked of human life, to rend and tear the ground itself.

How long had I been walking ? I didn't know. Half an hour ? An hour ? All morning ? I thought of my wrist-watch and peered at the dial, but the glass was off and the minute hand missing—broken in the fall, probably.

The hour hand pointed to nine o'clock. I looked again a few minutes later, but it was still in the same position. I couldn't remember whether I had wound it up lately either.

But a change had taken place in the mist. It was dry now and its greyness had changed to a silvery hue as if on the other side the sun was trying to break through. I went on, staring anxiously over to the left, but the hut was nowhere to be seen. I was beginning to be afraid that I had gone too far when, without warning, there was a rush of flame, followed by a violent explosion almost in my face. I glimpsed a great steel cylinder sinking smoothly into the ground at the side of the road. A wave of heavy air struck me full in the chest, almost lifting me off my feet, the breath left me and a feeling of impotence possessed me. The mask acted as a gag and in a panic I clawed at it and let the air into my lungs.

The feeling that I was alone had grown on me steadily.

When a man appeared at the side of the road and waved his arms excitedly I looked at him blankly before going over.

" By God, mate, the luck's hanging out of you. Did you not see the battery ? " he yelled in my ear.

My head still rang with the concussion. Pulling myself together I shouted back :

" Do you know where the R.E. signal hut is about here ? "

The gunner shook his head.

" Take my advice and don't go much farther up the road. Jerry's up there," he shouted, jerking his thumb.

I looked at him. Jerry ? I had forgotten about Jerry— Jerry who was responsible for all this.

" But what about you fellows ? What about the gun ? " and I pointed at the round steel drawn back now below the edge of the road. How would they be able to save a thing like that in a hurry ? There must be some way, of course, but it wasn't in evidence. I had a vision of madly galloping horses saving the gun in the nick of time, although more likely an ugly jolting tractor would grind its way to the rear with its precious burden. The gunner stirred and, stooping, put his hand on the ground preparatory to vaulting into the gun-pit. His lips moved, and bending down I caught the answer above the noise of the shells.

" Blast the gun," he said, and disappeared.

Folding the mask I had worn so long, and so hastily discarded, I walked on up the road. My face, and consequently my whole body, felt bare and unprotected without it, as a man would feel who had just shaved off his beard. A feeling of greater freedom, of being more in touch with what went on about me more than made up, though the pungent smell of high explosive burned its way into my nose, released now from the irritating nose clip.

I was tired, but went on hesitatingly. The friendly gunner was already far away—dead by now, perhaps—and what was the use of going on any farther.

The mist kept pace with my lagging steps and a feeling of hopelessness possessed me. Every step was an effort and every few yards won with death all round. In my heart I knew that I was very near the end of my resources. My teeth began to chatter uncontrollably. Again the premonition of death came, strong and insistent.

And then a new sound reached me faintly from in front, all but lost in the wild clamour of the guns. I stopped, straining my ears. There was something oddly suggestive about the sound, a quality at once intimate and unutterably fierce, as if there at the heart of the battle shells were disregarded and forgotten, and men were engaged in a blind struggle to the death of their own.

I went another few steps. Again it came, louder this time —the hot rhythmic beat of machine-guns ominously near.

I had come to the end of the road.

Completely at a loss what to do, I stood like a fool waiting for a shell to plunge down on top of me. To grope forward was madness. To go back along the way I had come was unthinkable.

I stared about irresolutely, ready to weep, and my eyes lit upon a little sunken lane branching off at right angles to the road. It offered more cover, and I went along it cautiously, half expecting to see it turn to the front where the machine-guns pulsated wickedly.

The lane led across the deserted ground for a couple of hundred yards and then, with relief, I saw it curve to the right, away from the front, and quickened my step.

" This is better than before," I thought, as I went along keeping close to the little bank, which gave some shelter from flying splinters and stray bullets. A feeling of comparative safety crept over me as I bent double and went on with renewed hope.

The lane turned again until it must have been roughly parallel with the road. There were no troops about, and I wondered where they all were. Battles seemed to be curiously lonely affairs. There were bound to be hundreds and thousands of men getting killed or wounded and yet the broken-down ambulance on the road was the only evidence that the R.A.M.C. existed.

And then the guns. There had been two or three—a battery, perhaps—back there where I had spoken to the gunner, but I had expected to see the place alive with them.

The lane went up an incline and then down into a shallow depression. In the centre was a big shed with open sides and a high corrugated iron roof. A group of men stood under the roof. I left the path and went over to them gladly. They hardly noticed me, so deeply engrossed were they. I looked at them in astonishment. They were gabbling away without attempting to listen to each other and here and there one burst into laughter and pointed excitedly ahead.

I looked, too, expecting to see something extraordinary, but the encircling mist jealously kept the secret of what was happening there. The men's faces were flushed. They breathed as though they had been running. Their eyes sparkled. I thought they were drunk.

The one nearest me turned and, grasping my arm convulsively, shouted hoarsely in my ear:

" Jerries. Coming over in thousands—marching along— not even deploying—saw them myself ten minutes ago—a break through—a break through."

I accepted this news rather sceptically. He was an artillery-man, I saw, and I had been as near the fighting as he had, and probably a lot nearer, without seeing a sinner, not even our own infantry, let alone the Germans.

" It's the truth," he cried. " The front and second lines are taken and hardly a man got away. Lost dozens of guns already—nobody to hold them up—a break through."

I began to be impressed. Had not the gunner along the

road looked calmly forward to deserting his gun ? Questions surged to my lips and in turn I grasped the man's arm and sought enlightenment :

" Where is all our side ? " " The Infantry ? " " The guns ? " " The Haig Line ? "

The group gathered round me, mouthing and shouting. I caught scattered words here and there : " Not enough guns—batteries knocked out of action—guns captured—cut off—battalions disappeared—blown to hell—Divisions—Jerries everywhere—millions of them—wash-out—break through."

Their strange excitement was infectious. I gave up attempting to hear what they said. Without cause, I, too, pointed and shouted, stamped my feet, and nudged my neighbours without knowing what I wanted to tell them.

The strident guns seemed to share our excitement. Waves of sound beat into my face, into my blood, and mounted to my brain until, like the others, I was drunk with noise.

The little circle where we stood staring into the white walls of the mist was a last refuge in an exploding universe. Outside it the guns raged unceasingly, swallowing up battalions, divisions, armies in a monstrous cataclysm of steel and blood.

G

THE TRENCH

I CAME to my senses to find that one by one the men were slipping off. They were mostly artillerymen and were going back to their batteries—if they had batteries—I supposed.

I wished I were in the artillery and had a gun to go to instead of this aimless wandering about by myself. I could stand where I was and wait till somebody else came along, but the high thin roof seemed to offer itself as a target. It was strange that it hadn't been hit long ago.

An officer might come along and want to know why the hell I wasn't with my battalion or doing something.

Again the faint staccato came from the mist ahead with its story of men at death-grips. I listened with slack jaws. The machine-guns again!

How could that be when I had left them up on the road?

Running from under the roof of the shed I went along the lane, my head bent to the storm and my useless rifle, with its naked bayonet, slung over my shoulder. As I went I sniffed the air suspiciously, but there only seemed to be the hot fumes of high explosive.

I would have thought twice about putting on the mask again, anyway.

The path meandered on, turning and twisting until my weak sense of direction failed altogether, and I wandered along automatically, the mist opening up in front and closing in behind.

The banks on either side gradually became lower until the path was hardly distinguishable from the bare ground. A few paces and it petered out altogether.

I stopped, undecided. About to wander off at a tangent,

I spied in front of me a half-made trench, ugly and naked, running roughly in the same direction as the path.

It was a bit of the Haig Line. Jumping in thankfully I walked along with bent knees and stooped shoulders, trying to reduce my lanky body to half its size. Even so, I was uncomfortably aware that I was half exposed. But I plucked up heart. It was better than walking along the lane, and I was bound to end up somewhere if I just followed my nose.

The mist didn't appear to be so thick.

For a long time the trench went on in a straight line, but for some reason or other it came to an end every hundred yards or so. I had to climb out and run two or three yards to where it started again. When this happened the same fear always came over me that it had stopped altogether. There was the danger, too, that I would be caught in the open.

The fact that I had walked for miles along an open road a little earlier in the day didn't offer any consolation when I scrambled over the intervening ground.

Great shells kept bursting on either side, sending up dense columns of black smoke. Each time they came I knelt down with head bowed as if in prayer, glancing fearfully to where the smoke hung as if loath to drift away.

I performed this manœuvre many times. The shells fell clear of the trench. I could hear individual explosions now as the great fountains spurted up alongside.

"Perhaps there's another trench running along over there," I thought, watching them burst at a regular distance out to the right. If there was, I hoped earnestly that the German gunners would stick to the target and that my own trench would escape their notice.

For the most part I went along stupidly as if my chances of surviving were increased by a kind of silly self-deception. When a shell swooped down I pretended it was a long way off. When I knelt to escape the splinters I tried to make

my mind a blank. When I slouched along I fixed my eyes
on the floor of the trench as if I had lost something there
and was just walking back that way to look for it. All the
time the fear of death was on me, catching at my throat and
making my knees feel weak, ready to send me babbling and
crying once it gained the upper hand.

As if the German gunners had decided I had gone far
enough a big shell burst with an ear-splitting crash almost
directly ahead. I dropped like a stone and lay quaking,
waiting for the next one to come nearer—wondering where
I would have been by now if by chance I had been walking
along at a slightly quicker pace.

The shell had fallen nearly a hundred yards away I judged.
After a short wait I got gingerly to my feet and went forward
step by step with downcast eyes, ready to drop at the first
warning. Where would the next one alight ?

The trench deepened a little and curved into a shallow
bay. Turning the corner, I stopped short. There were men
in the bay. Silent men. Ten, twelve, fourteen—who knows.
Such men as I had never seen before. Some lay in simple
attitudes, their arms raised protectingly to shield their
faces, like tired children on a summer day. Others sat back
with drooping heads as if asleep, their hands falling limply
by their sides.

I raised my head, and there in a shallow crater in the
trench floor, a little apart from the rest, lay the key to the
sorry riddle. A pair of stout boots, and puttees snugly
wrapped. Trousers, neatly turned over at the knees, clothed,
swelling thighs and lean hips. A tunic, creased naturally at
the waist rose cleanly to a pair of broad shoulders. There
was nothing else. Nothing but blood, and bloody, mangled
flesh.

For a long moment I stood taking in every detail of the
horrid tableau, then cautiously, almost mincingly, I advanced.
The world of war, the shells and the loneliness disappeared.

The sides of the little bay fell away into infinity before me, and only the obscene, bloody stump remained, barring my path.

Not to stumble, not to touch—Christ, not that—and not to look.

I came close with my head at an awkward angle and my eyes staring rigidly to the front as if on parade. Steadying myself carefully, I stepped over. Another ten yards and I would be round the corner of the bay. Averting my head now I drew level with the sleepers one by one and passed each slowly by.

But one was still awake. A tiny fluttering movement caught my eye, and I glanced round fearfully. The last man in the row looked at me. His lips moved :

" Water, water."

Without surprise I recognised him—the smart young sergeant of the draft I had come out with to France, and lost sight of since. His brown face was dirty grey now, and streaked with blood. His mouth hung open. Maybe he was dead after all. But as I looked his black-lustre eyes brightened, his lips moved, and again the word formed itself sluggishly.

" Water."

He tried to move, and his half-clenched hands fell away from his stomach. Glancing down, I saw a fearful wound through which his intestines came swelling.

Horror possessed me. I went through a meaningless pantomime. I touched my water-bottle, shrugged, pointed ahead, nodded encouragingly. Without altering my funereal pace, I reached the corner and went on.

Once out of sight I broke into a staggering run. Waves of nausea overwhelmed me. I tried to vomit, but I had had nothing to eat since the day before, and only a thin spittle dribbled from my mouth. I lurched on, bent double, fighting the sickness.

And then the dying, mournful eyes above the poor torn stomach, the headless, armless thing, and the huddled cadavers became inextricably jumbled. I slid to the ground, my reason trembling.

Gradually my brain cleared. I lay back on the crumbly earth, my shoulders resting against the side of the trench. The bombardment went on relentlessly, but with an impersonal roar, like some gigantic waterfall. I felt obscurely that what I had encountered in the bay represented in miniature all the blind bestiality of war, and that I had stumbled accidentally on the open, and yet carefully hidden, secret of war, its hideousness, and wantonness and the helplessness of its humble victims.

A man's baptism of fire is of no consequence. He has only been lucky to come through it alive, and there is no guarantee of luck the next time. But the baptism of death is a great ordeal which nobody passes through unscathed either in war or in peace.

Sitting there in a deserted trench I had a dazed feeling of having been in the bay when the shell came, and of having escaped it. Almost I felt at home in the trench. It seemed a haven compared to what lay behind. I could go so far as to imagine, and resign myself to death from a bullet, but never to be blown apart. That was indecent and unnecessary, an affront to being human. I would always hate and fear the shells. And, almost unawares, I had bridged the gap between those who had experienced war and those who hadn't. There was nothing mysterious or exalting about war. There was even nothing of the jungle law of kill or be killed. Even that small appeal was denied it. You were just exterminated, or you just survived. In individual cases it was a matter of luck. Taking it broadly, it was a matter of mathematics.

My ears, subconsciously attuned to the thunder of the

guns, detected a falling off. The battle appeared, to my little knowledge, to have reached a new stage which did not require the indiscriminate mauling of the ground. The black columns were not so much in evidence. The frightful screaming and roaring of the shells blended into a monotony of sound, all-pervading still, but less nerve-racking and overpowering in its effect. The guns seemed to be concentrating on the immediate front and the back areas. What this presaged I hadn't the faintest idea, and didn't care a damn, so long as it remained that way.

I continued on my way with not so much need for the fearful alertness of waiting for the next shell. My mind, more free to think, went back to the men I was to have met at the signal hut. I wondered what had happened to them. Their chances of ever getting to the hut were very small, as was the chance of the hut being still intact. If everything had gone according to plan, what good would we have been ? It didn't seem possible that fragile wires buried one, two or three feet in the ground could survive the countless heavy shells that had rained down since early morning.

I remembered the Corporal, stout and black-haired, who had been awarded the M.M. for his gallantry in repelling the Prussian Guard—and wished him well. He was now earning his medal in real earnest, whether he would or no. Dug-outs had not been considered necessary in the Haig Line.

It never occurred to me to ponder over the fate of the battalion as a whole. I had never set eyes on the Colonel, the Second-in-Command, the Adjutant. One Captain, whose name I didn't know, I had glimpsed on the pay parade at the Chalkpits. The battalion was only a name, an abstraction, and the little I had seen of it hadn't enamoured me of it.

The whole day was a mystery.

When the day and almost the hour of the attack were known beforehand why hadn't we been marched in peace and comfort to our positions the previous evening when not a gun sounded ? Then we would have been ready where we stood and known exactly what to do. The lives of hundreds of good men might have been saved. Then there were our guns ? The thunder of the bombardment must have been a one-sided affair. Where were there any men, except the few that the mist had hidden up where the machine-guns had stuttered ? With platoons acting as companies I knew they must have been very few.

But my childish attempt to understand came to an abrupt halt. Surely those were men ahead in the next bay. Moving men this time, for I could see their heads and shoulders above the low parapet.

I broke into a jog-trot, and came up with them.

A Sergeant and half a dozen men lolled about the trench near a squat, ugly gun fixed into the trench wall—a trench-mortar, I hazarded.

They straightened up in surprise when they caught sight of me, and then relaxed. I looked at them hungrily and then thought of the men I had left behind in the other bay— the dying man's plea for water. I would go back there if someone came with me, but not by myself.

" There is a trench full of men back there," I burst out breathlessly. " A whole lot of them. It was a direct hit. They are nearly all killed. There must be over a dozen of them. It's terrible—— "

I stopped. The men were regarding me quizzically. The Sergeant was puffing easily at the cigarette he had taken out of his mouth when I ran up.

" Well, well, well. And what about it, sonny," he said. " There's a war on, ain't there ? That's what shells are for."

" But I think three or four of them aren't dead yet," I stammered, exaggerating in an endeavour to impress them. " One of them was moaning when I passed by. He is hit through the stomach."

" And what do you want us to do, sonny ? " asked the Sergeant.

" Why, if you come along I'll show you the way. There is one of them lying in the trench with his head blown off."

" We can't stick his head on. We've no glue with us," said one of the men, and laughed.

" But, but——" I began, and then stood silent.

" Sorry, mate, but we've got this gun to look after, and daren't leave it," broke in the Sergeant. " We'll be going into action any time now, and if some nark of an officer happened along and half the gun-team away we'd be up against it."

" Up against a wall," added one of the men.

I stared at them, and they stared cynically in return.

I gave it up and turned to go.

" Maybe there is a dressing-station or something farther down," I said, curiously at a loss.

" Don't you believe it, mate. There's damn all in this do except shells. The dressing-stations and the doctors'll be blown up long ago."

" Or blown off," said another, raising a mirthless laugh.

I was silent again, not knowing what to say to this strange reception.

" Well, so long, boys," I said at last, and went on down the trench, my hand mechanically holding the butt of the rifle, which kept bumping against my thigh. Just as the trench straightened out again I looked back.

The gun crew once more lolled carelessly against the low trench wall, smoking and chatting as if they hadn't a care in the world. There was something unnatural about their cynical calm, something that was the reverse of reassuring. They were like men about to embark on a forlorn hope who knew beforehand that it was all hopeless, and that in a few minutes or an hour or so they, too, would be dead.

I tramped on, preoccupied with new and strange ideas of war.

Instead of running almost in a straight line the trench began to wander over the deserted landscape as if in doubt where to go. The ground appeared to share its uncertainty, and became broken into gullies and hillocks of chalky grey.

Gradually the trench got shallower and broader. It disappeared into a hollow, and became a slippy, uneven path.

I went down carefully, shoulders hunched, taking a tiny pleasure in placing each foot securely to prevent my slow walk from becoming a sliding run.

Reaching the level floor I looked round casually and was about to go on when I saw a tremendous gun over to the left, partly hidden by a crazy patchwork of rags. A single soldier was busily engaged doing something about it, and going closer I examined the great steel monster attentively.

It was the first gun I had ever had a good look at.

Its massive, rivet-studded carriage lay half embedded in the earth. About the breech little wheels and odd-looking bits of mechanism stuck out incongruously, giving the simple contours of the gun an unexpectedly complicated air. The thick slatey grey barrel projected high into the air.

The preoccupied gunner seemed not to notice my presence. After gazing my fill for a couple of minutes I turned to resume my journey.

When I had gone but a step or two I heard a shout. Looking back I saw the gunner standing with one hand grasping a thin wire running just above his head.

He was smiling. He had the exaggerated, theatrical air of a professional photographer who has at last succeeded in getting a client nicely posed.

I looked at him inquiringly as he gave the wire a jerk.

The gun moved.

There was a flash of lightning-like fire and a shattering explosion, which echoed and re-echoed against the sides of the hollow. The great barrel of the gun slid smoothly down, smoke wreathing from the muzzle.

I felt a sharp pain in the ear nearest the gun and, too late, covered it with my hand. My head became congested with blood, almost ready to burst with the pressure. The echoes died away. I stared round wildly, a sound like rushing water in my ears, hardly knowing whether I was on my head or my heels.

The smoke cleared, but the pain in my head and the roaring noise continued. My hand seemed to be holding someone else's ear. I rubbed frantically at it, but it felt dead, and the side of my face was numb.

The man at the gun saw my startled movement and dazed face. He laughed at the success of his effort, slapping his thighs. I looked at him blankly for a moment—then realised with a rush of rage and despair that he had had me for a fool. "You've burst my eardrum or something, you rotten bastard," I cried The voice, like the damaged ear, seemed to belong to somebody else.

He stopped laughing and took a threatening step forward, clenching his fists.

I felt a wild desire to grab my rifle, with its naked bayonet attached, and rush at him. Instead, I turned away impotently. In place of the rage that had filled me a moment before an instinctive urge came to cover up, to pretend that he hadn't hurt me after all, even to attempt to smile—until I was out of his sight.

There was the tremendous uselessness of telling him that he shouldn't have done a trick like that, that there was enough surely for one day of stupidity and hurt, a vast impersonal outpouring, without puny individual human beings acting as he had. It sounded naïve what I wanted to tell him.

Still holding my ear I made my way slowly up the opposite

side of the hollow. I kept on rubbing at it for a time, but it remained painful inside. The rushing sound, as if a large seashell were pressed against it, seemed a fixture too.

Reaching level ground again I went on without looking back. As I went I mumbled curses upon the gunner, but by and by my rage at him turned against myself. Why hadn't I changed his tune by sticking my bayonet into him. There had been nobody but the pair of us, and he had had no rifle to defend himself with. He had asked for it, but I had been too cowardly. That was what it boiled down to.

I fell to playing with the idea of what I should have done, if I had had the guts of a louse. A false glow of satisfaction filled me.

His laughing, jeering face suddenly changed as I flung at him all the meaningless, filthy words I had learned since joining the Army. He took a step forward, clenching his fist. But I was in a frenzy of rage and fright—rage at his senseless joke and fright at the terrible prospect of going blundering along without even my hearing. Pulling my rifle from my shoulder I rushed at him. For a breathless second he stared at me, open-mouthed. Then realising his danger he turned on his heel and made to run round the side of the gun. But too late. Automatically long hours of practice at sand bags bore fruit, and the point of my blackened bayonet sank into his backside. There came a wild yell, and I was alone with the gun. The point of the bayonet was wet and sticky with blood. Then I was running like a hare, expecting every moment to see a mob of mad artillerymen at my heels. When nobody came I dropped into a trot and then into a walk. I had a deaf ear as a memento, but the gunner also had a souvenir of the occasion. Probably he was now on his way to a dressing-station wondering how he could explain to an incredulous doctor how he came to have a bayonet wound in such a spot.

Comforted, I went on.

THE RECKONING

THE path became broader and more used-looking. Two or three other paths converged on it, and going down a steep incline I found myself at the base of a chalk cliff, into which a line of shelters were built. A little in front of these some men sat bunched together round the lip of a shell crater. I recognised the battalion colours on their shoulders. They stared curiously as I walked over.

" What's this place ? " I asked.

" Why, this is battalion headquarters," two or three of them answered together, and proceeded to ply me with questions.

" What is it like up there now ? "

" Where's Jerry ? "

" What company were you with ? "

Their excited questioning nonplussed me. What did I know about it ?

I stood awkwardly, and then proceeded in face of their expectancy to tell what little I could.

" I belong to ' A ' Company, you see, and started off first thing to meet three other fellows and start the signal station in a hut somewhere for ' D ' Company. I don't know what happened to the others, but I never saw them or the hut. Walked up the road for miles without seeing a sinner and then nearly into one of our guns as it went off. Wandered about after that looking for anybody at all, until I heard the machine-guns going just in front, and turned back. Came on the new trenches and followed them back. There's a whole squad of dead men back there in a bay."

I paused, overcome by the recollection, and pointed

vaguely over my shoulder. The idea of describing what I actually thought and experienced on my wanderings was all at once ridiculously out of the question. About God, and all, on the road, and being unconscious and sick, kneeling in front of the shells, fear, and how I had tried to conquer it, the trench mortar crew, the gunner and the pain in my ear.

But the men were waiting, hanging on my words, and I went on haltingly.

" Some artillerymen told me that Jerry had broken through and was coming over in thousands, not even taking the trouble to spread out, but marching along in column."

" There you are," broke in one of the men in I-told-you-so fashion. " It's true enough."

" The artillerymen said they had lost hundreds of guns," I went on, glad to have created some impression, " and the whole front line had been captured. Later I heard the machine-guns going again, so our side must have retreated a little more. But I saw none of the battalion except the men in the bay."

Suddenly I felt very tired and sank down in a vacant space on the lip of the big crater, anxious to escape further questioning in case colossal ignorance of everything should be exposed. I had been wandering about for hours and at the end of all had arrived at the battle headquarters of the battalion. I couldn't understand how it had come about. How far away were the other battalions ? Where was our own ?

The men left me alone and talked in scared voices. I listened greedily, staring from face to face.

They were young fellows, but their faces were grey and drawn. Most of them sucked eagerly at cigarettes as if their frayed nerves demanded some consolation from the horrors of the bombardment. They crouched close to the ground and to each other, and their eyes moved uneasily as they listened to the guns. Two or three of them belonged to the signal section and the rest were probably runners.

" I could understand a few of them being caught napping or even a company, but the whole battalion—— ? " said a signaller, reverting to some topic that my arrival had interrupted.

" The luck must have been hanging out of them. Fancy just waking up to find they had been taken prisoners. All over for them before they knew it had properly started, and all without a shot being fired."

" Did that happen to-day ? " I asked open-mouthed.

" Ay. They were captured in their dug-outs early on—taken by surprise, officers and all. We only heard of it a few minutes before you came along."

A man appeared at the entrance of one of the shacks and came towards us slowly. It was the big signal Corporal. The others leaned forward eagerly to hear what he had to say.

" Not a single line to the companies," he said heavily in answer to the questioning looks thrown at him. " Nobody knows a damn what's happening in front, now."

" What about the brigade line, Corporal ? " asked one of the signallers.

" It's gone again, and God knows if it will ever be fixed again. As far as we can make out the Division beside us has let Jerry in on them and left us in the air, though nobody knows whether it's true or not. The mist has everybody messed up. Just before the wire went we heard that ' A ' Company was getting it bad. A good many of them must be goners by now. Everything is in a mess."

" Any more news about the Redoubt, Corporal ? "

" Not a word, but it will be holding out, you bet. They got orders to hold out to the last, no matter what happens. Jerry must be getting it hot there, damn him."

" If the Redoubt goes it will be a bad business," said one gravely.

I listened stupidly. What was a redoubt and why should it be held to the last ? I did not know, and dared not ask.

But the talk about " A " Company interested me, seeing that it was my own company. At least I had been in the line with it once, or rather with one of the platoons.

" What is that about ' A ' Company, Corporal ? That's my company," I asked.

" Well, you'll probably never see them again in this world," replied the Corporal. " They've caught it hot up there, and the Lord only knows if any of them will get away with their lives. All their officers are reported killed and there was a Platoon Sergeant in command when we got word of them last."

My thoughts went back to the young officer who had called me out to drill the squad and had told me about the vacancy in the signal section. I was sorry for him. But after a vain attempt to remember the faces of some of the men I had shouted " Form fours " at I gave it up. Only the determined face of the Platoon Sergeant and the fat Corporal's came to me, and I had a fleeting hope that the Sergeant was the man in charge of the company, or what was left of it. The rest faded into the gloom of the Chalk-pits, where at long intervals the guttering candles had limned pictures old Dutchmen would have loved—sunken eyes, pallid cheeks, grimy hands holding cards—men bending awkwardly, pen in hand, over sheets of writing paper—all preoccupied, living in the minute. Dim rifles. Equipment. And, over all the dug-out, shadow.

The men about me moved and cowered closer. Perhaps they, too, had memories, or glimpsed what the future held in store—the whisper, the rising whine, and the shell that was meant for them alone, or the hum of the bullet that carried their name.

The Corporal turned to go back. Remembering suddenly that I was a stranger at battalion headquarters I asked him should I report to anybody.

" Let them go to blazes for a while," he replied casually.

" Just take a rest for an hour. It's the whole battalion we're looking for now, not you."

The Corporal went off, leaving me pleasantly relieved. It was nice to be sitting in comparative safety with comrades around me. I felt ravenously hungry.

" You don't happen to have anything to eat here ? I'm absolutely starving—nothing to eat all day," I inquired diffidently of one of the signallers sitting beside me.

" Come over here and I'll see if there is anything left," he replied. And I got up thankfully and followed him over to the shacks.

" Of course, there can't be very much, but what about the emergency rations. You've still got them, I suppose ? "

" But I—I didn't dare touch them," I replied, surprised. " Aren't they only for emergencies ? "

" Many a man has ate them for far less, and no questions asked," said the signaller.

We walked over to one of the shelters, and my companion rummaged about a wooden ledge, littered with odds and ends of wire, message-pads and dirt.

" Don't see a damned thing. I'll bet that some of those lads outside have wolfed the whole issue. Here, what's this ? " he said, holding up a round tin. " There's all there's left—a tin of pork and beans, if you can eat them, that is. Hate the look of it myself."

I seized it eagerly and ripped it open with my jack-knife.

" I'm afraid there's no fire to warm them up, or du pain," he added apologetically, " you see—— "

" That's all right," I broke in. " It'll do fine the way it is." Grabbing my spoon from its resting place at the top of my puttees I swallowed the cold, sticky mess ravenously, enjoying every mouthful. Then, searching my pockets, I came across a crumpled packet of cigarettes, also forgotten all day, and, lighting up, drew huge mouthfuls into my lungs.

When I rejoined the group outside they were squabbling

H

over some trivial thing. With a feeling that I was now only a spectator I listened appraisingly to the guns. They were certainly not nearly so bad as they had been in the morning, but they still banged away mechanically as if the German gunners who served them were wound-up automatons, in no danger of running down for some time to come.

The men, or more correctly, youths, stopped their futile quarrel and embarked once more on their gossip of disaster.

" The Redoubt is still holding out," someone reported.

A lean fellow with a hard, reckless face started discussing the attack and the others listened to him with respect. I noticed that he wore the D.C.M. ribbon. His name was Jenkins.

" I've been in every big do since the first of July and seen some shell-fire," he said, " but, by God, I never saw the likes of this."

" We thought the first of July was bad—couldn't imagine anything worse—and yet after our bombardment the Jerry machine-guns opened up and knocked us down like nine-pins as if nothing had happened. The other shows were much the same, except that each one got a bit worse, specially Ypres with the mud ; but Jerry must have brought every gun in France up for this do."

The others muttered profane assent.

" And yet our smart-Alec airmen never saw them, although we had only to cock our ears every night in the line, for weeks past, to hear the guns rumbling up all night long."

He stopped for a moment and lit the butt of a cigarette. " Why, by God, the ammunition must have been piled up mountain-high. And they never saw it. They'd rather be out of the line and telling the mamzelles what fine fellows they were and how many Jerries they'd brought down— like hell, brave boys."

The little audience growled in sympathy.

" Ay, that's the way of it. There hasn't been a single one

of our Johnnies up to-day and damned few any other day for that matter."

"You're right there, Jenkins."

I, too, thought of the peaceful days which had followed each other with hardly a shot being fired, the flag drill and telephone practice carried out as if the front was a hundred miles away. It was only yesterday that we had marched up the St. Quentin road in broad daylight to be warned off to the battle positions without a shot breaking the stillness and without the hum of a single aeroplane. All the time Jerry had been laughing up his sleeve and his guns had been wheel to wheel a few miles away.

Jenkins went on : " And the louts should have been going over in hundreds, blowing up the dumps. Why is it, too, that our stinking artillery have hardly fired a shot for days past and all that stuff lying praying for them a mile or two away—ready to be blown up, asking for it ? "

Nobody knew.

" But what about the fog. How on earth could the planes see a day like this ? " asked the signaller who had given me the beans.

Jenkins was adamant.

" They didn't need to see," he snarled. " They knew where our line was and where Jerry's started. They had only to go over and drop bombs and they were bound to hit something, weren't they ? And besides, the Jerry storm-troops must have been lying on top of one another for nights past, not to mention the guns. Haven't us chaps to fight no matter about the weather. We don't get told to put up our umbrellas or hoist a white flag if it's raining, so why the hell should the airmen, when they knew what was coming off ? They'd only get done in anyway if it went to the worst— the same as us, and a damned sight easier."

" But what does it matter, anyway ? " he ended bitterly. " We're the mugs, not them, but I hope to God Jerry reaches a lot of the twisters down the line and cuts their tripe out."

The audience treated this as a grim joke, and there was a scattered laugh, which sounded slightly forced, but Jenkins did not join in.

A Sergeant appeared from one of the shelters and beckoned Jenkins over imperatively.

" I bet I'm for up the line again looking for the Bat. See you later, boys," said Jenkins, and lighting a fresh cigarette he went off slowly.

A feeling of pride possessed me. " The biggest bombardment of the war," he had said. And he knew. The long, drawn-out strain and terror of the day, which had appeared hysterical and exaggerated sitting there, now returned softly and were justified. I could, should, have been killed a thousand times, but I was still alive where thousands more experienced and better men than I had died in scores, dozens, or alone.

A long hour passed.

" The Redoubt is still holding out, but the men are nearly all killed," went the rumour.

A movement amongst the men caught my eye and looking up I saw a man coming unsteadily towards us. He wore the Red Cross armlet of a stretcher-bearer, and his clothes were stained with dark patches of blood. His face, although pinched and wan, was that of a young fellow. He walked slackly, over at the knees. On reaching us he sank down heavily without speaking.

The man nearest to him made room, and offering a cigarette inquired with rough sympathy : " Bear up, mate. What's doing up there now ? "

The new-comer stared vacantly at the ground and made no offer to reply, or to accept the proffered cigarette.

We looked at him curiously, each realising that there was something ominous about his demeanour.

" Come on, mate, buck up. What the devil's the matter ? "
said one, adding for the others' benefit in a lower voice :
" What's biting him ? "

One of the signallers reached over and patted the stretcher-
bearer on the back encouragingly.

" You're all right, chum."

The man stirred and looked round dully and started to
speak, keeping his eyes fixed obstinately on the ground :

" ' D ' Company got it in the neck. And we couldn't get
the wounded down."

There was a moment's silence.

" ' D ' Company ? "

" My God, them too ? "

" Old Captain Thompson's crowd."

A runner got up hurriedly, his sense of duty aroused.

" I'd better go over and tell them," he said, pointing to
the officers' shelter, and went off.

The stretcher-bearer took no notice of the interruptions.

" The Captain sent runners down, but they mustn't have
got through—none of them came back. Then he was knocked
out—got a shell to themselves, he and Mr. Bell. You could
have put what was left of them on a shovel."

" Did Jerry come over on you."

" We never set eyes on Jerry the whole time," said the
stretcher-bearer vacantly. " He was supposed to be just in
front of us and then he was reported to be between us and
the company on our right. We couldn't see for the mist, and
it didn't matter, anyway. We were caught in the bombardment. One of the officers tried to get in touch. He disappeared, too. No, we never saw Jerry—never set eyes on him.
The Lewis-guns ran out of ammunition—they had kept
firing into the fog."

" Couldn't they have made off out of it ? "

" That's right. What was the sense of sitting there,
anyway ? "

The stranger looked up fleetingly.

" Some of them tried that," he said, " but it was no good. It was worse farther down, and, anyway, it was better in our bit of trench than in the open. Then a big one caught Mr. M'Donald's platoon. He was the only officer left. Jerry must have been very near after that for he turned a machine-gun on us—or else some other company did. ' B ' Company, maybe. I dunno. We couldn't see. Mr. M'Donald was badly wounded in the head—blinded, and what was left of the boys kept firing on at nothing. I tried to get the officer down the line. I had no bandages left, but he could walk all right. We didn't get far till a big one burst almost on top of us. I was knocked stupid. When I got up the officer had run away. I went after him and caught sight of him once or twice, then lost him in the mist. I searched about for a long time, but it was no use. He's still up there."

The runner came hurrying over with the Intelligence Officer, and we got to our feet. A couple of men helped the stretcher-bearer up and the officer led him away, plying him with questions the while.

We sat down again silently. How should this news be received ? Disaster was in the air and the dazed man's fragmentary recital kept repeating itself in our thoughts.

" Companies smashed up before the Germans come up ! " I thought. " What must it be like where men have lived through the shell-fire and the Germans come slinking out of the mist about ten to one and with no great desire as like as not to take prisoners—not time to take prisoners back and afraid to leave them to wander into the mist and escape ? "

I had heard tales of how Germans had been done in by our side in similar circumstances. The men who told the tales had been looked upon as tough fellows and admired accordingly. A whole battalion captured together would be safe enough, but it would be different when little groups and

Lewis-gun posts were taken, especially if they had held up
Jerry's advance for a time or knocked some of them out.

"So M'Donald got his packet," said a young fellow beside
me. "It's funny how things turn out sometimes. He had
me on the mat for not saluting him last time up the line.
In the front line, mind you."

"M'Donald," I repeated, and then remembered. The
blinded officer that had run into the mist and got lost.
Perhaps he was still wandering about the shell-holes—an
officer no more, but only a blind man without a guide. Or
had a shell, as blind as its victim, put him out of his pain ?

The Signal Corporal came over to us from the shacks.

"It's beginning to look bad, boys. That's two companies
that have got it pretty hot, and the other two must be in
much the same boat. We've lost touch with the battalions on
either side, and the one that was holding the line in front has
went off the map altogether. There's millions of Jerries.
When one of them's killed a dozen take his place. They're
everywhere, and the whole blasted Division seems to be
about napoo. Jerry has made a clean sweep. We've hardly
a gun left."

"Who's holding the Jerries up now ? " asked a man in a
scared voice.

"What's left of the old Div., I suppose," answered the
Corporal slowly. "Very likely the Jerries are mopping up.
It will be getting dark, and they'll be expecting counter-
attacks, though there's nobody left to make any that I know
of. The reserve platoons were sent up, but it must have
been like buns to an elephant. Imagine a handful of our
chaps counter-attacking whole battalions or more of Jerry's
best troops in the face of that bombardment ? "

"But, good God, Corporal, there's bound to be a lot of
our fellows up there yet," said the man who had cause to
know the blind officer, forgetting his wonder at the workings
of fate in this new emergency.

" Well, tell us who it could be ? " jeered the Corporal.
" The Bats in the line are all dead long ago—or taken prisoner
if they're lucky. The rest of the Division must be up in the
air, seeing that Jerry is through at the side. Nobody knows
just what's going on up there, but if you notice, there's
practically no shells falling now, in front, I mean. That's a
bad sign.

I cocked my good ear and found that he was right. Heavy
shells rumbled overhead on their way to the back area.
From up in front, where before there had been bedlam,
came the beat of machine-guns blended with dull, subdued
explosions as though some gigantic beast of prey was snarling
deep in its throat as it slobbered and tore at its kill.

It was colder. Gradually the evening shadows were closing
in on us. We huddled together fearfully in the immense
graveyard that a little earlier had been the field of battle.
The air seemed heavy with the sadness and mystery of the
day.

We talked in monosyllables, looking timidly over our
shoulders to away where skeleton battalions, companies and
platoons still fought doggedly their lost fight.

A Sergeant came up and ordered us shortly to get ready to
move.

We obeyed docilely, wondering what the move was to be,
and filled with vague forebodings. Other men joined us from
the shelters—orderlies and odds and ends of headquarter
details whom I had not set eyes on before—until we numbered quite a fair-sized squad, about twenty or thirty
strong, including the N.C.O.s.

For half an hour we hung about uncomfortably in loose
formation.

The Colonel appeared with three or four other officers,
amongst whom I distinguished the Intelligence Officer and
the spick and span Signal Officer, his cheeks not so pinky

now. They talked together in low tones and then the Colonel came slowly towards us, accompanied by a powerfully built, black-moustached, rather truculent-looking Captain, who, I learned, was the Adjutant.

The Sergeant called us to attention. We stood stiffly as the tall Colonel looked at us for a moment with kind, weary eyes, and away to where the rest of his battalion was—or had been.

" Are the men ready ? " he asked.

" All present and correct, sir," replied an officer, saluting jerkily.

There was a pause while the Colonel, lost in momentary study, stood silent with bent head.

" Let us go, then," he said gently, and taking the lead, the officers following respectfully behind him, and the squad bringing up the rear, we set off, stumbling over the broken ground in the darkness.

After a few minutes we reached the road—the road to St. Quentin—and, turning our backs on the front, went down it.

The guns had stopped completely now and our footsteps made a hollow, shuffling noise on the metalled surface, intensifying the strange silence.

Death was everywhere.

The night closed in on us threateningly, shutting out the scene of the massacre from our downcast eyes, filling our hearts with awe.

I thought of the men in the little bay, staring into eternal darkness instead of into the mist, and of the unnumbered thousands who lay with them in other little bays and bits of half-dug trench. We were trespassers.

We pressed on. Who knew but what the shells would start again any minute.

We passed through the village where the canteen was, but the groups of gossiping beer-drinkers had vanished. The place had already been looted by passing troops and empty chocolate and cigarette-boxes lay about.

We looked longingly at the inviting wreckage, knowing that there were still pickings to be had, but our looting propensities remained unsatisfied for the present. Only the mutters of the men testified to their desire as we passed by without slackening step.

" There's a box half full there."

" Any amount of fags."

" Why shouldn't we have it instead of Jerry ? "

We left the road and halted two-deep in a field which had apparently been selected as a rounding-up ground for troops from the front. Everything was in the wildest confusion. Stragglers roamed about aimlessly, breaking the ranks of our disciplined party.

Hoarse officers and foul-mouthed N.C.O.s stood here and there shouting orders, which sounded more like entreaties.

" All men of the 10th Battalion over here."

" 13th Battalion this way."

" Fusiliers to the left, Rifles to the right."

" R.E.s, Artillery and all other stragglers this way."

" Halt there, what's your mob ? Fall in here quick."

We halted in a clear space, and our officers joined in the bidding.

" 1st Battalion form up here "

" All men of the 1st Battalion this way "

" Fall in the 1st Battalion."

The squad stood at ease, and the N.C.O.s spread out a little, halting and questioning all that came their way.

At first there was little response to the officers' shouts, but they persevered. Then in ones and twos and threes men came—straggling, limping, roughly bandaged, grey-faced and worn. They gathered round us, looking hungrily for familiar faces, begging for water. The N.C.O.s pounced on them and fell them in, disregarding their puzzled questions.

Hours passed, and still the work of sorting out the broken

units went on feverishly. Three or four Lewis-gun teams joined us, cursing their heavy charges.

A field-kitchen made a welcome appearance, and forming into single file we received a meagre portion of stew, supplemented with hard tack. Ammunition was served out. The sense of urgency increased, and the shouting died down. We were counted half a dozen times at short intervals, and at length marched off, leaving the remainder still at the field.

" Where is the line now ? " I asked the man beside me, one of the latecomers.

" We're the line, such as it is," he answered.

" But I mean who is behind us now holding Jerry up ? "

" Nobody, matey, not a sinner. We left them to it as soon as it got dark and pushed off. That was the order that came. Jerry is supposed to have broke through in some other part of the line. So they say, anyway. Jerry's a couple of miles back, or maybe less, taking a rest. He's done enough for one day."

This was something to digest, along with the stew, and I asked no more questions.

We trudged across country, cursing the heavy ammunition strung round our necks. By and by we got on to a narrow, uneven road, deserted except for ourselves, and went along it for a mile or two until we came to a farmhouse. There was the usual delay, and we stood about shivering. The officers seemed undecided what to do, but at last the order came, and we trooped into a great barn, half filled with hay, and settled down.

A couple of headquarter signallers, whom I knew slightly, lit a candle-end, got out a cooker tin and set a dixie of water on the thin, blue flame. In a surprisingly short time the water was boiling, and from a screw of paper one of them tipped in a couple of spoonfuls of cocoa and sugar.

A warm, appetising odour came off the dixie.

Blowing out the flame the pair squatted down in the hay,

ignoring me, and tried the cocoa. It was too hot for them. Making the best of a bad job they grudgingly offered me a drink.

I accepted eagerly, and although the dixie burned my hands I put it to my mouth and swallowed, the resultant glow more than making up for scalded lips and tongue.

Seeing me drink, the pair reached for the dixie and tried again, but had to admit defeat. Taking another sip I thanked them and went off to my corner, leaving them alternately sipping gingerly and swearing.

The coarse straw jagged my face, but following the example of the others I pulled armfuls of it over me in lieu of blankets, and with my tin hat for a pillow went off to sleep.

THE BRIDGE

WE were awakened, and tumbled out of the straw, shivering and blinking in the raw morning air. There was absolutely no gun-fire. But instead of being peaceful the silence pressed heavily upon us. The officers had a gloomy, preoccupied air. The men were silent, knowing by right they should have been dead along with all the rest.

We fell in down in the cobbled yard, and after a few minutes' delay, which we spent in stamping our feet and slapping our shoulders in an effort to get warm, we moved off.

There was no sign of breakfast, but somehow we hadn't expected any, and weren't disappointed. Still, we were hungry, and hot tea would have worked wonders.

The short sleep had not given our frayed nerves time to recover. Once out of the farmyard we looked about, uneasily aware that for three or four hours we had been out of touch with what was going on. We knew without being told that there was no such thing as being relieved—not yet, at any rate—and we wondered how far Jerry had advanced in the meantime, and where he was.

It was misty again, but the mist was not so blanketlike as it had been the previous day, and gave promise of breaking up sooner. It didn't seem to matter so much either whether it was misty or not. We had the place to ourselves and took courage, stepping short and sharp to overcome the morning chilliness. We were upwards of one hundred and fifty strong, I judged hastily, and our iron-shod boots rang out with a solid comforting ring on the frosty road. Jerry and the battle might well have been a nightmare, but nevertheless our minds were troubled.

The rest in the barn had been useful if only because it definitely marked off in our minds the past from the present. From when the Sergeant-Major had kicked me awake in the Chalkpits to when we had sank into the straw was one day, complete and indivisible—and already fading in my memory.

Some things stood out sharply and would never need any effort to bring them back, but others would be hidden away in some mental Chalkpits, down which memory would go groping its way along gloomy tunnels, with here and there the guttering candles shedding a dim light on a forgotten face, thought, experience.

We were bewildered by what had happened and looked at each other covertly to see what attitude should be adopted. It was too soon yet to grouse or be cynical, so we kept quiet and stared into the mist.

At the end of an hour's brisk marching we left the road and went over fields. The ground rose and fell gently. The short cropped grass was white with frost and felt springy underfoot. There were no other troops about, and I wondered what had happened to them all.

Leaving the road spelled action of some kind, and we looked round inquisitively, wondering from what direction the trouble would come, and what it would be.

Topping a little rise we halted. Before us the ground fell away to a hidden river flowing along between deep grassy banks. Directly in front, about a hundred yards away, I made out a grey stone bridge, very solid and peaceful-looking.

The officers drew apart and the Colonel and Adjutant pored over a map, talking eagerly. The men lay down on the grass and smoked, wondering whether this was the end of the march or a temporary halt. It didn't matter a damn to us either way so long as things were quiet. Better on the march, perhaps, for the ground was cold.

The question was soon decided.

Orders rang out. The men of the companies were posted out in front, fan-wise round the bridge. The signallers and runners weren't included in the order so sat tight, until, catching sight of us, the Adjutant ordered us down the slope, where we lay contentedly with the silent river for company.

There was nothing to do, and still no sign of anything to eat. The march had made us ravenous with hunger and we crunched the hard tack from our emergency rations. Then, as no one objected, we got our bully beef and ate it as well.

The tall slim Colonel and the barrel-chested Adjutant stood up above and searched the ground in front with their field-glasses, the signal officer and the intelligence officer, who commanded the runners, a few paces behind waiting to transmit instructions.

All four seemed excited and the Colonel continually emphasised his remarks with jabs of his cane to different points of the compass. Sometimes he turned and stared over our heads at the bridge, as if to fix its position more firmly in his mind before pointing to the front again.

We began to think there was something exciting going on and crawled up the bank and looked too, but only the grey-green fields met our eyes and we soon came down.

The mist got thinner and presently the sun came breaking through. Its warmth put us in good spirits. We sat smoking and talking in low voices. It began to get monotonous sitting staring up the bank and watching the officers.

" It's a pity we hadn't a telephone to make ourselves useful with," I thought idly, remembering the days at home when we set up practice stations in quiet woods and fields. Suddenly, from far ahead, a few scattered shots sounded and a moment or two later a harsh, intermittent rattle. Machine-guns were coming into action out in front.

The officers strained their eyes anew as the noise gradually increased in volume with shorter intervals between the bursts. The men around me became excited and talked quickly, breaking off in the middle of a sentence to listen intently and exclaim :

" We might have known old Jerry wouldn't be far away," said one disgustedly, as bullets whined overhead. Sometimes a sharp hiss came and without being told I knew that it was caused by bullets coming near.

I kept my head down. The firing got fiercer, and from being thrilled I became uneasy.

The fellow beside me plucked my sleeve and looking round I saw three men setting up a heavy machine-gun right in the centre of the bridge where it rose over the water.

The three men worked quickly and methodically. In a surprisingly short time they had the gun up and proceeded to fire heavy bursts over our heads, the reports sounding very loud coming from a mere machine-gun.

Although it was one of our own guns its vicious pulsation was unnerving, and the now familiar sense of impending danger came over me. Oddly enough, it wasn't altogether an unpleasant feeling this time.

" After all, they aren't shells," I thought, as the gunners got down and worked and the bullets roared over.

Jenkins, the runner, came over to where I lay in a little circle with the other signallers.

" We mightn't have any artillery behind us, but we've got the suicide squad to make up," he called out, laughing.

For a long time the bullets roared triumphantly overhead, slaying the enemy somewhere ahead as they advanced to attack the bridge. Then something went wrong with the gun. It stopped firing and the gunners worked over it feverishly.

" It's always the way," said the man nearest me. " They jam just when they're wanted. They're nearly as bad as the Lewis-guns, and they're no blooming good at all. Same old story all the time."

Bullets began to fall in the dip, and we crouched down, little haphazard jerks in the grass warning us to be careful. Then an officer came running over the bank with his hand on a man's shoulder. We stared, flabbergasted.

It was a German prisoner, tall and thin, with a small, peaked face, and trousers and boots much too big for him.

The idea of taking a prisoner after yesterday's debacle struck my companions as supremely ridiculous.

" Maybe we've won the war after all," said one hopefully.

" No such luck. That poor specimen was never captured. He just gave himself up."

" He's one of these 'ere refugees," hazarded a fellow who answered to the name of Butcher.

" No fear. If he was a refugee he'd be wheeling a pram or a handcart with a poor mongrel underneath pushing its heart out," expostulated another gravely.

" Well, anyway, he's a funny looking customer," replied Butcher. " He ought to be stuffed and sent home to show what brave fellows we are. To the nearest museum, indeed, for it'll be a hell of a long time before we take another prisoner."

The others went on with their facetious comments, but I paid no attention. I could hardly believe that here was one of the men who had fought on the other side the day before. To me they were some kind of supermen who revelled in blood and slaughter and bursting steel.

As the prisoner passed by his scared blue eyes lighted on us and then dropped timidly. His helmet was shaped like a coal scuttle, and, like the rest of his outfit, was far too big for him. His papery grey uniform had a poor-house air. The tucked-in trousers and clumsy boots reaching halfway up his calves gave his legs a massive, navvy-like look, which his bony knees and thin shanks belied.

He disappeared over the bridge with his escort and I turned away wondering.

I

" He's only a young skitter," said Butcher Brown

" Yes, only a youngster, and you can see he's scared to death," went on Butcher, disregarding the fact that he himself was only a youngster. " He very likely thought he would get a bayonet in his guts on account of the way his pals cut the tripe out of us yesterday."

" So he should, too."

" That's what I would do with the bastard. He would never have got this length if I'd caught him," said Jenkins.

" They want to get as much information out of him as they can first," said the signal Corporal.

" What good's his information to us, I'd like to know," replied Jenkins cynically. " I'd far rather hear that our relief was coming, or that the rations were coming up— something useful. Besides, our artillery seems to have done a bunk, so what good would it do if that lad let out that the storm troops were coming over in thousands in five minutes' time ? "

Further conversation was interrupted. The machine-gunners on the bridge got going again and sent out an almost continuous stream of bullets.

A runner sitting a few yards away was wounded in the head, and two or three crawled to his assistance. In a couple of minutes he was roughly bandaged and getting shakily to his feet went off at a stumbling trot for the bridge, his helmet at an awkward angle.

He seemed a long time making the short distance. The machine-gunners stopped firing to let him past, but just as he reached them his arms went up and he sprawled full length and lay still. One of the gun crew reached over and fumbled at his chest for a moment and then shrugging his shoulders turned to the gun, which went on firing harder than ever.

" Hard luck, he stopped another, or else one was enough," said Butcher in my ear.

The officers still searched the ground in front with their glasses, but I saw that they knelt now, sheltering as much as possible behind the bank—all except the Colonel, who stood upright.

" There's something very odd about all this. Where are the trenches," I thought. It didn't seem like any warfare I had read of in France. " And where are the troops that should be on either side, and the artillery ? "

Suddenly the machine-gunners stopped firing—for good this time, and began hastily to dismantle the gun.

I nudged Butcher, but he and the others were already staring over, attracted by the sudden cessation of the clatter.

" So that's the game," he said disgustedly, and one of the gunners kicked a pile of empty drums and made the " Wash-out " signal for our benefit.

" What game ? " I asked mystified.

" Don't you see that they've used up all their ammunition as fast as they could, firing at anything or nothing, so as to get an excuse to leg off and leave us. The only gun we had, barring the Lewis-guns with the companies."

The sight of—as I had thought—three resolute men doing their best to help us beat off the Jerries had heartened me wonderfully. Their viciously-spitting gun had been as good as a battalion of rifles. Instead the bullets had been going harmlessly into the ground somewhere ahead and all the time the crew had been looking forward callously to leaving us in the lurch.

In a minute they had finished their packing and disappeared over the bridge without a backward glance. The men about me swore.

" Let's hope they die with their guts hanging out," snarled Jenkins.

" What are we here for anyhow ? " said Butcher to me savagely. " Are we expected to hold up the whole German Army on our own ? "

I shook my head, surprised that anybody should ask my advice on anything connected with the war.

"Probably it's that bridge," I replied, fervently wishing myself over it.

The fire in front got hotter. Wounded men began to trickle down. They passed us without a word or glance, their eyes fixed hungrily on the bridge. Beyond the bridge they saw golden visions of safety, comfort and Blighty. Some had not waited to get their wounds dressed. They trudged past with blood dripping from their fingers or soaking into their uniforms. We stared at them enviously.

"How does it come that they can all walk?" I asked stupidly.

"Well, you see, these are the lucky ones, but there's bound to be a few unlucky ones back there," said Butcher pointing to the bank.

"You're right there," broke in a runner. "I was up above a few minutes ago. I tell you it's no joke. Old Jerry is sweeping the place with bullets. There's a few of the lads up there that have stopped two or three, or else got it in the chest or belly. They'll have to stop there till Jerry comes over or it gets dark enough to get them away. It's a good job Jerry didn't come up until the boys got time to dig in a bit."

"Where could we get them to?" put in another. "We've no stretcher-bearers and there's no dressing-station that I know of about here."

"It's hard luck, but what is there to do? It'll be a good thing for them if Jerry does come over soon—the sooner the better."

"Unless he just sticks a bayonet in them to save himself any trouble."

"That's the worst of it. He might do that."

"Maybe one or two of the boys are 'sou'ing' themselves

when they've got the chance," said Butcher. " They'll be lying out there with only one or two officers. A single shot couldn't be heard in all this racket. A bullet through the foot, or a pal to put one through the arm and the trick's done, eh, boys ? It's not as if they were up the line where they'd be easily caught."

Some of the rest muttered assent. Others looked incredulous.

" If I was up there, I wouldn't be five minutes till I was down with a nice Blighty and over that bridge like a whippet."

" Like hell you would ! "

" More likely you'd be court martialled and shot," I said doubtfully. " Doesn't a shot fired from a rifle held close up against you leave the wound and the clothes about it all singed ? "

Butcher laughed contemptuously and leant over. " Why, man, all you have to do is fire through a full water-bottle, and the bullet might as well come from a hundred miles away. Not a mark, see—except on the bottle, of course, and that's easily planked somewhere out of the way."

I thought of the men lying in front badly wounded with no one to look after them and soon to be dependent on the tender mercies of the Germans, and knew I would rather " sou " myself and chance getting off with it than be in their position—if I could screw myself up to doing it.

The Germans came closer. The machine-gun fire was heavy and continuous. The officers looked worried. After a short talk with the Colonel the Intelligence officer called a runner and set off over the bridge.

" Perhaps there are some troops back there in reserve," I thought.

There was very little talk now, and we lay hugging the ground wondering how it was all going to end.

Presently the officer came back at the double and reported to the Colonel, who listened gravely.

His runner hesitated a moment and then came over to us.

" Anybody behind us ? " his mates asked eagerly, but he shook his head.

" Not a one that we could see. The blamed country's deserted."

We crouched down, glancing uneasily out of the corners of our eyes, listening to the leaden hail. With surprise I noticed that the Colonel remained upright and swished his cane against his leg. The Adjutant and he kept staring anxiously to the front, and then back to the bridge. They seemed to be waiting for something to happen, or watching the progress of a neck-and-neck race. But the contestants in the race—if it was a race—were invisible to us.

" We've had about enough of this silly stunt," said Butcher jerkily. The rest nodded agreement, but there was nothing to be done about it, and nobody spoke. The thing was would we get away alive, and that took most of our thoughts.

The two officers stared backwards and forwards with set faces. The bridge was the goal and Jerry was very near it.

Suddenly things began to happen. Several stocky, black-moustached French soldiers came into sight at the far end of the bridge and began clambering about like monkeys. They seemed too intent on some job, or in too much of a hurry, to notice the bullets. They took no notice of us.

" Runners this way," came an imperative shout. Half a dozen men were dispatched to the companies.

" Come along, lads, get ready to move," ordered the Signal Sergeant, who had been sitting morosely by himself, but who now was very wide awake. The Signal Officer stood beside him, still chubby looking, except that he needed a shave.

We sprang to our feet, hardly able to believe our ears, and then ducked hurriedly as bullets hissed past.

The bridge suddenly looked bare and forbidding as I envisaged the possibility of having to cross it.

The Frenchmen completed whatever they were doing on top of the bridge and then slipped underneath the single span out of sight.

The men began to crawl back from the companies, slithering into the shelter of the bank headforemost, their eyes popping with excitement. Some of them, including the Lewis-gunners, were made to line the bank. The rest of us got loosely into fours and stood bending down.

There was no attempt to bring in the badly wounded and no one mentioned them.

I kept looking towards the bridge. It was the first time that I had seen French soldiers, leaving out the old wrecks we had passed at the base. My heart warmed to them. We weren't left completely in the lurch. They were our Allies and it was fine to see unknown foreigners risking their lives to let us away.

" What exactly are they trying to do ? Going to blow up the bridge ? " I asked.

Butcher Brown, who was next to me in the ranks, snorted.

" They look as if they're not a bit sure themselves the way they're hopping about."

" Let's hope they don't get the breeze up too much and blow it up before we get across," said Jenkins. " I never swam a stroke in my life, and I'm not going to start now."

" It's mined already, and they've only to make sure that everything's all right."

" Look. They've got the wind up about proper," exclaimed the Signal Corporal.

We looked. The two Frenchmen had reappeared and were running about fussily, shooting panicky glances over their shoulders and ducking their heads continually. They were going through the motions of laying a wire.

Long minutes passed. Cursing broke out, and we made little uncontrollable movements as bullets filled the air and swished the grass at our feet.

The Germans seemed to sense that we were on our last legs and the fire reached a crescendo.

A young officer who had been out in front and who was now acting as lookout, suddenly collapsed and came rolling down the bank—dead before his body had stopped moving.

A rising shriek, and then a heavy crash beyond the bank, momentarily drowned the rattling machine-guns. We winced, and bent lower.

Fear caught at my throat and with it came the vision of being blown to pieces.

" Surely I can escape a shell or two now after yesterday's avalanche," I thought, but that was a poor argument where shells were concerned. An almost overpowering desire to take to my heels possessed me, but I didn't dare move a step. The men about me were in little better case.

Again a shell shrieked and burst, nearer the bank this time. Clods of earth rained down on our helmets. We were lost.

I dropped to my knees. The ranks became jumbled. Men started to edge towards the bridge, their looks only a remove from being openly mutinous as another shell plunged into the top of the bank.

But what was this ? The Frenchmen waved invitingly, and turning their backs made off.

Immediately a loud command came from the Adjutant.

" Righto, men. Over you go."

Hell for leather we made for the bridge.

" Take it easy, take it easy. Don't be in such a hurry," shouted the Colonel. Glancing back I saw him and the black-browed Adjutant advancing at a walk. The Colonel was flicking his leg with his cane, as if beating time.

We surged over, trampling the dead runner. A shell lit where we had been standing a minute before, sending the earth flying.

Rather sheepishly we re-formed ranks. The men broke into confused talk, their faces perspiring, but happiness at having escaped the shells another time rendered me dumb.

A little distance off to the right were the French engineers. One squatted down, holding on gingerly to a little black box. From the bottom of the box a wire ran back to the bridge. Another stood on tiptoe to see the last man safely over.

The Colonel and the Adjutant came up leisurely. Under the eyes of the Sergeants we got into fours, with our backs to the bridge. The Colonel was in good spirits, and laughed and joked with the officers.

"Quick march," came the order, and we started off. Behind us the officers still stood in a little group round the Colonel.

We had barely gone a dozen paces when a muffled boom sounded, and every man jack halted of his own accord and looked back.

A cloud of oily black smoke was already in the air over the bridge, hiding it from view. It billowed lazily, and then hung motionless for a moment before slowly settling. We stared expectantly.

"Move. What's the matter with you?" shouted one of the Sergeants.

Out of the corner of my eye I saw the two Frenchmen making off across the field, bobbing up and down like rabbits as they bounded along rather than ran.

The smoke disappeared. Hoarse laughter came from the ranks.

The bridge was still there, apparently not much the worse.

THE OLD MEN

IT was cold in the field at first, and the sweat dried on us. We had marched many kilometres the day before and a good part of the night and we were very tired.

We hung about, unable to rest, but when the sun began breaking slowly through the mist we were quite cheerful. It was pleasant to sit on the grass and rest and talk of yesterday's doings, although they too were becoming dim in our memory.

We were hungry. The lucky ones who had biscuits left gnawed at them ravenously, each trying to give the impression that he was at the last bite in case someone should ask for share.

" I'll bet old Jerry wouldn't have called the bloomin' Kaiser his uncle when he saw that bridge left open for him ! " said the Corporal.

" Aye, talk about hands across the sea, but give old Jerry a bridge across the Somme and he's laughing," said Butcher Brown conversationally.

" If I was at those Frenchies' behinds I would put my boot in them. Weren't they proper saps ? All they had to do was to blow the thing up and chase off."

" That's right. All our trouble for nothing. And a few good men killed and wounded, too, when they might as well have given themselves up straight away for all the difference it made in the end."

" And we'll be blamed for it," said a Lewis-gunner, who, having lost his gun, stayed with the signallers. The signallers had no telephones, so were equally at a loose end.

" Hanging on by the skin of our teeth," said the Corporal,

" for half the day. And all for nothing. First the machine-gunners did the dirty on us. Then the froggies had to make a mess of it—there'll never be a word about that in the papers, and if you tell anybody about it they'll say you're a liar—engineers they would call themselves. What a hope. I'd like to kick them, too."

" And so would I," said Jenkins, and added reflectively : " That is, if I hadn't my bayonet handy. I don't like putting my foot in dirt if I can help it."

" Maybe they were spies. They say the place is alive with them," broke in another. " Jerries dressed up as Colonels and Majors. They come up and order men to retire, or say the situation is hopeless and they should give themselves up. Why shouldn't they dress up as Frenchies and pretend to blow up bridges and roads ? "

We had been warned the day before against listening to any but our own officers, and to be very suspicious of strangers, especially staff officers giving orders for retirement, so this suggestion was well received. An order to retire would have been received even better.

In a day or two it would take its place with all the other rumours which circulated amongst us—spies leading battalions away—men running away without putting up a show of resistance and leaving others in the air—artillery that had fired all day on their own men, that had got the wind-up and sent thousands of shells harmlessly into the ground before the Jerry waves came over and, when he did, gave battalions and whole Divisions of the attackers a free passage into our lines—batteries that had deserted their guns long before they should have—battalions in the front line that were sacrificed for nothing and of whom no trace was left—posts slaughtered by their own machine-guns.

Mismanagement, misdirection, breakdown, chaos.

Nearly every man had some dark story of his own to account for the big defeat, but who was to blame we didn't know and didn't ask. It was none of our business, and we didn't worry. Some big bugs, likely, had made a mess of things. We were only the mugs—not a very enlivening prospect.

Our humble thoughts, concerned more with our empty bellies than the fortunes of war, blamed nobody, and praised nobody except the Colonel who had walked after us coolly when we broke and ran for the bridge.

Rumour was the only thing we were well supplied with. Nobody knew where the battalion transport was. They appeared to have lost us completely, or we them, so we had nothing to eat except the remains of our iron rations. The three or four Lewis-guns we had had used up nearly all their ammunition defending the bridge, and on the long march following that episode a good many of the men had surreptitiously dumped bandoliers of rifle ammunition.

Part of the night we had spent in an unknown village. We had sat huddled together for warmth or prowled restlessly through empty houses looking for food, wine and loot, but without getting more than a few musty books, mostly Bibles, and faded daguerrotypes of peasants in their Sunday best.

Now we were in a bare field, with an empty farmhouse behind us to relieve the monotony. Where the field was, and why we were in it in preference to any other field, were mysteries which we made no attempt to solve. The sun would soon be shining. There was no firing, and we were still alive, although for how long we didn't know.

The house behind was a poor affair with walls of wattle and daub, but it became popular as the men got thirsty and trooped to the rusty pump in the old yard to fill their water-bottles.

An hour passed, calm and peaceful, as we sat and talked or lay stretched out on the grass smoking. Those who had no cigarettes watched eagerly as the cigarette grew smaller in a comrade's lips, waiting on the promised butt. Smoking took precedence of hunger. War and shells seemed things of the past—right enough in their proper setting of muddy, grey trenches, evil-smelling dug-outs and rusty barbed wire, but alien to the healthy unspotted earth of the fields.

The ground about us rose and fell in gentle undulations like the breasts of a woman, and the memory of the girl at the camp at home came back to me as I lay curled up and half-asleep. Once again my lips pressed hers in the darkness of the old shed by the roadside, and my hands wandered timidly over her smooth tender flesh, I smiled wryly as I pictured my attempt to bring away a sweeter, more enduring memory of her when I had the chance, and a poignant sense of loss crept over me that I made a mess of it. The wild struggle on the bank that last time with her. How easily, in retrospect, I could have won. Would there be any more chances ? With a woman, sometimes, who would not struggle and fight like a wild thing. Or were all women like that ?

The questions disturbed my reverie. I tried to shake them off and think only of the hour we had spent in the shed and of what might have come of it, but they persisted, and putting aside my brooding thoughts, I turned to the others, sadly aware that they were all strangers to me.

They were sitting up stiffly, their faces screwed into expressions of strained attention. I stared at them in surprise.

A single rifle-shot sounded from in front.

" There it is again," cried Jenkins triumphantly. " What did you think it was—somebody letting off a squib ? "

" That's a signal of some kind, I'll bet," said a runner and started up to tell his officer. But the officers had already heard and were gathering about the Colonel. In a few moments the men who had been replenishing their water-bottles at the pump came running back at the double, followed by the Adjutant.

" Come along, lads, get into line and lie down. Three paces—quickly, now."

We bustled about obediently and spread out across the field, lying down at full length, cuddling our rifles against our cheeks.

The harsh rat-tat of machine-guns came from the front, where the mist still lingered. Heavy explosions made us shrink down.

" They've still got their big guns with them," said a hoarse familiar voice in my ear. I looked round to find Butcher's broad, homely face at my side.

I nodded, pleased that for some reason or other he had attached himself to me, even temporarily.

The men about me were looking apprehensively ahead and sending little questioning glances at each other. We had no stomach for shell-fire. Bullets were bad enough.

" Who is up there ? " I asked, knowing beforehand that he knew just as much as I did—which was damn all.

Our Lewis-gunners hadn't started to fire yet. They had too little left to fire indiscriminately.

Suddenly the machine-guns crackled with redoubled violence and shells thundered and screamed, filling the air with their vicious, metallic clang. For about five minutes the uproar continued and then it stopped as if by magic, and only a few scattered rifle-shots came.

" What is happening ? " I asked Butcher, afraid to say more in case he should notice the tremble in my voice. There was something awesome in that sudden murderous fire, so close and yet not directed against us, and about the silence, too, which the scattered rifle shots intensified.

" It sounds like an attack, but who can there be up in front ? " said Butcher, scratching his head.

The answer came.

" Steady, men," bellowed the Adjutant, dropping to one knee beside us. His jaw was thrust out and he gripped his revolver, finger on the trigger—a fighting animal, ready for anything.

Excited cries reached us and bearing down on us came a crowd of men, running helter-skelter, their forms rendered indistinct by the dissolving mist.

A ragged volley rang out from our line and some of the oncoming men dropped.

" Don't shoot. Don't shoot," they shouted and came stumbling on.

" Who told you to fire ? " roared the Adjutant as the men came up. They were British.

Their faces were distorted with fear and they panted for breath. Most of them were unarmed.

As they ran between us the Adjutant reached out and caught hold of one of them, a Sergeant. He made no attempt to halt the others. Only a brick wall, or a machine-gun, would have stopped their headlong flight.

" What the devil's the matter with you ? " said the Adjutant as the Sergeant, with working face and eyes which did not appear to see what was keeping him from running on with the others, tried to break free.

We stared round curiously, for some reason ready to look away quickly. The Sergeant's panic seemed a private matter—not meant for prying eyes. He had a lean, bony face, almost handsome in its own way, and was of medium height and build, just such a man as could have been found by the hundred in every battalion in France. He was a thing apart now. He made an effort to pull himself together and seemed to notice the officer for the first time.

" He came over on us, sir," he stammered. " Came over on us just back there. We had dug ourselves in a bit, but he crept on us in the mist and had us nearly surrounded before we knew. It was so foggy. Then he turned his machine-guns on us. All our officers were killed and we had no ammunition left. Then he shelled us—knocking half the lads out—they're all up there."

He swallowed and pointed vaguely over his shoulder.

" Then they came over on us. Hundreds of them. They had flame-throwers, too, and we thought we had run into him again when you started firing at us. It was awful— awful." His voice cracked.

The Adjutant noticed our inquisitive glances.

" Look to your front, you stupid fools," he shouted angrily.

" Well, buck up, Sergeant," we heard him say gruffly, but with an entirely different inflexion in his voice. " You did your best, I'm sure, and nobody can do more than that."

Out of the corner of my eye I saw him patting the Sergeant on the back reassuringly, and talking away to give him time to recover before reaching the Colonel, who was standing outside the farmhouse. Butcher uttered a string of fearful oaths and ended with an allusion to the Adjutant.

" Fools, indeed ! We know that without him telling us. But he's all right—a real hard case, but all right, and don't you forget it, matey."

Our turn came, and bullets began to search us out. Our Lewis-gunners joined in and sent out thin streams of lead, but there was nothing for the rest of us to do but to stare to our front through the grass stems.

Runners came and went, and the mist disappeared completely. A man near me cried out and set off for the rear with blood streaming from his forehead, into his eyes and on to his chest.

Butcher nudged me with his elbow. " There's going to be dirty work soon, and not at the cross-roads either. That's number one."

" What's the sense of trying to stop Jerry here, anyway. There's nobody on either side of us and the bastard has only to walk round us," grumbled the dispossessed Lewis-gunner beside me. " We've no artillery or supports."

" You would think I was a staff officer that didn't know his knee from his elbow," retorted Butcher. " How the hell do I know ? "

More bullets came hissing round us and the hubbub grew louder. It was closer too, and faces became strained. A couple more men were wounded and went off round the farmhouse.

Shells began bursting in plain view up the field and columns of black smoke sprang up and towered hugely in the still air before wavering and drifting away, as if loth to bare the ugly crater underneath.

" What's the matter with you now ? "

" Take my advice and get ready to run like blazes," he muttered, taking no notice of my irritableness. I saw that he had one knee drawn up beneath him and one hand pressing the ground, ready for a flying start like any athlete, except that his back was turned to the way he was going to run.

" What about the officers ? " I said, glancing involuntarily over my shoulder.

" They've got a good start on us when the time comes, ain't they ? "

But I made no attempt to follow his example and remained prone on the ground, holding my rifle to my cheek mechanically.

The man who jumped to his feet first and made off would be a coward, a man who deserted his comrades, leaving them in the lurch in face of the enemy, but he would be a braver man than I would ever be. And leaving shame out of it there was the danger of the officers behind—the hard-faced Adjutant who would whip out his revolver and shoot as an example to the rest without a moment's hesitation. I knew I would carry on obediently and do just as the rest did, run back, stay, or even advance. I knew also that for all the good I would be I might as well be sitting at home in

K

an arm-chair, or lying in front of the fire reading a book.

And I knew, too, that for all Butcher's preparations my long legs would cover the ground faster than his if it came to it.

Discipline still held and we lay tense, watching the falling shells come steadily nearer our thin line and listening to the chatter of the machine-guns. Our own guns were only firing an occasional burst, so that most of the noise was made by the attackers.

But I paid no heed to the bullets. The shells held all my attention, and I stared at them stupidly, unable to move.

" They're close behind those shells as sure as fate," said the Lewis-gunner with intense conviction. " They'll be on top of us inside ten minutes."

The din increased and clods of earth began to fall about us. The field which a little while before had been calm and peaceful in its bare greenness was charged with menace, although the sun shone brightly overhead now and made the grass sparkle. The hateful smell of high explosive, with its power to induce terrible memories, enveloped us and made me cower down. We were only a few men in a field ringed in with things we couldn't combat.

I thought of the panic-stricken Sergeant's talk about flame-throwers and wondered if they were as bad as the shells. The shells came inexorably nearer, and I knew they were the worst, with their metallic roar which I hated and feared and their hungry search for soft human flesh. I forgot about Ginger and the Adjutant, the girl and the battalion, and lay supine, waiting.

A little noise separated itself from the uproar with marvellous distinctness.

" Here's one coming," shouted the Lewis-gunner and hid his face.

A little whispering sound, inconsequential, impersonal,

came from far away. It rose into a moan, changing its impersonal note for one of imminent, inescapable disaster, and then with a rising shriek burst in the line of men.

I lay like a log as the fragments tore through the air and the last of the earth came pattering down. Silence followed the clamour. My face in the grass and my ears ringing I lay pressing into the ground, seeing nothing, hearing nothing, waiting for death. When the earth stopped raining clods I still lay gazed and stupid.

Someone jerked my arm, then caught me under the arm-pits and tugged.

Dimly I recognised Butcher's voice, hoarser than ever and almost unrecognisable with its urgent pleading.

" Hey, Corporal, Corporal ! For Heaven's sake wake up. Are you hit ? Corporal, Corporal ! "

I stared about. Hit ! " Was I hit ? "

Butcher kept tugging, and I got drunkenly to my knees.

" Come on. The rest are all away," he shouted bending down to make sure that I heard.

Leaning on his ready arm I got dizzily to my feet and staggered along. When we reached the farmhouse a thought struck me and I looked back.

" What happened to the shell ? "

" Come on," repeated Butcher.

" Where's the Lewis-gunner ? "

" Ah, to hell with him, and the shell, too," cried Butcher roughly. " We're all right, and that's the main thing. Hurry up, or we'll lose the rest of the boys. It's ' damn you, Jack, I'm all right ' in this show."

The morbid fear of mutilated men was on me again and lent wings to my feet. In the fleeting glance I had sent behind I had spied a little group of motionless men lying in crude attitudes, curiously lonely and remote.

"Did the gunner get his?" I asked again, but without any great curiosity now.

Butcher nodded. "Five," he added succinctly.

"Did the rest run after all?"

"Well, no. The officers got the order to retire in first."

I began to laugh, and Butcher looked at me doubtfully.

"And you are the fellow that was all fixed to run, with your knee drawn up and all ready."

"Ay, and so I would have," he replied, his face reddening, "only I was knocked half-rotten just like yourself." He started to laugh in his turn. "I know shells can do all sorts of funny things, but that's the first time I've ever been rocked to sleep," he said when he stopped.

But I didn't believe him.

"Here we are," he exclaimed after a short silence, and I saw the rest of the battalion a little ahead in a fold of the ground. The shell-fire had stopped.

They were just forming into fours as we came up and we fell in behind. The men were excited and talked quickly without waiting on replies. Everyone appeared to be in good humour.

We set off through fields. Reaction came, and we remembered that we were hungry and tired as we plodded along. We had escaped the shells another time, though our luck was wearing thin.

Walking along with heads bent we came unexpectedly on a line of men lying at full length in the grass. Some of them had scraped little holes for themselves with entrenching tools. Their rifles were pointed to the front, as ours had been a little while before, but there the resemblance ended.

There were men in stained uniforms which could only have belonged to cooks, men in oily overalls who would have been more at home with spanners in their hands, old men, grey-haired and wrinkled—so old that they never should have been in France at all—a few smart-looking bandoliered gunners, who had lost their batteries, A.S.C. lorry drivers, forgotten motor goggles cocked jauntily above the peaks of their caps—the only jaunty thing about them—a few Military Police wearing the brassard of their ugly calling, robbed of their erstwhile dignity. Then more old men. Many of them were without equipment.

The motley line held their rifles gingerly and stared at us with frightened, questioning eyes as we stepped through them. There was something forlorn and resigned about the old fellows, who could have been our fathers, as they lay stiffly, holding on to their rifles with unaccustomed hands, already sunk in the sad, introspection of men who divined that they were about to die.

" Who's up there now ? " asked one of them. He had a grey puckered face with straggling grey moustache that had once been smart, and as he raised his shoulders to put the question I saw a row of faded ribbons on his chest, marking some half-forgotten wars.

" The enemy," we answered, and went on.

THE MARCHING SONG

WE tramped along a narrow, uneven road. The ground on either side was bare and stony, and gradually became steeper until we were over at the knees with weariness.

Searching through my pockets I found a Woodbine packet crushed almost flat between some old letters. There were two dried up cigarettes in the packet, and they were worth far more than a thousand times their weight in gold. I slipped one into Butcher's hand and lit the other, only to nick it regretfully after a couple of long mouthfuls and put the butt carefully away for another occasion. Smoking and eating, and sitting doing nothing were the infantryman's principal pleasures. Having enjoyed the one I longed for the others.

We caught up on wounded making their way slowly to the rear. Nobody bothered with them, and they hobbled off the road to make way for us without looking up. Some of them seemed to be making heavy going of it on the bad ground. Here and there one had given up and lay at the side of the road, asleep or unconscious.

We overhauled others who were not wounded. When they caught sight of us they hurriedly cleared off the road as if afraid of being ordered to fall in behind. Most of them had thrown away their rifles and slouched along, with occasional apprehensive glances back.

We took no notice of them either.

The road brought us on to a bare plateau. We stared in amazement at a strange scene. The place was alive with men straggling along with bowed shoulders and slack knees, their eyes fixed hopelessly on the ground. Some of them were in groups and some in pairs, but the majority were on their own. There was no confusion and no bustle. There were no officers to be seen, and nobody shouted orders. The men straggled along silently, almost orderly in their disorder. They all kept the same pace, lurching along exhausted and dogged in hopeless rout. Ammunition and bits of equipment were strewn over the ground.

When the Adjutant cursed and threatened they moved slowly out of the way without looking up. We marched along, surrounded by the rabble.

They wore strange shoulder markings, and did not belong to our Division. It didn't occur to me to ask where they came from or what crowd they belonged to. Probably none of us knew, and certainly nobody cared.

Farther along we came on a few harassed officers shepherding squads of unwilling men into some kind of order. The men were like sleepwalkers, moving sluggishly in response to the hoarse commands of the officers.

We left the road and halted, forming two-deep and facing the way we had come. For a while we stood at ease, leaning on our rifles, and stared, awed, at the slouching men. There was little talking in the ranks, but a rumour passed from mouth to mouth that Jerry had smashed up a lot of our fellows in a big engagement somewhere ahead.

In front of us the squads got slowly bigger as more men were gathered in, but the majority of the stragglers still stumbled on doggedly.

The Colonel and his shadow, the Adjutant, stood apart and talked together earnestly. Without waiting to be told we sat down, tired out already, though the day was still young. Those who had cigarettes left smoked. Those who had biscuits ate them wolfishly. Those who had nothing squabbled half-heartedly with their luckier comrades for a share.

In a few minutes it seemed quite natural that we should be

sitting there. Wherever our backsides touched the ground there was our camp, and we had no desire to move on again until the order came, and often not then.

We had no imagination, and none of us worried much about what was happening around us. We had enough worries of our own. I looked at the stragglers and wondered whether, after all, they weren't better off than we were. They were moving, and in the right direction, and had no officers to order them about. On the other hand, there was something to be proud of in the fact that we were still under discipline and could march in step and in rank, with our Colonel at our head.

" Those lads must have got it in the neck about proper," said Butcher, nodding towards the road. The rest looked uneasy. A runner spoke up. The runners knew more than anyone else now that the signallers had lost their telephones.

" They say he came over in Divisions. Didn't give them an earthly. You may guess how bad things are when they brought up all the old men they could scrape together down the line and stuck rifles in their hands.

" Some of them looked as if they didn't know which end of the rifle the bullet came out of," said Jenkins with a sneer. " Old Jerry'll just about massacre them before they know what it's all about."

" Good luck to the old codgers, but all the same I'd rather they were lying here than us," said Butcher.

" It'll soon be all the same. Listen to that," said another, as shell-fire started somewhere up the front.

We listened anxiously as the shells burst steadily, subtly increasing the number of leaderless men passing us on the road, and got to our feet. As the explosions came nearer the old sickening apprehension that I might be blown to bits possessed me, and I shuffled uneasily. It seemed suddenly to have got darker and colder on the bare plateau, although it was scarcely midday.

Horrified exclamations came from the men around me as a squad a few hundred yards in front of us became enveloped in flame and smoke.

" Jesus, a direct hit—right among them."

Men came running, shouting incoherently. The smoke drifted away, leaving a number of crumpled forms where the squad had been. Some of them moved. A faint cry came, " Stretcher-bearers, stretcher-bearers."

But there were no stretcher-bearers.

A heavy droning added itself to the rising tide of sound. Looking up we saw the sky alive with aeroplanes. They came in some sort of diamond-shaped formation, and then swooped down until the black crosses were plainly visible on their wings and tails. The bodies were painted scarlet, giving them a curiously ferocious appearance.

Above the noise of the engines came the rattle of machine-guns going full blast. In front, where a moment before had stood squads of ordered men—islands in a sea of disaster—all was confusion and panic.

It was a target that couldn't be missed, and even as we looked men fell in heaps, helpless under the storm of bullets and shells. The survivors broke into a mad stampede, striking out blindly at whoever got in their way, trampling on dead and dying alike.

Overhead roared the triumphant planes, darting, wheeling, diving, skimming along the ground like swallows over a pond, rising abruptly only to come down again in headlong dives until it seemed they would crash nose first into the ground.

Our ranks broke, and in a moment I found myself carried along in the mob of fleeing men, blind and deaf to everything but the need to get away from the pitiless hail.

The red planes had passed on. I tramped along the road surrounded by strange faces. I was separated from the others and stared round wildly, forgetting the thought of danger, for the shoulder colours of the 1st Battalion.

Drawing out from the press I stopped and examined the men about me, but they belonged to strange units, and I went on, wondering sadly what would happen to me now. Instead of being a soulless machine, the battalion, what was left of it, was a living thing, warm and friendly, and somehow safer.

Why hadn't I watched which way the others went and stuck close to them ? If only Butcher had been with me it would have been all right. I stared again at the press of men, but there was no Butcher, only men intent on getting to hell out of it and saving their own skins. Unutterably alone, I slouched along like the rest.

A jam developed up the road.

The men about me cursed savagely and elbowed their way forward, only to halt, undecided in their turn.

Standing on tiptoe I looked over their heads, and recognised a familiar figure. In a clear space in the centre of the road stood the big Adjutant. He had his revolver in his hand, and looked as if he were on the point of using it. His eyes were bloodshot, and his under-jaw, covered with black stubble, was thrust out.

" Fall in men of the 1st Battalion," he kept repeating harshly.

Looking over his shoulder I saw a double line of men drawn up at the side of the road, amongst them Butcher. Overjoyed at seeing the familiar colours and familiar faces, I ran over and clapped my mate on the shoulder, edging myself into the rank beside him.

" Where the devil did you get to ? " I cried—as if it mattered now that I had found him.

" I got out of the way as fast as my legs could carry me until I ran into the Adjutant there. What the hell do you think I did ? "

I stood flushed and excited and didn't answer.

" Would you for God's sake take a dekko at him now," said Jenkins, his eyes snapping with excitement. " Isn't he a proper bloody caution ? "

We looked over. The Adjutant still dominated the scene, and in ones and twos men detached themselves from the throng and joined us, sheepishly, unwillingly or happily, according to what their feelings were.

The aeroplanes had disappeared, but the shells still crashed down, I looked at them bursting a few hundred yards ahead, and saw far beyond a long line of mounted men stretched motionless across the skyline. They were widely extended. They sat like so many bronze statues, facing the oncoming masses—implacable, impotent. The strange sight brought a lump to my throat. There was something heroic about that thin line, a series of dots rather than a line, something at once heart-stirring and despairing, a sort of still-life, no wild charge, but cold massacre. There was no attempt at concealment, and I knew that a single machine-gun could mow them down inside ten minutes—and would.

I turned to draw Butcher's attention, but he and the others were looking elsewhere.

Almost in front of us, less than a hundred yards away, three Frenchmen had appeared from nowhere with a tiny gun and were already in action.

One stood on an ammunition-box and directed operations. The second commenced tossing little shells, hardly bigger than hand-bombs, into pigeon-holes about the breech. The third jerked a string. A little popping explosion came with each tug. The barrel of the gun was hardly thicker than a machine-gun's.

The whole outfit looked ludicrously toylike and automatic in the midst of the disorder and turmoil all round. The neat sky-blue uniforms and handsome helmets of the Frenchmen looked out of place too. They seemed completely oblivious to everything but their little gun, and carried on—directing, loading and pulling the string—as if the whole course of the war depended on them and their puny efforts.

The sight tickled the irrepressible Butcher.

" Send one over here, mates. There's a louse been biting me all day where I can't get at it."

The Frenchmen did not deign to look round, if ever they heard, or understood.

" Hey, you blokes," he tried again, waving a cigarette-end, " just one, s'il vous plait. I'm out of matches."

" Put a sock in it, Butcher," growled the Signal Corporal. " You weren't so hellish funny a while ago when the planes were on us."

" Ay, you'll be laughing out of the wrong side of your gab before it's all over," said the Sergeant as the shell-fire became heavier.

" If you ask me those planes belonged to that big airman of theirs, Baron somebody or other. They say he paints his machines red," added the Sergeant morosely. " He damned near painted us red as well."

The Adjutant left the road and came over to us. He still had his revolver in his hand. His eyes bored into us malevolently.

" Battalion, 'shun," he roared, as if on the barrack square. We sprang to attention, with a rattle of rifle butts.

" As you were. 'Shun. More smartly, you blighters."

" Right dress."

We looked at him horror-stricken, scarcely believing our ears, and then made haste to obey. A couple of Sergeants, as flabbergasted as ourselves, ran to the right of the line and commenced dressing the ranks.

" Up a little."

" Back, you there. Not so much, damn you."

" Hurry up. That'll do it."

The subalterns stood looking in amazement. All the Company Commanders had been killed the first day and there were only the two senior officers left, one of whom seemed to have gone mad.

" I'll teach you bastards a lesson," raved the Adjutant, waving his revolver.

" By Christ, I'll shoot the man that moves."

" All correct, sir," reported a Sergeant.

" Number."

Voices rose and fell and then were lost as a shell burst a scant hundred yards away. The ranks flinched as crumbled earth pattered down on them.

" As you were. Number," ordered the Adjutant harshly, and voices rose and fell again, only to be drowned in more explosions. A Sergeant saved the day by running along and counting us himself, and the Adjutant was satisfied.

We stood—but not at ease.

Another shell roared down and a wild desire to turn and run seized me, but my feet remained glued to the ground.

The ranks swayed.

And then the tall figure of the Colonel detached itself from the remaining stragglers of the road and hurried over, his face a study as he noticed our dressed ranks. The reason for his delay in putting in an appearance was evident. His right sleeve was partly cut away and a clumsily made, bloodstained bandage took its place on the forearm. The hand rested inside his partly unbuttoned tunic in lieu of a sling.

The Adjutant's revolver, by a species of legerdemain, returned to its holster. Calling us sharply to attention, he saluted briskly. The Colonel acknowledged the salute with his left hand and looked at us silently for a moment, and then at the disappearing rabble.

We read his mind like an open book and stiffened, almost forgetting the shells. The Colonel was a man to be followed, and to earn his appreciation seemed an end in itself. We admired him for his sonorous name, which fitted him like a glove, although it would have sounded theatrical on other men, and for his handsome, kindly face, lined with pain and fatigue.

The Adjutant conferred with him for a moment and then, stepping back a pace, saluted punctiliously and turned to us.

" By the right, form fours."

" Right."

" Quick march."

Off we went down the road, quivering like hounds on the leash, but forced to observe the regulation step of the two leaders in front. The shells thudded down behind.

For once Butcher was speechless.

The ground sloped down gently and the road became broader with a shallow ditch at either side. Just before the plateau rose out of sight we looked back, struck with a sudden thought. The pop-gun had been silent for the past few minutes, and we saw the reason why. Two inert forms in field blue were humped over the gun. A few dozen yards away, making for the road, the third member of the trio was crawling painfully along on hands and knees. Another great billowing column went up, its base shot momentarily with an angry red glare, and the crawling Frenchman lay still.

For a few minutes it seemed as if we were going to get away in peace. The shells were falling well behind us, savaging the empty ground, and we were out of sight of the bursts. But, loath to let us go, the German gunners began dropping great black fellows to the right of the road, keeping pace with us, but going up just too far away to do us any damage. Our taut nerves flinched unbearably. A tiny change of direction and we were caught like rats in a trap. Surely Jerry knew that his shells were falling just a little bit out while his prey went on unharmed. Or would it occur to him before the next one came ? I was ready to scream with the strain, and the grey drawn faces of the others showed how they felt, each counting his chances. It was uncanny how the shells lit exactly abreast of us.

But we had forgotten the planes—and the target we made marching along in a disciplined body. The air became filled with the triumphant droning, and once more we scattered, skulking, this time, in the ditch.

They came at us wickedly, leaping and tumbling with unnatural adroitness. There were only two of them this time, and they took turns to dive at us with viciously spitting guns, reckless in their immunity from our harmless weapons. I lay doubled up, my arm shielding my face, with a dull acquiescence in whatever fate held in store, almost conscious of the fact that this continual " Wolf, wolf " existence had blunted my instinct of self-preservation. Turning my face upwards a little I stared at the whirring planes only to hide my head and shrink closer to the earth as they dived down. The fact that I didn't see them at the most dangerous moment seemed obscurely to make me less of a target for the bullets. Some of the men started firing as they crouched in the ditch, working their rifle bolts like madmen, but the airmen took no notice.

In a couple of minutes, tiring of the sport, or perhaps spotting better quarry elsewhere, they drew off and disappeared as rapidly as they had come, the hum of their engines growing fainter and fainter until it faded away completely.

We got shakily to our feet, and men whose cries and groans had been drowned in the din now made themselves heard. The wounded were hastily bandaged and most of them set off at once down the road, possessed by the anxiety of wounded men to put the greatest possible distance between them and the war in the shortest possible time.

Half a dozen remained where they had fallen. Two had

legs broken, and another, shot in the chest, was dribbling blood. The others were dead.

We re-formed and started off, leaving the three wounded propped up beside the dead in the ditch, disregarding their supplications.

" Have a heart, mates, drag us along," they pleaded.

" Take us with you, boys, Jerry'll bayonet us."

" Hey, for God's sake don't leave us behind."

In a moment we were out of range of the despairing cries and catching up on the walking wounded. They were already strung out on the road, handicapped according to where they were hit. Their comrades in the ranks called out rough encouragement as we passed by, but they took no notice or answered with a brief nod, hardly bothering to look round, the invisible barrier between men who were out of it and men who were still in already there.

In a very few minutes they, too, were left behind. The shells still fell out to the right, but sullenly now, as if they knew they were balked. The chance of survival appeared suddenly immeasurably greater, but we marched along with our minds blank, hardly daring to think, let alone put into words, our new-born hopes of safety, in case the shells should read our thoughts. We had outdistanced them before the actual fact that we were out of range dawned on us. The road turned sharply to the left, making safety doubly sure. We went on in silence, thinking disjointedly over the crowded events of the morning, dully congratulating ourselves on being still alive when we might, so very easily, have been dead. Gradually a feeling of well-being came over us as our feet came down rhythmically on the firm road. The sun beamed down warmly. It was good to be alive and marching along in step, instead of lying dead somewhere behind. The dead hadn't achieved anything. They might as well have lived. There was no merit in having died. The Germans came on inexorably and invisibly. Their aeroplanes rained death and destruction, and we were helpless. Their shells thudded amongst us unhindered. Their machine-guns made a way for them willy-nilly. And yet we were alive.

Our keyed-up nerves relaxed. We broke into false-sounding laughter. We compared notes excitedly. We contradicted each other and cursed each other's forgetfulness and obtuseness. We searched our pockets for ends of cigarettes and poked our fingers into the corners of our haversacks for crumbs of hard biscuit. Someone in front tentatively started an incongruous ditty.

One by one the ranks joined in. Coming to the chorus our voices rang out hoarsely. Even the Colonel laughed at the gusto we put into the last line.

> We haven't seen the Kaiser for a hell of a time.
>   Perhaps he's gone up in a mi-i-i-ne.
> They say that he's the leader of a German band,
>   So b—— him, he's no cousin of mine.

L

THE ESTAMINET

THERE were half a dozen of us in the trench, but it was so dark that we were almost invisible to each other. The trench was a slit in the earth, like a long grave waiting for the body for it to be filled in. It was so narrow that a broad-shouldered man would have found it difficult to stand sideways in it, but it was better than being in the open, and none of us were so very broad.

In front stabs of light appeared, followed by the noise of bursting shells. The harsh, yet intimate, rat-tat of machine-guns told their eternal tale of the eager enemy.

Still, it was quiet in our little trench. We talked in low voices, standing in awkward postures. It was less than five feet deep. Occasional stray bullets forced us to keep our heads down.

The battalion was practically on its own. There was some mob in front of us, but we hadn't seen them and didn't know who they were. We hoped they would stick it for a while, and stamped our feet in a vain effort to keep warm.

We had been marching most of the day along deserted roads with occasional stops in deserted villages, which bore traces of having been hastily evacuated by their inhabitants. The rations had come up, and stew and bread had been served out and a fistful of biscuits to each man. But we were hungry again and swore as we gnawed at the hard tack, wetting it first with spittle to soften it a little.

The country we had marched through seemed to have been new ground for British troops, although, of course, I didn't know. It was a pleasant country of rolling hills and little valleys through which the road wound, white and dusty. Once, after exchanging shots with the Germans, we passed through a village and heard the high, cracked voice of an old woman.

" Allez, allez," she screamed from a little window, shaking her fist.

" She may be a bleeding ally, but it's a pity she wasn't a bit younger," said one sourly, taking her cry up wrong.

We were out of cigarettes, and irritable accordingly, but sometimes we struck luck. Butcher found a goat tethered in an outhouse and shot it out of hand. Starting a fire going, we fed on tough, strong-smelling meat, half raw. Another time we found French cheese, white and soapy, looking and tasting like curdled milk. The others fastened on it ravenously, but I could hardly get my share down my throat so strong was my dislike of it.

It was a cider country, and nearly every farmhouse had a pile of rotting apples outside the door. In a village we came across a whole cellar-full of cider and filled our bottles. The Adjutant came on the scene and wouldn't allow us to have any more, so, regretfully, we left the casks, after making sure that they were emptying their contents on the ground. The enemy was not far behind, and there was no sense in leaving it for him.

For the same reason we broke into the houses, forcing open cupboards and drawers, strewing the contents wantonly on the floor and laughing mischievously as we pulled bedclothes and mattresses to the barn where we were resting for an hour or two before pushing on.

On such occasions the officers quietly removed themselves. The N.C.O.s took no notice, or else joined in the fun. A foolish feeling that we were loutish intruders spoiled my zest somewhat for looting, but I laughed with the rest when a wag, discovering a chamber-pot, solemnly proceeded to urinate—only to kick the pot over on to a bedroom mat when he had finished.

Our entrenching tools made excellent jemmies, and we soon became adept. Every receptacle was made to give up its secret, and we exposed the hopes and fears of many a careful housewife for the treasures she had been forced to leave behind.

Discipline grew lax. It was hard for tired, hungry men, who were being harried remorsely, to stand to attention and salute when spoken to by grimy, unshaven officers in stained uniforms. Perhaps that was why the subalterns left us as much as possible to ourselves. The Colonel never bothered us, but we always made a point of saluting him. He was as unkempt as the rest, but in his case dirt only served to make him more soldierly-looking.

It was rumoured that the Adjutant had tried to prevail on him to go down the line with his wound, and that he had refused point-blank.

" Lord God, if we had only his chance," said the men softly looking down at his injured arm.

The Adjutant was in a class by himself. He was domineering, and not particular how he expressed himself, but he was popular after a fashion. He never made the slightest attempt to fall back on his rank to enforce commands, but instead gave a strong impression that he was ready to throw off his tunic and fight the piece out, man to man. The result was we never questioned his orders, especially as at bottom he seemed to like us far better than he did the subalterns. We harked back to the grim memory of having to dress and number off under shell-fire, and at once feared and admired him.

He would come over when we were resting in the village or at the roadside and inquire heartily could we stick it, but always with an unspoken threat that it would be the worse for us if we couldn't. On such occasions he waved us down half-angrily if we started to rise off our backsides to stand to attention.

The signal Sergeant and Corporal who were along with us in the trench got restless and wandered off into the darkness to scrounge round. They were absent a long time. We were wondering had they got lost when they returned laughing and talking thickly. There was a deserted estaminet a couple of hundred yards away, they told us, with many hiccoughs, as they bit into a roll of du pain.

Leaving two fellows in the trench to keep an eye out for officers, Butcher and I crept away, and after prowling about in the dark found the place. Butcher had a stump of candle with him. By its light we saw that it was littered with dusty bottles. To our disappointment, however, we found bottle after bottle was empty. Many soldiers had been there before us.

It was nervous work—for me at any rate—rummaging about in the candle-light. Jerry might take it into his head to attack, or a sudden order to withdraw would leave us stranded. If one of our officers came along we would be in for trouble, perhaps serious.

When we had almost given up hope we came on full, long-necked bottles, and without waiting to see what was in them we grabbed a couple of each and stumbled back to the trench. We shared the bottles with the men who had remained in the trench and drank queer-tasting wine that seemed to require a pinch of salt to make it more palatable.

The two N.C.O.s made another visit to the estaminet and came staggering back, arm-in-arm, singing and shouting. After a while they reeled off into the darkness, and the snatches of song, punctuated by shell-fire, gradually faded. Long afterwards we heard they had been caught and court-martialled for being drunk in the line, but what the sentence was nobody knew. They didn't come back.

The strange wine went to my head, too.

"Why, you were dead-drunk," laughed Butcher, as towards morning I found myself walking along in the ranks half-stupid. But at the end of three or four hours' marching I was sober enough.

THE CAVALRY

THE battalion was completely on its own now. The other battalions of our brigade had vanished. The Division seemed to have dissolved into thin air. We forgot that we belonged to a Division. We marched and counter-marched by day and by night, covering uncounted kilometres and fighting obscure rearguard actions without hope of winning or being relieved.

But in some mysterious way—mysterious to us in the ranks, that is—messages reached us from unknown sources and at the oddest times, messages that generally turned out to our detriment. It was all a muddle.

It was afternoon. We were disposed in the peculiar, narrow trenches which always appeared to have been freshly dug for our benefit by persons unknown. We were on the edge of a wood.

The Germans, as usual, were somewhere about, marking time for a while, and, as usual, we knew, without being told, that they were somewhere in front or at either side. But that was the full extent of our knowledge.

If I had been told to face about in the trench and look the other way it would have been all the same to me. I would still have known to go in the opposite direction when he came over, and that was all I really required to know. There was no such thing as a front line, or any kind of line.

In front of us was a stretch of clear ground, and then the trees began again. There was some desultory machine-gun fire going on somewhere near, but no shelling, so we paid little attention. We had travelled out of the shell zone, and I had no great fear of bullets unless they were coming thick, or from the air. The Germans had apparently advanced too quickly for their artillery to keep up with them, for which I was devoutly thankful, and hoped their infantry could stick the pace.

Our own artillery was a thing of the past. From the day of the big attack scarcely a single shell had gone over our heads in the direction of the enemy. Not one of our planes had put in an appearance.

"But surely there must be some guns somewhere! They weren't all left behind at St. Quentin," we argued.

Butcher, greatly daring, had scrounged a cigarette from the Signal Officer and was in a good humour. I was expecting the butt, so I was in good humour too.

His idea was that England had gone out of the war and we hadn't been told.

We were all lousy and scratched industriously, but that was as far as we could go. We had no opportunities of getting rid of the pests. We didn't dare take off our shirts in case something happened and they would have to be left behind in the hurry. Lice were a new thing to me, very tickly but endurable. I hadn't seen them yet.

My puttees, loosened with the constant marching, had slipped until they were half-way down my legs, but I never thought of re-winding them. The other men were in the same case. Nothing mattered.

We were crouching down in the narrow trench talking casually of when we had had a square meal last and, what was more important, the chances of getting one in the near future, when a jingling sound made us look round. We stared incredulously as a crowd of horsemen emerged from the trees. They took no notice of our heads bobbing up from the ground and manœuvred their mounts into some kind of order. They were Colonials, and their uniforms were spick and span. The horses snorted, and their coats shone. The men were big fellows and their bronzed faces were keen and oddly intent. They were very splendid compared to us.

"What the blazes is coming off now?" we asked each other. At least the others did—I was all eyes and said nothing.

We ducked in alarm as the squadron spurred their horses into a gallop and came straight at us. With a thunderous drumming of hoofs they took our trench in their stride. From the bottom, as I cowered down, I had a momentary glimpse of a horse's belly and powerful haunches as they were over and away like the wind, sword in hand.

They spread out as they went into two lines and were half-way across the open when there came a sudden pulsating blast of fire, and gaps appeared in the double line. Bullets came hissing about our heads. A man a couple of yards away from me slithered down to his knees, and then sprawled full length on the floor of the trench. Realising our danger we ducked. Looking down I saw blood gushing from a wound in his throat. Butcher who was next to him dropped down beside him, but there was nothing to be done. I felt relieved, because for a moment I thought Butcher had been hit.

Then uncontrollable excitement possessed me and, defying the bullets, I raised my head and looked at the cavalry. Their ranks were much thinner now. Just as the foremost of them reached the trees they hesitated, turned and came racing back, lying low in the saddle.

The machine-guns barked triumphantly at their victory over mere flesh and blood. Only a handful of the once proud squadron put their blowing horses at the trench and lunged across to the shelter of the wood behind. Others tailed away on either side and in a moment were hidden from view among the friendly trees.

The whole thing, from when we saw them first, had only occupied a bare five minutes. We stared at each other in amazement. The fire died down. Looking over the top we saw that the ground in front, which before had been bare, was dotted here and there with shapeless mounds.

The screams of horses in agony pierced our ears with

shrill intensity. As we looked animals struggled convulsively to their feet and galloped off at a tangent. Some of them swayed drunkenly and fell back, with their legs in the air. Smaller, more feeble movements showed that some of the troopers were still alive.

Single rifle-shots sounded, whether from our side or not I didn't know, and by and by the horses were mercifully silent, but men moved at intervals—crawling behind the horses for cover, perhaps.

What sense there was in pitting men and horses against a hail of lead we didn't know. It was only another mystery on top of many others. What particular reason there had been for a charge over that particular bit of ground was another mystery. The foolhardiness of the affair prevented us from feeling very sympathetic towards the men lying out in front and the idea of doing anything for them, or attempting to bring them in did not occur to us. We could have done nothing for them anyway.

" I think they might have had more bloomin' sense than try that mug's game," said Jenkins slowly.

" For all we know they thought the same thing," said Butcher, " but orders is orders. Likely enough they had to go through with it knowing all the time they were up against it."

" Tha-at's right. And they hadn't a dog's chance."

" Any fool would have known what the result would be," said Jenkins. " It was only a case of two or three Jerry machine-gunners turning their guns on a target they must have dreamed of many a time, and there you are ! They had only to press the trigger."

" They must be having a hell of a laugh to themselves this minute," said another, spitting disgustedly.

" Poor old Harvey there isn't laughing," said Butcher, pointing to the dead man on the floor of the trench. " Their charge did for him all right."

" Throw a sheet over him, for it's about all he'll get in this god-forsaken hole," said Jenkins.

" It's their funeral," said the dead man's mate angrily. " They should have known what they were up against as well as us. Besides they're cavalry and it's about time, when you come to think of it, that the cavalry did something to earn their keep—eating their blinking heads off behind the line while us fellows have to do the dirty work."

It was quiet again and I stared over at the dead men and horses. That stretch of ground between the trees didn't strike me as very valuable. Any one of us would have given it away cheerfully, with a few dozen buckshee acres thrown in, for a single packet of issue cigarettes or half a loaf of bread, or even a tin of pork and beans.

If it had been valuable from the military point of view only a lunatic would have thought of putting cavalry at it, for what chance had they against lead ?

Butcher read my thoughts as we skulked in the trench.

" I'm no staff-wallah, but I'll swear a new recruit would have known better, even if he didn't know his arse from his elbow.

" Aw, let them alone," interrupted Jenkins crossly. " They'll be dishing out bows and arrows next, the stupid bastards."

" All the same," said Butcher wistfully after a pause, " I wish I had a horse—and could ride. . . . You wouldn't see my heels for dust."

" I wish old Harvey was still alive, no matter a hoot about the others," said his black-browed mate resentfully, " he was worth a ton of swanking cavalry."

For the rest of the day we kept very quiet in our narrow stretch of trench, hoping that Jerry would be satisfied with his easy victory. We knew that after the way he had polished off the cavalry that he was there in strength, a

thing we hadn't known before, and that he could come over
and oust us whenever he felt the notion.

For that matter there didn't seem any reason, as far as I
could see, to prevent him walking round us and taking us in
the rear. The remnant of the cavalry had disappeared and
we were left to ourselves again.

It got quickly darker, and with the coming of the night our
nerves grew tauter. Nobody had any Verey lights and there
was no barbed wire in front of us. The machine-guns had
stopped entirely, but the silence only added to the menace
of the night. Somewhere in front was Jerry, strong and
confident. We were only a handful of thrice-beaten troops,
officerless and ready to take to our heels. The rest of the
battalion was somewhere about, but we didn't know exactly
where. We began to get jumpy.

" They've gone off and left us."

" No, they wouldn't have the hard neck to do that."

A hushed argument ensued, broken from time to time by
a muttered " Shut-up," from those who were straining their
ears for sounds in front. The trees rustled, and the darkness
was our enemy.

We fingered our rifles and wondered what to do, as little
abrupt noises reached us from the bare ground where the
horses and troopers lay. That was the way the Jerries would
come, unless they crept round behind us.

The hopelessness of the situation must have occurred to
the Colonel for presently we were hailed softly :

" Retire without making any row."

A pin could have been heard drop as we carefully placed
our rifles on the parados and squirmed out of the trenches,
making for the shelter of the trees on hands and knees.

The rest of the mob came up quietly and we marched away,
leaving behind what had been an empty clearing in a wood.
Now it was a makeshift graveyard for British cavalry.
Canadians, the others said.

THE NAIL IN THE BOOT

WE grew more footsore and weary as the days passed until we were indifferent where our officers led us. Leaving villages without a backward glance, we marched to unknown destinations, and away again on other futile journeys when for all the good we did when we arrived we might as well have been sitting on the roadside at our ease. The men cursed and groused, but none fell out, no matter how long or how hard the road. Falling out meant capture or death.

The officers might have known what the idea behind it all was, why we wandered over the deserted country-side, and where we were, but we doubted it, if ever we thought of it at all. If they did know they kept the knowledge strictly to themselves.

The days were wonderfully fine and dry. In the morning it was misty, but always the sun came out and we became warm—too warm on the dusty roads. Nevertheless, the air was sharp and the nights were bitterly cold without our greatcoats.

From being spruce and well-turned-out we had become dirty and ragged. Our battalion, strong in the traditions of the Regiment, had made a fetish of smartness. The faces of the older men were covered with heavy stubble, which daily grew heavier and more beardlike, giving them a peculiar appearance of hardship and suffering. The faces of others, young like myself, developed a downy covering that irritated the skin and felt strange to the touch.

One night we stumbled on a scene of intense activity.

We were marching sullenly along a narrow road when we

heard a distant rumble which got steadily louder as we went on. Turning a corner we debouched on to a crowded road.

It was packed with French transport. An unending line of clumsily made carts, each creaking and groaning to its own rhythm. They were more like big, high, country carts than Army transport. But the drivers, hardly visible above our heads, were uniformed. They urged their horses forward in low voices. When jams occurred, as they did every few minutes, they cried out to each other anxiously.

We formed two-deep, and then into single file, and trudged on in the darkness, moving in the opposite direction to the transport. The drivers took no notice of us. We were excited by the strange half-companionship and called out rough greetings, slapping the straining horses and catching our hands in the spokes of the big slowly-revolving wheels. A warm, steamy smell came from the animals which more than made up for the discomfort of stumbling and bumping in the darkness along the narrow strip of road open to us.

For a couple of kilos we edged along uncomfortably and then turned off to the left. In a few minutes we were back again in our customary loneliness.

" Wonder where they were going—up or down ? " said Butcher reflectively. None of us knew where we ourselves were going so the question was unanswerable.

The closely packed transport moving along in the darkness and the anxious men perched on top of the high loads boded no good. At the end of a couple of hours' marching we arrived at a deserted town. It was being heavily shelled. Some said it was Noyon. The name conveyed nothing. They were probably wrong, anyhow.

I passed the news to Butcher. He was limping. He had been complaining for a few kilometres back about a nail in his boot, and had already made several attempts to reach it with the haft of the entrenching tool when the fall-outs came. He was in a quite excusably bad temper.

" Noyon," he repeated angrily, " I wish to Hell it was Boulogne. If I can't get this nail out of my boot at the next halt I'm going barefooted, so help me God."

I had offered to carry his rifle before, but he would have none of it. Now I renewed the offer.

" Wait till we get past this lousy grip," he answered.

We came to the first scattered houses of the dark town.

" By the uproar that's going on we'll be damned lucky to get past, rifle or no rifle," broke in Jenkins.

" Where can those shells be coming from ? " I asked nervously.

" The only people that know that are the stout lads that are sending them over," said Jenkins cynically, " and they're only doing it by rote because someone else is giving them the order."

We marched into the dark main street. Shells were bursting just beyond the houses on the right-hand side. Every detonation was followed by the threatening clatter of falling bricks and masonry.

Fortunately the street was wide. We kept religiously to the left. We even tried to edge on to the footpath, but soon found that that was out of the question. The footpath was littered with dead Frenchmen and dead horses. They lay in grotesque shapes, almost hidden in the shadows.

Little tremors of fear ran through me. I stared at the dead men in silence, fascinated. The old instinctive stupidity descended on me and dulled my thoughts. Still, I found it hard to turn my head away. It was strange to see men and horses lying dead in the main street of a town with nobody near them except ourselves passing through.

" Transport," said Jenkins, as if that explained everything.

" How does it happen they are all together on the pavement ? " I asked, with a last look at the cadavers.

" They would be in the way on the road, wouldn't they ? " he replied, changing his rifle wearily from one shoulder to another.

We went on. I glanced over to where the shells were falling, but their fitful glare only intensified the darkness. Gloom and death were everywhere. We pressed on fearfully with bent heads, sometimes skirting and sometimes stumbling into great crumbling shell craters on the cobbled street.

In the little, desolate silence following each crashing explosion our footsteps took on a hollow, ghostly sound in keeping with the place. The tall, narrow houses, their shuttered windows deep in shadow, leaned together with a mysterious, womanish air, as if deliberating helplessly whose turn it was to be violated next.

We left the town of ill-omen and slogged on steadily. We knew roughly by the number of fall-outs how long we had been on the march. Jenkins and I said four hours, or about sixteen miles. Butcher swore blind it was six hours and twenty-four miles. Without being too certain of our own figures we allowed him a few miles for the nail in his boot, and forebore to argue. He still refused to hand over his rifle.

We fell out at a place where two roads met. As usual in a minute or two it got too cold to rest and we lounged about, cursing disgustedly. The lice bit into us where we had sweated on the march. We tore savagely at our bellies and chests until the lice had open blood to feast on. When we were cold they ceased to trouble us.

We had no cigarettes and longed all the more for a smoke as we caught the faint aroma of fragrant tobacco from the little group of officers and saw the glowing tips of cigarettes lighting up their faces momentarily. We had nothing all day but a few dirty crumbly biscuits and were ravenously hungry. Thinking of white bread, crisp bacon and scalding tea, we cursed our missing transport for a pack of cowardly creatures, too windy to look for us, or too greedy to share the rations once they had them.

The regulation halt seemed to have become very long.

We began to look inquiringly to where the officers stood apart, by the way not tired enough to think of sitting down although, like the rest of us, they were over at the knees with fatigue.

It got steadily colder, hanging about a bleak crossroads. Men who a few minutes before had been grousing about the eternal sweaty march, march, march, now began to grouse for a different reason.

" Why don't they get a move on, or stop near a farm-house or some cursed village where we could kip down in peace ? "

" Are they mad or what, stopping at a grip like this, the bottom of nowhere ? "

" Damn and blast them."

Time dragged on. It was a full half-hour before the answer came. When it did, it came in a way we would never have suspected. A tiny humming noise, scarcely noticeable at first, reached us. We stopped grousing to listen, thinking of the German planes. The noise became steadily louder. The hum became a pulsing throb, magnified by the stillness of the night. Far away down the road a tiny gleam appeared. In a moment we distinguished the headlight of a motor-cycle.

On it came with a rush, but the driver slowed and pulled up with a jar of brakes beside us. Jumping off his machine, he saluted the officers briskly. A bit of paper changed hands. The dispatch rider, with a commiserating look at us, straddled his machine and roared off into the night along the road he had come.

There was silence while the Colonel read the message by the cupped light of a match. We looked on blankly, seized with foreboding. A low-voiced conversation ensued amongst the officers. An order came :

" Fall in ! "

We obeyed with alacrity, glad to be doing something

M

again. Anything was better than slowly freezing. The Colonel, the blood-stained bandage showing up dimly, stepped forward. The Adjutant called us harshly to attention, and although the Colonel waved his hand deprecatingly we stood stiffly. He spoke quietly and solemnly.

" I have just received a dispatch, men. I thought we were relieved—that you were going to get a rest. You have earned it, everyone of you, if ever soldiers did. But the order says we must go on for a while longer, and we can only obey. I want to see you stepping out. All that I can say is that it is an emergency, and we must do our best. We are British soldiers. This will be a forced march. But there must be no falling out, for every man is needed. Throw all unnecessary stuff away, and I pray to God we will soon be relieved."

The Colonel stepped back. We looked at each other, wondering what else Fate held in store. But the Colonel was a pukka soldier, and we knew he would stick by us, come what may. We should have been relieved—that was news— but he wanted us to see it out and do our best. None thought of hanging back, though our thoughts were gloomy. There was nothing to be done about it, anyway, but obey. Without hesitation the few that had carried blankets from the looted villages dumped them on the side of the road. Other things followed—souvenirs : a motley dump they made—hand-mirrors, framed photographs, women's underclothing, silver-backed hairbrushes, mother-of-pearl boxes, plaster Madonnas, crucified Christs, silver candlesticks. Even the little inconsequential things that soldiers hold most dear were thrown away with the rest, swelling the dump.

A large beautifully illuminated French Prayer Book which I had fastened on in one of the houses and had intended to keep, both for reading practice and as a souvenir, went with the rest. " Very likely I'd never live long enough to get reading it," I thought.

" By the right, quick march," came the friendly order

from the Adjutant, and we started off, keyed up for one last effort.

We knew we were for it again. A forced march meant stepping out hard and fast, with perhaps a short halt at long intervals. Above all it meant that somewhere, many kilometres ahead, things were in a bad way and that we, bad and all as we were, were being rushed up to fill the gap. We marched silently for a while, each man trying to imagine what lay in store, averse to putting his thoughts into words. At the end of the road an obscure death was waiting for some of us. We wondered dully who it would be. We had escaped death a lot of times.

At the end of an hour we felt tired again. But the Colonel had struck the right note, and we responded, for the time being at any rate, in the way he would have expected— cheerfully enough and without grousing. It was a marvellous night for marching. Our iron-shod feet rang out sharp and determined on the hard road stretching before us, silvery, unending. The night air, that had chilled us sitting down, now felt pleasantly cool and refreshing. The Adjutant dropped back a step and slyly suggested starting up a song.

There was a moment's hesitation, and then a man in the leading file responded in a good tenor voice which rang out sweetly and clearly above the tramp of feet. The song was taken up by a hundred throats. It was a filthy song about nothing in particular. The burly Adjutant laughed heartily at the response to his request. The junior officers carried on without looking round. " Dirty beasts," they were very likely saying to themselves, but what did we care. The words had a far-away austere sweetness in spite of their lewdness.

When it came to an end others contended with the tenor for the honour, and we were off again with a full-throated roar. All the favourites of marching men followed, with scarcely a pause in between for a breather. But by and by the strain of the march descended on us and more and more men were silent.

The Adjutant dropped back again and spoke to the tenor, but the response was so poor that the singer stopped after a line or two. Left to themselves our footsteps pounded dully and lifelessly on the frosty road stretching into infinity before us.

Butcher still limped. Without asking his leave this time I pulled his rifle from him and slung it over my free shoulder. After covering a few hundred yards he said he could march better with it, and I handed it back.

" It gives a chap something to hang on to," he explained, and I knew he was right. The rifle acted as a kind of balancer. Pulling at the strap gave a measure of comfort which more than compensated for the extra weight.

Our steady pace ate up the miles, and still there was the road ahead and the cold, blank fields on either side. Our legs moved under us automatically, as if outside our control.

We fell out for five minutes at long intervals and lay on the road exhausted. Instead of being rested our joints stiffened and the sweat dried on us. We could hardly scramble to our feet when the order came to go on. We were too tired now to waste our time in grousing, but set faces showed the strain of the long march. Hours before we had come through a town that was being shelled. Hours before that again we had passed French transport. March. March. March. Now we were on a forced march. Was it hours or days ? We no longer felt hungry. None of us cared now where we were going. Our minds were concentrated on the ever-increasing difficulty of getting one foot before the other. It got steadily colder as our energy became used up. My body was warm and the lice fed, but my face and hands were numbed. Opening the neck of my tunic I bent my head and breathed the warm air rising from my chest,—and fell asleep on my feet, only to waken again with Butcher's hand on my shoulder and his voice in my ear.

" Hey, Corporal, stop bumping into me. You'll have the pair of us down." He kept his hand on my arm encouragingly, but I shook it off, half ashamed of myself. I had no nail in my boot to worry about, but no matter how I tried it got more and more difficult to keep my place in the ranks. One moment I would be too far in advance, taking the heels of the man in front. The next I was lagging behind, lurching along drunkenly. Butcher's limp became painful to watch. It was a kind of dot-and-carry one progress, like that of a man with a bad cork leg. His face was screwed up, and the breath hissed between his clenched teeth. A sudden fear came to me that he would have to drop out, and I didn't want to lose him.

" Stick it, Butcher," I said.

" Ah, b—— you, shut up," he snarled.

I was silent again, but a warm feeling, something like what I felt for my mother when I thought of her at odd times, and had once felt for the girl at the camp at home, came chokily. They were far away, but he was beside me on the road. And he had singled me out from the rest to muck in with. I tried to imagine a rusty nail cutting its way into my foot for hour after hour, but couldn't. Any time that I had ever had a nail in my shoe I had been able to get relief at the end of a few minutes or else stop walking. It was such a simple thing.

The marched dragged on endlessly. How far had we gone ? How far had we to go ? Other men began to roll drunkenly, taking up more than their fair share of room, bumping against their mates, who cursed them savagely. My legs felt paralysed, but the dread of dropping out and lying alone on the road kept me from giving up. At last only vile blasphemies, sounding the depth of obscenity and despair, came from the reeling ranks.

THE SHOT BETWEEN THE EYES

WE went on quicker than ever when the march ended. A grey smoky dawn was breaking when we came on a line of A.S.C. lorries drawn up at the side of the road waiting for us. We were so far gone that the drivers had to leave their seats and hoist us in.

Twenty men to each lorry was the order, and we stood clutching and swaying as they moved off quickly. Jenkins pressed the others back and made room for Butcher to sit down and take off his boot and sock, squelchy with blood. The continual jolting of the lorries as they sped along excited us. We recovered our good humour after a fashion, cursing and wrangling as we lost our balance and stood on each other's tender feet. In between times we wondered what was happening ahead.

The sky grew rapidly lighter, and it was a new day when we dropped stiffly to the ground in a little deserted village. The A.S.C. men turned their cumbersome vehicles and drove off without a word, eager to ditch us and get away. We marched along the single street, the question of what we were in for looming larger with every step. About a mile outside the village we left the road and stepped to the left into a newly dug trench. It was fairly deep and so broad as to be more like a sunken road.

"We've got room to stretch ourselves and have a kip down," said Jenkins approvingly.

We lost no time in making ourselves as comfortable as possible, surprised that this quiet spot should be the cause of all the trouble, but well content that it should be so. Another and more welcome surprise was that the rations had come up. Breakfast would be ready shortly. Things were looking up. The sun came out, and we luxuriated in its warming rays. We lay back, everything forgotten but our present ease. There was another trench or two farther up the field and about half the men were sent to man them.

The rumour went that other units of the Division were somewhere nearby, but we didn't know, and didn't see any sign.

The headquarters cook, a big stout man, made his appearance. He was laden with good things. A fire was started in the side of the trench and rashers of bacon laid in a shallow dixie lid. The tea was made in the dixie proper. Soon it was ready, hot and steaming. The marvellous aroma of bacon frying in the open air allied itself to the smoke of burning wood to make our mouths water. We fell into line, and each man was presented with a thick round of white loaf bread dipped in boiling fat with a strip of golden brown bacon on top and a canteenful of strong tea, well coloured with condensed milk. Afterwards Butcher cadged a cigarette from the cook and shared it with me.

Signal flags had come with the rations. We looked dubious as they were handed round. Nevertheless we greeted them like old friends and wagged out alphabets to get our hands in, although the fags would have been much more welcome. The runners laughed at us.

" Didn't I tell you they would be dishing out bows and arrows soon ? " jeered Jenkins. " Signal flags on the Western Front ! Who ever heard of it before ? "

" They're to keep in touch with the men in front," said the Signal Officer non-committally.

" Yes, sir," we answered, glad to be back at our trade, no matter how antiquated the tools.

In front a flag appeared above the ground and waved a message in the clipped, unauthorised, but rapid movements and spelling that signallers employed for unofficial messages :
" How r u off for sox ? " we read.

" Go to L urself," we replied.

" She is his sister," waved the flag in front, a time-honoured sentence which consists entirely of dots with the exception of a single dash.

" Send her along anyway," answered Butcher, sitting on the parapet.

The war reared its ugly head jealously.

Jerry machine-guns opened in front, and our Lewis-gunners, with a plentiful supply of ammunition, replied at length. The bullets droned high overhead, but we lay low, listening to the fire as it gradually got heavier and better directed. A man farther along was hit. Three or four of his mates busied themselves round him for a minute with first-aid bandages, and then turned away, the bandages still in their hands.

The men about me commented.

" Kicked the bucket."

" A bad start."

" Who is it ? "

I was getting hardened to such everyday occurrences, and let my eyes wander over the dead man, but I could not entirely conquer the repugnance that badly wounded or dead men aroused in me, and looked away. There was something mysterious, too, in the spectacle of a man who an hour before had been eating dip bread and bacon in the bright sunshine now lying blind, deaf and dumb to what went on about him, no longer caring whether bullets thudded into him until he was full of lead—or into us. The body was there with its dirty uniform. The man had disappeared into thin air. It was a pity, too, that a good slice of bread and bacon had been wasted. . . .

" Listen to them," said Butcher, " this is going to be a picnic, I don't think. I wish to God I had joined the Navy."

Butcher had solved the problem of how to reach the nail

in his boot by the simple expedient of cutting off the toe-cap
to get at it. He had thrown away the sock and his dirty toes
protruded, a bandage round the big one.

"It feels better than it looks," he said with a grin. "We're
all a lot of bloody scarecrows anyway."

"Wonder would there be another chance of scrounging
another cigarette out of the cook," he added wistfully.

"Wait awhile, or he'll think you're going to skin him
altogether," I counselled.

"To hell with that for a yarn. If we cop a bullet we'll
be thinking more of wooden crosses than Woodbines. If
the fool of a cook stops one the lads nearest him 'ill have his
pockets picked before you could say ' Jack Robinson.' "

I sat listening to the firing as Butcher crept away determin-
edly. We seemed to be gradually getting encircled by rattling
machine-guns. They were invisible, but the air was full of
hissing bullets. Suddenly the signaller who was doing
look-out, bent down and shouted excitedly :

"Here come the lads in front."

As they spoke they came racing along and tumbled into
the trench, their eyes popping and their mouths open, filled
with the wild energy of men expecting bullets in the back
every second. They lay gasping on the trench floor.
Realising that they were still alive they tried to return to
normal and appear collected.

"It got too hot up there," said one, his breath still going
and coming in gasps. "Jerry started to——"

But what Jerry had been about to do I never learned.

A louder, heavier noise imposed itself on the hard rat-tat
of the machine-guns. It came from the air above us and
we knew, without looking up, what it meant.

The noise came rapidly nearer. We crouched down
against the trench wall as a familiar-looking, red-bodied
plane appeared. Its engines stopped. I looked up fleetingly,
hugging the earth again as it swooped down, amazingly

large and close. Its machine-gun sent a stream of bullets hissing down about us.

I lay stupidly, my mind a blank, all the nerves in my body concentrated in my exposed back, awaiting the impact of a bullet. The plane swept upwards with a roar.

One or two wounded men scrambled out of the trench and made off over the open, forgetting about the machine-gunners on the ground. The plane turned and came towards us again. The Lewis-gunners sent bursts of hot lead upwards, but without result. It dived, engines shut off, a great man-made bird of prey, spewing bullets the while. Again we lay quiescent, hiding our faces, until the roar of the engines told us that the headlong swoop was over for another time. He would get us next time sure.

The Lewis-gunners, mad with excitement now that they had got a real target to shoot at, worked their guns for all they were worth as the plane rose gracefully and seemed to stop motionless for a second before making another swoop. A long trail of oily black smoke and red flame appeared behind it as it came at us for the third time, gun spouting. The pilot seemed to sense something wrong. The engines had hardly been shut off for the dive before they were going again full blast. The bullets didn't come our way.

"He's down. He's down," came the cry as the plane wobbled and, with long tongues of fire shooting out behind, went to earth over a fold of ground in front and disappeared.

I looked down the broad trench. Nobody at our end was hit. Farther along men busied themselves about huddled forms. Still, we seemed to have got off lucky enough. Perhaps a single trench was a hard enough thing to hit from the air, especially when Lewis-guns were spraying the plane from the ground.

Butcher came running, bent double, with a packet of issue cigarettes in his hand.

"What's up down there?" we asked, our eyes on the packet.

" About half a dozen of the boys got hit," he answered.

" Where did you get the fags ? " put in Jenkins, more to the point.

" Well, the cook was one of the unlucky ones. Just as he had the packet out to give me one, too. So I got the whole blasted lot."

The others exclaimed enviously. We gathered round, hands outstretched.

" What about divvying ? "

" Come on. Do the decent ! "

" Don't be in such a flaming hurry, you pack of lousy scroungers," said Butcher, and handed out three or four cigarettes unwillingly.

" There, that's all," he said, handing one to Jenkins. " There's only three left and we want them for ourselves. Some of you would smoke cow-dung just so long as you had to scrounge for it."

Our gunners, full of their victory over the plane, blazed away. It was a battle of machine-guns again. The rest of us were non-combatants to all intents and purposes, with nothing to do but listen.

" They're mad now because we busted up their dirty plane," said Jenkins, as we crouched down, sucking eagerly at our cigarettes. " The important thing is how are we going to get away from here ? There's not an inch of cover, and Jerry's sweeping the whole place. They say none of the wounded that ran for it got away."

I looked round uneasily, but didn't dare put my head over the parados. There was nothing to be done about it. Anyhow, the future—even the immediate future—could take care of itself. " Minute, mind thyself," was one of war's chief teachings.

After a while the men sat silent, filled with a growing apprehension, which the warm sun overhead could not dispel. Once more things seemed to be working to a climax.

The Jerries wouldn't let us hold them up much longer. " They must know that we're only a handful," I thought drearily.

The end came suddenly.

Away on the left a machine-gun commenced enfilading the trench and in a moment men sprawled, screaming and twisting as bullets found them. We cringed, helpless and unprotected, as the bullets swept hissing up the trench.

" Here it comes," I thought, thinking of death, and the man who had been first killed. In another moment we would be out of it all like him.

The sides of the trench came alive as particles of earth spurted and crumbled down about our shoulders and down our necks. We struggled blindly with each other to get into the base of the parapet. The line of crouching men made a living shield.

Then the stentorian voice of the Adjutant made itself heard over the clamour. I strained my ears, hardly comprehending what he said.

" Every man for himself. Run for it," he roared.

There was a mad scramble out of the death-trap trench. In a moment we were running for our lives across the open, making for the road to the village we had passed through in the morning. Bullets fanned our cheeks, buzzed about us like a swarm of angry bees, slapped into the earth about our feet. They came from behind and either side, converging on us until the air was alive and it was a miracle that we still lived.

A man running, bent double, almost in front of me, gave a jerk as if he had received an electric shock, straightened up, and tumbled on to the broad of his back. Before I could change my step or swerve out of the way my foot crunched sickeningly into his face as he lay spreadeagled in the dirt. I stumbled, half-stopped, then ran on with the others. It was Butcher, with a hole between his eyes.

"He didn't feel my boot," I found time to think.

THE BUGLE CALL

WE sat on the grass in front of a solitary deserted farm-house.

It was a pretty, homely-looking place with three wooden steps up to the door. A pile of rotting apples lay on the porch and gave off a sweetish, rather unpleasant smell. The officers were not visible. They sat in one of the rooms talking, and we were left to our own devices.

The ground near the house was divided up into neat rectangular fields with wire fences. Farther on it rose and fell irregularly, and in the hollows were little dense planta-tions which remained shadowy and cool in the bright sunlight. The men spoke in subdued voices, as if afraid of being overheard. Their faces were hollow and strained. From time to time they glanced uneasily about—towards the house, where the orders to move would come from, at the N.C.O.s sitting a little apart, and away to where the sunbeams played hide and seek with the trees. We knew only too well that the sun, the quiet farmhouse and the peace-ful fields were not for us. They were alien things, mocking our misery and making it more apparent.

" The weather is on Jerry's side again. If it would only rain the advance would stop," the Adjutant had told us, gritting his teeth and cursing God.

And yet there was a certain comfort about the present. For one thing we were not on our feet slogging into the kilometres and swallowing dust. We had stopped estimating the number of kilometres covered at a stretch and instead developed a faculty for forgetting, like children, what we had done the previous day. Sometimes half-hearted wrangles

started about what day it was and how many days we had
been retreating, but they always ended nowhere for we had
lost count.

We were famished as usual, but there was nothing new in
that. Our inimitable transport had lost us once more, and
seemed in no hurry to find us. Very likely it wasn't their
fault. They might have had nothing to bring us, or else
were wandering about looking for us in places we had left
hurriedly days before and were forced to dump the grub on
the side of the road for Jerry's benefit. We cursed them,
anyway.

The last debacle, on top of so many more, had robbed us
of the slightest desire to hold up the Germans. It was like
trying to keep the tide back with a pitchfork and we had had
about enough of it. We had been betrayed in the first
instance and now we were deserted.

" They knew we'd be massacred in the big attack, and
nobody cared a damn.

" Ay, there was nobody to back us up. Us that held out
all day in the battle positions, too."

"Tha-a-at's right. If there had been two or three Divisions
behind the line in reserve it wouldn't have happened, this
stunt."

" They're having us for a lot of mugs. Even with just a
few more guns and such-like we could have put up a show, eh,
boys ? "

" You bet we could. But where are they all now ? There
must be thousands of our fellows somewhere, and guns,
too ! "

" Of course there must. But where are they ? "

" In the name of God, where ? "

I sat a little apart from the rest, lonely and sad at the loss
of Butcher, not knowing that in a day or two I would forget
him almost as completely as if he had never been. When
a mate went West he was only a dead man, to be forgotten as

soon as possible. It was a bad thing to have a long memory in the infantry.

Two or three of the junior officers had gone off sick or wounded, and we hardly noticed their absence. The Colonel and the Adjutant and the few remaining N.C.O.s mostly Regulars, were the ones we looked to and obeyed. We were all more like tramps than soldiers. The hair on my face felt strange. It was crinkly and itchy as if the lice were in it, as probably they were. The Colonel—tall, stooped, emaciated—was like a man in a dream, or a fever. He seldom spoke to us, and at times I thought I detected something very like despair in his weary eyes. But always, in spite of his wound, he kept his place at our head on the long marches, and issued calm orders when things were at their worst.

The black-bearded Adjutant mixed amongst us, his haggard face and bloodshot eyes never at rest. He was more like a gorilla now than an officer with his great barrel chest and black muzzle, and he frankly took us into his confidence, ranting against the staff of the Division, the Fifth Army, and the whole B.E.F. with equal impartiality for a set of incompetent bastards who should be stood against the nearest wall and shot out of hand.

" He would do it, too, if he got the chance," we thought.

" The enemy holds all the cards," he said, grinding his teeth, " but by Christ, we've given nearly as good as we've got so far. The battalion has gone to hell, but that's all that matters. Cut their hearts out any time you get a chance, boys. No questions asked. That's my motto."

When he went away we looked at each other. Jerry had a hundred men for every one of us. He had machine-guns, and shells, and flame-throwers, and food and aeroplanes. We had nothing but our rifles, and nobody could prevent us throwing away our ammunition on the interminable marches. Attackers lost more than attacked, but had it been that way this time ?

We had lost our Lewis-guns, and most of their crews, in the last fiasco. The order " Every man for himself " did not include Lewis-guns, the survivors argued, and we accepted their dictum.

There was nothing to prevent us from quietly disappearing over the landscape—nothing, that is, except the Adjutant's ready revolver and the idea that we might be shot as deserters by whoever stopped us. Even without such deterrents we would have hung together. In spite of all our vicissitudes we were still a unit of sorts, and it never entered our heads to be anything else. As a newcomer to the battalion I pondered the matter over. Why? If the others had dispersed I would have made off too, without a moment's hesitation, but as it was, I clung the closer. It was an unanswerable question.

When I asked Jenkins about it he put another unanswerable question.

" Why does one bastard sheep follow another ? "

The sun's rays were coming to us in broad slants when the officers emerged and gave the order to move. We left the derelict farmhouse and went forward slowly, keeping to the bottom lands and skirting the trees. There was no firing, but occasionally walking wounded from strange units limped by—a bad sign, we thought, looking at them curiously. They were dusty and dirty and went along doggedly, taking little notice of us. They looked as if they had been walking a long time, and meant to keep on walking. Some of them used their rifles as crutches. Others were in pairs, holding on to each other for support. They were all famished-looking. Every few hundred yards we stopped and hung about aimlessly, only to go on a little bit farther.

" What's the dirty game this time ? " we asked each other without expecting an answer.

The trickle of wounded ceased, and we were alone. The sun went behind the trees, and the earth took on a more gloomy aspect more in keeping with our thoughts. We went slower. The men stopped talking, knowing that we were seeking contact and that, as usual, somehow and sometime soon, we were going into action, the usual action against impossible odds. By and by we skirted a wood, and started to climb. The slope got steeper. We groused mechanically. Coming to the edge of a road cut into the hill-side a halt was called. On the other side of the road the ground continued to rise. The road formed a natural breastwork so long as we didn't actually get on to it. We lay staring across to where some low bushes lined the far side, hiding the rising ground behind from our limited vision.

The Colonel, with a couple of attendant runners, got on to the road and explored first to the right and then to the left with negative results. There seemed to be nothing doing at the moment. We lay at our ease on the grassy slope. Again the rumour went the rounds that there were other troops in position somewhere around, but again the rumour was all we had to go on. Perhaps the officers started it purposely.

Time passed slowly and the Colonel becoming anxious for some reason or other, sent a couple of men tiptoeing off, first to the left and then to the right along the road. They soon returned, calling out softly as they came to guard against being shot by mistake. The prolonged silence began to get on our nerves. An occasional smothered cough and the nervous clicking of a rifle bolt drew low-pitched venomous curses. Jerry was somewhere about or we wouldn't be lying there. But where ? When a single rifle shot shattered the silence like the bursting of a heavy shell we reacted like prowling animals, holding our breath, frozen in whatever attitude the sound had caught us, striving vainly to pierce the darkness. Then, as if the chance shot had done away with the need for further caution, voices, strangely guttural, reached us. Drunken voices which

N

broke into snatches of song and roared out strange choruses
with drunken gusto. It was the Germans. Drunk with
wine or victory, or both. The real authentic Jerry who had
been chasing us for over a week, now only a few yards
away, though still invisible. The singing went on. I
listened intently to the unintelligible words of the songs,
getting a queer vicarious satisfaction from their full-throated,
carefree voices. How strong and confident they were!
How weak and helpless we were.

The Colonel crouched at the far side of the road, peering
through the bushes and listening. A runner knelt beside
him. A loud argument broke out in front, broken with
maudlin shouts and yells. It ceased abruptly, and then
came a roar of voices and the smashing of glass.

" Hoch der Kaiser."

Silence followed, and we stiffened. Silence was ominous.

Remembering another occasion I drew up one knee up
under me and pressed one hand against the bank to get
purchase for a quick start.

The little rustling noises commenced again. But where
before they had been all round us they came now from the
other side of the road. The Colonel crouched lower, his
bandaged arm showing faintly against the dark background.
His runner crept a shade nearer to us on hands and knees.
Then, as if undecided what to do, he stopped in the middle
of the road.

A bugle blared out shrilly, almost in our astonished ears.
There was a rush of heavy feet behind the bushes. A
bomb burst with a roar between the Colonel and the runner,
sending jagged bits of iron whizzing past our heads. Starting
to his feet the Colonel staggered off down the road to the
right. The runner lay motionless, a dark blob on the road.
A ragged volley came from the men around me. Another
bomb burst, behind us this time, and I felt something strike
the sole of my boot. The man alongside me, it was a pimply

youth named Spike, screamed piercingly and sprawled half on top of me. I threw him off, and jumping to my feet went flying down the slope with bombs bursting behind and panic-stricken men all round. The ground fell away so steeply at first that my legs had difficulty in keeping up with my body. My feet jarred each time they touched the earth like missing a step going down a dark staircase. A man beside me tripped and fell headlong. A second later another went head over heels.

" What's the matter with them," I thought distractedly, the invisible slope smooth and grassy now under my feet as I got into my stride.

Above my pumping heart-beats I heard the stuttering of a machine-gun and fled the faster.

We reached level ground. Dimly I made out ten men clambering over a wire fence. Fear still lent wings to my feet, and launching myself in the air like a steeplechaser I managed to clear it, but the trigger-guard of my rifle caught on the topmost strand of wire and wrenched the weapon out of my hand. For a second I debated going back for it, but for all I knew a horde of drunken Germans were at my heels, and I wasn't going to die for the sake of a rifle. It was too dark to look for it anyway. I ran on. Damn the rifle, and everything else.

We stopped at last, completely winded, and gradually got together, listening as well as our heaving chests would let us for the sounds of pursuit. All was quiet once more. The Adjutant appeared. With the help of the N.C.O.s he got us into some kind of order, and then made us extend in single file and lie down on the ground a yard or so apart. We lay down obediently, but all the yarns I had ever heard, or imagined, of men being shot for being found without their rifles in face of the enemy kept recurring to me. The Adjutant had his revolver in his hand again, and I didn't trust him, remembering his mad behaviour once before.

He would shoot me as soon as look at me. I lay for a time in an agony of indecision, but there was only one thing to do.

Getting quietly to my feet, I drew back a pace and made my way cautiously along the line of indistinct figures lying prone, facing their front. Creeping forward noiselessly I slid in between two and crouched at their feet. They didn't notice my arrival and kept on staring into the darkness. There was just a chance that one had left his rifle down beside him.

Leaning forward I groped about first with one hand and then the other. My fingers touched a smooth, rounded butt lying on the ground at the side of one of the men. Very gently I drew it towards me, inch by inch, and then withdrew as stealthily as I had come. Back in my place in the line I lay down and fondled my prize.

But I was troubled for all that. My own rifle had borne the single figure 7, which was rather unusual. Rifle numbers generally ran into the hundreds of thousands, and I had come to look upon the solitary 7 as a mascot of sorts.

There didn't seem any sense in making us lie in the hollow. If the Germans had chosen to follow up their success we would have taken to our heels as before. Rifles were worse than useless in the dark against bombs and machine-guns. We were fed up anyway with the whole business.

Two or three French soldiers came slouching over to us from amongst the trees on our right. They stood looking down at us in silence, their hands in the pockets of their caught-up overcoats. We stared back at them curiously, wondering what they were doing in the wood with the enemy only a few hundred yards away, and how many of them were there ? It was very odd. They stood for a while casually watching us, and lounging about aimlessly. Without a word they disappeared amongst the dark trees like so many ghouls.

" They look more like squareheads than Froggies."

" Spies, maybe."

" Well, let them spy. What do we care now."

A couple of the junior officers came up, the Signal Officer and the Intelligence Officer. We learned that the Colonel had been wounded again. He had refused to go at first, we heard, but had fainted from loss of blood and had to be carried away. The news disheartened us still further, and we began to get restless. It was bitterly cold, too, lying in the lush grass of the hollow.

I noticed an indistinct crouching figure now and then making stealthily for the left of the line, and drew the attention of the man beside me.

" They're doing a bunk, likely," he replied softly. " If we don't hurry up and get a move on I'm going too."

At last the Adjutant, assuming command, arrived at a decision and passed the word to retreat. We departed in single file, making as little noise as possible, holding on to each other until the ground rose and we could see better where we were going. Coming on to a road we reformed. After a long, nervous wait for possible stragglers to join us a low-voiced order came and we tramped off.

" Was that the ' Charge ' they sounded on that bugle before they come over on us, d'you think ? " I asked curiously after we had covered a kilometre or two in silence. Anything with a foreign touch to it interested me in spite of myself. The question tickled the men nearest me and they laughed jerkily, without replying. Too stupid, or too weary, to sense that the insolent bugle call rankled with them more than anything else, and made them feel ashamed I asked again.

" What the blazes do you think it was—' Come to the cookhouse door ' ? " said Jenkins derisively.

THE UHLAN

WE marched mechanically, dazed with hunger, fatigue and defeat. It was nearly midnight, and the cold bit into our exhausted bodies.

It was a long time now since we lost the Colonel. Two days, perhaps. So long that we had forgotten him. He was out of it and didn't count. So to hell with him.

There had been a faint rumour the previous day that we were going out. Nobody knew where it came from. Nobody confirmed or denied it. We were too apathetic to care. The gulf between life and death had almost disappeared. We lurched along, knowing that nothing was any use any more, no longer wondering where we were bound for. When would the next halt come, to let us slump down at the roadside? The Adjutant, in the lead, strode along tirelessly, setting the pace. His great shoulders were bowed until his helmet seemed to rest on them instead of on his head. He seemed to have forgotten our existence, as perhaps he had. The other officers brought up the rear, walking a little apart.

And then, once more, a dispatch rider sought us out. Once more—without the formality of a speech this time—we went on purposefully into the night.

A hoarse murmur came from the skeleton ranks—unheard, or unheeded, by authority.

" Where is it this time ? "

" For it, again ? "

" Lord God, what do they think we're made of ? "

We marched on doggedly, eating up the miles, mumbling viciously as we bumped into each other.

The road was a dim grey ribbon.

I had keen eyesight, and stared first to one side and then the other trying to see the fields, or a landmark of some kind to remind me should I ever return, that once I had passed that way, but I might as well have tried to read the future. Or I did read it, and the darkness showed what the future held in store.

Next I tried walking with my eyes shut, keeping my place in the ranks by instinct and the sound of the tramping feet and grunts of my neighbours. After an initial bump or two I succeeded wonderfully, despite the uneven, rutty road. My thoughts wandered. Life is a simple thing, a mere matter of spending energy, perhaps, to those who have no energy to spare for wondering about it. And yet, their desire for life was virile and sensible, an unspoken condemnation, deep and admirable, of their barbarous fate.

Butcher, too, had been full of the desire for life. Now he lay—probably still where he had fallen—his body swelling with foul gases, preparatory to sinking into the earth—stinking, worm-eaten, obscene. The rasher of bacon with its savoury smell, the white, dipped bread, and the hot, sweet tea he had swallowed a while before the bullet got him were rotten, along with the sore foot that had given him so much pain—all food for the worms. And the mark on his face, where my clumsy foot had rested. That would be there, too.

Would the crawling lice desert him, or would they remain sharing his body with the worms ? And what about the rats ? They would have to get their share. Big, fat-bellied ones with sharp, pointed teeth. But what way did it go ? Rats ! Rodents ! Hadn't they to keep gnawing continually or their teeth grew and pierced their lips ? Rats, too, Butcher, old man. Otherwise, it's cruelty to animals, you see, and all that. But why argue, even with oneself ? Butcher would know.

" Hey, Corporal, wake up ! What's the matter, with your

mumbling and bumping. Are the crabs biting you, or what ? "

I shook my head dizzily. " I'll carry your rifle for a while now, you old leadswinger."

I woke up and walked along, trying to pierce the surrounding darkness.

Sometime in the night we halted.

" Another charabanc ride," muttered a cynical voice.

Someone held a light while the Adjutant consulted a map anxiously. After a low-voiced conversation he went off followed by the Intelligence Officer, who called upon a runner to accompany them. Lying in a heap on the road, the men stirred sluggishly as the frosty air crept into their bones.

In about half an hour the Intelligence Officer returned alone and ordered us to follow, waiting patiently while we got slowly and unwillingly to our feet. Some, despite the cold, had sunk into deep sleep and had to be roughly poked with rifle butts. We slid clumsily down a bank at the left of the road and, finding our feet at the bottom, trudged along for a hundred yards parallel with the road until we came on a row of tumble-down shacks built into the bank.

" Why, they're old gun-pits," a man said.

At some period of the war's ebb and flow a battery had been concealed there with the road as a screen. It was too dark to see whether the walls of the shacks had succumbed to time and weather—the war was very old—or whether hostile shells had found the hidden guns and wrecked the pits. The darkness and loneliness of the place spoke of disaster. It was a dreary hole for men like us, cold and comfortless, but there was nothing to be done about it.

We kipped down as best we could, lying close together in a vain effort to be warm, and slept, only to be awakened in what seemed a minute or two by a flurry of shots somewhere near at hand. The drumming of horses hoofs came to us clearly, followed by the rattle and rumble of a heavy wagon going all out. The noise came, not from the road in front, but from behind.

Someone gave the alarm. We tumbled out of the shacks, shivering and wincing, as only men can who have slept in their clothes, who have not had enough to eat for a long time, and whose nerves are very ragged. No more shots were fired, but the protesting rumble of the wagon, going slower now, told us that we had not been mistaken. Presently this stopped too. We huddled together, fingering our rifles doubtfully, wondering what the sounds portended.

" The bastards must be all around us this time," we decided. A feeling almost of relief came to us. Better capture than any more of this dog's life. But were they taking prisoners ?

The raw misty air numbed our limbs and our eyes seemed full of sand. It sucked into our lungs and made us cough continually, but we stood stupidly, forgetting everything in the new danger. It didn't seem worth while putting up a show of resistance.

Then a hail came from the half darkness ahead and a hearty voice called out reassuringly, as if its owner was in no danger of being mistaken for anyone but himself :

" Ahoy, there ! Is that the 1st Battalion ? "

" Yes, yes," we shouted gladly. " Who are you ? " And without waiting for an answer : " This way. Over here. Mind yourself."

The big voice boomed back, with a self-confident chuckle somewhere in it.

" Rations, boys. Rations."

We listened, hardly daring to believe our ears. Then we burst into amazed exclamations.

" Rations ? "

" God Almighty, rations ? "

" That's the stuff to give 'em."

" Rations ! "

A burly figure materialised out of the greyness, and some of the men, recognising it, hastened to inform the rest.

" The Transport Officer."

He was a being from another world, someone who long ago would not have struck us as anything out of the ordinary —a smiling, healthy apparition out of the past, confronting us, as we stood in misery and wretchedness. He was fat and his neck was hard put to it to keep within the bounds of his collar. His cheeks shone from the recent application of a razor, and fawn-coloured riding-breeches and immaculate top-boots set off a well-turned leg—as if such things as shapely calves, or razors, or smart clothes, or health, or cleanliness still mattered. We were grey-faced, hairy and hollow-eyed—like men after a long illness. Our uniforms were torn, filthy and wrinkled, and we kept hunching and shrugging our shoulders with little unconscious, squirming movements as the lice crawled over us. The Transport Officer was excited and jubilant.

" You were damned nearly losing your rations after all, boys," he laughed. " We ran into a troop of Uhlans down the road there. They thought they had us, but we whipped up and galloped through them. I got one as he came alongside and blest if he didn't tumble into the limber right amongst the chuck."

We listened dumbly.

" So you'll have some Uhlan blood on your du pain, boys. It will make good kitchen, ha, ha."

He chuckled throatily at his own humour.

" The drivers are bringing him along," he called over his shoulder as, catching sight of the Adjutant, he left us and hastened over to report.

We looked at each other, the thought of the rations making our mouths water.

" Cavalry behind us on the road ! "

" So that's the way of it, boys ? "

" And trying to pinch our rations, the dirty tykes."

" He's a good man, after all, that Transport Officer."

A Sergeant detailed a squad to act as ration party. The squad went off with mixed feelings. Likely enough the Uhlans were lying in wait on the road, knowing they would come along, and ready to cut them down. On the other hand the ration party could easily sneak a couple of loaves buckshee on the way back, or a wedge of cheese, without anyone being a bit the wiser. It was a fair risk, but nevertheless I was glad I hadn't been selected. The party went off. They had hardly gone when two drivers made their appearance, dragging the wounded Uhlan between them by the arms, his heels acting as a brake as they scraped the ground. They were excited and breathless, but we looked on with impassive faces as they came up and deposited their burden at our feet and straightened up with sighs of relief. A dozen of us gathered round the captured trooper. The rest stood in groups apart talking, filled with warm anticipation of the feast to come.

" Would there be cigarettes ? "

" Would there be any rum ? "

I pressed forward curiously. I had never seen a Uhlan before and wondered what he would look like. The two drivers knelt beside him as he lay motionless on the ground. One of them removed a bloody bandage from about his mouth. I took one glance at what lay revealed, and stepped back hastily to the edge of the group of onlookers with a queasy feeling at the pit of my stomach. He was a young, clean-cut fellow, fair-haired and soldierly looking, his strange uniform heightening the impression of smartness and efficiency. His lower jaw was shot away and dark blood streamed down his neck and into the tight collar of his tunic. Already rivulets formed a dark pool on the hard ground about his head.

" Any of you boys got a field-dressing ? We've used both of ours on him," said one of the transport men without looking up.

Nobody answered or made a move to comply. The driver repeated his request in a louder tone, under the impression that we hadn't heard him the first time.

Jenkins, the runner, who was standing beside them, reached out his foot and moved the wounded man's head casually with his toe.

" I have," he said slowly, " but this joker isn't going to get it. Hell mend him. He's a goner, anyway."

There was a mutter of approval.

" Good judge, Jenkins. Let him go to blazes."

" Cop the bloomin' rations, would he ! "

The two transport men, still kneeling, looked up in astonishment. One of them started to say something and stopped. The others looked down at them, grimly waiting for them to speak. A variety of expressions followed one another on their upturned faces. Indignation. Doubt. The sudden apprehension that we had been passing through strange experiences. For the first time they took stock of our appearance, and all that it stood for. They looked fleetingly at their own spick and span clothes and shiny boots, and all that they stood for. Their faces got red.

There was a pause. The Uhlan's life-blood dripped on to the ground. The silence became unbearable, inhuman. The man was dying like a dog.

" Here, have a heart, you fellows. The poor beggar's bleeding to death," I broke in shamefacedly, and fumbling at the little stitched-up pocket of my tunic, where the emergency dressing was, ripped it from its resting-place and dropped it down beside the kneeling pair, craning my neck involuntarily as I did so.

The wounded man's head was pillowed now in his own blood. The pool was slowly spreading as if loth to sink into the hard earth. The blood radiated from his jaw in thin streams, streaking his cheeks and running into the hollows of his eyes. The skin in between was chalky white, giving his young face an odd likeness to an old circus clown's. The bandage was applied, and in a moment became bloody. His eyes fluttered open, and immediately blood blinded them. His body seemed to cave in. The death-rattle sounded, loud and harsh.

Jenkins turned on me angrily.

" You're a warm tin soldier, you are," he said. " Here we are, getting chased over the whole landscape, getting knocked to hell and gone every day for nobody knows how long now. The old Bat is away to scrapings and we're due for ours any minute. Well, you know it, too. And because we get hold of one of the beasts trying to steal our rations you act the fool and hand out your field-dressing. What'll happen to you when you get slugged yourself? Maybe nobody near you, eh? Left behind, say, in a rush. You'll put your hand down for it, eh? What about this moocher of an Uhlan, or whatever his name is, and you with no dressing. It's easy to bleed to death, eh, boys?"

" Ay, you're right there, but still—"

" Still, be damned. I'll bet the only field-dressing many a one of our lads got when the Jerries came up was a bayonet in his guts. That man should have got the same medicine."

I hung my head without replying, and then looked longingly at my stained bandage, wishing it safe back in its pocket. The drivers went silently back to their limbers. The group broke up, leaving the Uhlan alone, his face, what was left of it, turned to where a pale glow in the sky heralded the first rays of the rising sun.

I went back to the gun-pits disconsolately. Less than a month ago I would not have believed that men like Jenkins existed. Yet he was a decent fellow, and had sounded convincing when he stated his case. I knew that, because I had not only felt foolish, but had been made to look it. According to Sunday-school standards I was right, but Jenkins was right as well. He had a field-dressing and I hadn't. And we weren't at Sunday school. He was the more efficient. He had, leaving other considerations out of it, a double chance of survival and was therefore twice as good a soldier. I pondered the question, but could arrive at no decision.

" Perhaps there is something to be said on both sides," I thought, and gave it up. A bustle outside signified the safe return of the ration party.

Grub was more important than ethics.

THE RELIEF

W E dined wolfishly on crisp white bread, jam and strong Canadian cheese. There was no water and therefore no tea, but afterwards we paraded informally for tots of rum and cigarette issue. The Adjutant sat on an upturned case in a gun-pit and measured out good tots. He was in high good humour and his face was flushed, but his eyes were muddy and more bloodshot than ever. I got the impression that he had had more than one go at the rum jar.

Some of the men lay about in the sun swopping yarns and others went to sleep under the influence of the fiery liquor, but daylight revealed a French prisoners' cage just across the road from the gun-pits, and beside it, to the left, a deserted camp. Along with seven or eight other young fellows I scrambled up the bank and crossed over to explore. The rum made us reckless.

We went round the empty cages and into the huts, nosing about curiously. I was still enough of the new-comer to be thrilled by the fact that the place was French, but we soon found it was as bare as Old Mother Hubbard's cupboard. We went in and out of the dirty huts, I trying to fathom the ways of the people who had lived there, talking and laughing the while light-heartedly. It was adventure, with an out-of-bounds zest, and I enjoyed the casual rummaging.

Two of the party, Jenkins and another runner, wandered off by themselves, more to be in advance of the rest than with any great hope of finding anything. They made for the upper end of the camp, and after a while we forgot about them. The rest of us scrounged through what had been the camp stores where odds and ends of blue uniforms lay about, and an old, rusty stove.

Looting is an exciting business even when there is nothing to loot. We persevered. We came also on a rusty water tank and filled our bottles with scummy water against future emergencies.

One of the squad discovered a pile of old equipment. We were busy poking through it when we heard an explosion quite close, as if a bomb had gone off amongst the huts. Immediately afterwards there was a yell and the sound of running feet. With our hearts in our mouths we dashed helter-shelter through the door of the hut.

I was first out, and almost collided with Jenkins racing past with his mouth open and a panicky look on his face.

" Come on to hell out of it, mates," he gasped, " Jerry's at the other end of the camp. Quick, he got Johnston."

Without a word we took to our heels and slithering down the bank reached the safety of the gun-pits. There, alarmed by the explosion, officers and N.C.O.s were bawling orders and men were hurriedly seeing to their equipment and rifles.

We gathered round Jenkins, plying him with questions.

" We were just going into one of the huts—Johnston and I —when we ran into a squad of them. We ran like whippets. One of the Jerries must have thrown a bomb after us. Johnston was behind me and got it all to himself. I thought I was sent for, and that's a fact." He stopped abruptly to light a cigarette, his hands shaking with excitement.

" This way, you there. What do you think you're on, standing there chattering. That's right. Spread out a bit now. Get down."

The Adjutant came up buttoning his tunic. " No, don't lie down. Kneel, and you'll cover the bank better. Keep in lines, that's the way."

A couple of lines were formed, half a dozen yards apart, and we knelt as directed, facing the bank. An officer and a couple of N.C.O.s climbed up it and lay peeping over the road.

Nothing happened, and we began to get cramps in our legs. We got up and moved about. The look-outs slid down and a couple of men took their place. There seemed nothing to do. Jenkins, who had fully recovered, had a couple of candle ends in his haversack, and suggested drumming up with the water we had found. A couple more joined in, and the four of us slipped into one of the shacks. In about fifteen minutes the water began to show signs of coming to the boil. We poured a handful of tea and sugar and some dried milk into the dixie and sat licking our lips.

" A char and a wad is hard to beat," said Jenkins, pulling a grimy slice of bread out of his pocket, just as a shell burst with a roar outside. We stared at each other.

" Blast the luck," ejaculated Jenkins, " but we'd better get outside." Leaving the dixie of tea on the makeshift fire we ran out and joined the men below the bank.

No sooner had we taken our place in the line than a second shell fell about a hundred yards behind, sending earth and splinters flying in all directions. Another and another followed.

" Minniewerfers, by God. We're up against it now, for they're on top of us here before we can see them," muttered my neighbour.

The Adjutant shouted a question to the look-outs, but they shook their heads in reply. Nothing to be seen.

The shells came over at short intervals, all too far behind to do any damage, and then one burst near the second line of men. I was in the first line, nearest the bank. The smoke cleared away, leaving a couple of crumpled figures.

More shells came. The cries of wounded men allied themselves to the rising shriek of the explosions and the stinking fumes of cordite. The wounded were dragged under

o

the lee of the bank, and one or two men began rendering first aid, stopping to cower down with every detonation.

A shell burst over to the right and more men called out in agony. Splinters whined about our heads. The bright sun was almost obscured now by wreathing smoke, which hung close to the earth. Wounded men and mangled bodies lay about. Again some helpless kneeling men were enveloped in oily smoke, and again men screamed as jagged metal tore into them. It was more than baited flesh and blood could bear. With hoarse, inarticulate cries the survivors rose to their feet, filled with unutterable rage and despair. For a moment the foremost bunched together, pitifully few. Others joined in, and then, calling encouragement to each other, they surged forward in a leaderless, undisciplined charge with the bayonet against the hidden enemy, clawing and cursing as they forced their way up to the steep bank.

The remainder of us stood looking on uncomprehendingly, not knowing what to do. Affected by the strange excitement the N.C.O.s joined in the scramble up the bank, forgetting their duty in the wild desire to get at close quarters with the Germans.

" Come on, boys, we'll make them fight decent for once."

Like a madman the Adjutant threw himself forward, knocking men gone berserk right and left, pulling men back by their belts and shoulder-straps, tripping them up, exerting every ounce of his enormous strength.

With a bound he gained the edge of the road, and turned, revolver in hand, facing the frenzied men, ordering, threatening, pleading, kicking them back as they reached the top, sending them toppling on to the ones behind.

" Fall back in order."

" I'll shoot the first man that reaches the road."

" Stop, for Christ's sake, stop. Are you gone mad ? "

" D'ye hear. It's all right now, men. It's all right."

" Get back, you God-damned fools."

" Back."

Slowly and sullenly, baring their teeth and snarling, the men obeyed, their eyes fixed on the towering figure of the Adjutant with the unwinking glare of animals at their trainer.

The other officers asserted themselves, and the N.C.O.s, coming to their senses, lent their aid, but the Adjutant, forgetting his perilous position, stood, straddle-legged, looking on with a queer, almost rapt expression on his fierce bearded face. Passing a hand over his eyes, he shook his shaggy head and came slowly and clumsily down the bank.

" Get them into two lines again," he directed, and we jostled about.

" First rank kneel, and the second retire fifty paces."

I was in the first line and knelt obediently as the second moved off. The shells kept bursting near and I kept my head down as the hysterical excitement passed, leaving us apathetic. " Let them burst away," I thought. " What does it matter now where they light." The cries of the wounded scarcely penetrated my dull understanding and, disregarding them, I fixed my eyes on the ground. Our turn came. We rose stiffly and fell back through the second line, whose turn it was now to kneel facing the bank, their rifles at the " Ready " and their fingers on the trigger, but no enemy appeared.

Some of the wounded hobbled after us, but a few lay under the lee of the bank, oblivious to everything but their pain, or absorbed in the contemplation of death. One or two remained crumpled up where the shells had caught them. After a couple of hundred yards of alternate kneeling and falling back—all to no purpose, for no enemy showed over the bank—we all went straggling along, giving our whole attention to dodging the shells, which followed remorselessly. Gradually we broke up into little groups and separated, each group on its own. I found myself with half a dozen others trudging down a newly ploughed field, crouching and running according to the whim of the falling shells. It was heavy going over the raw earth, but our little squad was well in advance. By and by we got out of range and proceeded slowly down the field, looking over our shoulders at the men behind who were still playing a game of hide-and-seek in the sunshine. Sometimes we held our breath as a fountain of earth and smoke spouted skyward near a little group of plodding men and their forms were obscured for a moment, but nobody was hit so far as we could see—not that we cared overmuch either way.

We were slouching along slowly, heads bent, dully content at having outdistanced the shells, when a voice with a strange accent, a sharp authoritative voice, made us look up.

A tall thin officer stood before us, immaculately dressed, a little cane under one arm and gloves in his hand. He was a full Colonel. A glinting monocle added to his foppish appearance, but there was nothing foppish about his voice. Behind him was a stretch of narrow, freshly dug trench about twenty yards long. It was manned by British infantry, young, clean and well-groomed, who stared at us with round eyes. A little farther back to right and left were other strips of trench lined with the same chubby, doll-like faces, all turned our way. We came to an unwilling halt, facing the Colonel. He looked us up and down contemptuously.

" What is the meaning of this ? " he demanded, his face set in stern lines.

We only stared, trying to comprehend that here were fresh troops at last, when we had least expected them, dazzled with a sudden, wonderful vision.

Relief !

" Are you all deaf ? " shouted the Colonel, stamping his foot. " What does this mean ? Where are your officers ? Where is your battalion ? What regiment do you belong to ? "

We shuffled and moved closer to each other uneasily. Where were our officers ? Where was the battalion ?

" We are all tired out, sir," I said as none of the others attempted to answer the rain of questions. " We belong to the——"

" How dare you speak to me, Corporal, without saluting ?" rasped the Colonel. " You are a disgrace to your uniform, the lot of you."

We looked at him.

" Get down into those trenches," he went on harshly, " and try and act like soldiers if you can. I'll have the whole damned lot of you court-martialled for cowardice. Disgusting."

The vision of relief faded as quickly as it had come. In its place came despair. Every man of us still alive was the representative of a dozen or more. Our luck was too far strained as it was. Each of us knew in his bones that another day would mean the end. I started to expostulate as we went slowly towards the trench. The angry officer raised his cane and struck me on the face.

We lowered ourselves stiffly into the little trench, the spick-and-span occupants silently making room, as if fearful of being contaminated by such scarecrows, and fixed our eyes on the officer.

He glared until we were all down, and then turned away to deal with another ragged group coming along with bent heads and sagging knees.

Immediately his back was turned we looked at each other. Without a word we scrambled up and commenced edging away. The new troops looked on woodenly, making no effort to stop us.

The Colonel chose that moment to glance round.

He came hurrying back, fumbling at his revolver-pouch with one hand, waving the cane threateningly with the other. The shells which we had temporarily outdistanced sounded nearer now, but there was nothing else for it. Once more we lowered ourselves into the trench.

"If you move out of that trench again without my permission I'll shoot you without waiting for a court martial," he stormed.

And then, when all seemed lost, a loud familiar voice fell on our ears. We looked up joyfully.

"What the devil is coming off here?" asked the Adjutant brusquely.

"What's the meaning of this? Come away from those bloody trenches, you men. Did I tell you to get into them?"

We got out hastily, knowing that somehow we had a chance of getting away in spite of the strange officer—filled with sudden love for our wild Adjutant.

"Are you in charge of this rabble?" asked the Colonel cuttingly.

The Adjutant looked his interlocutor up and down, as if noticing him for the first time. Drawing himself up, he saluted punctiliously.

"Sir, I have the honour to be temporarily in command of the 1st Battalion of this Regiment," he replied. With a wave of his hand he took in our little group on the edge of the trench and the rest of the limping, ragamuffin crew that had come up behind and stood silently watching.

"What do you mean by allowing your men to straggle along in this disgraceful fashion?" asked the Colonel, not returning the salute.

The Adjutant stood like a ramrod, without answering.

"Have you no control over your men, or over yourself. Are you lost to all sense of what is expected of you? Are you——"

The Adjutant's face became congested with dark blood. He took a step forward. We closed in behind him trustingly.

"Are you aware, sir, that these men were in the line at St. Quentin, that they have been up against it ever since, every day, that this is what is left of a whole battalion, and that you and your men——"

A tiny movement caught my eye. I glanced at the Adjutant's right hand as it hung by his side, grasping his revolver. A little drama was being enacted there and I paid scant attention to what he was saying. The hand tightened convulsively. The blunt nose of the revolver rose slowly and surely, until it pointed straight at the immaculate Colonel's guts.

The Adjutant's voice, beginning to shake with suppressed passion, stopped for a moment. Hunching his broad shoulders, he made a step towards the Colonel and finished violently :

" These men are going out, d'ye hear ? Going out. And by the Lord neither you nor any other chocolate soldier is going to stop them."

Blank astonishment came over the Colonel's face. He seemed unable to believe his ears. He stared open-mouthed at the Adjutant. The monocle fell from his eye and dangled at his waist. In the act of retrieving it he caught sight of the pointing revolver, and started back.

" All right. Take your men away," he said in an altered voice. Turning on his heel he walked off hastily. The Adjutant waved his revolver encouragingly.

" Carry on, men."

We carried on gratefully, threading our way past neat trenches, each with its complement of young soldiers gazing at us in bewilderment.

I sensed something lightly supercilious in their looks. Not one of them spoke a word. I remembered that we had acted much the same way towards the crowds of stragglers we had met with on our travels, many days before, and dimly understood.

We left the new troops behind and went on down the gently sloping fields, only to come on another system of

trenches, manned this time by stout, elderly-looking Frenchmen, bearded and phlegmatic, all apparently about the same
age. They were a strange contrast to the slim, boy-faced
English in front of them and looked oddly out of place as
they lolled in their toy trenches. Their smart blue uniforms
and shiny helmets showed up conspicuously against the
brown earth instead of merging with it like the khaki. They
seemed to take us for granted. They were munching at
long French rolls and drinking wine, and nodded and smiled
good-humouredly, patting their bottles knowingly as we
passed by.

" Très bien, eh ! "

They were like so many fat burghers at a picnic.

We got on to a dusty road. After waiting for late-comers
we formed up and marched off, the Adjutant in the lead.
Shells were bursting in earnest about the little trenches and
only a blue helmet showed here and there above the ground.

" It's funny, isn't it, that old codgers like that should be
fighting along with those young soldiers in front. Like
fathers and sons," said one.

" They'll soon get shelled out of that," said another.

" Yes," I agreed, feeling my cheek, " but I hope that
Colonel gets a shell to himself."

" Fathers and sons," echoed Jenkins. " Ay, and they can
put my old woman in along with them so long as I get to
hell out of it."

Nobody laughed.

THE DUMP

HARDLY able to believe our luck, we swung along for what seemed to be a bare couple of miles, although it must have been five or six, for the sounds of war gradually decreased until we were left with the steady tramp, tramp of feet.

Before we had time to feel that a fall-out was due we arrived at a dusty village—deserted as usual—and halted. The officers betook themselves to one of the houses, or perhaps to what had been the village estaminet. We lay down in the middle of the sunny street and rested royally, our minds a blank to the past and future alike. Little by little it soaked into our consciousness that the harrying and killing was over, the machine-gun bullets, the shells, the bombs, the vicious planes. Little exclamations escaped us. We became human again, or nearly so. Our minds freed from the long-drawn-out apprehension of death took wing lazily. We were cynical, too, and found ourselves wondering whether any mention of what had happened had been allowed to leak out to the people at home.

" They are probably saying we retired a couple of hundred yards," said one, scratching contentedly.

" To positions previously prepared," added Jenkins sententiously.

A grizzled Sergeant spoke up authoritatively. He had received a splinter in the rear and lay in an awkward posture on the cobbled street, a dirty bandage, like the tail of a shirt, protruding from the seat of his trousers.

" Some big pot has messed things up, and they'll take

good care to keep everything quiet and save their own dirty skins and cushy jobs."

We agreed with this eminently sane reasoning, feeling at the same time an indefinable sense of disappointment and frustration that this should be the way of it.

" It wouldn't do for the people at home, you see, to know that the Germans had knocked the lights out of us," the Sergeant continued. " We have to win every time so as they won't lose their appetite for their ham and eggs in the mornings. Jerry shouts ' Kamarad ' at the right moment. Everything in the garden's lovely."

The Sergeant paused to spit. His audience waited approvingly for him to go on.

" I was at Mons," he said, " and it turned out to be an epic, whatever that means, so God only knows what this will turn out to have been in another month or two, or another year or two. They might give us a medal for it to show what heroes we were and all that. Whenever Jerry gives us an extra hard kick in the pants some genius gets the idea of making a great victory out of it. Give the blighters a bit of tin or an inch of ribbon and they'll brag about what they did till everybody else believes it too. That's their motto. Good luck to them while they can get away with it."

" It's funny they don't start asking why the war keeps going on in spite of all the victories ? "

" So long as they're making good money out if it some way or other, or on munition works, what do they care about us or what happens to us ? "

" Th-a-at's right. They don't know, and they don't want to be told."

For some reason I remembered the two brothers I had worked for before joining up. A picture formed before my mind's eye, a dim picture, very old, and musty and unreal. " Yes," said Mr. Samuel, softly rubbing his hands—or was it Mr. Silas ?—" a pound note in the plate every Sunday morning. It used to be a golden sovereign, but this terrible war——"

We got hungry again, and thought longingly of the rations we had left behind in the gun-pits. Enough for one meal only had been handed out, and the thought of the sacks of loaves, the slabs of cheese and the pozzy and beurre we had left behind for the squareheads to feast on made our mouths water. I thought longingly, too, of the dixie of tea we had left boiling, and tried to picture one of them calling out gleefully to his comrades to witness our kindness of heart.

" It only needed their slippers set out to make the toerags feel really at home," said Jenkins, to whom I had communicated my thoughts. " I hope to hell it chokes them."

" There was some rum left in the jar," said another, licking his lips.

It was pleasant to lie in the dusty street and talk, secure in the knowledge that somebody else was getting it in the neck up in front for a change. But after a time hunger moved us and we began prowling round, as usual, to see what we could find.

The others went into the houses. Happening to go into a big dark barn for my own purpose, I heard hens clucking, and investigated. In a corner I came on a big hen-house with a wire front and a little door into it. There were three or four sleepy hens inside on the roosts and snuggling into the strawed floor a couple of fat rabbits. In a minute I had half a dozen eager comrades round me. One of them, a farmer's boy, wrung the neck of the fowl. The rabbits—the big Flemish breed, somebody said—were quite tame and made no attempt to escape. I caught one by the scruff of the neck, and it lay trustingly in my arms like a cat. According to instructions, I tried to break its neck by giving it a sudden twist, but the big furry creature lay passive, and still alive, despite my efforts. I had never killed anything in my life, not even a rabbit.

" Choke it, then," said the fellow who had killed the hens, and I caught it by the throat and squeezed manfully, but the rabbit still lived, and still snuggled down in my arms.

" The damned thing has as many lives as a cat," I said desperately. " If it wasn't so tame I could do it better."

" Aw, bring it here," said the expert. " Reach it over and I'll soon put the kybosh on it."

The others stopped rummaging amongst the straw for more rabbits to jeer at my awkwardness. Afraid of being made a laughing-stock, I jerked my rifle, still with its naked bayonet attached, from my shoulder. Putting the rabbit on the ground at my feet, I dug the bayonet into it, and held it up, spitted, for one of them to pull off. The rabbit gave a last convulsive wriggle. I felt a sickly feeling.

" Here, can't you take the cursed thing," I said angrily, " or am I to stand here all day with it stuck to the bayonet ? "

A scrounger discovered an old boiler, and we filled it with water and started a fire going. The hens were plucked and the rabbits skinned, and after being roughly cleaned they went with a splash into the boiler and the lid was closed. Two or three chairs and a chest of drawers from one of the houses kept the fire roaring merrily, but for all that it was nearly dark before the half-dozen self-appointed cooks pronounced, after some wrangling, that the stew was ready. The appetising smell had drawn the whole crowd to the scene. They sat round the boiler with their dixies ready, sniffing and eyeing it hungrily. The officers came up, too, and stood looking on amusedly. They made no objection when one of the Sergeants offered them a chicken.

Where the remainder of the meat went was a bit of a mystery—perhaps the cooks knew—but the rest of us had to be content with the soup, and I had to close my eyes to get it down. Through haste or laziness we had omitted to clean the boiler, and it must have been dirty. A thick, greasy scum floated on top of the stuff. There was no salt.

Afterwards we huddled round the fire and slept uneasily, pressing together for warmth, half-expecting to see the troops in front come helter-skelter into the village with the Germans at their heels. In the morning we marched off, breakfasting as we went along on meagre supples of hard tack served out the previous day in the gun-pits.

Although relieved, we were a long way from getting a real rest. The first flush of gladness gradually faded as the miles passed and the dust swirled about us. We slogged along doggedly uphill and down dale, and through villages with not a soul in them. It bore every appearance of being a well-used road, but we had it all to ourselves. The population seemed to have fled *en masse*, taking their livestock with them. The silence had something uncanny about : Stranger still, there was a complete absence of troops, either British or French. No wagons rumbled along the road towards the front and there was not a sign of the activity one would have expected to see in a place even dozens of miles to the rear, let along a few kilometres.

The specimens that had relieved us were probably retreating in their turn. They had no artillery, no reserves, and nobody on either flank. They were only a handful, and a mixed one at that, of sacrifice troops. Somehow they weren't the kind that inspired much confidence in their ability to hold up the Germans. Some of the men commented on this curious state of affairs, but the most of us paid no heed. What did we care where it would end so long as we were out of it.

Our transport had gone off the map again. They were probably under the impression that they had left us enough grub for a couple of days at the gun-pits. We wondered would they be so stupid as to think we were still there, hanging on by the skin of our teeth, and if they would go wandering back again ? It wasn't very likely, of course, but we earnestly prayed that they would, and that the Uhlans would make no mistake about knocking hell out of them this time. We had a poor opinion of our transport.

Everybody stuck it, although many of the men's feet were in a bad way. Scarcely one of us had had his boots off since the show started. We were afraid to take them off now in case we couldn't get them on again. Many of them were ready to fall to pieces, anyway, and some of the men had hastened the process by hacking off bits of the uppers where they hurt their feet.

The sun got hotter as the long day wore on. Our skin was scalded by the sweat and dust. At every halt we left something behind. I still had my entrenching tool, but at last threw it away. The haft beating against my thigh with every step made my leg raw, and the tool itself weighed like lead. We discarded our ammunition and some dumped their gas masks and equipment. The officers saw them do it, but didn't say anything. The water in our bottles was warm and gave no relief, but we drank it, anyway, and sweated accordingly. We had no fat on us, so it must have been the water. We halted for an hour outside a village and gnawed the crumbled remains of our hard tack as we lay in the shade of some trees. Those who had cigarettes left from the last issue lit up and later grudgingly handed the butts to impatient comrades, who smoked them until their lips were burned. The thought that we were relieved came to us again and cheered us up. When the time came to start again we set off almost cheerfully, only to find ourselves, at the end of another few minutes' slogging, putting one foot before the other as wearily as before, waiting for the moment when we could go no farther.

Each halt became the end of the journey, each unwilling start the last that we could manage. It was a blind test of endurance that fresh well-fed troops would have baulked at, perhaps for the very reason that they would have been fresh and well fed. And behind it all, in some obscure way, we gloried in it and derived a strange satisfaction—comprehensible only to well-tried troops—in being able to stick it out, no matter a damn about anything else. That was the thought, all unacknowledged, that kept us on our feet, and made us force one foot before the other until all else was blotted out, the retreat, the relief, and the dusty kilometres ahead.

Some time in the night we fell out and lay in a shallow ditch, dead beat. We didn't know, at first, that we had reached the end of the march, but after a while the officers recovered sufficiently to consult a map, and we began to take notice. Opening our tunics we pulled back our shirts and let in the night air, which had suddenly grown cool. The officers argued in low tones and lit matches, the hoarse voice of the Adjutant dominating the others—the tiny light recoiling from his haggard face and sunken eyes.

We speculated fatalistically on what it meant, too tired to care overmuch. Our fitful attention was distracted by little drops of moisture falling on our faces and bared chests. Some said they felt it and others grunted incredulously, but in a couple of minutes there was no room for doubt. The drops multiplied and pattered down silently.

The rain fell heavier. Little spattering noises came from the road, and the unmistakable smell of rain impacting on dust filled the air. Buttoning up our tunics, we sat up. Our disjointed talk took a different turn as we marvelled at this phenomenon, which laid the dust so easily and quietly. In a minute or two we were regretting that which we had cursed so long and bitterly. Dust was better than mud, we decided, as the damp penetrated our bones. Instead of sweating, we shivered and turned up the collars of our tunics.

The rain increased until it became a regular downpour

which sizzled and swished about us. The ditch where we lay became wetter and wetter until it ran with water and we were forced on to the bare road. Some lay, as before, on the broad of their backs in the mud, disregarding everything but their weariness. Others, even more miserable, got to their feet and mooched about, shivering. Our waterproof sheets had disappeared long since—dumped by the roadside on some forgotten march, or handed over as shrouds for those who had been knocked out. The dust lying thick on our uniforms was changed into cold, slimy mud, and the soggy cloth clung to our flesh. A couple of Sergeants went off into the darkness and returned shortly with great news, which gradually percolated down to the ranks. We were beside a railway station, and our long march had been made to catch a train. We had walked too quickly, apparently, for there was no sign of the train. Some of the men wandered off to investigate, and returned with another wonderful story.

"Hey, boys ! but there's a tremendous dump in the railway station. Something fierce. Piles of everything. Stacks and stacks of it, and not a sinner to look after it."

We made tracks for the railway station like one man, and found that it was nearly all true. It was a gigantic dump—thousands and thousands of pounds' worth of valuable stores lying derelict waiting for Jerry. It was amazing, too good to be true outside a fairy tale. Yet there it was, piled high in the deserted station, streets and lanes and culs-de-sac of boxes, cases, bags, packages, in orderly confusion.

But the things we wanted were hard to find. We hacked open case after case and package after package, only to find them full of soap, rice and flour. There was lime juice, barrels of it, but our bowels had had sufficient inducement to move lately, and we left it severely alone. Bayonets were poor substitutes for entrenching tools for opening boxes, but we persevered. There was plenty of tea, but no fire was allowed, and there was no water except the rain. We tumbled the tea on to the ground. Sugar—no good either —met a like fate. There was everything in the dump but eatables.

We were coming away in disgust at not getting anything substantial when one of the fellows with me spotted a man sitting under a high-built railway wagon out of the rain. He held a naked bayonet in his hand and slashed the air with it. He appeared to be drunk. He had rigged up a seat for himself with a plank and a couple of cases. He stared about him with a stupid, pugnacious look. Underneath him was a big cardboard package, and every other minute he stooped down and fondled it lovingly as if it held something very precious. We were curious and arranged a plan. Some of my companions went to the wagon and shouted gibes to attract his attention. The man waved his bayonet at them and swore horribly, daring them to come on. The others kept his attention distracted while, very carefully, I crept under the wagon from the rear. With my heart in my mouth I stole the package from between his feet and retired. I had perforce undertaken the most dangerous job because I was the only Lance-jack in the squad, and felt elated at my success. With my package under my arm I rejoined the others. It was full of cigarettes, and we stuffed our pockets. Drunken laughter reached us from a corner of the dump. We went forward to where a little group of men lay, stupid drunk on ration rum. One or two were too drunk to speak coherently and stared at us with glazed eyes as we searched eagerly for a share of this priceless loot, but there was no trace of the rum jar. At last we gave it up and retired baffled to the road and hung about miserably, as before, with only cigarettes as consolation.

When the train arrived, as it did eventually, two or three men were missing. After the N.C.O.s had searched perfunctorily around we left the missing men behind.

P

" They're stretched out somewhere paralytic," we whispered as we smoked our stolen cigarettes.

" They might never wake up," said a man shaking his head.

" Ay, d'ye remember the big dump down Cambrai way. The boys got soaked, and died without a whimper. Even when it was pumped out of them it was no good.

" And the rain and the cold night. They'll not have an earthly."

" And their empty bellies."

" Ah, well, that's as good a way as another, eh, mates ? "

THE ADJUTANT

THE train trundled on through the night, creaking and jolting as if ready to fall to pieces. Instead of being in cattle trucks we were crammed into old third-class carriages, crowded together on the hard wooden seats and on the floor, although for that matter there must have been plenty of empty carriages. We dozed fitfully, waking up each time shivering and cursing our sodden clothes.

At dawn the train stopped. No order came to get out and we sat on, too miserable to scrounge round and too fatalistic to do anything but accept what came. An hour passed slowly, and then another. The hopes that had buoyed us up the day before and kept us on our feet through the long march were gone. Out last square meal had been in the gun-pits, a round forty-eight hours before. Before reaching the gun-pits we had starved and marched another couple of days. Ant that was only four days. It was probably twice as many days before that again since I had bade good-bye to the Signal Section that was, and sat in the Chalkpits waiting for the bombardment to commence. Like a schoolboy, I remembered dimly, about to sit for an examination.

We sat pillowing our heavy heads upon each other's shoulders, waiting patiently for something to happen. We no longer felt hungry. Presently a little doubt gnawed at us. Were we relieved ? Or had we been rushed to some other part of the caving front ? It was like something that would happen.

" Ah, well, they can do whatever they like with us," we mumbled, uncaring.

" They're waiting now till the troops are too dog-tired to run away before shoving them into the line, likely," said Jenkins with a flash of his old cynical humour. " Some blasted staff-wallah has discovered the fresher they are the harder they run."

The rain had stopped and the sun was shining again when we got the word. We clambered stiffly from the high, old-fashioned carriages on to the railway track. The officers came along. We formed a rough double line, shivering and twitching. We were at the entrance to a fair-sized, unroofed station. Many lines converged or wandered off into sidings. The steel rails glittered like molten silver, dazzling our eyes. In front of us, a little to the left, and half hidden by the carriages of the train, was the main platform. There was no sign of life about it. We were dully disappointed. That meant we were still in the danger zone. The inhabitants had been evacuated. To the right, just beyond the station, I caught sight of a great wheel, black and motionless against a gleaming white-washed wall. Behind it were red-tiled roofs, mellowed by time and weather, clustered round a grey church spire. A sound came to us sweetly on the fresh, rain-washed air. We stopped shuffling our feet and mumbling to listen with childish pleasure, hardly believing what we heard, or realising what the sound portended. Again it came. The sweet measured peal of bells stealing softly and peacefully, each lovely ever-lessening sound caressing us with ever-increasing beauty until it died away and was re-born in the grey church spire. We listened eagerly, with ears that had grown used to the harsh music of the guns, nudging each other, awed.

The Adjutant stood in front of us. The N.C.O.s tried half-heartedly to dress the ranks.

" It's all right. Leave them alone," he said heavily. " Just get into fours, men. That's the way."

We obeyed slowly, and stood steadying ourselves with our rifles, awaiting the next order.

" It's the rain last night that has made my legs so shaky," I thought, although it might have been the bells.

" Come alone," said the Adjutant, placing himself at our head.

We stumbled over the shining rails, that a child could have negotiated with ease, reached and passed the deserted platform. A right incline that took us towards the water wheel. Passing the wheel, we turned a corner into the main street of a little town. There were people in the street. An enormously fat, knock-kneed priest, black-gowned and wearing a funny little music-hall hat on his shaven head, was waddling majestically along on the far side. A squad of children followed behind in some sort of procession, very subdued and solemn-looking. A few women, dressed in black, brought up the rear. The houses and shops were drawn and shuttered as if it were a Sunday. Attracted by the noise, the priest glanced up. He stopped short and stared at us with slack jaws. A golden crucifix which he had been fingering devoutly a moment before slipped from his fat hands and swung, unheeded, about his knees on a silver chain. The children, after one terrified look, huddled behind the priest's voluminous gown and tried to hide. One or two, more daring than the rest, peeped round at us fearfully through their fingers as if trying to avert the evil eye.

" March to attention ! " came a muttered order from the Adjutant.

We tried to obey, and pull ourselves together in front of the civilians, but in spite of ourselves our knees sagged. Giving up the attempt to dress the ranks and march in step, we shambled along, filthy, emaciated, heedless of the panic our coming had caused.

The women conquered their fear. They came running towards us, arms outstretched, uttering little cries of horror and pity as they took in our woeful plight. Doors opened. More women came running carrying little offerings of bread and wine, breaking our ragged ranks without ceremony as they thrust their gifts into our hands, pausing to stroke our arms endearingly or help us on our slow way for a few steps before running back for more. The children, deserting the fat priest, ran alongside. They stared at us, all eyes, uncomprehending.

A young woman in widow's weeds thrust a piece of bread into my hand. Then putting her arm on my shoulder she drew my face down and kissed me on the cheek.

" Pauvre garçon. Pauvre garçon."

We took everything gladly and humbly, surprised that such kindness existed in the world, wondered what there was to be so excited about in the spectacle of a handful of beaten British soldiers.

What of all the others who had started out when the bombardment opened on the 21st of March, and who now lay dead in bits of trench, in fields, in nameless villages, and by the wayside, here singly and there in heaps—mute witnesses that the First Battalion had once passed by ? The wounded we had left behind—— ?

We left the town behind, and still, by some magic of sympathy, women came running from scattered houses with the same tender, brimming eyes.

The road became lined with tall trees. We travelled alone, but the memory of the women remained with us.

The gable of an old, ivy-clad farm building came into view, the crumbling stone pierced with tiny rough-hewn slits, like mediæval windows. A lane, almost hidden by lush grass and bushes, ran alongside.

A spick and span Quartermaster-Sergeant stood in the middle of the road waiting for us. A halt was called. The quarter-bloke wore the battalion colours on his shoulder, but I had never seen him before. He wore a cap, with the gleaming regimental badge on it, instead of a steel helmet. The Adjutant conferred with him and then turned to us.

" Fall out the signallers, runners and observers," he said gruffly, and we hastened to obey. " Not much farther, lads," he encouraged the others and led them on up the road.

" This way," ordered the quarter-bloke, and led us down the lane.

The billet was a massive, untidy barn. It was divided in half. The back part was filled almost to the low, crudely beamed roof, with dry, sweet-smelling hay.

There were no parades, and no officers came near us. In the daytime we lay on the sun-warmed cobblestones of the yard, our bodies filled with pleasant restfulness. When the sun went down we transferred ourselves into the barn and lay in the hay with our minds at ease. There was plenty of grub the first couple of days. Each man got an unbroken loaf and about a pound of cheese and a dixieful of rich stew—dead men's rations, but none the worse for that. Afterwards we got the regulation allowance and squabbled over its division, feeling hungry after every meal. There were no baths, but we washed at the pump in the yard and shaved, tidying ourselves up as best we could. A large part of our time was devoted to de-lousing. I took off my shirt and drawers for the first time since leaving the Base. I still wore the flannel belt issued there and took it off as well to have a look at what was going on underneath. In the process I disturbed a squad of lice, which ran about the belt at a surprising rate. I had always been under the impression that lice were sluggish things.

" The best thing you can do with that belt is burn it," said Jenkins and I followed his advice, looking on gloatingly as the lice tried to escape. My cardigan jacket, which originally had been brown, was dirty grey with lice eggs and dust. It was a hopeless job to try and clean it, so I put a match to it as well, watching the eggs swell and shrivel as the flames reached them. The seams of my trousers and tunic crackled as copying the rest I ran a lightèd candle down them.

It was my first battle with the pests, I felt like vomiting. The others seemed to think it all in the day's work. I did my best to follow their example, setting my teeth and holding my breath when my throat moved spasmodically. When it was all over and my underclothes were on again, dotted with the squashed and roasted bodies of the lice, it took all my fortitude to bear the touch of them against my skin. I felt itchier than ever.

" I would sooner have the live ones," I thought, feeling, if possible, more unclean.

The Post Corporal, who had been with the transport, came on his rounds, burdened with letters and parcels. We formed an eager circle. He fumbled about for five minutes as if sensing his importance and wishing to make the most of it. After arranging and rearranging the letters he cleared his throat and began calling out the names. The Signal Sergeant's name was called and then his Corporal's. We grinned, remembering the state they had been in when last seen, and hastened to tell the Corporal, who put the two letters on the ground at his feet.

" Pte. Clarence H. Brown, a letter and a parcel."

We looked at each other. Who the devil was Clarence H. Brown ?

" Oh, Clarence, kiss me quick," said one of the runners in a shrill falsetto, and raised a laugh.

The Corporal fingered the letter, and frowned as he looked at the pile he had to wade through.

" Do none of you know him at all ? " he asked sharply. " I haven't all day to stand here."

" Why, I'll bet that'll be old Butcher," Jenkins burst out.

" Yes, yes. Didn't he stop a bullet ? "

" That's him all right. He went West."

" Old Butcher—a damned decent chap, too."

" Well, why on earth couldn't you say that at first ? " said the Corporal pettishly, and called another name.

" Pte. M. Murphy."

" He got it the second or third day, didn't he ? "

" The first it must have been," I said. He was to have been on a station with me. " Wasn't he the small chap with a brogue ? "

" He's not here anyway, Corporal."

Name after name was called. The men became quiet as they searched their memories for what had happened to each one, until the Corporal, getting wiser, commenced calling two or three names at a time. Like Judge Jeffreys, the men had no mercy.

" Gone West."

" Missing."

" Wounded and left behind."

Now and then, as if to relieve the monotony, a man stretched out an eager hand and went off into a corner, like a dog with a bone. My turn came and I received a newspaper and parcel from home, and knowing that there could be nothing more lost interest in the proceedings. It was not the brave who got the spoils, but the survivors. The Post Corporal disappeared and the others gathered round me as I cut the string of the paper, the only one received in the billet.

" I'll bet five francs out of my next pay that there won't be more than a line or two about the whole do," offered Jenkins, but there were no takers.

I spread out the paper, a local weekly, and turned over the first page after shaking out a letter, which I put away unread. Half a dozen pairs of eyes searched the columns, first the headings and then the bottom of the page, but there was nothing but advertisements and local news. I turned over a page, with the same result.

" What did I tell you ? " said Jenkins triumphantly, getting to his feet. The others slackened their pressure on my shoulders.

Disappointed, I turned the last inside leaf. Great inch-deep letters leapt at us.

GREAT GERMAN BREAK THROUGH
FIFTY-MILE BATTLE FRONT
GREATEST IN HISTORY

We looked at each other in shocked silence. When we spoke again our voices had dropped to whispers.

" Is that our show ? "

" The biggest battle ! "

" Fifty miles ! "

We realised afresh how lucky we had been to get away with our lives.

The paper drew our eyes like a magnet. Fiery captions dazzled us. " Battle of awful ferocity. Fearful Scenes of Slaughter." " War's Heaviest Bombardment." In wild excitement we read the official communiqués. But they seemed to deal with another battle altogether. Only once or twice did we come on names of places we had passed through— so long before that we had almost forgotten about them. " It was thought advisable or found necessary for such and such a reason to withdraw to such and such a line," they ran coldly and primly as if it all had been a game of chess. The anti-climax came. We looked at the last page of the paper and more great headlines met our eyes.

THRILLING BATTLE ACCOUNT
" WE HELD THEM," SAYS WAR CORRE-
SPONDENT

We rolled helplessly, writhing our bodies. No sooner did one get his breath than the yard rang with delighted exclamations, which sent us off afresh, holding our sides.

We recovered with many lapses, and read on. It was all Germans, it appeared, who had been slaughtered. The writer painted glowing word pictures of lion-hearted officers snatching a brief respite from shooting hundreds of Jerries in order to tell him confidentially that it was the finest show they had ever been in and they wouldn't have missed it for worlds.

" For God's sake stop," wailed Jenkins, but the others shouted for more.

" The complete dominance," I read, " of the British in the air has been one of the brightest features of the great battle. Our airmen have been untiring in bombing troops and transport at all times, and turning Lewis-guns on them from low altitudes. The enemy made marks that simply could not be missed."

We paused to savour this amazing news.

" Read it again. It must be the Jerry airmen he's talking about. If he'd been with us he wouldn't have wrote that."

I dumped the paper and opened the parcel. What did a lot of eyewash for home consumption matter to us.

None of us had any money except a few dirty notes of small denominations belonging to particular villes, and not negotiable anywhere else, but our poverty didn't trouble us much. We were under strict orders not to go into the town. A travelling canteen paid us a fleeting visit, carrying a stock of chocolates, cigarettes and other delicacies, which made our mouths water, but there was nothing to do about it. After it had gone I discovered a half-franc piece in one of my pockets, and went over the road from our barn to where a French creamery was in operation. I knocked at the door and a young Frenchman in blue dungarees, the only one

I had seen so far not in uniform, opened it. I held out my
canteen in one hand and offered the half-franc with the
other.

" Du lait, m'sieur, s'il vous plaît ? "

The young man, clean-shaven and pale, stared interroga-
tively, smiled, and took the canteen, returning in a moment
with it filled to the brim with warm, foaming milk, fresh
from the cow. I still held out the half-franc, but he waved
it away with an expressive shrug.

I drank half the milk—to keep it from spilling, I told myself—and gave the remainder to Jenkins and a couple more,
telling them gleefully about the half-franc.

Half an hour later Jenkins borrowed it and went across to
try his luck at the creamery. He came back with a broad
smile, more milk, and the money. We had another slug.

The news spread, and the half-franc circulated amongst
the men in the barn. Before we left every one of us had
tendered it to the smiling Frenchman, always with the same
result.

" There can't have been any British troops in this part of
the country before," the others decided.

Our fifth day in the old barn proved to be our last. In
the morning we went to where the rest of the battalion was
billeted a little farther along the road and got a new outfit
of clothes and equipment from a couple of A.S.C. lorries,
and when we were all served, started back again, our new
boots creaking, with orders to be ready to move.

Some of the boys kept wondering where we were bound
for, betraying a strong belief in rumours about Italy,
Palestine and Mespot—anywhere in fact but the Western
Front—but in reality none of us cared tuppence. We
knew that all places were the same when it came to the bit,
and with the advent of new uniforms our thoughts took
flight and past doings were relegated to the scrapheap of
memory. We had lived through the great retreat and that

was all we cared about. Soon we would be on the move and putting our luck to the test again, not once or twice but many times.

" Will my luck hold out ? " I asked myself doubtfully. We were like so many unwanted puppies thrown into a pond with bricks to our necks. Momentarily we had reached the safety of the bank, only to be pushed back again.

We were ready to move, and busily engaged in adjusting buckles and chaffing each other on our changed appearance when the Adjutant's favourite runner, who had not been with us in the barn, came slowly into the cobbled yard. There was a scared look on his face.

We stopped our idle talk and looked at him expectantly, with a curious fore-knowledge that he was the bearer of bad news.

" Wot cheer, Bill ? " cried Jenkins with forced humour. " Why, man, you look as if the wife had just had triplets. Where are we bound for ? "

" The Adjutant——" said Bill, and stopped.

" Well, what about him ? "

" He has gone mad—completely off his nut. Put his revolver in his mouth and was just going to blow his brains out when I ran up and knocked it out of his hand."

There was a shocked silence.

" It took half a dozen of us to hold him down," went on Bill dully. " He's back there raving, as mad as a March hare."

We gathered round, plying him with disjointed questions. He turned away dispiritedly.

" You chaps are to fall in on the road and join the rest of the Bat when they come along," he said over his shoulder.

We let him go, recognising with rough sympathy that his grief was a personal affair.

" He was a wild 'un, but we'll never have an Adjutant like him again," spoke one.

" Aye, mad or not mad, he was the best one of them all."

Speaking in hushed voices, we straggled out on to the road.

BOOK II

THE VETERAN

THE cattle-wagons making up the train jolted to a stand-
still. Outside, shells were falling with an echoing
clatter. In response to the bawling of the N.C.O.s we opened
the clumsy doors, grabbed our tangled-up equipment and
rifles and formed up on the dark platform, shooting apprehensive glances over our shoulders in the direction of the
explosions, taken unawares by this sudden reintroduction to
the sounds of war. We waited impatiently while the formalities attendant upon the movement of troops were gone
through, stamping and shivering in the night air, vainly
regretting the stuffy discomfort and safety of the wagons.
We marched unwillingly into an empty street, each man
peering about anxiously in an endeavour to spot the shell-
bursts. Only indistinct flashes and the heavy rumble of
falling masonry rewarded our efforts. That and the old,
familiar smell of high explosive. It was an ugly place, what
we saw of it, apparently, being battered out of existence
piecemeal. It was a dangerous place to loiter in. We
passed windily along the twisting, cobbled streets lined with
dark, forbidding houses. The place had a subtle atmosphere
of its own, which I felt, but could not explain. In spite of
the shells it had a certain gloomy solidity and impression of
permanence, of being doggedly held against the enemy,
which boded ill for troops who had become accustomed to
hastily evacuating towns and villages.

We left the town, and disgusted murmurs came from the
ranks.

" Back to the graveyard.

" The bastard frying-pan into the fire."

" Shoving it on to us proper, and us only out a bleeding week."

" What place is this ? " I inquired diffidently, ashamed at having to show my ignorance.

" It's the place where you can't budge without running the risk of getting a splinter up you—and even then you don't know where it's coming from," said Jenkins morosely. "Why, old Jerry himself is fed to the teeth with it. D'ye remember the last time. They used to commit suicide before they'd go into the line. We were ready to do the same, or ' sou ' ourselves."

" Tha-at's right. Good judges, too. They might have picked us a cushier place after the last stunt."

" But who cares a rip what we think, mates ? "

We covered a good few kilos, marching along sullenly. During the fall-outs the men who had been there before lay silent, directing lowering glances to where the officers congregated on the road.

At last we arrived at a camp and halted before a number of huts laid out in neat rows, hardly visible in the darkness. They were elephant huts—semicircles of galvanised iron sheeting set on raised wooden floors. The front of each hut had a small square window, innocent of glass, alongside the door, for purposes of ventilation. Each hut was capable of housing anything from twenty to fifty men, according to how many men there were, and how many huts. We had plenty of room. The signallers and runners dumped their packs in a hut and lay down, filled with the curious discomfort of men who might receive orders to move off again at a moment's notice.

A strafe started up in front and gradually spread until guns were firing from behind and on either side. No shells came our way, but I didn't know how far we had penetrated into the front areas and the roar was unnerving. I wanted to ask if we had been thrown into another big battle, and why we weren't in trenches instead of thin, unprotected huts, but kept silent, hugging my fears. An obscure vanity kept me from asking "rookie" questions of the men around me. The simpler the question the more ridicule it generally brought on the luckness inquirer. There was the possibility that experienced men knew there was nothing to get the wind up about. On the other hand their experience might tell them they were "for it" and make them all the more apprehensive and snappy.

No rations came up. I was initiated into an old soldier trick. Four of us got into a corner.

Each contributed a biscuit from his emergency rations. These were soaked in water until they had swelled to twice their usual size and were correspondingly softer. One wise fellow, with just such an emergency in view, had scrounged some bacon fat and kept it carefully in a cigarette tin. When this was sizzling over a fire made from a cut-up candle, the biscuits were dipped in the fat and a spoonful of plum and apple spread over each.

Delicious.

Afterwards we tried to sleep, our tin hats taking the place of pillows. Some succeeded in spite of the hard floor. A shell might come in through the roof and catch us unawares, so I lay awake in the darkness, snuggling into my greatcoat. What good being awake would do me if a shell did come I didn't know. The feeling was there, very strong, and it never occurred to me to question the sense of it. The snores of my companions increased my loneliness, but gradually a false feeling of safety comforted me. It didn't seem possible that a shell could come crashing through the roof of my particular hut amongst so many. I felt that because I lay in it it had a better chance of escape, almost as if the shells had tacitly agreed to fall somewhere else.

The firing outside got heavier. Sleep struggled with instinct. I got the bright idea of putting my helmet over

my face instead of using it as a pillow, and strangely comforted by this additional protection, dropped off—but not
for long.

The most appalling racket suddenly broke out amongst
the huts. We started up fearfully.

We huddled on the floor, keeping close to the sloping
sides.

One man—braver than the rest—ran to the door and
looked out. After staring about for a moment, his body
fitfully outlined by flashes, he came back swearing.

". . . our own artillery . . . guns between the huts."

" Using us as their camouflage, eh ! The twisters."

" It's a pity there wasn't a C.C.S. about ; they'd go
there."

Acrid fumes filled the hut.

" What's a C.C.S. ? " I wondered, that they should go
there.

We lay down again, trying to accustom our ears and
nerves to the noise, and after a while fell into an uneasy sleep.
The others still used their tin hats as pillows, but I stuck to
the idea of covering my face with it just in case.

In the morning we quickly forgot the night before. A
mild strafe went on intermittently, but it was too far away
to trouble us. After breakfast we paraded with rifles,
ammunition and towels and went for a bath. It was my
first bathing parade with the B.E.F. We went along gaily
laughing and joking. Everything was different in the day-
time. A mile tramp down the road brought us to a big,
seedy-looking brown hut. We piled arms and sprawled
about for an hour in the sun. When our turn came and we
trooped inside, the place had a sour, steamy odour as if all
the dirt and sweat of the squads of men who had gone before
us had dissolved into the atmosphere. We crowded into a
small ante-room and undressed higgledy-piggledy, squabbling over where to place our little belongings for safety

while we were separated from them. We didn't trust the bath attendants overmuch—or each other. Our underclothes, by direction of an attendant, we threw into a corner and our uniforms were taken away to be fumigated.

Shivering we went into a big barn-like room with a slimy floor on which we walked gingerly. Pipes in the ceiling opened and trickles of lukewarm water fell about our shoulders. Forming into a shivering queue we received steamy grey underwear. Our uniforms, fresh from the fumigator, were wrinkled and damp. We dressed hurriedly, eager to get out into the sunshine.

Rows of shrivelled grey eggs lined the seams of our shirts and drawers and uniforms promising another loathsome generation.

The battalion became unrecognisable.

Big drafts arrived from home—young fellows with pale faces and thin shanks. A good many of them were Cockneys.

"We were at our breakfast when we got the word," said one in an injured voice. "We were put in the train without a medical inspection or draft leave."

A cavalry mob that had been engaged on some cushy job down the line had been disbanded, and we got a number of disgruntled troopers.

"The lousy infantry," they groused, looking for sympathy and getting none.

Men who wore the shoulder markings of one of the service battalions of the regiment landed with us. Their battalion had been disbanded.

"It was better with the old lot," they said sadly. "We all knew each other and came from the same place. Not so much spit and polish—more like chums, you see. You don't know where you are in this crowd."

Stragglers who had "lost" us in the Retreat rejoined.

All these were not sufficient to bring us up to strength.

We received a curious mixture of men combed out from jobs down the line. There were R.E.s straight from the docks at Le Havre and Calais, where for years they had been engaged on unloading grain boats and assembling machinery and motor cars. There were A.S.C. men and other odds and ends.

A grizzled Corporal stopped me and asked some questions which betrayed his greenness. He had a thin, pasty face.

" I've been a baker, you see, all the time, and I know nothing about all this," he said with a quiet, helpless air. " I'm forty-five and never had a rifle in my hands until to-day."

I listened to his garbled tale of how he had suddenly found himself in the battalion. He didn't know how or why, except that there he was. His white, knobby hands fluttered ineffectually as they tried to eke out his muttered words to express his amazement and non-comprehension. He took off his cap to scratch his head, and I thought I saw traces of flour in his hair. Either that or his hair was whitey-grey.

" Do you know anything about what a Corporal has to do in the trenches ? I mean what is he supposed to—what are his duties ? How does he look after his squad and tell them what to do ? What do you do when there's an attack ? "

I looked at him. He was asking questions that I hadn't had the courage to ask when I was in his position. As regards age he could easily have been my father. Perhaps that only made things more difficult for him. I didn't know how to answer, for the good and sufficient reason that I didn't know myself. I secretly sympathised, but as well felt anxious to get away from him. His naïve questions were disturbing.

" Well, you see, it's like this," I said. " There'll be some lad in the section, or the Lance-Jack, maybe, that knows the ropes. Get hold of him and he'll tell you."

" But they are all just out in my squad. Young Londoners.

I can hardly make out what they're talking about when they do speak to me. I'm North Country."

" Ah, well," I said, " you'll soon pick it up. It all depends what it's like where we are going."

" Thanks. Thanks, very much," he called after me.

I felt ashamed of myself for not returning confidence for confidence and telling him that he knew as much as I did.

I felt sorry for him, too. He was a kindly, harmless old fellow, worried more about his mysterious responsibilities than of his own skin, which was what he ought to have been thinking about. It didn't matter much, so far as I could see, whether a man knew much or little. The more an infantry-man knew of the war the sicker he was of all connected with it.

We were warned off for a general inspection. When the hour came we paraded in a narrow space between the huts and the road. We were all spick-and-span and after being minutely inspected by our own officers stood waiting patiently for the General.

He was a long time coming, as is the way with Generals.

At last the General Salute sounded. We presented arms as a big motor car drew up. A hard-faced man, all red tabs and ribbons and with a bristly grey moustache, got out and came towards us, followed by some other brass-hats. When the inspection was over we received a little homily.

" The Division, I am proud to tell you, has been highly commended for its work. I wish to take this opportunity of congratulating all ranks. Your battalion did as much as could be expected considering the circumstances. In doing that, however, they were only livnig up to long and honour-able traditions of the regiment, which, I know, are dear to every one of you. But get it into your heads once and for all. There is to be no more retreating. Retreating is a shameful business. You are a regular battalion and I look to you to show the new battalions an example of smartness, discipline and steadiness, no matter what you are called upon to do. I expect you to lead the way when there is hard fighting to be done. Harass the enemy in every way you can."

The General paused to blow his nose on a fine white handkerchief.

" Give him no rest. And remember, no more running away. Any man who does that will be shot for cowardice. No excuse will be taken. Put the events of the past month out of your mind completely. Start with a clean slate. I know you will try to follow my wishes. If you die you will have the satisfaction of knowing that you died in a great cause. What man can ask for more ? The Huns are unfit to live and must be exterminated at all costs. I look forward confidently to hearing a good account of you in the Salient, or wherever else you may be sent. God bless you."

We stared stonily before us as the General damned us with faint praise. I was no thought-reader and wondered what the old Corporal baker, late of the A.S.C., knew or cared about the traditions of the regiment, or the R.E.s or the ci-devant cavalry or the young Cockneys. But I knew that every man-jack who had been in the retreat was thinking the same thing. " What did he know about the retreat and what we did or didn't do ? " He wasn't there.

After the parade my prophecy was borne out to the letter and the General was cursed contemptuously—all in two words.

" And did you twig him blowing his nose in the middle ? "

" Ay, he's got a cold. Got his little feet wet somewhere."

" Who is he exactly ? " I inquired as we made tracks for the hut to dump our equipment and get a smoke.

" Why, that's old What's-his-name, our General," said Jenkins. " There's one sure thing and that is he hadn't to run for his life half a dozen times and Jerry at his heels. A motor car takes you along quicker."

" I never saw him before," I said.

" No, and you'll never see him again, unless we're away somewhere training for a show. This is about as far as he'll come."

" Did you hear him at the end, too, with his ' God bless you ' ? "

" Oh, that's all right. He meant God curse you, only he didn't like to say it. And it's all the same to us," retorted Jenkins with a sneering laugh.

" He said it like a Scotch minister blessing the congregation after they had all put pennies, buttons and threepenny-bits in the plate."

As a make-weight for the General's visit we had a pay parade. Afterwards, along with Jenkins and Corporal Mundy, our new signal Corporal, we went down through the camp, which straggled along for a couple of kilometres.

Mundy was an oldish man as far as years went, but his black hair was only lightly streaked with grey, and he was as hard as nails. He had been a commercial traveller in London before the war. He spoke reminiscently of the many women he had known intimately and of the many ten-course Masonic banquets he had attended in the good old days. He had come to us from one of the service battalions.

" Isn't it hell when a fellow doesn't know when he's well away ? " he asked with an exaggerated expression of regret, his sense of humour, fostered by long practice, making game of his own feelings. " That's what the trouble was with a whole lot before the war. Just too bloomin' well off. There I was with a woman in every port, as you might say, when I went on my rounds, and money to jingle in my pocket. It's a poor commercial who can't make pocket-money out of his travelling expenses. If he hasn't enough brains to do that he'll make a poor order-getter. Then when I arrived home at the week-end the missus would be waiting for me. She would have all the things I liked best in the way of grub, and fuss over me and have on her newest blouse and her tightest skirt, and I would know what she was after. Haw, haw, haw. And here I am now, ready to eat potato-skins with anybody."

The Corporal was proud of the fact that he needed to shave twice a day to keep his face smooth. He looked upon this as evidence of his virility and bewailed the absence of women, but the only result was that having shaved in the morning his chin was stubbly in the evening. His teeth were long, yellow and curved—like a horse's, I thought— and he had a great horse laugh, which often came unexpectedly. When he laughed his cheekbones became more prominent and his big, beaked nose took on a sharper curve, giving his lean face a Mephistophelian air which his boisterous humour belied.

A Divisional concert party was giving a show and we elbowed our way into the hall. A group of pierrots sat in a row on the stage. A " pierrette " was reciting some patriotic piece and the audience was restive. It was all old stuff to my two companions, who derived their principal enjoyment from making highly uncomplimentary remarks on the shapelessness and general uselessness of the leading " lady."

After some patter the troupe broke into a song. It was " My Little Grey Home in the West," and a lump rose in my throat and my eyes smarted. The men joined in and dwelt longingly on the simple words.

Other songs followed, but reaction came and soon we got tired of joining in familiar choruses at the behest of the actors. It was organised jollity, dull and hearty, artificial and natural at one and the same time. The dullness and artificiality were on the stage and the heartiness and natural- ness in the audience. The two front rows were reserved for officers. Despite the small size of the hall and the crush a clear space preserved them from too close contact with the lousy rank and file.

Some of the officers kept glancing round to see how the men were enjoying the jokes, as if ready to order them to laugh and be happy by numbers. A padre, the first I had set eyes on in France, sat amongst them. He had a strong, fleshy face and broad shoulders. When some of the jokes were on the blue side the other officers looked at him quizzically, but he laughed as loud as the rest and turned his face towards the men, inviting them to notice how broad-minded he was.

When the show was over the troupe paraded about outside. Some of them hadn't bothered removing their fancy dress, but others sported tunics and slacks. The tunics were waisted and tight-collared, after the Continental style, and the pants nicely creased, but even so the khaki went oddly with their soft, rouged faces and big sparkling eyes. Taking no notice of the passing troops they called out to each other in clear, high-pitched voices. Several of them stopped close to us and chattered gaily, looking about them with a supercilious air.

We wandered down the road through the camp. Reaching the last of the huts we went on a bit farther just for the sake of something to do. When about to turn back we came on a little cottage. A box of dusty Woodbines was displayed in the window.

We went in and bought a few packets, more for the sake of spending money than through any desire for fags. We had plenty at the moment. When we were getting our change Mundy had an idea. Drawing the old woman serving us to one side he whispered hoarsely into her ear, with the air of a heavy conspirator. She looked at him doubtfully at first and then slyly, although it was hard to tell what her expression signified. She was very old, very ugly and very dirty.

Mundy redoubled his efforts. He shrugged enormously, his eyes rolled, and he waved his hands as if trying to mesmerise her. To wind up he thrust a ten-franc note within an inch of her face, went through the motions of drinking, and gave vent to his great haw-haw.

The old woman hobbled into a room at the rear and returned with a bottle and three glasses. There was a table in a corner and some upturned boxes. We sat down. Mundy poured out wine with a generous hand.

" My God, that was a near thing," he said. " The old 'un is Flemish and either deaf or can't parley the bat. She's r t supposed to sell booze here."

" What kind of stuff is it ? " I asked diffidently.

" It's the one and only, the real simon pure, vin blanc. Guaranteed made from water and vinegar."

We had a second bottle, but I contrived to escape drinking my full share. It was bitter stuff, with a nasty chemical taste. On the way back I thought I was going to vomit, but managed not to. It would have looked very silly. Nevertheless I was happy and that night didn't hear the guns belching between the huts.

In the morning I listened with surprise when the others told of an air raid. A rumour spread that a bomb had caught one of the huts farther along. Later we learned it was true enough. Some men had been hit, but as they belonged to some other unit we didn't worry.

Our Signal Officer had gone off sick and the new O.C. arrived just in time to go up with us. He was a tall, pleasant-looking chap. A new Sergeant had been posted to us and most of the section were new. I found myself one of the battalion veterans. Hardly anyone knew but what I had been out for months instead of weeks and I didn't attempt to spoil the illusion by telling them. For that matter I felt that I had been out for years. At odd moments it came to me with a shock that I had only been once actually up the line. My memory seemed to be at fault, and I banished the thought. It seemed ridiculous that I had been out a bare few weeks. It was like looking at a long procession of years through the wrong end of some kind of mental telescope which transformed years into days.

THE TIN OF BULLY

WE paraded in full marching order and set off for the line. It was almost a pitch-dark night, but quieter than usual as regards shells, which was the main thing. We went along at a good pace and soon had the road to ourselves. All round us pale glows came and went with the sullen boom of guns, but nothing came our way.

We progressed along the dark road into the heart of the gun flashes. There was little talking in the ranks, each man tramping along with his own thoughts for company. We had no idea of what part of the line we were bound for, or what it would be like when we got there. It was no joke going into the line in these parts, we had been told more than once by old-stagers with long and sorrowful experience of similar journeys.

I felt depressed. It was an anti-climax going into the line again as if nothing had happened. I had no stomach for it. Somehow, subconsciously, with the end of the Great Retreat I had looked upon the war as being at an end so far as we were concerned. I hadn't bargained for going on and on as if nothing had happened, and I realised dimly what the feelings must be of men for whom the Retreat had been only another " do " on top of all the others they had been in.

I was afraid of the dark, let alone shells.

And then a new sound reached us, and we pricked up our ears. From somewhere in the air above a low musical hum came, so softly as to seem part of the night itself— just such a sound as a heavily laden bee would make on a hot summer day in a garden, lazy, inconsequential—slightly unsettling. In front a flare appeared magically and floated slowly earthward. The hum grew louder and became more engine-like. Another flare appeared—nearer this time, lighting up the ground ahead.

" Halt. Into the field on the left," came an urgent order.

We dived off the road.

" Lie flat."

We dropped to the ground, but around me men raised their heads and stared curiously into the sky, their faces grey blobs in the darkness.

A raging order came.

" Don't look up, you hopeless fools. He'll see you."

We lay like dead men, faces pressed into the damp grass, as the enemy plane cruised directly overhead. A third flare turned night into day and descended with sickening slowness. The drone of the engine filled the universe with dire forebodings.

We held our breath, waiting for the bombs. The form of the men nearest me became clearly outlined.

The light went out, leaving the darkness blacker than ever. Imperceptibly the drone lessened until, once more, it was a low musical hum. When next a flare floated down it was well behind us.

" Fall in on the road," came the sharp order, and we obeyed silently.

" Could he have seen our faces ? " a lad asked me, but I didn't know.

Coming to a cross-road we turned to the left and then executed a half-right on to a road paved with railway sleepers and camouflaged on the left with rags strung meagrely on high wire netting, signifying that the Germans were on our left as well as in front. By and by I made out the dim shapes of big guns at the side of the road, each with its own particular canopy of fluttering rags.

The man beside me said we were going up towards the

ridge. He didn't mention what ridge and I wasn't curious enough to inquire. It didn't seem to matter much whether it was a ridge or a hollow we were bound for.

We were beginning to get tired when a halt was called. We stood passively with our rifles grounded behind us taking the weight off our packs. I was with " C " Company and when their turn came we formed single file and turned off the road in a half-right turn again on to a narrow wooden track, each man holding on grimly to the one in front. It was like walking on a never-ending ladder laid on the ground, only the rungs, instead of being round, were flat and more closely spaced, and I was too much occupied holding on to the man in front to pay any attention to where I was going. Stagnant pools of water lay on either side of the duck-board.

The track wandered at will over the swamp, but always forward. Shells began to fall with a smothered, squelchy sound into the mud, glowing redly for a moment before going out, like damp squibs.

" We must surely soon be at the front line," I thought innocently.

Shells began to burst near us, but there was nothing to do but stoop, hoping for the best. Once off the duck-boards a man was as good as lost. Every few yards muttered instructions came down the line.

" Broken duckboard here."

" Round the edge of a shell-hole."

" Halt for a minute."

Once, after a shell had burst directly in front, there came a message.

" Pass the word to stretcher-bearers."

A hundred yards farther on I passed two dim shapes lying motionless, half in and half out of a slimy pool. But whether the word ever reached the stretcher-bearers or not I don't know. " Stretcher-bearers " after mouth-to-mouth travel down a couple of hundred indifferent, plodding men could became " Stretch out a bit " with fatal ease.

Wounded men, I learned later, had a habit of sliding into the water and disappearing. Until the next shell resurrected them. Nobody seemed to care very much what happened to them, and becoming rapidly acclimatised I didn't care either. The company had to go forward no matter about incidentals, and there was room for one-way traffic only.

It was the devil take the hindmost—or the foremost, as the case might be.

After a long drawn-out game combined of blind-man's-buff and follow-my-leader we arrived at Company headquarters. I caught a glimpse of a revetted trench round about a dug-out entrance. I thought the journey was over, but presently found myself with two other signallers, one of whom carried a telephone over his shoulder, following a taciturn guide, who led the way on past the dug-out.

At the end of a couple of hundred yards the duckboard ended and we found ourselves stumbling along the slippy, insecure edges of the craters, trying to put each foot where the man in front had put his, but not always succeeding. Before we had gone another dozen paces we were mud up to the thighs, balancing desperately at every other step to evade total immersion and possible extinction in one of the endless shell-holes. The ground was a gigantic honeycomb, with mud for honey, each filthy waterlogged crater forming the sides of so many more. We stopped trying to see where we were bound for, indifferent to everything but the task of keeping on our feet and following the leader.

I wasn't experienced enough to know what reaching the end of the duckboard signified, and the guide didn't volunteer the information.

We arrived at last at what he assured us was Sword Farm —the end of our journey. It was a tiny burrow among the waterlogged shell-holes with a couple of sheets of galvanised

R

iron, covered with mud and rotting sand-bags, for a roof. The silent guide stopped for a moment to get his breath back. Then, with a muttered " Good luck, mates " he went off the way he had come, leaving us peering at each other.

We crawled in and connected up the telephone.

It was an S O S post. Our job was the extremely simple one of tapping out three dots, three dashes and three dots on the sending-key of the instrument if the enemy attacked unexpectedly. In such an eventuality it was left to our imagination what we were to do about saving our own skins. We decided unanimously, without interchange of words, that none of us would attempt to earn a posthumous V.C., or even the Military Medal.

Warning off my two comrades for first duty I wrapped my greatcoat round me and went off to sleep in the mud, tired out with tramping half the night. There was no use being a Lance-Corporal if a fellow couldn't get to sleep first.

When the morning came we lay half on top of each other, unable to move from under the flimsy shelter. Our range of vision extended to about 20 yards behind us, but it might as well have been 2000 yards for all there was to be seen, grey craters half filled with slime.

From the side of a hole a few paces away a stump stuck out, which at first I took to be an old barbed-wire stake. Looking closer, I made out the rough outlines of a human foot.

Maxwell, tall, broad-shouldered and heavy-featured, was a survivor of the retreat and had been in the section when I joined it. I had scarcely spoken to him as yet. He was religious and had been one of the few men, if not the only one, in the old battalion who refused his rum ration. When spoken to he answered in monosyllables, his face took on a stupid, uneasy expression, and he looked away, flushing.

On the other hand he was conscientious and always ready to do anything he was asked.

Beck was even more stupid than Maxwell. But it was a likeable stupidity. He was much smaller than the other, and had only arrived in the section on a draft a few days previously. He was untidy in his dress, and shambled along rather than walked. All the drilling in the world would not have made a peace-time soldier out of him, but as it was he did all right. He perspired around the nose a lot in warm weather, especially when eating.

The long day wore on. In the evening hunger swamped all other feelings. I kept looking at the signal watch and wondering when the rations would come up. At last Maxwell volunteered to go down for them. I was surprised that anyone would of his own free will attempt the weird journey over the craters on the off-chance of reaching the beginning of the duckboards, but he said he thought he could find his way, and I didn't trust Beck. For that matter I wouldn't have trusted myself. The other two seemed to accept it as natural that I shouldn't go, and I was only too pleased to let it go at that. With the three dixies in his hand and three water-bottles slung over his shoulder he set off gingerly into the darkness.

A long hour went by. The shelling, which had been going on intermittently all day, got heavier. At intervals Verey lights went up, their pale light only heightening the mystery of where we were. Beck and I lay low, whispering to each other. I was on duty and kept my hand on the telephone, ready to send the S O S. As soon as it had got dark we had put the candle out. Earlier we had kept it lit for the sake of the warmth of the flame, which we used as a stove to warm our hands at.

Famished and miserable we listened for Maxwell returning, but only faint rustling noises came, as if the dead were stirring with the coming of the night.

Hidden machine-guns began to sweep the swamp. I thought anxiously of Maxwell, stumbling, sliding and crouching as stray shells came near, and the bullets whined closer, and then going forward again searching for the track.

" Will he find his way, d'ye think ? " asked Beck stupidly.

" Well, haven't we got our emergency rations, anyway ? "

" There's no water, and besides there isn't much heat in hard biscuits, is there, Corporal ? "

A damp breeze blew over the torn earth. It got steadily colder. First my feet and then my legs began to grow numb. We hadn't sufficient energy or desire left to stand up and stamp about, and lay on in the mud.

" What the hell's keeping him. He could have been down to the camp and back by this time ? "

" Maybe he lost his way going down," suggested Beck ; " or maybe he's lost his way coming back."

" I forgot to tell him to be sure and bring the rum issue, and it would be just like him to forget it."

" I've never tasted it," returned Beck. " Would it warm us up, d'ye think ? "

I kept silent.

We had given Maxwell up for lost when a faint rattle of dixies came and a low voice hailed us. We called out eagerly and the heavy figure of the wanderer came blundering towards us.

" I was sure I had walked past you," he whispered breathlessly. " I was going to turn back, and then I thought I would go another three or four yards to make sure. I tell you, it's dark out there."

" Did you bring the rum ? "

" There was none. It's stopped, and they were dishing out lime-juice instead so I didn't bother bringing any."

Maxwell insinuated himself into the burrow. " I've lost some of the stew, but I've got nearly a whole loaf and some cheese and jam. I fell two or three times."

We examined our mess-tins and found one about a third full of thin, lukewarm stew and the other with the same quantity of boiled rice in it.

" I took mine before I started back," said Maxwell as Beck and I looked rather blue.

I cut the bread into three parts. Maxwell put his share away, but I was still ravenous and ate half of my share of the bread. Beck following my example.

" Better keep some of it for to-morrow," advised Maxwell.

" But we're hungry now," expostulated Beck.

" Ay, we didn't have our whack down at Company headquarters."

" I hadn't much more than you at the end of all, and, anyway, I went for it while you two sat here at your ease."

We squabbled until, feeling better, I put the remains of my du pain away.

" Better leave the rest for to-morrow right enough. It's not your fault that the stew was spilled."

The night dragged on the same as the first, except that we had less inclination for sleep. In the morning Beck and I finished our rations and looked hungrily at Maxwell's larger portion, part of which he kept for later in the day, like the careful fellow he was.

The sun came out and we brightened up in sympathy as its warming rays reached us through the thin roof. It was enjoyable enough in the burrow after a fashion. There were no parades and no officers to worry about. We were so filthy now that we took a certain amount of pleasure out of wallowing in the mud, beginning to get used to its damp embrace. The man on duty curled his body round the phone, but the likelihood of an attack in daylight was *nil*.

It was odd. We were in advance of the whole British Army but we felt quite out of the war. The Germans were not such fools as to try any tricks over the shell-holes with everybody looking, so to speak. Barring accidents we were as safe as the Bank of England for a few hours. Except for the filth it was better than doing fatigues and parades back in the camp. Even the nights were safer.

" Haven't they a cool nerve putting the guns between the huts ? " I remarked apropos.

" So they have," said Beck, as if it had just occurred to him.

" Of course, you know, likely they have to do it," said Maxwell, as if that explained everything to everybody's satisfaction.

The minutes slowly mounted into hours.

As the sun got stronger a horrible stench rose from the ooze, but we bore it stoically on account of the additional heat. The way we looked at it was that only our noses were affected, whereas the cold affected our bodies.

In the afternoon the sun disappeared in a leaden sky, which seemed more suited to the landscape. The craters became a uniform slimy grey, with a strong suggestion of corruption and decay, as if the earth were poisoned beyond redemption. Foul, syrupy water was everywhere, lying in stagnant pools and forming little slow-moving channels.

Lying close to the ground one saw two or three dozen shell-holes ; raised a little, two or three hundred ; kneeling, two or three thousand—each one a replica of all the others. Every other one was the resting-place of rusty rifles, rusty barbed-wire, or rusty dead men.

There was an order in force to the effect that any man who did not salvage an old rifle or coil of wire when relieved and shoulder it down the line along with the rest of his burden of equipment would be crimed. The useless carcases showing a wasted foot here and a gnawed face there in the mud, which lay swollen and rotted at the bottom of the pools, were not worth bothering about.

The whole place was an immense graveyard, silent and brooding over what had gone before. Yet it was here that in some small measure I conquered my horror of mutilation and death. Death was more at home and more natural than life. It was all around. In the earth, in the water, and in the air. The living were trespassers. The foot that stuck out from the side of the crater near where we lay told more of war than a whole library of books, and epitomised it better than any book could ever hope to do. Ugly and sad and useless and stupid was what it seemed to say.

Somewhere underneath a leg was attached to the foot and a body to the leg, with a face on which the grey mud pressed heavily, shutting out the sky. Or the body that owned the foot was yards away in another shell-hole. Or in tatters, and the foot was all that was left to tell that once a man had crouched there, knowing that death was near, but never dreaming for a single instant that a shell fired from a hidden gun miles away would catch him, and that his body would slowly rot on that chance spot until it became part of the ground itself—the little, nameless, unnoticed plot on which he had stood, thinking in his own little doubtful thoughts of what the future held for him.

Most soldiers refused to admit the possibility that a shell would get them. For all that the thought was at the back of the minds of all but the dullest. A maggotty thought. It frayed the nerves and made men preoccupied and silent in spite of themselves when shells were falling near. They knew they were utterly helpless, which made things worse. A soft flesh and blood creature armed with a puny weapon and protected by an inverted steel saucer on his head set up as a knocking-block for clanging, rending metal that ripped and tore his body like a child tearing up a newspaper.

" There must be something else to it that I don't understand or don't know about," I thought humbly. " But doesn't a bullet or a shell kill the brave men without giving them a dog's chance, just as easily as it kills the cowards ? And the men behind the line escape simply because they are behind the line. The men up the line get killed just because they happen to be up there. If we had our way we'd all be down the line like a shot, so it's not true that the base wallahs are cowards. They're just the same, only lucky. If they were pushed up the line they'd be as good any day as the fellows in it. Why is it that the war doesn't stop immediately, seeing that nobody wants it ?

" War was senseless and ridiculous. The worst of it was nobody seemed to realise that but me. There was no use in individuals thinking that way, anyhow.

" If I knew for certain I would survive the war I would be willing to die at the end of ten years," I thought again. The long vista of ten years stretched before me enticingly, an eternity of time.

My sad speculations were interrupted by the sight of Maxwell bringing out what was left of his bread and cheese, which he proceeded to demolish with thoughtful deliberation, spending an unconscionable time over every mouthful.

" We'll have a biscuit out of the iron ration, no matter a damn," I said, and, Beck agreeing, we crunched one apiece, savouring its hardness.

Another hour, and we were hungrier than ever.

A hard lump in the dirt under my shoulder had been annoying me for a long time. Almost unconsciously I had been trying to shift out of its way, but without success in the confined space. With nothing else to do I arched my body and set to work at it with my jack-knife. After scraping and digging for a couple of minutes I found it was an old tin that was causing the trouble. I succeeded in unearthing it, and was about to throw it away when I noticed that it felt solid.

Scraping the mush off it an ancient tin of bully beef disclosed itself.

Suddenly interested, I took the top off with the aid of the key which was still attached, and found the meat discoloured and smelly on the outside. After cutting off the putrid parts it didn't seem so bad. I was too hungry to be particular. I sliced off a hunk, and offered to share the remainder. Beck took a bit and eyed it doubtfully. Maxwell refused to touch it.

" As sure as goodness you'll get ' potomaine ' poisoning after eating that dirty stuff," he said.

" What's that again—is it dangerous ? " asked Beck in alarm.

" What ? Why, it'll kill you," exclaimed Maxwell.

" Let him rave away," I encouraged. " It won't do you a damned bit of harm. Besides, if it does you'll get down the line, so you needn't worry."

Beck looked rather uneasy, but hunger conquered his prudence. We finished the tin, without being very particular about the black parts.

For the rest of the day Maxwell kept looking at us from the corner of his eye as if expecting rigor mortis to set in any minute, but, fortunately, or unfortunately, nothing happened.

Thoroughly convinced that ptomaine poisoning was a bogey Beck spent the time poking into the mud with his jack-knife on the off chance of making another find. There was nothing doing.

I had only a sketchy idea what ptomaine poisoning was. But I had no great fear of it. It was almost with disappointment that I found I had no unusual symptoms. It would have been nice to go down the line on a stretcher even if, when I did recover, I would not have been entitled to pin a golden wound-stripe on my sleeve.

THE LETTER HOME

WE were relieved from the S O S. We ploughed through the mud with intervals spent in crouching down as bullets swept our way, and reached the duck-board track, which led down to Company headquarters, now located in another farm a bit farther back. It, too, boasted a little, well-revetted stretch of trench.

For some reason or other which I didn't understand every inhabited hole hereabouts was a " farm," though where the analogy came in wasn't clear.

Company headquarters was a small, damp dug-out, reached by a dozen steps. In it there was room for little more than the Captain, his bed, his batman, and the signaller on duty at the phone. It was a palace compared with the place we had left, with its sandbag-protected entrance, firm floor and a roof supported by massive beams.

After we had reported I spied in the trench one of the petrol-tins used for bringing up drinking water. I was very thirsty and made a grab for it. It was nearly full. Tilting it above my head I opened my gullet and swallowed greedily.

Next moment I had my finger down my throat trying to get some kind of evil-tasting oil up again, but despite all my efforts at retching it refused to come. I felt squeamish as the stuff went down into my stomach.

Jenkins, who was hanging about the dug-out on some errand, came over to see who was making the noise.

" You're not the first that has been caught that way," he laughed.

" I'm glad you lifted it first. I was just going to," said Beck gratefully.

"It won't be a very good mixture for that rotten bully beef we had a while ago," he added.

"You weren't wolfing your iron rations, were you?" asked Jenkins, and then went on without waiting for a reply. "The grub's getting worse and worse in this ramshackle mob of ours. I'm going to start in on mine, no matter if they shoot me for it."

I gave up hawking and spitting, and told him about scraping off the putrid parts of the tin of bully we had found, and eating the rest.

"Between that and drinking rifle-oil you must have a stomach like an ostrich," he said.

"I wish I was an ostrich, I'd fly away to hell out of this grip," said Beck, scratching his head.

"Ostriches don't fly, you damn fool," I said, recovering.

"You should be back at school, if you ever were at one," said Jenkins, peering to see who the speaker was, evidently not very impressed with his appearance.

"I wish I was back at school," said Beck. "When I was there the old master used to hammer the life out of me for not knowing anything, but I'd let him knock the tripe out of me now without grousing. Ay, every day in the week and twice on Sundays."

"Ah, well, maybe you're right enough," rejoined Jenkins. "I dare say if an ostrich was here it would damned soon learn to fly."

Maxwell was taking first turn on duty at the phone, so there was nothing for us to do but hang about the dug-out entrance waiting for the rations to come up. They proved to be the usual sloppy stew, the fatty part of which had congealed by the time it reached our dixies. An old barrack-room saying about a certain thing, when erect, having no conscience occurred to me as I devoured my share. Hunger has no pride, which was much the same thing.

I had already learned that all the time I was to be with the battalion I would go hungry. After every meal I could easily have eaten as much again, sometimes twice as much. This eternal hunger was not confined to myself, or the three or four other young fellows I mucked in with. Everybody in the ranks suffered from it.

Most of the blame, rightly or wrongly, fell on the A.S.C., who were accused of eating more than their share, and whacking what they couldn't eat for wine and women. Some held that it was because some high-up bastard laboured under the delusion that the more we thought of our bellies the less we would worry about the Germans.

On the odd occasions when we got Maconochie instead of stew there was one tin between two and often three men. Our breakfast was a round of loaf, a rasher of bacon and tea. Tea was another slice of bread with cheese or jam. Where we were the bread was often wet and muddy by the time it reached us, and the stew cold or seriously depleted. The rum ration was about the half full of an egg-cup and was apparently replaced by lime juice in the summer-time.

The officers didn't as a rule dislike rum, and neither did the Sergeant-Majors and Platoon Sergeants. We got what was left. I remembered reading wonderful yarns about the British Army being the most expensive and best fed in the world. It did not now seem to be true. The French and Belgians were better done for. They always appeared to have a supply of rolls in their haversacks, and vin rouge in their water-bottles. On the odd occasions that we fell in with them we begged bread.

I relieved Maxwell to let him get his stew, and sat in the dug-out at the phone, carefully adjusting the earphones. They had a habit of catching in the hair and pulling some out by the roots.

The Captain had just finished a snack, and sat back in an improvised arm-chair. He was a small man with a serious, repressed air and a disproportionately long chin below a thin mouth. His black-rimmed glasses matched a trim black moustache.

His batman cleared away the dishes, and set out a whisky bottle and a box of cigarettes, and went off into a corner without speaking.

I eyed the amber liquid and the cigarettes and wished I were an officer. I had run through my scanty supply of fags, and didn't like lime juice.

Runners clattered up and down with routine messages. The Sergeant-Major, a quiet, compactly-built man, appeared and dealt with them. The Captain sipped and smoked and chatted.

After a while things became quiet in the dug-out.

The C.S.M. went off to see about something. A portly Corporal peeped into the dug-out and I glanced round.

" Oh, hello, Corporal. Come in and close the door," said the little Captain perkily.

The Corporal, a stranger to me, insinuated himself into the cramped space and saluted as best he could. I noticed that his uniform was quite clean.

" Well, what have you brought this time ? " demanded the officer.

" Well, sir, I've some sardines, and a tin of peaches, sir," said the Corporal eagerly, " and I've got a loaf and some tea biscuits and some not bad cheese."

" Good man," said the Captain. " But did you bring any——"

" And I've a couple of little jars of chicken, ham and tongue, sir, if you think you'd like it," hastened the Corporal.

" Great," said the Captain, " but——"

" I'm very sorry, but I couldn't get any of the other, sir," went on the Corporal with the frank air of a man who has put all his cards on the table.

" Oh, well, it can't be jolly well helped. We really cannot expect to get everything, y'know," replied the Captain.

I smacked my lips at the enumeration of such good things, and bent forward a little to be more in the light of the candles.

" But I brought another bottle of the Black and White, sir."

" You'll really have to do a little better in future, Corporal, but I suppose it will have to do this time."

The Corporal looked contrite.

" Yessir, yessir—but you know how it is ! The mess—I'll bring what I have along directly, sir."

" Right ho," said the Captain airily.

The Corporal backed out, his face turned resolutely to the officer, and disappeared up the steps, giving a strong impression that only physical impossibility kept him from springing to his full height and saluting with clicking heels. A minute later he was back with his arms full of good things. First he laid the bottle of whisky reverently on the table and followed it with an assortment of tins, glass pots and parcels and the loaf.

My mouth watered. Surely the little runt of an officer couldn't eat all that. Our own rations had been skimpier than usual that night. I envisaged my teeth sinking into the fat chunk of cheese.

The Captain became quite jovial—but not with me. I seemed to be covered with the invisible paint of the fairy story for all the notice he took of me as I sprawled over the phone, all eyes and ears and mud.

" You've earned your keep for another night, Corporal," he laughed.

The latter smirked and flushed. He muttered something liberally interspersed with sirs.

" This Corporal must have a nice cushy job somewhere," I thought, eyeing him enviously.

" Yes, sir. I must say the mess has been fairly lucky, considering everything that has happened lately."

" Perhaps you are right there," replied the Captain as the Corporal, with a muttered " Mustn't miss the transport, sir," wriggled out.

The Captain sat for a time eyeing his treasures like a spoilt child its toys. Motioning to the batman, he proceeded to give him minute directions about the next meal.

I coughed, moved restlessly and stared, almost ready to ask point-blank for the heel of a loaf or a tin of sardines, but the officer's sublime indifference to my presence awed me. The efficient batman, who eyed the comestibles with a superior air, had them all packed away out of sight in minute or two.

" Some people are well away," I thought as the little Captain replenished his glass. " And maybe if I'd asked him he would have given me something."

Later I heard that the Captain was decent enough as officers went, but, like so many more up the line, disinclined to move from his comfortable dug-out. This was his first tour with our battalion, but his men seemed to have weighed him up without losing any time—not bad, but windy up the line.

" Why is it," I wondered, " that officers are far better fed than the men for doing much the same thing, and why should they be able to get hold of ration rum and mess whisky—as much as they wanted—when our share is doled out like attar of roses. More leave, more food, more booze, more pay." I couldn't find a good reason. I put my failure down to my own denseness, as usual.

The Captain started writing a letter. I listened to occasional shells thudding into the mud outside and the distant clatter of machine-guns. Very likely the duck-boards were being sprayed, but the fire sounded lifeless and haphazard, as if neither side had much hope of making much impression on the all-pervading mud.

The Captain finished writing and began to nod. A cigarette between his slack fingers sent a thin spiral of smoke up his sleeve. A peculiar peacefulness reigned in the dug-out, which the occasional noises outside only served to intensify. There was something satisfying about being up the line on a quiet night which needed to be experienced to be understood. The dug-out was strongly built. There was only one chance in a thousand that a shell would come its way. The atmosphere was pleasantly muggy, and the candle-light sent formless shadows up and down the rough walls and beams.

The officer snored, jerked awake and then nodded again. The smouldering cigarette dropped unheeded to the floor. Reaching forward I picked it up and finished it.

Yet, being a newcomer to war, the thousandth chance was sufficient to give me an uneasy sense of danger, but the corresponding alertness added to my well-being. Just to be alive and breathing the warm air of the dug-out was sufficient inducement to enjoy life. Outside men were lying in the mud.

A young Second-Lieutenant came in from one of the platoons. The Captain woke up and treated him to the whisky. They discussed the latest musical comedy in London, the chances of getting leave in the near future, and then the mud, and how soon the Division would move to some more comfortable sector.

All leave was cancelled, it appeared, owing to the parlous state of the B.E.F.

The conversation was carried on in a schoolboyish jargon so different from the direct Anglo-Saxon of the rank and file as almost to constitute another language. Things were " too utterly priceless " or " too perfectly fearful " for words.

So-and-so was a " splendid chappie." The acting C.O. of the battalion, I learned, was " rather a stiffish old top," according to the Captain, to which sentiment the Lieutenant answered : " Rather."

The talk became desultory. After another spot from the bottle the Lieutenant rose to his feet. " Well, cheerio, sir ; I think I'll amble along," he said and saluted.

" Chin chin, mind the step, old bean," said the Captain.

Although I had been sitting almost cheek by jowl with the pair of them the invisible paint was still in action. " I know they're officers, but they could have looked at me instead of through me once or twice or even offered a fag," I thought in slow anger. " A couple of clerks, probably, not much better than myself, trying to act like public-school boys or leaders of men."

When Maxwell came back a few minutes later I went up on top, bidding the Captain farewell in my turn, but silently —the soldier's farewell.

There was an old German cemetery a few yards away from the tiny shelter we occupied when not on duty at the phone. Drawn by curiosity I went over to it next evening and tried to make out some of the names.

It was a dreary spot. There was a little of dignity about the few blackened crosses that remained sticking out of the slimy earth at all angles. Legs and arms and bits of rotting flesh, still covered with tattered field-grey, lay here and there, almost indistinguishable from the ooze. A sweetish, sickly stench rose.

The Captain's batman joined me as I was about to turn away. It was dangerous, too, to walk about upright.

" They're in a hell of a mess, eh, a regular Chinese puzzle. And it's their own guns that knock them about. That's the joke of it."

" Well, probably enough our guns are doing the same to our men in the German lines," I said.

" That's right. What does it matter anyway ? They're all stiffs together, aren't they ? They don't care a damn,

s

and we don't care a damn, and everybody's happy. It's only when Jerry starts making more recruits for the boneyard that we get the breeze up." I turned to go back to the shelter, but the batman caught my arm in sudden excitement. " Look at that one over there. There, in the hole, with his arm sticking up. I'll swear that's a good ring he has on his finger."

I looked in the direction of his pointing finger and saw a legless cadaver, partly covered with rotted cloth and mud. A bony arm stuck out over the edge of the crater, so near that I could have blown a spittle on it. Looking intently I saw a tarnished ring on the little finger.

" You're surely not going to take that ? " I asked, shocked at the idea of robbing the dead of a little intimate thing like a ring.

" Keep your eye skinned for a minute, and you'll soon see."

I stared in horrified fascination as he stepped among the crosses, his eyes fixed on the prize. Reaching forward he tugged at the little finger.

" For God's sake come away," I cried involuntarily as the arm came away from the rotting trunk.

The batman swore and, opening his jack-knife, hacked at the skeleton hand. I turned my back on the scene and started picking my way over the shell-torn ground alone, but in a minute he caught up on me.

" What's all the hurry about ? " he asked in surprise. " I got it without any trouble. Look." I didn't look, and left him without a word.

Later the batman displayed a bright gold ring on his little finger, and one or two more expeditions were made to the cemetery by other souvenir hunters before we moved farther back. It paid to be tough.

The signal station was reinforced by the addition of a little Cockney named Hopkins—Nigger Hopkins we called him. He had a pinched, sallow face, almost invisible beneath his helmet and black hair, which needed cutting. His meagre body was not designed for carrying equipment, an infantryman's equipment. Like his face, it was almost invisible beneath its load. His belt was awry with the strain of badly balanced straps connecting up a jumble of pouches, bags and buckles. He had an odd habit of rubbing his skin with the tips of his fingers until it was inflamed and sore-looking. When spoken to he replied briefly and non-committally, but with a wise little placating smile that took the place of many words. When on the march the strap of his rifle and equipment straps were continually slipping off his narrow, sloping shoulders. But always the little smile disarmed gibes and criticism.

" You see how it is," it seemed to say.

If he was very tired he became quite silent. The smile became a grimace, and then a mere writhing motion of bloodless, compressed lips.

The post came up and I got a small parcel of food. Maxwell was on duty, and the other two looked covetously at the home-made bread and apple tart which I sat gloating over. It seemed a shame that I couldn't have it all to myself. I shared it unwillingly with them, only keeping the lion's share of the tart by right of ownership.

We decided to drum up, and contributed a pinch of tea and sugar each out of our iron rations, only to discover that we had no water. We were strictly forbidden to touch the stinking shell-hole water.

" It'll be all right when it's boiled," suggested Beck. After some demur we allowed him to creep out for some. He soon returned with a dixieful of thick brownish liquid. When the tea was made we drank it up and ate the good things.

Afterwards Nigger said there was a dead man at the bottom of the crater where Beck had drawn the water.

Beck had received a letter and sat studying it, his lips unconsciously mouthing the words as he went along. When he had finished he glanced round and caught my eye.

" It's from the old woman and she's a bad hand at writing," he said, his face reddening, but I knew without being told that it was about as much as Beck could do to read and write, for his letter was written in big angular letters with about a dozen words to the page. Any child could have read it with ease.

I got hold of a message-pad and dropped a note home. When I had finished Beck leaned over cautiously, so as not to awaken Nigger, who had fallen asleep. " When you're at it, Corporal, you might drop a line for me, will you ? The old woman's a bad scholar and nearly blind, and always says she can't make out my writing."

" Well, what'll I say ? " I asked.

" Oh, just whatever you think yourself," murmured Beck, wiping the sweat from his nose with the back of his hand. " You know how to put it. Tell her I'm all right and to send me a parcel as soon as she can, now that she knows the address."

" Yes, and what else ? "

" That'll do fine, but be sure and write it plain," said Beck, as if that was more important than what was said.

" And how will I finish it ? "

" How d'ye mean ? "

" Will I say ' Your loving son,' or what ? "

" Aw, Corporal, do you want her to have a fit. Just put ' Sam,' and she'll know," said Beck blushing.

" No, you had better put something more than that. It doesn't sound right, somehow, just the bare name."

" All right then, Corporal, put it in," said Beck shame-facedly.

I had stumbled over the same problem myself. I had never been before farther away from home than the camp and with week-end leave there had been no necessity for writing. In my first letter from France I had pondered on how to end it. We were not a demonstrative family. I had signed a diminutive I only got at home. Then, feeling that something more was required, I had nerved myself up to putting " Your loving son " and hastened to get rid of the letter before I changed my mind and struck it out.

I didn't like writing home, anyway. I couldn't say what I thought and had to use dull, meaningless phrases, which bore an odd resemblance to what I had written for Beck. In reality my parents were farther away from me than if they had been dead. Sometimes I wished they were dead when I thought of them grieving if the next blind shell got me instead of one of the other fellows, who had mothers too. Whenever the thought of home came to me I tried to put it away as quickly as possible, and usually succeeded, but whenever I got a letter or a parcel full of the little things I had once liked and packed with loving hands anxious for my welfare, the thoughts were harder to chase. What good were letters that took it for granted I would be there to receive them ? What good were parcels with their little wedges of cake and fancy stuff when all I wanted was another hunk of loaf and cheese or a tot of ration rum ?

THE HOLY BIBLE

WE landed in a different camp this time, for which we were duly grateful. Bucket Camp—which the old-stagers had called the last camp—was too suggestive of kicking the bucket for our taste. We were at the side of a main road and whenever I was free I sat watching the traffic. The weather was warm and sunny. Once out of the line I became almost superhuman in my enjoyment of life, living every minute in a careless enchanted way that took no heed of time. There were plenty of parades and kit inspections and fatigues, but no actual drill such as there had been before St. Quentin. There was probably some good and sufficient reason for it, but we didn't inquire. Perhaps it was because we were too near the line, although where we were, exactly, I hadn't any idea. Wherever we were it must have been very near the end of the British line, for just below our camp there was a crowd of Belgian troops. They had a canteen of sorts and in it we spent whatever money we had, which wasn't much. I wasn't particularly fond of beer, and the stuff they sold was very watery, but always I was fascinated by hearing a strange tongue and seeing people of a different nationality. Why, I did not know. Most of the Belgian soldiers spoke English, some of them very good English. They were ridiculously English in appearance, too, with their fair hair, blue eyes and everyday faces. I had always thought of the Belgians as a tragic people who had been so raped and robbed, and generally ill-treated by the Germans, that the whole nation was a symbol of suffering and misfortune, but these ones were a jolly lot, who seemed quite contented with life.

When we spoke to them they gathered round smiling and good-humoured, each one trying to show off by picking up what we meant before the others had. Their physical likeness to Englishmen was increased by their khaki uniform, only the different collar with its touch of red and the different cap and boots showing that they were foreigners.

They seemed to accept the war in philosophical fashion. "There it is and make the best of it," was their motto, delivered with an expressive shrug which made light of the whole thing. They might have been acting for our benefit, of course, or they might have had cushy jobs.

Their infantry seemed to be all cyclists, which I thought a very good idea, especially when one evening a battalion of them went flying past in a cloud of dust, each man pedalling for all he was worth and paying no regard to keeping in line. They waved to us light-heartedly as they streamed out along the road, for all the world like a cycling club out for a Saturday afternoon run into the country.

"They're well away, you see," said Jenkins, who was sitting beside me. "They've only got a little stretch of line to hold and nobody bothers them. It runs among the sand-dunes on to the sea and they have most of it flooded. All they have to do is man the trenches and see that the water doesn't run into them. There's never anything doing on their front and the yarn goes that they used to make quite a lot of buckshee cash showing our base wallahs round so as they'd be able to go back and blow about having been in the front line."

"Go on," I said, "tell it to the Marines."

"It's a fact," said Jenkins, "many a lad round about Dunkirk in '16 and '17 has been up for two or three hours at any rate and sometimes for a day or two, all according to what money they had to splash. They saw the Belgeek idea of no-man's-land and went away thinking they knew all there is to be known about the whole front from Ypres

to the Somme. They were nearly ready to put up wound
stripes as a souvenir."

The way took us over a railway line and up a straight road
that led into the enemy line and beyond. Great flashes lit
up the sky and disappeared to make room for others crowding
behind. They seemed to be carrying on an eerie, bloodless
war of their own with the darkness, each side alternately
advancing and retreating, never tiring of the silent struggle
until day came and put them both to flight.

A pretty, story-book war it was on the part of the gun
flashes. Many a gallant charge up the sky routed the
darkness, only to be followed by headlong retreat leaving
not a trace of the battle until it started all over again. The
sullen roar of the shells was a thing apart.

We came to a bridge over a river or canal. The bridge
was being shelled and there was congestion on the road.
Limbers going up with rations and faced with the necessity
of getting back before daylight ran the gauntlet. The
horses were unruly. The drivers, lashing them and themselves into a frenzy of excitement and fear, clattered over
hell for leather. After a short, uneasy halt we went over at
the double by parties. There were no casualties, at least
not in our company, which was all we cared about ! We
went on for an hour or more, the ground rising gently as we
progressed. It was very bare ground from what I could
see of it, but firm and dry. A cautious hail reached us.
We left the road and groped our way through the darkness
until we arrived at, of all things, a little group of elephant
huts. One of them was the signallers' stopping-place.

We took over and connected up the phone. Squatting on
the floor we wondered whereabouts the front line was and
why the huts had not been knocked to bits long ago. The
company Captain came in with the Sergeant-Major. He
was loud-voiced and domineering. He was a Regular Army

ranker officer, which was sufficient in itself to damn him in
the eyes of the men. He knew too much and didn't hesitate
to make use of his knowledge. He had a reputation for
hectoring and bullying and a " Don't-dare-to-tell-me I-
know-it-all " style. His men swore he was more or less
drunk all the time and that he had a strong partiality for
ration rum. He was also popularly reported to have robbed
a château somewhere of valuable paintings and bric-à-brac
and sent the stuff home.

" Have you got a signal lamp here, Corporal ? " he
demanded harshly.

" No, sir," I said, more than a little astonished. What
use could a signal lamp be ?

" Well, you'll have to get one. I want a signal lamp."

" We've got the phone, sir," I pointed out.

" I know that. Damn it to hell, do you think I'm blind ?
The line to battalion was cut half a dozen times yesterday
I'm told, so your phone isn't much good. Have they any
lamps down at headquarters ? "

I hadn't the faintest idea, but made haste to placate him.

" I'm sure they have, sir. I'll send a message down at
once."

" You'll do damn all of the kind. You can send a man,
can't you ? He can bring it back with him."

" Yes, sir," I said obediently. I had no more notion
where battalion headquarters was than the man in the
moon.

" If there was an attack here the wire would go phut
inside five minutes, and I'm not going to be left in the air
with no means of communication. I don't want it to-night,
but see to it to-morrow or by God I'll want to know the
reason why."

The Captain fumed some more. Muttering something
about bastard signallers he turned on his heel and went out.
We discussed bastard Captains.

" A signal lamp up here ! That means getting out into the open to send."

" Jerry'll blow it into the air when he sees it."

" And there'll have to be one at Bat headquarters as well. What'll the Signal Officer say to that ? He's supposed to decide things like that, or the Colonel, or the Adjutant."

We looked at each other. And perhaps the Captain would prove right and an attack would come !

" Do you fellows know how to work lamps ? " I asked, remembering the sketchy training given at the Signal School at home, mostly devoted to flag-wagging and telephone work. I saw visions of having to work the lamp myself. It seemed a bad idea to use powerful electric lamps right in the line, but the officer had looked on it as quite natural. He might have been drunk, of course. On the other hand I didn't have enough experience to know.

Maxwell nodded half-heartedly, as if only his stern conscience made him admit it. The other two shook their heads decidedly.

" I remember getting taught about them, but blest if I could ever understand them—how to get them focused and why they used different slides to change the colour," said Beck. " They used to have two kinds of lamp, too, and that made it worse. You know, Corporal ? There was the big ones that kicked up such a row that if you couldn't make out the flashes you could read the rattle of the key going up and down eedy-umpty. Then there was the electric ones, but I never got much practice with them. There wasn't enough of them to go round where I was."

" I could send a message all right, but I couldn't read the one at the other end very well," said Nigger. " My eyesight isn't very good. I used to wear glasses before I was in the Army."

" Well, you and Beck can look after the phone then and

keep repairing the wire," I told them. " Six times it was broken yesterday, the Captain said. That's one thing about a lamp. There's no wires to look after."

" Maybe I could work one all right if I had a shot at it. I remember something about them," said Beck, wiping the sweat off his nose.

" You can damn well forget it," I retorted brutally.

" There you are. That's what you get for coming the old soldier," said Maxwell reprovingly.

The hours passed slowly. No messages came to an us and the shell-fire died down with the coming of daylig Nigger was at the phone and the other pair slept, curled up uncomfortably on the hard floor. I should have been asleep too, but up the line I found it hard to sleep—to let myself sleep, that is.

And then, from far away, a faint, unmistakable whisper came to life. Nigger and I dropped to the floor, filled with sickening apprehension. The whisper became a murmur, changing imperceptibly into an ominous whine. The whine rose to a shriek and a tremendous explosion sounded outside the hut. The sleepers awoke with a jerk. We pressed against the floor-boards, waiting. Earth and stones thudded down, making the iron roof clang. A jagged hole appeared in the door. Silence came. We looked round.

" It's all right. It was only a chance shot," said Maxwell. " It must have burst just outside the door."

Getting to his knees Nigger bent over the phone again, his black eyes staring fixedly upwards at nothing as he strained his ears.

Another tiny whisper came. We hugged the floor help-lessly as it changed to a rising clamour, spelling imminent disaster, and ended in another shrieking explosion. The hut shook crazily and splinters rang against the flimsy side. Again the earth rumbled thunderously down, scaring us almost as much as the actual burst.

" Come on, for God's sake. He's trying to get the hut," cried Nigger, tearing off the earphones.

A horrible indecision possessed me. Where we were we had a roof over our heads. We might no sooner be outside the door than another shell would come. The hut was already familiar, and I didn't know what outside was like. It had been too dark to see when we took over.

" But what about the phone, Corporal ? We can't leave it," said Maxwell, pointing at it to help make me understand. The others looked at me for direction. I was in charge of the company station. I thought of the Captain.

" We daren't leave it," I said. " We'd only be up against it if we did."

We lay huddled together, waiting for the next shell. Maybe this one would get us. We shrank down as the roar came. The clattering and banging on the roof followed. Not that time. This one ?

A newspaper had reached me from home the day before. It was squeezed into my tunic pocket. Taking it out I sat up and opened it up. Holding it up before my face I pretended to read.

Again the murmur rose and grew, and again the rushing, piercing scream of the shell ended in rending steel. My hands jerked instinctively to protect my face. The door of the hut fell in. Rents appeared in the galvanised iron side.

Again I held the paper before me and tried to read, but the print was blurred and as meaningless as Greek. I threw the paper to one side. Instead of screening my fear it was only giving me away.

The shelling went on, and we either plucked up heart or our nerves became deadened. Our bodies jerked uncontrollably with each shattering explosion, but for the rest we were silent and motionless. The hut was a sounding-board.

None of us knew how long the ordeal lasted. Our ears missed the little warning whisper. We looked at each other furtively, scarcely able to believe that we had escaped. I felt parched and shaky, and then thought of a cigarette. In a moment I was inhaling furiously, hardly taking time to dispel huge lungfuls of smoke. We spoke disjointedly, in voices hardly above a whisper, unwilling of meeting each other's eyes.

A young Sergeant with a grey face appeared in the wrecked doorway. His eyes took us in and wandered expectantly into the corners.

" Anybody hurt ? " he asked gruffly.

We shook our heads, staring at him. He was a man from the outside world. We had almost forgotten about it.

" That was hot while it lasted," said the Sergeant. " The Captain's hit and about half a dozen of the boys killed. Two more have caught bad packets and'll kick the bucket."

We ran over to hear more, with the exception of Nigger, who had put on the headphones again.

" But what was it all about ? What started it ? Everything was quiet. These old tin huts——"

" It wasn't the huts he was strafing, or you chaps wouldn't be here," said the Sergeant. " It was all the fault of the crowd we relieved. Some fool of an officer of theirs made them dig a new trench here. Some of them don't know what to be at. Jerry spotted it, of course, and waited until they had made a good job of it. Then he started in and made a mess of it. You wouldn't know there had been a trench now unless you had been told. The worst of it was that we took over in the meantime."

" It was good shooting," said Maxwell.

" Look at that. That was good shooting, too, eh ? " said the Sergeant.

We looked, and exclaimed. There was a tear in his left tunic pocket. He pulled out a pocket Testament and some letters. The letters were pierced. Embedded in the Testament was a shell-splinter.

" I was born to be hung," said the Sergeant with a strained grin. " When a Bible saves your bacon, eh ? Felt a tap, just. As if somebody had poked me in the chest with his finger. Didn't even bother looking till after the shelling was all over. First bit of practical Christianity I've ever seen."

We watched him as he replaced the letters and book in his pocket and buttoned the flap. The little khaki Testament was a souvenir worth having. It was a very powerful charm.

" And we were getting the wind up for nothing, Corporal," said Beck when he had departed.

" Oh, no. We were doing it for practice," said Hopkins, with his pallid smile.

" It was a near thing, anyway," said Maxwell shyly. " Things like this happen to nearly everybody some time or other up the line. They're planted somewhere where they can't move, and they get shelled for half an hour and think every minute is going to be their last, and when it's all over they haven't got a scratch or a mark."

" Ay, that may be," said Nigger, " but they never forget it, do they ? They're marked up here." He touched his head.

Maxwell and Beck peeped out to inspect the smashed trench and the smashed men, but I wasn't sufficiently curious. Instead I felt in my left breast pocket to make sure that my Testament reposed there. Without having been told it was the custom I had carried mine there from the day I got it.

A thought struck me.

" I forgot to ask the Sergeant did the Captain get it bad. We'll very likely get out of that lamp business, anyhow."

" It was a bit of good luck him getting hit," replied Nigger. " Everybody will be glad to see the last of him. I bet the lads of the company are hoping he never sees the dressing-station let alone Blighty."

THE LUCKY LAD

THE signal station was a small sandbag hut, with a fairly substantial roof. The weather had suddenly become very warm and sunny. Inside the hut it was dark and cool and cramped. Outside was much more pleasant except that it was open ground and shells fell at intervals. I wanted to lie in the sun and have the protection of the hut at the same time, so I was in a quandary. The shells weren't falling so very near, but they might. Beck sat out in the sun scratching, and Nigger sat in the hut rubbing. Maxwell at the phone was writing a letter. I envied them their preoccupation. I pretended to be occupied too, but the shells were uppermost in my mind. They spoilt the sunshine.

The Signal Officer and Sergeant appeared. We sprang up. The officer looked to see that things were as they should be, then drew me to one side.

" Are you anyway well up in visual-signalling, Corporal. Lamps and flags, and so on like that ? "

" Lord save us, is he on lamps, too ? " I thought.

" You've got an instructor's certificate, I see," he went on, pointing to the crossed flags on my arm. A certificate entitled me to wear them above the stripe, otherwise they would have been on my cuff.

" I was good at it, sir, at one time, but I'm afraid not so good now. I was doing clerk for a long time afterwards, so I've got out of practice."

" Just the man I want," said the officer, smiling, and nodded to the Sergeant.

The latter took out his note-book and inquired my regimental number.

" I'm sending you on a six weeks' course for visual-signalling down to the Army School," continued the officer. "You and Corporal Mundy. Go off as soon as it gets dark and pick him up on your way down. There's no one else I can send, so off you go."

The officer and Sergeant departed.

"Six weeks!" exclaimed the others, looking at me as if I was a stranger. "Six weeks!"

A Frenchman driving down in a high, old-fashioned cart, painted blue, gave us a lift. Mundy sat with him, practising his French, and I sat behind. The horse went at a jog-trot. Well content to be left out of the conversation, I stared about at the quiet, darkening road and trees, trying to realise my luck. How decent the officer had been choosing me! God knows what would become of the battalion in the long space of six weeks. How easily he might have picked someone else! And how pleasant the road was, and the shallow, grassy ditch on either side.

It was quite dark when we thanked the driver, and shouldering our packs sought our divisional headquarters. It was strange to be in a bell-tent again. In the middle of the night there was an air-raid, and the roar of bombs bursting nearby, but not near enough to seriously get the wind up over. Men who have been through a bombardment or two up the line are not inclined to worry much over nearby air-raids down the line. The fact that you are down the line more than makes up.

In the morning we visited a quartermaster's store and drew what we wanted in the way of clothes and underwear. Then to an orderly-room where we were presented with stamped vouchers authorising us to be away from our unit. Then a pay, and a visit to a dry canteen for cigarettes for the journey. After that there was nothing to do but lie on the grass at the roadside and wait for the lorry. The sun shone in a cloudless sky. We had discarded our helmets for caps— sign-manual of being down the line—and were happy. I lay back, not so much luxuriating in the sun as in the sense of security.

The officers and men moving about the divisional head-quarters were happy, too. There was quite a lot of them. Each one seemed prepared to endure the hardships of war for an indefinite period. R.E. linesmen working back to corps or " forward " to brigades. A.S.C. storemen and drivers. Ordnance Corps officers with bands on their arm. Military police.

It was my first view of life at a headquarters. I was greatly taken with it. I turned to Mundy, feeling quietly expansive and sure of myself as anticipations of the good time to come flowed in on me.

" Do you know, I'd rather have a job here than one at the base or even in a camp at home. It's more enjoyable here somehow. Now and then there's an air raid and a bomb drops sufficiently close to make you thank your lucky stars you're still alive, and give you an appetite for the next meal. You're near enough the line to enjoy being free from lice and keeping your cap badge and buttons clean and looking smart. When you hear a heavy strafe going on up the line at night you snuggle down and pity the poor chaps in the trenches. And you could even——"

" Yes," broke in Mundy, eagerly taking up the pleasant tale and embroidering it to suit his fancy. " And there would always be a good wet canteen handy where a chap could go and get a slug of real beer in the evenings. And these lads are never stuck for a woman when they feel like one. There's always a village not too far away, and they can flog the troops' rations if they're short of cash. And when they go home on leave—well, aren't they with a Division and not at the base ? They can swing the lead about the number of times they were blown up by shells— though it was with beer—and how lucky they are to come through all the shows they were in. The yokels at home swallow it all. The old women snuffle when they hear it and say, ' God in His mercy has spared our Willie ' ; and the village parson looks down his nose and says, ' God be thanked, it's a miracle indeed that ·Willie is still alive,' when, if he only knew it, it would be a damn sight bigger miracle if he wasn't."

Mundy paused for breath and then his own humour got the better of him. We both burst out laughing.

We got another meal and loitered about. I spotted an anti-aircraft gun and a few minutes later saw it in action. It was a bright, brassy affair in a little patch of level ground surrounded by a low wall of clean sand-bags. There was a tent, gleaming white, at the rear of the gun.

A man with a telescope on a tripod searched the sky. Another man sat at a little table. An aeroplane sailed over high in the air and the gun crew tumbled out and got to work. White puffs appeared near the plane, which appeared not to notice at first. Then it side-slipped clear of the Archies and the game started all over again. The gunners didn't seem to be at all put out by their waste of good ammunition. The airman didn't seem to be at all put out by the puffs. The details passing and repassing on the road, to whom this was an old story, looked up casually, and as casually away.

The dismal town was being shelled, as usual, when we passed through the cobbled streets lined with mean houses. A shell screeched and burst on the road behind, and then another. Our lorry swayed and shook as the driver put on speed. For a long minute the shells followed us like hounds on the scent. The driver seemed a superman as he hurled us along. The lorry was alive with speed and fear. A last crash made us shrink down, and then we had left the town and the shells behind. For six long weeks, I thought joyfully, gloating over the minutes and hours and days. Every second was golden. I gloated over my wealth. Millions of seconds. Thousands of minutes. Hundreds of hours. Forty-two days.

An immense exhilaration filled us. We sang, allying our voices to the loud hum of the engine. When the others stopped I made childish crooning noises to give vent to my ecstasy, my mouth half-opened to catch the rush of air.

The road, deserted at first except for ourselves, became full of colour and life as we sped on. It was really two roads, set side by side. One, to the right, was rutty and dusty. The other was laid with great stone blocks, pavé.

Creaking and grunting the lorry forged upwards to where a small town perched like a mediæval castle on its hill. A funny little double tram with smart, well-set-up soldiers and a few drab civilians inside jolted along the main street. A tram in such a tiny town tickled my fancy. I stopped humming in tune with the engine to laugh contentedly. Light motor ambulances scurried up and down. Heavy lorries rumbled along enveloped in dust. Dispatch riders wormed their way through the traffic. Smart motor cars, equipped with klaxon horns, with red-tabbed supercilious officers reclining at their ease on padded seats, claimed right of way.

Overhead the sun was a molten mass in the clear sky, but on the road the white dust eddied and swirled.

A jam developed ahead. We slowed down to a snail's pace. The driver had known how to put on speed when the shells were falling and now something required him to go slow. I felt the respect which a passenger always feels for the driver.

The leading columns of a battalion on the march appeared. The men trudged along with heads bent, their knees sagging wearily, taking everybody's dust and in everybody's way, to judge by the impatient honks. Their tunics were unbuttoned at the neck and a thick white layer made each man almost indistinguishable the one from the other. They were all very young looking, even the Sergeants and officers. Their small, sweat-streaked faces were screwed up into an intensity of effort.

I knew it all, green as I was, and felt somehow self-conscious sitting at ease on the lorry. They were heading towards the line and extinction, while we were safe and going in the right direction.

The difference was so great that my quick sympathy, born of experience, evaporated in a twinkling. I was an individual with life ahead and they were dusty automatons whose obscure fates were of no importance. It seemed ridiculous that each marching man should have his own little, private aspirations to live.

I looked at them as they slumped past, and then at Mundy sitting beside me, his long, muscular legs beating a tattoo of impatience on the tail-board. His face was dusty too, but the dust couldn't hide his great beak of a nose and strong, bluey chin, or the twin clefts running down his leathery cheeks. He was like a scarred old dog watching a flock of sheep.

Glancing round he caught my eye. He was as sharp as a needle in some ways and sensed what I was thinking.

" Poor creatures," he said, jerking his thumb at the marching ranks. " There's not one in twenty could grow a moustache—not a damn one. Haw, haw, haw."

I was silent. I couldn't have grown one myself.

" Not that I blame 'em," said Mundy, quickly. " They's only a pack of youngsters—look at them—that should be at home with their ma. Are there no men left in England at all ? Look. There's not even a few old ones here and there to stiffen that crowd. Even the blinking officers and Sergeants—all kids, and they're expected to go in and hold the Germans. A good Jerry battalion could eat them alive before breakfast and still feel hungry. And dekko the way they're marching—as if every step was going to be the last."

" Well, we don't know how many kilos they've covered ! "

" Ah, what can you expect. It don't matter how long they have been hoofing it. A fool could see that they've only had about three months' training—if they've had that. These youngsters. They've no big bones, and the flesh melts off them in no time. It hasn't had time to harden. Don't pay any heed to yarns about boys of eighteen and nineteen being better than men of thirty and forty. It's all bunkum. A healthy man of thirty or thirty-five, say, is a better man any day in the week. For soldiering, that is. He has more guts in him. I'm over forty—ay, well over it— and I'll guarantee to slog longer, and booze harder and play with the Mam-zelles oftener in between than any two of those young fellows. I'm not bragging or blaming them. It's not their fault."

Mundy was talking about the marching men—taking me into his confidence as if I were an equal—but I applied his remarks to myself, and knew them to be true.

" Mind you," he went on, full of his subject now. The object-lesson was still before us, trudging along in silence. " It's not that I want to run that mob down, bad and all as they look. But they're not the right kind. First, you have what I call the original kind—the ones that when the war came rushed to join up, thinking they would like it. Mostly tough characters, able to muck in and carry on—the kind that are as good as any German that ever existed, and far better, for that matter, because they took everything as all in the day's work and didn't brag or chuck out their chests about it. I don't come from the same part of the country as our Div., but take them. The Divisions were all much the same in those days. In 1916, as regards physique and guts, ours was the equal of any Division in the whole British Army, or any other army. And why ? They had what's called esprit de corps. The Bats were always up against each other. When they went on the spree on pay

days they would end up by going for each other with fists
or belts. They kicked the guts out of each other at football.
On the Somme they went as far, and farther, than any other
Division, and the same in 1917 at Cambrai and Ypres.
They were what's known as shock troops now, but then
they didn't know it. They are nearly all dead. Even at
St. Quentin, what was left of the old crowd put up a good
show. On the first day they held out until ordered to leave
the battle positions. Other Divisions just faded out. In
the days that followed they went to pieces, of course. There
was only a handful left, so you can't blame them. At that,
they were used to fill the gaps left by some of the other
Divs.—some that had been less knocked about. Now the
Division's a hotch-potch—not worth a tinker's curse. Old
Jerry could wallop us again any time. What's left of the old
crowd is fed up. They've had enough, and they're almost
ready to tell the Brass Hats that and damn the consequences.
Once there were fighting men, but——"

The lorry jerked forward and Mundy subsided, rather
shamefaced at letting himself go.

We went on, passing a constant succession of sprawling
dumps, depots, aerodromes, gun parks, workshops, horse
lines and attendant men. It was all very imposing and
businesslike compared with the sketchy trenches, the shell-
holes and the scattered platoons and companies that made
up the front line. It was all so very stable, too, as if the
front line was some fabulous place, more of a legend than
anything else, instead of a real thing of shreds and patches
where young, inexperienced troops lay, waiting for the
German masses to come over on them.

The battalion we had just passed was composed of the same
material—worse looking, if possible—as our lot. Anyone, with
eyes to see, would have seen that they had no stomach for the
war, didn't know what it was about and didn't want to know
—victims of the powers-that-be. A poor thing to fight for.

The romantic idea of war started at the wagon lines and grew as it progressed backwards to the bases. Out of range of the shells men were men indeed. Smart uniforms could set off broad-shouldered, soldierly figures.

It was a curious thing that such men were content to hide behind a screen of young fellows in their teens with small, unformed faces and boy's physique. Had I been one of them I would have been ashamed of myself, but they seemed to bear up. The war—in 1918 at least—was only the business of those who were pitchforked into it.

Probably I would have borne up, too.

Suddenly we left the noise and bustle of the war behind and traversed an empty, tree-lined road. Here and there solid farm-houses nestled amid green fields. I began to feel unaccountably sleepy. Along with Mundy and a couple of others I was sitting swinging my legs at the back of the lorry. We were coated thickly with dust. The stink of warm petrol enveloped me chokingly.

My companions raised voices and the steady roar of the engine became inextricably jumbled.

Someone emptied a water-bottle about my face and down my throat and I came to. I was lying on my back on the road, but in a couple of minutes I was all right again—the fumes from the exhaust were to blame, the others explained. I had been sitting just above the pipe. For the remainder of the journey I travelled in front with the driver and got the benefit of the breeze. The little accident didn't damp my enthusiasm for long—I had fallen on my shoulder and not on my head—and when we drew up at the Signal School and found tea, bread, jam and cheese awaiting us I mucked in as heartily as any.

" You were lucky you didn't break your bleeding neck," said Mundy.

" Not at all, man, I couldn't have," I answered, shocked at the idea of meeting such a simple death.

THE TELESCOPE

WE were a cosmopolitan crowd at the school : English, Irish, Scots and Welsh, along with a few Australians and New Zealanders.

We were in bell tents. We kept the flaps wide open and rolled up the bottoms. Even then it was too warm and at nights we removed outside and slept on the grass. There was plenty of food, generally served up in the open under the shade of convenient trees. On Sundays, to remind us that we were still in France, dinner consisted of bully beef, hard tack and pickles.

The instructors, most of whom were R.E. Sergeants, were sharp and competent without driving us too hard. For that matter they could have driven us as hard as they liked and we wouldn't have complained. All they could do on us was child's play compared to what we were escaping.

All day long we flag-wagged and flapped and helio'd, and at night there was lamp-reading. It was a visual signalling course and in between we listened to lectures on how to keep up communication in open warfare. These in our humble opinion were a lot of nonsense, but good fun. It was laughable in a way to hear lectures on a subject on which a good many of us could have lectured the lecturers. Their ideas and maxims came from training manuals.

In the tent with Mundy and I were a couple of smooth-faced " Highlanders," whose speech betrayed the fact that they had been born within sound of the Bow Bells, a young Yorkshire sergeant, a quiet reserved R.E. signaller and a handsome, reckless-looking young Australian. Mundy and his " Jock " townsmen quickly became bosom pals and his great horse-laugh was continually sounding.

There was nothing very surprising in Cockneys in kilts. Cockneys were being drafted into nearly every corps and regiment of the British Army. They were young, thin-faced and often of poor physique. Their advent in an infantry battalion was a sign that that particular crush was on its last legs as regards replacements.

By natural gravitation I knocked about with the Sergeant, the R.E. and the digger. The last named had left his mob with another Corporal, but only the one had reached the school.

Digger's explanation was somewhat garbled, but we gathered that they had got drunk at some village on the way down the line and lost each other. There had been a girl mixed up in it somehow.

" He will be all right. He'll wake up sober some morning and go back to the battalion or lorry-hop down to the school here," he said off-handedly.

Put that way it seemed an affair of no great importance, and yet I marvelled. In our lot he would very likely have been shot as a deserter.

" He's a nice fellow, isn't he ? " I said to the merry-faced Sergeant. I liked the Sergeant and didn't mind letting him see that I was rather raw, although I wouldn't have let the R.E. see it for worlds. Engineers weren't entitled to the confidences and friendships of infantrymen.

" Why, of course he is," said the Sergeant. " Take my tip, and you'll find that it's true. You couldn't meet a nicer, decenter fellow than an Aussie in France—when he's on his own, that is. But put two or three of them together and you wouldn't find bigger blackguards anywhere."

Knowing nothing about Australians I accepted his word at the time anyhow, but for all that there was a glamour about an Australian that was sadly lacking in home troops.

They preserved some idea of freedom in the serfdom of the war and refused to bow down blindly to stupid authority. They carried on a feud with the Red Caps and according to rumour had killed not a few. In the Jock mutiny at Etaples they had been sent to restore order and had joined forces with the mutineers against the common enemy. Then the Guards had been sent.

Digger wore a beautifully made uniform and expensive boots. In addition he was well supplied with money, even for an Aussie. At the weekly pay parade he drew an enormous fistful of notes in comparison to our meagre allowance.

After " pay," which was every Saturday, the " students " invariably celebrated by getting drunk.

The first time I set off with my three chums for the village nearby. As usual, I was shy in front of strangers, more on account of one being a Sergeant and another a wealthy Australian, but the feeling quickly wore off. The Sergeant was as unaffected as man could be, with a shrewd, kindly humour that demanded response.

The Digger was a harum-scarum fellow, always up to some devilment. Invariably when in his cups he insisted on telling us that his father either was or had been Lord Mayor of Sydney—I was never sure which—a statement which we always believed implicitly at the time and wholeheartedly disbelieved when we were sober and in our right mind. The odd part of it was that he might have been telling the truth for all we knew.

We crowded into the local estaminet and were soon well and truly drunk. Digger insisted on ordering champagne and the Sergeant and R.E. Corporal, not to be outdone, ordered vin blanc. A compromise was arrived at by filling each glass half full of vin and then pouring the champagne on top. Seeing that I was only a Lance-Corporal in the infantry the others objected to my paying anything, but I insisted on going my whack—of the vin blanc. That was a compromise, too, but things were hazy by then and we ended up by drinking more of the bubbly than we could well hold. We reeled back to camp. The others were sick and lay on the grass retching. At first I wasn't a bit sick, but the sight of the others made me think I should be, so I put my finger down my throat and vomited in company. The four of us became bosom pals. Although the Digger had compatriots in another part of the camp he stuck to us. The R.E. was the butt of much good-natured sarcasm, but as he was on a Brigade Headquarters working up to battalion there wasn't much sting in it. Each of us gave free rein to his personality and fitted in wonderfully well considering that we were total strangers and would be dispersed to what corresponded to the four corners of the earth in a few weeks' time.

I was by far the least colourful of the four, and wondered why they seemed to like me. The handsome young Aussie was a figure of romance with his slim figure and feathered hat. He was generosity itself and hated nothing more than being told that he was paying for more than his fair share.

" Us bastards have the money and you bastards haven't, so we are all bastards together," was the way he put it.

When with them I hardly knew myself. I lost my self-consciousness and when half fuddled delivered myself of all manner of curious ideas that I hadn't known were in me until the wine brought them tumbling out. The others clapped me on the back and the fun would end with us staggering back to camp singing.

Even when we were vomiting the drink up we were able to laugh at each other. I belonged to the front line fraternity at last—if only for a time.

On occasion I was as reckless as Digger.

Rumour had it that a young war widow, the village laundry woman, was complaisant.

One velvety summer night, inflamed by a long day in the burning sun and the mixture of champagne and vin blanc, we dodged past the camp guard at the risk of being caught and sent back to our units, and proceeded down to the village.

The laundry woman lived in the end house. We knocked cautiously at the window of her bedroom—it was a single-storey cottage—and waited impatiently for a reply. None came. We knocked again—a little louder.

An overmastering excitement seized me as I pictured the pretty Frenchwoman being awakened by our tapping and coming to the window in her thin white night-gown. There would be a complaisant " Que voulez-vous, messieurs ? " I suddenly felt sober. My throat felt dry, and I had difficulty keeping my teeth firmly set.

But it was not to be. A woman's voice sounded certainly, but querulous, as if her good name was in danger. The window jerked up and a man's gruff tones came.

" What do you think you're on ? Go to hell out of this."

I thought I recognised one of the instructors' voices.

" Go to hell yourself, you perishing base wallah," roared Digger, and put his elbow through the glass, spoiling for a fight. The woman screamed.

A volley of oaths came from the room. Looking through the window I glimpsed a half-naked man with his back turned feeling his way along past a bed.

There was the sound of a door being unbarred. In the next cottage a window went up and a head peeped out. Grasping Digger by the arm I made off at a staggering run which lasted until we had reached the other end of the village street. We halted, breathless, and strained our ears for sounds of pursuit, but none came.

The sun burned us to a mahogany brown. We sweated at flag drill and lay on the baked ground taking practice messages. We went on long excursions, keeping up com-

munication by various means. We became expert helio-
graphers and at night we winked code messages, five letters
to a word, to each other by electric signalling lamps. It was
tiresome enough work, but we enjoyed every minute. It
was all child's play to the likes of us. The instructors were
the ones who sweated most. I loved the hearty meals in the
open and the long lines of trim tents. I loved our tent,
where we foregathered in between times. At night after
returning from the village, when candles were lit, a far-off
tent would start a song. Others joined in and the simple
melodies pierced us to the heart in the friendly darkness as
every man added his voice.

But best of all I loved the silence at night and the murmur
of hidden voices raised in friendly argument. When it was
too hot for the tent I lay outside listening contentedly.
Regretfully I would go to sleep, thinking of the hours of
pleasant consciousness I was missing, but consoled by the
thought that in the morning early when Reveille blew there
would be the joyous skelter to the wash house and afterwards breakfast at the long trestle-table. Once a week we
went down to a big barn and splashed each other in tubs filled
with lukewarm water.

One night the distant thunder of heavy gun-fire came to
us from the front. At the bottom of the dark horizon faint
flashes rose and waned in an unending succession. We
gathered in little groups and commented in low voices. The
days were flying and already the course was at the beginning
of the end.

Next morning we were served out with telescopes for
reading distant flag stations. As we lay in pairs on the
ground waiting to start, a curious idea came to me. It was
midday and the sun scorched us.

" What would happen if a fellow looked through the
telescope at the sun ? " I asked the Engineer who was with
me, as if it was only an idle thought.

" Why, it would roast the eye out of you," he said, surprised apparently at the simplicity of the question.

I lay and considered. Up the line men were lying in shell-holes, being killed off like rats. In another fortnight I would be up there too, and the school would be a thing of the past. Life at the front would be harder to bear because I knew better how to enjoy it. They were only passing friends at the school, but they afforded some proof that I wasn't really a solitary fellow, or a complete failure at being a man. The Sergeant liked me, I knew. So did Digger. The R.E. was more taciturn and therefore harder to understand, but he was, after all, an R.E.

" What would happen if a man looked through the telescope at the sun ? "

I looked at the instructor. He was fairly stout, with a trim black moustache. He wore a Jock cap-badge and a smart tunic, and rolled his r's. He would continue to eat good food and live in safety till the end of the war, and draw good pay for it. Perhaps he would be instructing a fresh squad when——

I lifted the telescope, filled with sudden resolution, and then put it down.

Which eye was the rifle eye ? It was a long time since I had fired a so-called musketry course. I was left-handed' which somehow complicated matters.

Which eye ? It would be stupid if I looked at the sun through the wrong eye and found myself still able to aim with the other.

I debated the matter. In imagination I closed one eye and then the other and stared along the sights in a vain effort to remember. And then a host of difficulties came. How would I explain that I had felt a sudden desire to look at the blazing sun through a telescope ? What accident could I think of to work the oracle ? The R.E. might be wrong about the blindness, and it would only hurt without doing any actual damage. And how was it that nobody else had tried the same stunt before ? Otherwise we wouldn't have been trusted with telescopes. Regretfully I gave up the idea. The sun shone mockingly, a ball of fire in the grey-blue sky. I would have sacrificed an eye cheerfully if I could have got away with it.

THE HARPY

THERE were no parades on Sundays at the school. We had made it up to walk into Boulogne, but at the last minute the Sergeant and the R.E. were too lazy and refused to go. Digger and I started off by ourselves as much out of bravado as anything else. Boulogne was twenty-five kilos away, and the day was hot.

"That lousy grip isn't worth walking five kilos to, let alone twenty-five," jeered the Sergeant with the air of a man to whom Boulogne was an old story. "And you'll have to horse it back, remember, when you get out of the Red Lamp."

"We can have as many fall-outs as we like," I said, struck by the novelty of route-marching at our own pleasure and being able to stop, go on, or turn back, according to how we felt.

We went off after breakfast and walked leisurely for an hour, smoking and yarning. At our first halt nature called us off the road. When we had finished I discovered hundreds of tiny creatures scurrying through the grass carrying things on their backs. Digger said it was an ants' nest, and I knelt down staring at them fascinated, forgetting about Boulogne.

"Look, they're actually carrying packs," I said excitedly, wondering where they were bound for.

"For Heaven's sake come on, or we'll never get there," said Digger.

I got to my feet and went on regretfully, making a mental resolve to visit that field again. Ants were interesting things.

The road was as straight as a die and lined with trees planted at regular intervals.

Gradually march discipline ruled us, and we tramped doggedly on and fell out for the regulation halt for all the world as if we were marching with a battalion. Villages were few and far between, and we felt guilty when we stopped at one along the road and drank a couple of glasses of vin rouge.

When we arrived at last we had an uncomfortable sense that the Sergeant's estimate was about right. Instead of being thronged with people, as we had fondly hoped, the streets were almost deserted. Here and there a wrecked house testified to a successful air-raid. The few British troops strolling about were different from the troops we knew. They wore natty, waisted tunics and sported creased slacks and mahogany brown shoes, with belts to match. They had an air of calm assurance, as if each of them spoke French fluently, and was quite at home among French people. Our dusty uniforms looked raw and ugly.

Occasionally a woman in widow's weeds glided past with downcast eyes carrying a prayer book. They had pale, secretive faces, and their indifference made me feel like a stupid barbarian. With my handkerchief I wiped my face, and then my boots, and tightened my belt. My uniform wasn't a very good fit, and my puttees looked rough. It took a fairly big tunic to fit me about the shoulders, but I wasn't stout enough to fill it properly. I was uncomfortably aware that it stuck out in an ugly pout behind. Digger, being an Aussie, naturally looked better, but he was angry.

"And we put one foot in front of another for umpteen kilometres to look at that there," he said morosely as one of the dandies stopped for a moment in front of us. We had sat down to rest on a bench under a tree. We watched him draw a piece of gleaming white cambric from his sleeve and blow his nose delicately into it. He replaced it so as to leave the hem sticking out, and moved on leisurely

U

I sat silent, glancing about me with hungry eyes, loath to be utterly disappointed.

"I'd cheerfully do ten years just to get rolling that lad in a dirty shell-hole," muttered Digger.

After a while the high boulevard where we sat became more popular as the inhabitants woke up or came out from Mass, but still we were completely out of it.

We got up and wandered about aimlessly. Even in the daytime the town seemed a dark, repellent place except for the high tree-lined boulevard leading into it.

I noticed a place down a side-street with a notice in the window that French lessons were given free, and felt a momentary pang that I could not avail myself of the offer as my old love of languages recurred to me.

"Well, we'll have steak and chips, anyway," said Digger. "I could eat a man off his horse."

We left the main streets and halted outside a mysterious-looking little café. It was somehow more French-looking than the others we had passed. Hunger decided us.

A sharp-featured woman, rather elderly and dressed in a prim black gown that rustled, came towards us from the rear of the premises. A bright silver crucifix hung on her non-existent breasts. She had a well-defined moustache.

"Avez-vous pommes de terre frites, avec bifstec?"

"Qu'est-ce que vous dites?" said Madame.

"Avez-vous——" commenced Digger hesitatingly when Madame interrupted.

"Steak and cheeps, eh?"

"Oui, oui, madame."

"Vin blanc? Vin rouge? Champagne?"

"Vin blanc," I put in quickly.

"Champagne," said Digger.

"The vin's enough," I said in a hoarse aside. "I'm no Aussie."

" Aw, have a running race at yourself," replied Digger, also aside, and then, to Madame :

" Vin blanc et champagne, s'il vous plaît."

" The same damn mixture," he said to me, laughing, in the same tone.

Madame looked puzzled for a moment and then bobbed and smiled.

" Oui, oui, messieurs, tout de suite."

The old lady disappeared and presently returned with the bottles.

" C'est beaucoup tranquille, ici—it's very quiet here, madame," said Digger restlessly, speaking in both bats to make sure that she understood.

Madame shrugged her shoulders expressively, and smiled a thin smile to show that she understood—both ways. Coming closer she looked at us sharply, her dull black eyes lighting up momentarily.

" Vous desirez mademoiselle, messieurs ? " she asked with a sharp, upward inflexion.

" What about it ? " said Digger, turning to me. " She wants to know do we want a couple of girls."

Then speaking very quickly so that the old woman wouldn't catch what he said, he added eagerly :

" We can see what the floosies are like and beat off if we don't fancy them, eh ? What about it ? "

I nodded dumbly, making a brave pretence of being casual. The little tables in the gloomy room, shut off from the sunlight outside, had a sinister air and I shrank from the shadows that wavered across the smutty ceiling and hid the far corners. Passion, cold and bedraggled and commercial, and yet strangely alluring, rose before me almost like a living thing. I wanted to run and wanted to stay, knowing that every passing second made the circumstances more irrevocable. It was impossible to go because we had had no food yet and had barely touched the wine.

Raising the bottle of bubbly Digger filled my glass and his own. I emptied mine and, lighting a cigarette, smoked furiously, my mind made up.

A couple of girls appeared, each carrying a tray of food, and came laughingly towards us.

One of them was tall and robust. She had blunt, rather handsome features, and bright red hair. The last struck me as comic in a French girl. The other was very young—not much more than sixteen or seventeen, I judged—and was darkly, childishly pretty, with a pale oval face and regular features.

" Ginger," as Digger immediately dubbed her, struck me, for all my inexperience, as being a dame with a good eye to the main chance, and no chicken to boot. She made no bones about laying claim to him. In a minute she was helping herself to his glass.

She knew where the money was.

The other girl was different. She set the plate down in front of me, and, like myself, seemed at a loss what to do.

Ginger glanced at her sharply. She sat down beside me and put her hand on my arm with a little deprecatory smile.

I was stupidly aloof. It was odd enough to be eating food after the civilised manner. The girl looking on turned my fingers into thumbs. I ate without knowing what I was eating, stealing glances at her when I thought she wasn't looking. She sensed my shyness, and seemed to derive courage from it. More and more often I caught her dark eyes fixed on mine. I thought I detected a little spark of friendly encouragement in them.

Suddenly she nestled up beside me, and said something in rapid French.

I shook my head ruefully.

We looked at each other nonplussed, and then smiled, our eyes leaping the barrier of language.

" If I saw it in writing I might know what she's driving

at," I thought, and produced an old envelope and stub of pencil.

I leant over her shoulder as she wrote in round, ill-formed characters :

" Mais comme vous êtes jeune ! "

" Vous aussi," I wrote back, and we laughed a little breathlessly.

" Quel est votre nom ? " I wrote slowly.

" Yvonne. Et le vôtre ? "

Pushing my plate away I slid an arm round her, bending down until our lips were an inch apart. For a long moment we stared into each other's eyes and then a slight pressure on the back of my head brought my mouth to hers. A fleeting glance at Digger showed me Ginger ensconced on his knee. Pushing the table out of the way I drew Yvonne unresistingly on to mine and held her close.

Whether it was her dark hair and red lips set in a pale oval face, or the contact of her warm body I couldn't say, but for the first time for long enough I thought of the girl in the camp. They were each of an age with slim bodies and immature curves covered by a wispy frock, but there the resemblance ended. The one at home had been a little wildcat. The girl on my knee was firing my brain with passionate kisses and running her fingers caressingly through my hair to the accompaniment of murmured words that I hardly needed to understand. My unsatisfied longings came back with a rush. Here was the opportunity at last. Another few days and it would be " Up the line and the best of luck," as the base wallahs said to the drafts.

I drank glass after glass of wine, and remained sober. Yvonne sipped delicately each time before I drank. Her eyes sparkled and then grew humid.

Digger and Ginger had been hitting the bottle more than we had. They were rather dishevelled.

He started a broken conversation with her, which ended

in his pulling a wad of ten-franc bills and passing several over. Ginger seized on them avidly. Pulling up her skirt, she pushed them down the top of her stocking.

" How much are you giving her ? " I asked in alarm, and in turn pulled out my stock of wealth, three soiled five-franc notes. I eyed them disconsolately.

" Find out how much your dame wants. I'll make up the difference."

I looked diffidently at Yvonne, knowing in my heart that we had gone beyond money, but with a sudden doubt that maybe that was all it amounted to.

" Combien, mademoiselle ? " I asked with downcast eyes.

" She has to earn her living, so it's not really her fault," I thought as a chill came over me at the thought of money. " I'll not look at her till she answers."

She was lying with her head on my shoulder, hot and flushed, her eyes half-closed. Disregarding her I reached over and, filling my glass, tossed it off at a gulp. Reckless-ness welled up in me, and I mumbled a string of unmeaning oaths. For a long moment Yvonne was silent. Then she broke into a rapid patter, getting more excited as she went on. She didn't glance my way and I wondered what it was all about. Ginger listened, stared, shrugged her shoulders, and laughed indulgently before relaying the message to Digger.

" Lord, but you're lucky," said the latter enviously as he got the purport of it. " The kid says she won't take any money. She only wants five francs to pay the patronne for the bed. She'll do the rest ' pour l'amour '."

" Pour what ? "

" For love, you fool."

A glow, which had nothing to do with the wine, came over me. If I had had a thousand francs I would gladly have slipped them down her stocking " pour l'amour."

I felt suddenly sorry for handsome, reckless Digger as he

stumbled up the flight of dark stairs before me, half dragging and half hanging on to his companion.

" He deserves another Yvonne," I thought, and stole another kiss as we followed slowly behind.

We came to a dark landing. I stopped irresolutely. The pair in front disappeared into a room off it. Yvonne pressed my arm and led the way along a narrow passage and into a little room at the end. We went in, and she closed the door gently behind me. A small window adorned with a pair of dingy curtains admitted some light to the room. There was one chair against the wall, one narrow bed opposite it and a chipped washstand in a corner. There was a strip of old lino before the bed. Some soiled underwear hung on a nail behind the door. Yvonne pointed silently to the chair. I sat down and commenced fumbling at my puttees. She busied herself about the bed, patting out the creases and shaking the pillow. My puttees came off and I fumbled with the laces of my boots. With a quick movement Yvonne drew her thin dress over her head and draped it over the rail of the bed. I lowered my eyes and made a great show of taking off my boots. She had on a lacy petticoat. Waves of shyness and self-consciousness swept over me. I realised with a shock that I was actually alone with a girl in a bed-room. The bed, which at first glance had seemed a common-place piece of furniture, was an ominous, almost menacing thing. In sudden panic I wished myself back listening to the Sergeant and talking of bygone battles and escapes. But, try as I would, I couldn't keep my eyes down.

In a moment Yvonne stood before me in her long black stockings and shiny shoes—a study in black and white, straight, slim, and yet rounded, and infinitely desirable.

THE UNLUCKY LAD

DIGGER was sober, and rather quiet, as we started on the long tramp back to Camp. It was getting late and we knew we would have to step out briskly to get in by midnight. We left the town behind and slogged along the broad straight road. The rays of the setting sun were pleasantly warming. The road was deserted except for our two selves. It looked strange, somehow, as if our stay among bricks and mortar and paved streets had lasted a long time and we required to be freshly introduced to the dusty way. I was in no mood for talking, and Digger was the first to break the silence when we got into the country.

" I wonder was she all right ? " he said, more to himself than to me. The question seemed to be the culmination of a long and involved process of introspection.

I didn't reply.

After a while he repeated it—as if I knew. But I could see that he was worried and did my best to put the notion that she wasn't out of his head.

Digger became silent again.

I looked at him affectionately as he strode along beside me, slim-hipped and debonair, his fine, rather rakish uniform setting off his suppleness. Aussies always reminded me of pictures of cavaliers.

" Maybe it's because they're dressed differently that makes them good fighters—that and the big pay," I thought. The very idea of him contracting some loathsome disease because of an hour's adventure was ridiculous. I laughed at his fears.

" How did you get on with your dame ? " he asked after a pause, but I shied at replying.

" Oh, not so bad," I said casually, as if being with a girl was mere ham and eggs, as the married men used to say in the camp at home after a week-end leave.

" You had to buy your fun, so you're at liberty to talk about it as much as you like," I thought to myself, " but mine was ' pour l'amour,' and that makes all the difference in the world."

It smacked too much of treachery to give a cold-blooded recital of the little intimate ways of Yvonne.

" I promised faithfully to go back next Sunday," I added, to give a slightly different twist to the conversation.

" You'd be a mug if you didn't, lucky lad," said Digger.

" But what about you—are you going back to see Ginger?"

" I'll be able to tell you better by next Sunday."

We stopped at a wayside estaminet and had a couple of drinks to buck us up. It was pleasant to sit in the cool room and watch gnarled, corduroyed labourers eating crisp white rolls and coarse salad from a dish, and drinking vin rouge as if it was an everyday affair. From time to time one would utter hoarse, nasal sounds, and the others muttered " Way, way " without looking up. A buxom woman looked at them maternally and a mangy dog nosed about patiently for scraps.

It was a simple, peaceful place and I felt curiously sorry to leave it. It was odd, too, to hear old farm labourers talking in French, because it was their mother tongue and not a painfully-acquired accomplishment. It didn't seem right.

We walked on. Digger became livelier and we talked disjointedly of everything under the sun, except of when the war would end. The idea of it coming to an end some day never occurred to us or we might have discussed that too. It was only natural that we had lived through some of it, that at the front it was going on that evening, and that some time in the near future we would have to go back to it.

By and by Digger monopolised the conversation, but I was a poor listener. No matter how I tried to keep my mind fixed on what he was saying my thoughts kept returning to Yvonne.

I edged Digger on to the topic of Australia and what a fine place it was, but for all the heed I paid he might as well have been talking of China or Timbuktoo.

" Is that so ? "   " Go on ! "   " You don't say ? "   I encouraged him at appropriate intervals and carried on with my own surging thoughts.

It was with a start that I recognised the dark outlines of the village near the camp on the road ahead and heard Digger still talking by my side.

Wednesday came, and I was beginning to forget the events of the preceding Sunday in contemplation of the Sunday to come when a new factor upset everything. Several of the men in our squad didn't put in an appearance at the morning parade. In the afternoon a few more were absent. On Thursday the parade was about half its usual strength. A feeling of surprise, tinged with alarm, possessed us. It was the 'flu, whatever that was. Ambulances were soon making hourly visits to the school. The victims were carried into them and taken away to places unknown. Men who were the picture of health one minute dropped off their feet the next as if they had been poleaxed. In the space of a day or two instruction became a farce. The mysterious plague became the sole topic of conversation.

My turn came and I was whisked away after developing an amazingly high temperature in a remarkably short time. One minute I was all right and the next I was burning and shaking by turns. The ambulance ride was a blur. Then I found myself stretched out on the grass in a crowded bell tent. There was no sign of a doctor and I suffered from an all-consuming thirst. An overworked orderly brought round hot milk in a bucket and dished out drinks. I went to sleep. When I awoke it was only to gulp down more hot milk. More sleep.

It was all over in forty-eight hours. The convalescents sat outside sunning themselves in deck-chairs. We exchanged milk food for ordinary grub and felt hungry after each meal. When we got up to walk about we felt weak.

It was a pleasant place. I would willingly have sat in the deck-chair for the duration, feeling the sun on my face and staring at the green grass and the shady trees. It was as quiet as being in church listening to a drowsy sermon.

The orderly told us that some men had died, but it was hard to believe.

For a couple of days we lived like gentlemen of leisure, but it was too good to last. We returned to the school the way we had come. I felt about half a stone lighter, but otherwise there were no ill-effects.

The school was a thing of the past. Most of the tents were down and most of the men had disappeared into hospitals or returned to their units. Ugly, circular patches of yellow withered grass marked where the tents had stood. Only a few of the staff of instructors remained. They had the preoccupied air of men who had received bad news. All the snap had gone out of them.

They had to go back up the line to their units, it was rumoured.

Mundy still remained—waiting for me, he said—so why the devil hadn't I stopped in hospital and swung the lead for a few more days. The Yorkshire Sergeant was there, too. We hung about at a loose end. There had been no pay-out on the previous Saturday and consequently nobody had any money. There was no use in going into the village. I inquired about the Digger.

" He went off with the rest of the Aussies who were at

the far end of the camp," said the Sergeant, laughing at some memory. " What were the pair of you up to down at Boulogne that Sunday, eh ? You've a lot to answer for. That's you young fellows all over. You don't know what to be at." He spoke with mock severity.

" We were with a couple of girls—they were in a café we went to for some grub."

" A couple of trollops," broke in Mundy, and launched into a great laugh.

" And I promised faithfully to go down and see mine on Sunday. That was last Sunday. She'll think I was only laughing at her."

A poignant sense of what I had missed obsessed me. I felt sad, but the well-developed instinct to hide my feelings came to my aid.

" Why, what about them ? Had Digger the 'flu, too ? What's the joke ? "

" The 'flu ? " echoed the Sergeant. " No fear."

" Well, what was it ? "

The Sergeant shrugged his shoulders.

" Use your imagination," said Mundy, with his great haw-haw.

The time dragged heavily. The deserted camp was an omen. When we were ordered to take down our tent and hand it into store we knew it was time to bid good-bye. Late in the afternoon a lorry arrived and Mundy and I, along with a couple of Corporals, climbed in and deposited our packs and equipment. The other two were Scotsmen from a strange Division who were going in the same direction as we were. Our chum, the merry, red-faced Sergeant, shook hands and wished us luck.

When we departed he stood in the middle of the road waving.

" He was a fine lad, that Sergeant," said Mundy.

I didn't speak, but ever afterwards I looked upon Yorkshiremen as friends. The lorry gathered speed. I took a silent, fond farewell of the school and of the village, and of the big, spotlessly clean farm-house up the lane where we used to go on Sunday mornings and drink glasses of sweet milk until we were almost ready to vomit.

It had struck me as remarkable that a man's capacity for sweet milk is strictly limited. I had thought that applied only to liquor.

I bade farewell to Yvonne. " The Kid," as Digger had called her. It seemed strange that at that very minute she was in her dark, shabby café in a Boulogne side-street. I hadn't turned up, and she would be a little bit more cynical now. If she thought of me at all, that was. Probably she would be perched on someone else's knee, egging him on to drink wine. There would be a long, long succession of customers for her charms.

The unlucky lad !

THE RETURN

THE setting sun shone redly. The familiar landscape was left behind. The lorry sped on, rattling and bumping. The country-side lost its old-world peacefulness and took on a gloomy, threatening air. We reached the main road leading to the front and mingled with a stream of traffic moving up. The sound of the guns which for weeks had been little more than a rumble became ominously louder as every turn of the wheels brought us nearer and nearer, instead of away from the front as they had done a few short weeks before.

" There must be a big strafe on somewhere," said Mundy, cocking his ears.

" Is there ever anything else where we're going, nowadays ? " said one of the strangers morosely. " The war has gone to hell. I remember the time when it was cushy enough—in and out, in and out with only a few shells at night and some sniping in the daytime."

" Aye," said his mate, " but July, 1916, tore it, Bill, and it's never been the same since. Now, a mob gets it in the neck somewhere and you get a crowd of perishers scraped up from anywhere and in you go again. The Bat is supposed to be as good as ever. Half of them couldn't beat eggs."

" That's the truth," said Bill. " There's hardly a single unit in France, but what's full of kids who don't know a whizz-bang from a 5·9, or else they're made up of any ragtag or bobtail they can lay hands on. We've got about a hundred R.A.O.C. all the way from Paris. They were sewing buttons and stitching patches on dead men's tunics and trousers there. That's all they knew about the war. If it wasn't for the artillery banging away at Jerry all the time, ay, and ready to smash into us if need be, the war would have been over long ago. In 1916 our Red Tabs made a mess of it and the same in 1917. They get away with it, but if some fellow up the line goes off his head and makes a break for it he's shot."

The guns came louder. The Signal School and all its ways faded into the past. The others smoked and went on with their bitter, impotent talk. I paid no further heed.

" There won't be any more courses and a fellow can't expect to escape the shells all the time," I thought as the sky darkened and far ahead flickering lights appeared, white and ghostly, on the horizon. I felt very insignificant.

It was night when we drew up outside a big wooden hut with a tarred, sloping roof. We gathered up our kit and got out stiffly, looking inquiringly at the driver.

He poked his head round the hood.

" All out, Corp ? " he said to Mundy.

" What are you stopping here for ? " asked the latter, perplexed. " We've a goodish distance to go yet, you know."

" This is where you get off," said the driver, grinning maliciously, and started off with a roar down the street.

The other two talked for a moment and then went off with muttered so-longs, leaving us on our own.

" The Division must be about here," I said optimistically, staring about the dark street, half expecting a guide to materialise.

We stared up and down, but nobody came. We looked at each other.

" To the devil with this for a stunt," said Mundy crossly. " Do they think we're thought-readers and know just where to go ? It's six weeks since we left and the Division might be in hell for all we know. I wish it was."

We went into the hut. It was taken up by long rows of trestle tables and their accompanying forms. An old orderly man pottered about. He looked at us suspiciously when we went over to him, and shook his head when we asked where the Division was. We might have been a couple of tramps on the bum the way he eyed us askance.

We went into the street again and loafed about uncomfortably, but nobody passed and we moved along slowly, beginning to think more of a bed-down for the night than finding our unit. We came out on to a broader street. On the footpath on the other side a long line of men were queued up. It was odd in that dark town to see men lined up for admittance somewhere. Some Divisional show, or a Red Lamp, perhaps. They gave me an impression of remoteness standing there patient and silent. I made no effort to go over to them.

Mundy went over, but came back shaking his head.

" No luck," he said shortly, and although I knew he must have asked what the hell they were waiting for I did not ask what the explanation was.

" Let the Division go for the night," he said. " There should have been a guide to meet us, so it's their own look-out."

We sought out the old man in the dining-hut and scrounged a dixie of tea and some bread and cheese. Afterwards, with his grudging assent, we threw off our equipment and, pulling our greatcoats over us, selected a table each and lay down and slept.

In the morning we inquired right and left for the whereabouts of the Division, but all we got in return was blank stares or curt negatives.

" They don't know and they don't care," I said at last.

" You'd nearly think they'd never heard of the Division," said Mundy. " But what can you expect of a lot of dud mechanics and A.S.C.—a pack of line-dodgers. These R.A.F. pretend they're not in the same Army."

We cadged a scrappy breakfast of the orderly man. He

was already tired of our importunings, and made no bones about showing his feelings. We left under an immense debt of gratitude.

"The old skinflint—you'd think he was paying for it," said Mundy when we had shouldered our packs and departed.

"They'll know farther on," Mundy said hopefully. "It's nearer the line, so we're going in the right direction, worse luck."

It was pleasant enough to be slouching along in the sunshine at our leisure with the feeling that we were our own masters for the last time. We were going nearer the line, so naturally were in no great hurry. The dry ditches looked inviting after every couple of kilometres.

"I wonder how the battalion has been going on since we left it?" remarked my companion thoughtfully on one of our frequent rests. "It all depends, of course, where they've been and whether they were in any big shows. They might even have been in some footling do and got knocked to scrapings. Many a time a mob is let in for something that's hardly worth mentioning in despatches—especially if it wasn't a success—and there's not a word about it, although they might as well have been in a regular full-dress affair as regards casualties." There had been no newspapers at the school, so we were completely in the dark.

A selfish wish came to me. It would be great if the Division had just got it in the neck the day before we arrived and had to be withdrawn from the line for a month's rest and refit. It would pass unnoticed that we two hadn't been there to share in it, and we would enjoy all the advantages. The Division was only an abstraction. I hoped that our luck was in. We had another rest and lay watching the lazy smoke from our cigarettes curling upwards, at peace with all the world. A big car appeared and came swiftly towards us. Behind it the dust billowed and instinctively I drew a deep breath of pure air. It was a big, open touring car with a

x

little flag in front. Two officers in the back seat turned and stared at us disapprovingly. They were young and red-tabbed. We felt uncomfortable and, getting to our feet, went on.

" Did they expect us to jump to our feet and salute like jack-in-the-boxes," said Mundy viciously. " Those lads give me the pip. They never had such a good time before, ordering men about, and they never will have again—men that could be their fathers."

We reached the little town on the hill, and sat down on a convenient doorstep for a blow. A little further down on the opposite side a smart sentry marched up and down before a long grey building.

" What's the idea of that ? " I asked.

" Who knows," said Mundy. " It's probably a head-quarters of some kind with some old General dug in."

A car came up the dusty street. The sentry sprang to attention. Some officers alighted, laughing and talking gaily. They were beautifully dressed. Their breeches were almost white and their boots and Sam Brownes sparked in the sun.

Mundy got hastily to his feet.

" Come on," he said, " or they'll send somebody along to find out what we're doing here. I don't know what the German airmen are thinking of that they don't drop a few good, hefty bombs here some time and blow their brains out, if they have any." We went down the long, straggling street and inquired of one or two passing soldiers, but without result.

" It's getting beyond a joke," said Mundy as we cleared the town and started down the hill.

" It's funny that nobody seems to know anything about it at all," I said. It was hard to believe that 7000 or 8000 men could be lost so easily."

" Would they have been sent to Italy, d'ye think ? There

was a rumour just before we left for the course that some Divisions were going to go there on account of the Ice-creamios taking to their heels when Jerry came over and shook his fist at them."

Visions of a long train journey came to me to a sunny, indistinct place where the war would be a more adventurous affair and British troops rare birds who would be received everywhere with open arms.

" It would be nice if that was the way of it."

" Ay, a cake-walk, you bet, compared to this God-forsaken front."

A heavy lorry lumbered past in a cloud of dust. Mundy spat.

We came to a cross-roads and wandered off to the left on spec. A little way along it we saw a crowd of French soldiers encamped in a field. We stood looking at them for a few minutes, and then went on. A hundred yards farther on we met a little group of the Froggies on the road. They were in pairs and each pair carried a bluish, cylindrical pail filled to the brim with red wine. They went carefully, laughing and joking the while, as the wine slopped from one edge to the other. I would have liked nothing better than a dixieful, and so would Mundy, but we didn't like to ask. It would have been too much like cadging. They took no notice of us, and, besides, they were foreigners. When they were past we stood looking longingly after them. Wine was an issue with them, like bully beef stew with us. The wine seemed more civilised.

We came to a tiny village and prowled about. It was a pretty place, and we looked about us with an indefinable sense of satisfaction. Each house had a little kitchen garden attached, and here and there a big barn. There were no inhabitants to be seen. We sniffed about like stray dogs. Some women's stuff hung drying on a line—a pair of cloth bloomers and coloured petticoats.

It was good to be alive, but our packs felt heavy, and we were hungry. We left the village reluctantly and went on. Still, we were on our own, and free.

" We're about due for another fall-out, Corp., aren't we ? " I ventured after covering a couple of kilos.

" Right you are. There's no use in horsing it," said Mundy magnanimously.

We sat down in the ditch.

" Yes," he said fondly. " Italy would be the stuff to give 'em—with knobs on. The Italian girls would be a change, too. We haven't an earthly. And then the booze. It's past all buying. Half a franc for a glass of French beer and you might as well be swallowing water, and the same for a mouthful of their rotten vin blanc. It would put you in the rats if you took a couple or three bottles running. The price of everything goes up every day, but our alleged pay doesn't. We'll get to Italy—I don't think. Some crowd that aren't worth their meat will be sent there out of harm's way and we'll be here for the duration."

" You'd be as well here after all," I pointed out. " You'd have to start in to learn the lingo a bit to be able to parley the bat with the Signoritas."

We were famished now, and thirsty. Being on our own had its drawbacks. I was for going back and reporting ourselves.

" We'll get a square meal, anyway," I argued. " We could go to the headquarters there and find out what to do, instead of wandering about like a pair of lost sheep."

" No fear," said Mundy. " Why, man, you wouldn't go very far from here until some lousy Red Cap of a policeman would have us arrested for desertion. We're all right so long as we keep going forward. Nobody bothers then. There's no such thing, as far as I ever heard, of anybody deserting from the base and sloping up the line. But just you try it the other way about and you'll soon wake up. The military police are all over the place. Why, I saw a couple of them back there in Cassel. Didn't you twig them looking at us ? "

I hadn't noticed them, but I took his word for it.

" They're all over the place, like lice on a soldier's shirt," repeated Mundy sagely. " If they weren't, a lot of the boys up the line would damned soon try their luck at getting out of it all. Too true, they would. A few try it as it is, and generally end up against a stone wall with a hanky round their eyes and the padre holding their hands and whispering the Lord's Prayer into their ears."

" But why do they try that game ? " I asked.

" Ay, it's all very well to say that, but that's just where you make the mistake. It's the hardest thing in the world to get away with nowadays," explained Mundy. " You see, a single rifle shot can be heard for far enough. Even when there is a strafe on some officer or Sergeant is bound to hear it and investigate."

" But couldn't a fellow do it when there was some rifle-firing going on ? "

" Did you ever hear any rifle-firing go on up the line in all your bleeding life ? " returned Mundy drily. " I haven't—very seldom anyway—and I've been out since 1916. Of course, you might have heard it during the Retreat, but that's about all."

" You might be right," I said, struck by the question. " I haven't been out very long."

" It doesn't matter. They used to make the boys empty their magazines at the stand-to every morning. They've cut that game out now. Some say it was because nobody ever shot anybody—except when the rookies accidentally shot themselves. But I wouldn't be surprised if it wasn't because the smart-Alecs took the opportunity of shooting themselves on purpose when bullets were flying about promiscuous-like. They had more chance of getting away with it, you see."

" But what do we have to carry rifles for then ? "

" Search me. Because they did it in the Boer War, or in the Crimean War—or when the howling Dervishes came up howling to be shot, so as to get to the bits of skirt in Paradise quick."

I joined in Mundy's hoarse laughter.

" There's damn few want to get to Heaven now," he said. " Not that way, anyway. Soldiers want to die of old age, you can bet your life."

A van came trundling along and drew up at a cottage on the opposite side of the road. The driver, an old bearded Frenchman, got stiffly to the ground. The door of the cottage opened and an old woman came out. The old man delved into the van and handed over a couple of great " cartwheels " to the waiting housewife. The pair gabbled to each other like familiar friends making the most of a short absence.

" I wish we had some cash. We could get that old devil to sell us some du pain if nobody was looking," said Mundy enviously, his mouth watering at the idea.

" If nobody was looking ? " I repeated stupidly.

" They're not supposed, you know, to sell civvy bread to the troops, though they do when they get the chance. Of course, the troops are supposed to get all they need in their rations—what a hope."

I looked on idly, yet hungrily, as the gossiping bread-server collected the money for his du pain. He held up his black bag to poke for change, still talking.

I gripped my companion's arm.

" He dropped something there, as sure as God—a franc piece or something," I whispered excitedly.

" Are you sure ? I didn't see anything."

I didn't answer. The two continued jabbering and gesticulating for a moment or two. I held my breath. Then the woman turned abruptly on her heel and went in, closing the door behind her. The van moved off at a walking pace.

A sigh of relief escaped me.

" Wait a minute longer," cautioned Mundy, half-convinced by my excitement that I was right. " The old chap might look back."

But I was already on my feet, moving as casually as I could across the road. Examining the ground where they had stood I spied in front of me a little white disc in the dust.

" Good for you. You must have weepers like a hawk," said Mundy slapping me on the back, and joyfully snatching the coin—a two-franc piece—out of my hand he ran after the van.

I watched him as he caught up on it and started haggling with the old man, hardly comprehending at first what he was in such a hurry about, but satisfied, with his praise ringing in my ears, that I had done my part.

The bread-server halted his horse and got down. Mundy's arms moved like pistons.

The old man looked timidly up and down the road.

In a minute Mundy came hurrying back. His face was wreathed in smiles. He held a " cartwheel " in one hand and a dirty franc note in the other. A distant rattle of wheels sounded.

" You missed your job," he said with his great haw-haw. " It's a sniper you should be, not a signaller."

" The old madame might have some milk or something in the house to wash it down," I said, eyeing the bread. There was still a franc left.

" That's a bon idea. We might as well eat like Christians for once in our lives."

The franc worked the oracle. Soon we were sitting down at a scrupulously clean table lapping up a big glass each of vin blanc. Mundy, as befitted being Corporal, lopped off chunks of the loaf with his jack-knife, dividing them impartially. The wine was like nectar.

" It's a great life—while you're still alive," he said a while later, stowing the remains of the bread in his haversack. " We won't starve for the rest of the day anyhow. If we had a couple of tots of ration rum now we could let the war go and chase itself for a while. If the old lady here was twenty years younger, and took a sudden liking for us, I wouldn't call the King my uncle. But what's the use of talking ? "

" Ay, she's too damned old for that," I said, thinking of Yvonne.

The day wore on. For all our good fortune our temporary freedom began to get irksome. There was no great fun, after all, in plodding along unknown dusty roads with the prospect of wandering all night or sleeping at the roadside. We debouched on to the main road and slouched along, our packs weighing heavily. It was beginning to get dark, but the steady stream of traffic moving upwards told us we were on the right road. Once or twice we waved at drivers, but they pretended not to see us.

We came to a half-ruined village where there was a cross-roads. It was Something-or-other, like all the villages thereabouts. We had another fall-out and wondered what to do. We had passed out of the civilian zone and broken roofs and gaping walls offered cold comfort. In the gathering darkness the houses took on the strange aloofness that all buildings had near the line.

" We are very old in war," they seemed to say, " so old that we no longer discriminate between friends and foes. Don't count on our bricks and mortar to protect you."

I squatted down on the deserted footpath and rested my

back against the wall of a roofless house. The sough and roar of bursting shells came distinctly from somewhere ahead. I wasn't very anxious to go on.

Once again war struck me as being a very stupid affair— but not so much stupid as blindly malevolent. There was nothing to hinder a shell plunging down among the houses and, incidentally, blowing Mundy and me to bits. And if one did, it meant nothing. The war wouldn't end a second sooner, the scale would not be tipped a fraction either way. We just wouldn't be missed. And the same applied exactly to every soldier in France. Individuals, whether brave or cowardly, were of no account. Only mass massacre satisfied the war-makers. Only mass resistance could destroy them.

We got news of the Division at last. A dispatch rider stopped a few yards from us and alternately cursed and tinkered at his motor-cycle.

" Yes, they're up here somewhere," he said casually in response to the usual question.

We pricked up our ears.

" They've just gone into the line. They were out resting for five or six weeks."

" What's that ? " said Mundy, astonished. " We were beginning to think they had been wiped off the map or had gone to Italy. Nobody knew anything about them, you see."

" Well, that's the reason. They were in Divisional reserve, I think. You'll probably find them on ahead if you just follow your nose. I'm not quite sure what particular sector they are holding, but it's somewhere about here. Inquire as you go along and you'll soon be on the right track."

The dispatch rider got to his feet and wiped his oily hands on his trousers. Straddling his machine he moved his hands expertly over the tank and engine. The engine started with a clatter, and we shouted our thanks as he drove off.

I looked after him enviously. Dispatch riders seemed to have a grasp of things. His casual, well-informed answer explained everything.

" God Almighty," said Mundy, " that tears the whole inside out of it. I see now why they sent us off on a course. The whole flaming Division must have come out the night we left it or the day after—and for six full weeks. The lads in the section have been having a cushy time in some nice village well behind the line, while us poor merchants were hard at it morning, noon and night—sweating away at flag-wagging, dot-dashing at blinking lamps, flappers and discs, squinting at old helios and through telescopes, and listening to a pack of louts yapping about open warfare. They knew more about bun-worrying and beer-burying. And there we were, listening to them, thinking all the time that anyway it was better than being up the line with the mob. Open warfare ! "

An empty feeling assailed me as the fond hope that the Division might have got it in the neck in our absence faded. I discovered dismally that I had been relying on it.

" We might have known there was a catch somewhere," said Mundy disgustedly.

We ate what remained of the du pain and then went on at a brisk pace, anxious to get somewhere before the usual nightly strafing of the back areas began in earnest.

The war came nearer as we passed a village just off the main road. Heavy shells were falling among the houses, sending the bricks flying. As we hurried past I got a whiff of the old, familiar smell of high explosive. A shiver went down my spine, but I kept a straight face. I was back at the old game of trying to hide my feelings. The clanging, evil explosions were like death knells. Mundy stopped for a moment to listen and I, perforce, stopped too.

" Jerry doesn't seem to like that village, eh ? " he said and went on.

When we were safely past I felt ashamed of my fears. After all, the road was a good hundred yards away or more, and there was no use getting windy for nothing with long weeks and months of the line to look forward to.

A couple of hours later we stumbled on our own wagon lines grouped round an old, crumbling farmhouse just off the road. There was no question of going any farther that night. We reported to the R.Q.M.S., who fixed us up with a meal of sorts and quarters in a rickety hayloft. In the morning we had breakfast of tea, dip bread and bacon in the cobbled yard. Afterwards we lay sunning ourselves.

The Transport Officer lived in state on the ground-floor of the farmhouse. The various sheds and stalls round the yard housed the Orderly-room Sergeant, the Sergeant Tailor, Sergeant Bootmaker, Sergeant Farrier, Quarter-blokes and so on—most of whom I had never set eyes on before. Without exception they each sported one red and four blue chevrons on their sleeve and the Mons Star on their chest— a tribute, I took it, not so much to length of service, as to the safety of their jobs. Their bearing suggested that they were pukka soldiers and the men in the line poor imitations whose fate was no concern of THE Battalion of THE Regiment.

The R.Q.M.S. was king of this Regular castle.

We did our dirty best to make a good impression on him, springing smartly to attention and clicking our heels when he addressed us, and sir-ing him liberally in reply. We had the idea that he could prolong our stay with the transport until the battalion came out of the line. We were beginning to catch at crumbs.

He was a peculiar-looking man, very tall and very thin. His complexion was brick-red, and he had the thinnest, sharpest face I ever saw on a man. His hair was red to match. When he spoke to me I tried hard to pretend that I thought him quite natural looking, and to keep the surprise out of my eyes. When he wasn't looking our way I kept staring at him furtively fascinated.

" Hasn't he a head like a Red Indian ? " I whispered to Mundy.

" Like what ! " exclaimed that worthy. " It's more like a bloomin' hatchet. It's the thin end of the wedge come to life, so help me God. Look. Isn't it just like a great, big flea sitting on his shoulders ? "

In spite of his face he didn't seem a bad sort.

" I don't know what to do with you, so you can stay here till I find out. I'll see you get rations. You're Signallers, you say ? "

" Yes, sir ; yes, sir."

It was good to be alive. We lounged about the wagon lines. It was like being in a gypsy camp. The transport men moved about in their shirt-sleeves grooming and watering the horses. Their faces perspired and the horses' coats shone. The only fly in the ointment for them was that they had to take the limbers up the line every night.

A youngster who seemed to have plenty of time on his hands kept us company for a while. He had come out on a draft, and it had been discovered that he was only sixteen. Now he was employed doing odd jobs in the store and acting as batman for the R.Q.M.S. He was a great favourite with the drivers.

" They're talking about sending me back to Blighty, but I don't want to go," he told us. " It's far better fun out here, don't you think. More like being a real soldier. It would be awful to be sent back home."

In the evening we were warned off to accompany the rations up the line.

" Ah, well," said Mundy philosophically, " we might get a ride up, and anyway we'll be able to dump our packs on a limber."

THE COMPANY OFFICER

I CAME on my three henchmen in a crumbling, wattle-and-daub farmhouse which loomed up out of the darkness after a long mile of stumbling over open country where shells soughed, whined and burst redly.

Whether it was through having had a rest from the shells I didn't know, or whether it was because none burst sufficiently near to make me duck and flinch, but I found myself not paying so much heed to them as I had imagined I would. Being under fire had seemed a hideous thing from the safety of the school. Once again, as when I had first heard them, an invisible armour seemed to cover me. I forgot for the moment—or rather it simply did not occur to me—that a shell could as easily light twenty yards away or even right on top of me as two hundred yards away. It just didn't seem possible.

Still, experience of what a shell could do was a part of me now. I went warily, ready to sprawl down at the first sign of danger. But moving in the open at night when a strafe is on is distasteful, to put it mildly, and I was glad when the journey came to an end. There was always the possibility, too, that the guide would lose his way and go wandering about ashamed to acknowledge that he was lost until chance proved him right or wrong, or death came swiftly to settle all doubts.

I pushed aside the sandbag curtain that served the dual purpose of keeping out gas and keeping in the light, and found myself in a small room. It was cluttered with a curious medley of carelessly thrown rifles, broken furniture, and a tangle of equipment draped anywhere. In the centre

333

stood a bed, complete with a strip of nondescript carpet before it. Mouldy wallpaper, bearing a faded pattern of fruit and flowers, peeled off the walls, exposing the grey, hardened mud. On a battered, spindly-legged table beside the bed were dirty dixies and a couple of lighted candles. Underneath it, to complete the tally, and looking ridiculously out of a place, was a dirty pink earthenware toilet pot half-full of urine, on which floated cigarette ends.

Maxwell was bent over the phone in a corner. He had a stub of pencil in his hand, and a message pad on his knee showed that he was ready for anything. He looked up fleetingly, gave a barely perceptible nod, and fiddled with the pad as if on the point of taking down a message. He appeared anxious to ignore that I was something of a stranger, and flushed a little as if he thought I might divine his dislike of acknowledging that I had not been with them all the time.

"What does he mean ? What kind of a fellow is he ? " I asked myself, struck by the strange form his shyness took. "He doesn't curse nor sweat. Is he afraid to ? He refuses his rum ration and won't say a word against the officers or the grub or anything. He believes all the things he was taught at Sunday School when he was a kid. Impenetrably dull, yet quiet and conscientious—worthy of respect."

Looking at him I had an uncomfortable feeling that I was looking at an old photograph of myself, that once upon a time I hadn't cursed or drank or done anything I shouldn't have done. I didn't know whether I had changed for the better or the worse. I was inclined to put the difference down to lack of will-power on my part or an unsuspected leaning towards bad things. And yet I knew in my heart it was he who was in the rut and that it was I who had grown up. He held fast to the old. I grappled with the new things as they came, with occasional secret misgivings about their worth—bad language, bad drink, bad women.

Maxwell might be right, but I disliked him, passively.

When I screwed up courage to think he was wrong I felt only contempt.

" He's a stupid bastard," I thought, taking my eyes off him, but with a secret misgiving that I was an even stupider bastard as regarded being of any use to anybody when there was a war on.

The little Londoner, pinched and miserable, as usual, was sitting on the edge of a chair with his back turned to me. He was absorbed in trying to reach some spot between his narrow shoulder-blades. His thin, clawlike hand stretched another inch as he squirmed and wriggled in a desperate endeavour to bring the itchy part within reach. He hadn't noticed my entrance.

" 'Lo, Nigger."

He looked round, startled, and I noticed that his small, sallow face had become smaller. His black eyes sparkled momentarily as they took me in and then dulled, taking on the downcast apprehensiveness of a dog with a cruel master.

He nodded and smiled, the womanish, intuitive smile of one who takes in everything and understands everything at a single glance, and carried on with the all-engrossing occupation of rubbing himself raw.

I was suddenly conscious that I had returned after a six-weeks' absence, and with the idea somewhere at the back of my mind that I was practically a stranger again and had some kind of s tanding to regain or attain.

" Has it all gone yet ? " I asked.

" Is what all gone, Corporal ? "

" Your damn skin, of course. What else ? "

Nigger smiled understandingly, but showed his teeth a little more this time, a grimace rather than a smile.

" Not yet."

What he meant was " I'm glad to see you back, Corporal, but you shouldn't try to make yourself feel at home at my expense, not too much at my expense."

I understood.

" He's a mysterious fellow," I thought, " with his eternal rubbing instead of scratching like anybody else would."

The bed was covered with a jumbled heap of dirty white blankets, left behind along with the bed by the departed owner of the house. Even by candlelight I could see the lice crawling over them. The end of a stained sheet hung over the bottom of the bed and on it rested a pair of ammunition boots. There was even a pillow, although its usefulness was nearly gone, judging by the amount of feathers and fluff it had shed upon the floor.

" Who's having the kip ? " I asked, not knowing what changes might have taken place in my absence.

There was a sudden movement under the blankets and Beck poked his head out. For a moment he stared at me with naive blue eyes as if he had never expected to see me again.

" Are you back, Corp'l ? " he exclaimed with an astonished, open-mouthed grin of welcome, rubbing his eyes and scratching his touzled hair to assist his scattered wits to digest the fact that I was really there. A bead of sweat gathered on his nose, catching the guttering candlelight.

Standing my rifle against the bed, I pulled off my equipment with a sudden feeling of confidence that I could carry on all right.

Beck sat up, pushing the blankets back. Putting a hand in his pocket he produced an inch of cigarette-end and then, without waiting to light up, slid out on to the floor.

" Here you are. Try a kip in our bed. It's great steam. Makes you think you're back home instead of up the line."

For a moment the thought of the lice, which I had been shot of for a month past, gave me a feeling of nausea, but Beck's friendly invitation, and the fact that I was tired, decided me.

" Right you are, though you have a hell of an imagination," I said. Loosening my tunic, I climbed into the vacant bed.

" He's a simple-minded chap," I thought happily.

" Did you have a good time ? " asked Nigger politely.

We were with the same company still. The Acting Company Commander was a new broom. He was tall and thin and bony, with a grey, hard face and sharp light blue eyes. He was a stickler for discipline and efficiency and had therefore plenty of work on his hands. His manner more than made up for his deficiency in rank. He had the cold, determined air of one whose goal lay clear and almost within his grasp, and was determined to reach it. To me he was an inhuman kind of man. I couldn't even begin to understand him. He was apparently without fear, and yet without enthusiasm or the capacity to inspire it.

No matter how close the shelling or how exposed the position, he immersed himself in the duties of command—filling up forms, sending messages, exacting obedience, asking what this or that platoon was doing, seeing to everything that concerned the proper conduct of the war, never satisfied, never excited—an exemplary commander of a company of infantry—and yet never thinking of the war. For him the war was almost a side issue, like breathing and sleeping, to be taken for granted.

Lieutenant temporarily commanding a company. Captain commanding the Company ! And, eventually, a battalion !

" He's a stinker," said Hopkins, baring his teeth helplessly. " All up on himself since he got a company. You couldn't look sideways at the bastard or he'd jump down your throat. Not arf he wouldn't. I hate the look of him."

" He made Beck wash his face, anyway," said Maxwell. " Or his neck rather. What's this he said, Beck ? "

Beck went red. " My neck was clean. It was washed that morning. What does it matter in the line if your neck is a bit dirty ? "

" We were only in reserve. ' Just because you're up the

Y

line is no excuse for being filthy,' he told him. And he had
to go and get a dixie of water and scrub it."

" When he's in a bad temper he always says ' Jesus wept,' "
muttered Beck. " What does that mean ? "

" It means that Jesus burst into tears," said Nigger
patiently, " and no wonder."

" It's the shortest verse in the Bible," explained Maxwell.
" He likely says it instead of cursing."

Beck subsided, mystified and somehow impressed.

Our stay in the farmhouse was pleasant enough except
for the almost continual shelling that went on. The room we
inhabited was more comfortable than a gloomy dug-out.
We took turns in the bed. If a shell came near we stopped
our idle talk to listen furtively, and then hastened to fill the
gap in the conversation as if nothing had happened.

At night, always at the same time, a lone motor-lorry
passed somewhere near. We listened for it, and if the shelling
was heavy, speculated on the driver's chances and what had
brought him so far up.

Once a shell caught a corner of the roof. We thought our
number was up. Part of the ceiling fell and plaster, dirt and
laths rained down on us. I doubled up like a jack-knife,
shielding my face with my hands, thinking it was a direct
hit. The room was full of dust. When the rubble stopped
falling we sat up coughing.

" I thought we were sent for," said Beck with his silly
grin, but nobody spoke.

We strained our ears for the sound of a second shell, but
none came and, when the dust had settled, cleaned our
rifles and tested the telephone to find out if the line still
held, avoiding each other's eyes.

The company moved forward and then back. In the line
we lived in holes, and when we moved back we set up our
station in a heavily sandbagged hut, the floor of which was a
couple of feet below the ground level.

The roof of the hut was built on what someone said was the new principle. First there was a layer of sandbags and girders and then a space where a shell was suppose to burst if it scored a hit. Below the space were more sandbags supported on stout beams. It looked strong, and I often glanced up with satisfaction, tinged always with doubt.

" It might stop a 5·9, but on the other hand, 5·9s take a lot of stopping," said a runner who was billeted with us. " It's all a matter of luck, no matter what's above you, should it only be the sky. You could be in a dug-out twenty feet deep and if it caved in you would be twenty feet deeper than you wanted to be."

The shell-fire went on steadily.

Not that it was heavy shell-fire. Monotonous was a better description. A few shells would fall, four hundred, three hundred, two hundred yards away. A single one would roar down quite near, and we would wait fearfully on the next.

A wait of long minutes and the game would begin all over again, except that we could never be sure it would end the same way. That was the rub. When they came near, the doubt about the safety of the roof loomed larger. Sometimes I found myself wishing that a shell would score a hit just to solve the problem.

Maxwell was nearly caught in the open. An uneasy peace had lasted a little longer than usual, and he went over to a pond fifty yards away to wash a pair of socks. A lone shell burst close to him. He came running back with his eyes popping, and minus the socks.

" You were nearly ' killed in action ' there," jeered the runner.

Maxwell flushed and said nothing.

After that I didn't stir outside if I could help it.

The runner was sent for to take a chit to Battalion H.Q., and went off grousing. I stood in the doorway watching him until he was out of sight. It was odd how ignorant most of us were up the line. We seldom knew where Battalion H.Q. was or where the other companies were, or even where the different platoons of our own company were located. I was seldom curious enough to inquire. We attached the phone to lines already laid and didn't stir a dozen yards from it unless the wire went.

The battalion never took over the same place twice. If asked the name of the sector we were holding I couldn't have told. When relieving, or being relieved, we caught a glimpse of the shoulder marking of one of the other units in the Division, but that was all we ever saw of them. Ostensibly we belonged to a battalion, a brigade, a division. In reality the infantry unit was a company and the rest abstractions. In every platoon different dialects could be heard, so that, in the 1st Battalion, even the company lacked cohesion. A dull, spit-and-polish discipline was our principal inheritance from Regular Army and regimental traditions.

THE COMPLAINT

WE took up our quarters in a big farmhouse surrounded by cultivated fields which were only beginning to show signs of shell-fire. Potatoes grew in the fields, but it was strictly forbidden to dig them up. It was a stupid order, and scroungers were always ready to defy it. We added potatoes, roasted or boiled in their jackets, to our scanty fare. " Drumming up " was one of our few pleasures.

When our turn came to go in again we went up a hill past a ruined monastery where a German prince was supposed to be buried, and away to a substantial village, only slightly damaged. The name of the village reminded me of the nursery rhyme :

> Little Bo Peep has lost her sheep
> And doesn't know where to find them.

A few kilometres beyond the village was the line.

It was the saturnine Jenkins who told me about the dead prince.

" If the Kaiser, and a few more high and mighty ones like him, were done in, the war would soon be over," he predicted. " But what a hope. Catch them taking their chance with us blokes."

" You couldn't expect them to come up the line," said Maxwell, more than a little shocked at the idea.

" That's it," said Jenkins sourly. " Nobody expects them too, so they don't come. They might fall like Nelson."

" Nelson wasn't a king, was he ? " pointed out Beck doubtfully.

" My God, man, put your hand out and see if you're

awake. Don't I tell you he was one of the other sort. He chanced his arm like a common five-eight."

"You said he was a king," said Beck doggedly, "and he wasn't one at all. He was in the Navy."

"Aw, shut up," said Jenkins, turning away, "that's where you should be—or in a Home. Some one of the two, it doesn't matter which."

It was up here that I committed what the Signal Officer described as "rather a blunder, y'know, Corporal."

We were in a little group of sod and sand-bag huts. The huts were poor affairs, damp, and only about four feet high, but we were quite satisfied with them because there was little or no shelling going on.

For all their crudity I liked them on sight. It was like a village in the Stone Age, and after all that was what we were living in, leaving out modern improvements like H.E. shells and poison gas. A little stockade or wall, which a tall man could have stepped over, surrounded the huts. The latrine was a narrow trench with a plank raised over it lengthways to sit on.

It was to this plank the company went when the spirit moved them to sit, gossip and de-louse themselves with their trousers down.

During the day the company slept, as was their right. The signallers, as was their duty, took turns at the phone. Up the line that was the main difference between signallers and the men of the company. The one rested in the day-time and took up active duty at night. They manned the trenches and dug and wired, patrolled and did sentry-go. The signallers did none of these things. Their job was to attend the phone day and night, and repair breaks in the wire. It was a fair enough division of duty.

Sometimes the platoons had the worst of it. They were in more intimate touch with the enemy to start with, and that was the thing I didn't like. It was no joke to start in at night to dig or deepen a trench, or stand on the fire-step for hours, or lie in a shell-hole all night long. But once out of the actual front line they had most of the day off. When they were unlucky, which was often, they had to go back in to work at night.

The signallers, on the other hand, had responsibility.

They had to keep the company in touch with the battalion headquarters by hook or by crook. They never got an uninterrupted sleep and when the phone wire went they had to follow it across country and find and repair the break. Shell-fire broke the wire, so it was generally under shell-fire the repairs were affected.

In the second line, or in reserve, their work went on, so many hours on and so many hours off, with the strong possibility of having to go out at night searching for a break through unknown country with only the wire as guide. It was not uncommon for one of us to be out for hours searching for the leak.

The first night in the little camp the Company Officer sent for me.

" Leave a man on the telephone, Corporal," he ordered sharply, " and the rest of you come along. There's some digging to be done up the line to-night."

I was thunderstruck at this curious order.

" But-but—what about the relief of the man on duty, sir. We've been taking turns all day," I stammered.

" Good God," said the officer, " don't you hear what I say. You have been told to come out on a digging party. Don't have me to tell you again, Corporal, or it will be the worse for you."

" Yes, sir," I said and saluted. Obey the last order, no matter how pig-headed, was the golden rule of the Army.

The others, with the exception of Beck, looked blank when they heard the news. Beck was at the phone.

" It's not a bit fair," said Maxwell, quite cross for once.

Hopkins shrugged his thin shoulders and cursed our Acting-Captain viciously, meaning every word.

We paraded with the working party, rifles slung over one shoulder and shovels or picks sloped on the other, and set off.

We marched along a deserted road, level with the bare ground on either side. The night was cloudy, but occasionally the moon appeared and sailed at an incredible speed across a clear patch of sky. Somewhere ahead shells plunged sullenly down. We listened anxiously, wondering where the road would lead us. Far away, towards the right, a bombardment was in progress and a sickly glow lit up one corner of the sky.

At the end of half an hour we halted. Verey lights went up in front. We stood staring mutely about us. The order came to proceed, and leaving the road we made our way carefully over broken ground, past a silent trench where blobs of shadow told of watching men.

We stopped, and low voices sounded at the head of the column. Somewhere ahead a machine-gun started tacking and we bent down instinctively. A man dropped his spade and his mates cursed him in undertones. The officer came along with a Sergeant and we got into single file.

" Spread out—a yard apart—and get stuck into it," said the Sergeant. We obeyed, laying down our rifles beside us.

In a few minutes my back was aching from the unaccustomed graft. Everyone dug with a will and soon we were a foot down. At intervals the machine-gun troubled us, but it was the shells we were afraid of. They came nearer and nearer as if of their own accord. Gradually, but with horrible certainty, the front came to life. The shelling increased until one of the aimless night strafes started.

" Our own artillery started it as usual," whispered the man behind.

A couple of shells fell with a shattering roar almost on top of each other at the top of the line of diggers. Dropping the spades we cowered down behind the little parapet of loose earth that had formed.

A hoarse, wavering cry sounded.

" Ah, ah, ah ! "

Another voice, thinner and shriller, like a boy's treble, came in a rising shriek and broke off to continue in little yelping cries. Then silence.

The tall form of the Company Officer materialised above us.

" Get on with it. Get on with it. What are you waiting for ? Get a move on or you'll be here all night."

His harsh whisper was not to be disregarded and we worked feverishly.

Some men passed by slowly carrying sagging, indistinct forms. By and by the news came travelling from mouth to mouth.

" Three caught it. One of them done in."

The stinking fumes of high explosive caught at our throats as more shells fell near, but clear of the line of men.

" Jerry must have us taped," said the man behind, but I paid no heed. Where would the next one light ?

For a time we were left in peace and the trench deepened. Then a faint plop sounded some distance off, followed by another and another. Once more we stopped, and sniffed the air.

" Gas," came the cry.

I clawed at my mask, so long unused, and got it on somehow. The gas shells came thicker.

" All right. Fall in. That will have to do for to-night," came the muttered order, and scrambling out of the half-dug trench we set off thankfully.

We reached the huts and dumped our shovels.

" Nothing like gas for putting the breeze up," said the Sergeant.

" Nothing like gas-masks, you mean," I thought, as the

three of us rejoined Beck at the telephone. The hut seemed very cosy and safe in the candlelight.

" Wonder who got hit ? " said Maxwell as we related the events of the night to Beck.

" What does it matter ? It wasn't us and that's the main thing," replied Nigger, sliding his hand through the breast of his tunic as if he knew he had arrears to make up. " But it might be us the next time, eh, Corporal ? "

" It's a damned shame," I said angrily. " The rest of the boys are kipping down now and we've still got to relieve Beck here and do our turn on duty."

" We'll be dragged out to-morrow night as sure as God," said Nigger. " That trench is only half-dug yet."

" Well, by God, he won't drag me out again if I know it," I swore. " Once is enough of that kind of dirty trick."

Reaching for a message-pad I wrote a service message, telling the Signal Officer what had occurred and asking for instructions.

" We'll see what happens now," I said and buzzed the message through. The others stood looking approvingly over my shoulder.

We waited anxiously all next day, but no reply came.

" He don't care a damn about us, that's about the size of it," said Nigger despondently.

" It's not fair. The Signal Officer should have reported him," said Maxwell.

That night, however, the company went back to finish their job without us. We wondered what had happened. It had been gone about an hour when the Signal Officer, followed by Corporal Mundy, made his appearance.

" Everything all right, Corporal ? "

" Yes, sir."

" Any more working-parties ? "

" No, sir."

The Signal Officer drew me to one side. " By the by,

about that message you sent. Any time you have anything to report of that nature it would—er—be better if you—er—waited until you could speak to me instead of sending it over the phone. It was rather—er—unfortunate the way it turned out. Always wait, especially if, ahem, it's an officer you are making a complaint against. You see?"

I listened, puzzled, as the Signal Officer rambled on like a man who had bad news to tell, and who hesitated to blurt it out, depending on the acumen of his hearer to guess what is the matter.

" —so—er—always try to keep on good terms with the Company Officer, you understand, Corporal, and wait always till I come round."

"Yes, sir," I replied, not understanding a bit. Wait until he came round, indeed, when it was obvious that only the message had brought him.

The Signal Officer had hardly disappeared through the door when Mundy burst into his great horse laugh, slapping his thighs with glee.

"What was he raving about?" I asked, "and what the devil's biting you, Corp?"

"Oho, my lad, you're for it. Take my tip and watch out for yourself," said Mundy in a rush as he prepared to depart after the officer. "The Commanding Officer happened to be at the telephone waiting for a message when yours came through. He read it and kicked up an awful stink. Sent for your Company Officer straight away and nearly chewed him up. Showed him your message, too, and said that was no way for a Company Commander to treat his signallers and what the blazes did he mean by it. It was fierce."

Mundy went out and we looked at each other in awed silence.

Mundy stuck his head inside the door. He took in our dismay in a glance.

" I wouldn't be in your shoes for a Blighty one. A low, common lance-jack, a five-eights, getting his Company Officer told off by the Colonel. What a hope. Haw, haw, haw."

Mundy disappeared—for good this time—satisfied with the impression he had created. I felt blue.

" Hell mend him, anyway. He shouldn't have sent you to dig, the big so-and-so," said Beck loyally.

" He'll be up against us, right enough," said Maxwell. " Maybe you should have waited a bit, Corporal, before sending a message like that. If I had been you I wouldn't have done it. I thought you were a bit too quick on it at the time."

" Listen to Cuthbert," sneered Hopkins softly and, squatting down, tried to reach between his shoulders with grimy fingers, as if to signify, in his own peculiar ways, that the crestfallen Company Officer wasn't worth worrying over when the lice were on the job.

THE CURE

COMPANY headquarters had at one time been a farm-house. Our shelter was at one end of a paved yard. At the other end was a pile of mouldy bricks and rubble, all that remained of the farmhouse. A big iron gate, as yet undamaged, opened out on to a shell-swept road.

I took over from the outgoing company signallers and settled down for the first tour of duty.

On the ledge where the phone rested I found a book. It was George Borrow's *Bible in Spain*. I had read the first half of it some time, and given the second half up as too dry. Still, it was an old friend. I remembered how I had envied Borrow his mastery of languages and had pictured myself in his place, making, Portuguese, Spanish, Gipsies, thieves and Germans believe in turn that he belonged to their country, race or profession. I turned the leaves, but idly, like a patient in a doctor's ante-room, and threw it back on the shelf unread.

After a while the book caught my eye again. I remembered the curious, dark charm of it and how, somehow, he had been most interesting when hobnobbing with tricksters, thieves and smugglers who had always accepted him as one of their own kidney.

" Perhaps he was, too, under the skin," I thought, and took the book down again, and opened it, haphazard, at his first meeting with the old German. I forced myself to read a page or two and then gave it up in disgust. The words were stale and colourless. My eyes scanned the lines without my brain catching the sense.

Shells were falling not far away and the roof of the shelter

349

was very thin. Not to pay attention to the explosions was in some obscure way to defy them and invite disaster. Throwing the book into a corner, I concentrated on the shells.

Something else caught my eye, and I sat up and took notice. In the corner, where the book had gone, was a small rum jar. Rum jars were worth shaking. I shook this one several times before a faint swish told that there was something there. Taking out the cork, I sniffed doubtfully and was rewarded by a strong, rich odour. The other fellows were asleep. Getting my mess-tin lid I emptied the contents of the jar into it. There was barely a couple of glasses all told, but it was the bottom of the jar and more like treacle. For a while I sat looking at it. It would be dangerous stuff to take on duty. Overcoming my scruples I raised the lid to my mouth and took a sip. Immediately I felt warm and comfortable as the fiery stuff coursed through me. I took another sip.

When after an interval I found myself talking out loud I had just enough sense left to kick the nearest of the sleepers —Beck—into wakefulness before curling up on the floor and falling asleep.

In the morning I waited for him to blurt out something. But he had noticed nothing out of the ordinary except the smell of the rum, which still pervaded the shelter.

I had forgotten to replace the cork in the jar.

" I noticed it, too," I said, " and wondered where on earth it came from."

" It came from that old jar there, but it was empty," said Beck.

" You weren't soft enough to think that anybody would leave you some in it ? " said Nigger, with a slightly contemptuous smile.

Next night I sat at the phone. It was quiet, and the front seemed asleep. To distract my attention I started de-lousing. A sudden strafe started outside. When Maxwell came to relieve me he seemed a bit nervous as he put the headphones on.

"What's all the row about now?" he said crouching down.

"How the devil should I know?" I answered, feeling of a sudden very shivery and in bad sorts. I had been sitting with my tunic and shirt open and the shelter was a draughty place, and cold at night. Crawling over to the place he had just vacated, I lay down and was soon twisting and turning in uneasy sleep.

All next day I lay burning and shivering by turns, and unable to eat. The others lent me their great-coats, but it didn't seem to make any difference. As the evening came on I felt worse, and for once paid little heed to the shells. When the sun went down the burning sensation decreased, but the shiveriness increased.

"You'll be all right, Corporal," whispered Beck. "We're going out to-night, you know."

The prospect of going out didn't excite me. I watched apathetically their preparations to move. I would much rather have remained lying where I was.

"Buck up, Corporal," said the little Londoner.

"You can go down with the limber," said Maxwell. "Tell the officer and he'll let you shove your pack on it and walk behind, at least. When he hears that you're sick he'll let you ride down on it. I'll go to him if you like and tell him."

"Maybe you've got that flu again that you were telling us about," put in Beck sympathetically.

"I'll go myself," I said and got unsteadily to my feet.

The officer looked at me with cold eyes. I remembered the message I had sent to Battalion headquarters a few days back.

"Couldn't allow it at all, Corporal," he said. "There's far too much malingering going on here. Besides, the limber will have enough to carry as it is. There's my own kit and the usual stuff. Yes, I'm afraid you will have to walk like the rest."

I saluted, in duty bound, and turned away, not caring overmuch.

The Company fell in on the road and stood two-deep waiting while the usual tedious formalities of handing over were gone through. The shell-fire, which had been steadily getting worse, became heavy and almost continuous. Stabbing flames pierced the darkness, emphasising the bareness of the road. The shells screamed and whined and burst deafeningly. The men cowered down. The air, heavy with the hot, bloodthirsty smell of H.E., seemed full of flying steel. The Company Commander appeared before us and bawled querulous questions at his platoon officers, his voice almost drowned in the uproar. Shells burst nearer. Some men in the rear rank broke and knelt at the side of the road, shielding their faces. I was one of the first to make for the ditch. Self-control—the fear of giving myself away completely as a hopeless coward—deserted me. I was shaking with fever and my teeth chattered. I felt naked.

The Company Officer shouted angry commands. Along with the others I got into rank again, only to dive for the ditch as another shell erupted redly. He threatened, his words coming sketchily in the clamour. We understood their meaning and fell in once more.

" Court martial. . . ." " Cowardice. . . ."

Fortunately he couldn't see who was at fault. We stood still until the order came, and then moved off, wondering at every step would we get away safely. A sudden call, " Stretcher-bearers," told that somebody had been caught.

In the big village we found the rest of the battalion waiting for us.

Shells were falling among the houses down the street and

we sighed with relief when we moved off. We went on our way over the hill and down into the valley.

"We're going right out," said Hopkins beside me, but I paid little heed. My feet and head were as heavy as lead, and I was afraid of having to drop out. Guns boomed all round and away to the right a heavy bombardment was going on.

After a long time we came to a village. Bursting shells barred the way. The men hung back, terrified at the prospect of running such a gauntlet. The shells whined and shrieked. The clatter of bricks came to us menacingly after each explosion. The officers shouted orders, urging us on.

We went forward fearfully by companies, jostling each other one minute and pressing back the next, half-stunned by the crashes. A single shell among us would have blown up half the Company. The tall houses leaned outwards, ready to collapse. Heaps of masonry on the street tripped us up. The ranks became jumbled as men surged forward panic-stricken. Others huddled together helplessly waiting to be killed. Above the confusion harsh shouts came.

"Get on. Damn and blast you. Keep moving."

For the second time that night the cry sounded: "Stretcher-bearers."

By some miracle we got through the village, and coming on a narrow railway track, halted. A few yards farther ahead a line of tiny trucks stood invitingly on the line. Immediately the men's mood changed. The rumour that we were going right out was true, and on top of that we were going out by train. I brightened up with the others at things being so unexpectedly made easy.

The halt began to get wearisome. Grumbling broke out. There were the empty trucks and why the hell weren't we told to get into them. Some of the men edged along and clambered in, but were sharply ordered to get back. They retired, baffled.

z

Another rumour reached us. Our hearts sank. It was the railway rather than the village that Jerry had been shelling. The track had been torn up a few yards ahead of the engine. The Canadian train crew were trying to repair it.

We waited, hoping against hope, but at last the order came to fall in. Getting to our feet, we started off again. Soon I was sweating, and when the next halt came I dropped in my tracks and lay gasping.

The shells no longer troubled us, but I began to think there was something the matter with me. Marching I was all right after a fashion, but after a minute or two's rest I felt deathly cold and longed for the whistle to blow. In spite of their weariness and disappointment the rest were quietly content at being alive and out of the shell zone. They talked in cheerful monosyllables and cursed their luck offhandedly. I kept silent, saving my breath, finding a strange relief in withdrawing into myself. The march became a nightmare of slogging as the strain of forcing one foot before another grew. At intervals I staggered along slightly lightheaded, and when this happened I grew more afraid of falling out, and tried to concentrate on the dark road and the man in front. I was dead beat and stupid when we arrived at our destination. It was a big, draughty barn, devoid of straw. Without waiting to share the hot meal that was waiting for us I crept into a corner and, wrapping my great-coat around me, was asleep before my head touched the ground.

Next morning I awoke completely cured of whatever had been the matter with me, and ravenously hungry.

"It's a brand-new cure for the flu," said Hopkins. "You should get a patent for it and you'd make your blinking fortune—I don't think."

THE SIGNAL LAMP

WE went in again over the Canal bank.
To my surprise I found that Maxwell and I were detailed for duty with the battalion headquarters' station, a comparatively cushy job. To add to our delight at this unexpected good fortune we found that headquarters was in an immense dug-out. It was the largest British dug-out I had met with in my short career in the line, comparable only with the great chalkpit barracks where the battalion had been lodged when I first joined it before the Retreat. It was built of concrete and surrounded on three sides by a clean-cut, well-revetted and duckboarded trench, into which numerous narrow entrances gave.

The chalkpits, back on the Somme, had been the work of the French. It was unusual for the British to go in for such big affairs. They did not believe overmuch in providing dug-outs for the infantry. The Germans were the dug-out builders par excellence, and according to popular report the French were a good second and, in addition, strong believers in lying doggo whenever possible, particularly in the day-time. Perhaps the British Army was considered too brave for this kind of coddling, although any troops I ever met with seemed to have no great objection to a few feet of solid earth over their heads when this was available and the Jerry gunners were sending over their ration of frightfulness. Battalion headquarters generally had the best and safest accommodation going. The rest of the battalion had to shift for itself.

All movement in the vicinity of the big dug-out was strictly prohibited in the day-time. That is, notices to that effect were displayed at each entrance. With the exception of the trench the place must have been practically invisible from the air. Possibly the trench helped to camouflage it by screening the entrances and making it appear just a trench.

Down below the atmosphere was evil-smelling and damp and at one end the floor was under water. All the time we were there the pumps clanked monotonously. It was a maze of dark passages with slimy walls. From the ceiling, supported by great beams, dirty water dripped continuously.

With my bad sense of direction I was always losing my way and wandered round the trench trying to recognise the stairway I had come out by. When I had found it, or thought I had, and went down it was another job finding our particular room. The principal guide to its whereabouts was that the floor was six inches under water, the dry part of the dug-out, naturally enough, being occupied by officers and permanent residents.

Maxwell and I found that our fond dreams of a nice safe time with the headquarter signallers were only dreams. We had no sooner arrived than we were taken up on top and across some hummocky ground to where an old wooden shack with three sides stood on a little rise. Inside, on a tripod, was an electric signalling lamp pointing towards the line.

Our job was to take turns with the lamp.

" All you have to do," said the Signal Sergeant, " is once every hour, day and night, send a flash up the line. The lamp is trained as it stands now on another lamp in the line and you have to watch for the answering flash. Be sure and keep yours focussed correctly, but you can work a two-hour shift. D'ye see ? "

We saw. The Sergeant, leaving us to our devices, made a bee-line for the dug-out as a shell fell unpleasantly close.

We also saw that the lamp had been placed about two

hundred yards from the dug-out for reasons that were soon apparent. From the point of view of the inhabitants there the reasons were quite reasonable and proper. The lamp might draw fire.

" This is a devil of a job," I said, looking dubiously at the lamp, the shack, and then up the line to where Verey lights rose and fell.

Maxwell agreed, and I felt windy.

" It's not very healthy looking, right enough."

Going up to the lamp he pressed the key tentatively. A great beam of light shot linewards.

" For Christ's sake, cut it off," I shouted, clutching his arm. " Are you mad. Why, it's like a searchlight. Jerry could see it from his wagon lines."

" But it has to be done every hour. That's what the Sergeant said," exclaimed Maxwell.

" Damn the Sergeant," I said. " You can do it if you like, but I'll not. It's all very well for him to say it, but he took good care to push off as fast as he could, didn't he ? "

Maxwell took first turn, and I made tracks for the dug-out, wandering about until I found our wire bunk, reaching it at the expense of wet feet. I was sound asleep when Maxwell came and shook me. It seemed a very short two hours but the watch bore him out. Taking it from him I prepared to depart.

" Anything doing on top ? " I asked.

" It wasn't so bad, but there's a machine-gun nest just beside the shack. They kept hammering away all the time nearly. Jerry seems to know about it for he keeps trying to get them, you'd think. That or the lamp."

" What, is he shelling now ? "

Maxwell nodded. " It's cold outside, too. Not much shelter sitting in that place."

Maxwell scrambled into the bunk I had just vacated. His teeth chattered, but whether with cold or cold feet I didn't know. Filled with foreboding I edged along the pitch-dark passages and up the steps into the trench. For a moment I stood luxuriating in its safety, and then climbed out and went over to the lamp.

Sure enough a heavy machine-gun started to clatter five minutes after I arrived. Looking round the side of the shack I saw a little concrete nest about fifty yards away, and thought I could make out the dark forms of the gunners.

A stream of bullets roared into the German lines, the fiery tracers pointing the way.

In front the Verey lights and flares went up, picking out the bleached sandbag parapet of our front line. A ragged shell-fire was in progress and pale gun flickers came and went silently.

I had no intention of adding to the risk by sending flashes over the lamp. I sat down on the floor. Maxwell, the conscientious, could do it if he wanted.

" All the better for me if he does," I thought. " The lamp is firmly enough fixed to keep in focus while I'm on duty. If it goes a bit off he'll make it right when he comes on and think nothing of it, even if he has to send a few extra flashes in the process."

The gunners kept up their jarring rattle, but after a while I got more used to it. I stared up the line listening to the gun-fire and watching the star-shells as they spread out and sank slowly earthward. I could never get over the strangeness of it all and sat, all eyes, like a street waif peeping timidly, through a lighted window and half expecting a kick on the rump from an officious policeman for being where he had no business.

" It's a lively place, this," I thought, and then shivered and drew back as a shell plunged into the ground in front and exploded with a clang.

Minutes passed and nothing happened. I was congratulating myself on it being a chance visitant when without warning a rush and another explosion came, slightly to the left of the first, but nearer.

There was something malignant and purposeful about the sound this time. I crouched down. There was no reason in the wide world why it shouldn't have travelled a few score yards farther and sent me, the lamp, and the shack to blazes Exactly the same rigmarole of shriek and burst and red glare which had resulted in a crater in the ground ahead would have sufficed to turn me into a few pieces of bloody dirt. And the shell, the maker of the shell, and the gunner who had sent it whining on its way, wouldn't have been a whit the wiser, or a bit better off. The loss of the electric signal lamp would have caused more trouble and worry to the Signal Officer and the sergeant than the loss of half a dozen of its operators, let alone one. Lamps were worth their weight in gold in an emergency, ready to send out vital instructions to the men in front when telephone wires had gone bust in a sudden attack.

I felt very much alone. A splinter might get me. If Maxwell was sound asleep, as probably he was, I would have to wait all night before help would come. Another shell might come and finish me when I should have by right been on my way to the dressing-station.

Already I seemed to have been in the shack for a long time. I stared at the illuminated dial of the watch, the strong metal guard of which made it difficult to see the hands.

"It must be stopped," I thought, and gave it a shake, but the hands pointed inexorably to the same time. A faint but regular tick sounded when I pressed it to my good ear. Another shell burst over to the right this time, between me and the dug-out. A fresh complication occurred to me. When I had done my two hours I might easily get caught on my way in. The machine-gun carried on firing with a pause now and then to put on a fresh belt. I wondered what on earth they were shooting at so conscientiously.

" Very likely into some empty fields where there isn't a German within miles," I thought, speaking aloud for the sake of hearing my own voice, waiting for the next shell.

It took its time in coming. When it did it sent me sprawling, bursting with a roar right between where I lay and the machine-gun post. Splinters hissed over my head and clods of earth beat against the flimsy wall and roof of the shack.

A piercing scream from the post and I stopped quivering. The machine-gun ceased fire. In the heavy silence that followed I found myself speaking out loud again.

" Serve you right, whoever you are. Maybe you'll catch yourself on now for a while and give your gun a rest."

Two or three more shells came over at short intervals, but they went up a safe distance behind. I was left in peace again with the impersonal, almost friendly boom of distant guns firing on other targets.

For a long time I sat in dull content. By some subconscious process of reasoning the fact that at least one of the machine-gun crew had been knocked out seemed to make the chance of survival so much the better.

A morbid desire to see with my own eyes what damage the shell had done came to me. I visualised myself crossing over to the machine-gun nest and sympathising with the survivors of the crew. They would be busy bandaging the wounded man or going through his pockets for letters, personal belongings—and cigarettes, if he had been killed. I would realise all the better then that I had survived too, and was still warm and breathing in spite of the shell that had come and gone. But I made no move and debated instead whether I shouldn't send a flash, just a short one to show that someone was on the job. Getting to my knees I groped carefully for the key, and then withdrew my hand.

" Better see what time it is first. The time must be about up," I thought. " If it is I'll press the key and run like the devil for Maxwell."

The watch showed a long half-hour to go. I hunkered down, disappointed.

" You were nearly making a fool of yourself there. Yes. Send a flash and sit like an idiot for Jerry to send another clatter of shells, or turn one of his machine-guns on you."

Time passed.

Glancing idly to the front my eye caught a stab of light. It appeared and disappeared several times before its significance came home to me. In sudden panic I jumped to my feet and pressed the key hard, forgetting my own fears in the greater fear of what was happening, or had happened, in the line. The great beam leapt out before me like a river of molten fire. Releasing the key I stared breathlessly, questions hammering at my brain.

" How long had they been trying to attract my attention ? "

" Was it an S O S ? "

" Would they report me for not keeping in touch properly ? "

My fingers were groping for the key ready to send another flash, when from the front came a satisfied flicker. I sat down, feeling shaky.

I remembered the watch. Was it never going to let me away to the safety of the dug-out, or was I doomed to spend all night in this cursed place ?

Ten minutes to go. Not so bad ! The machine-gun, which I had almost forgotten, came to life with a roar. Again the tracer-bullets flew like sparks into the Jerry lines.

" Why couldn't they have kept silent for a few minutes longer," I thought, looking at the watch again.

Eight minutes. Seven and a half, say. They couldn't be very long going in now, surely to God ! For answer a shell burst fifty yards away. I pressed close to the ground as gravel and bits of earth spattered the shack. A second and then a third shell followed. The splinters hissed above my head.

I could nearly go any time now. I would probably lose my way in the dug-out and spend five safe minutes prowling about in the darkness for the bunk.

Still, better stick it out. No use taking advantage of the chap, although he was glum and stupid. Another minute would have passed now. 1, 2, 3, 4, 5–20, 21, 22, 23–40, 41, 50– That would be another. Should I look at the watch, or count again ? The machine-gun clattered and thudded in a frenzy of senseless hate. In a moment the shack was the centre of spouting earth and flame as shell followed shell. I lay with bowed head, forgetting the watch and what it stood for, thinking hazily of life and death, of the softness of flesh and the unyielding obstinacy of the ground beneath me which refused to give way an inch to my clawing fingers. Showers of earth and stones drummed against the sides of the shack and off my helmet. The machine-gun stopped.

In a minute the shells stopped too, leaving me with a dry throat and smarting eyes. For a while I lay supine, hardly believing that it was all over. Slowly gathering my scattered wits, I looked at the watch—looked again and commenced whispering meaningless oaths, rolling nameless obscenities on my tongue, pronouncing the words slowly as if loth to let them go. I had overstayed my time.

We led a strange, lop-sided existence at the big dug-out.

The pair of us were absolutely on our own. Battalion headquarters were hidden away somewhere in the maze of dark alleyways. None of the station bothered with us and we saw none of them. Dim figures passed without a word, or stepped to one side to make way as I groped my way up and down. The gloom made it impossible to make out who or what they were. There was no point in being curious.

Days and nights were a succession of two hours on and two hours off. Up above the shells fell with nerve-racking irregularity, sometimes near, sometimes almost on top of the crazy hut, at other times three or four hundred yards or more away. At night the machine-gunners in their concrete post rattled away at unseen targets. When the shell-fire got too hot the gunners stopped firing and disappeared into a small deep dug-out of their own beside the gun. At times Jerry gave the crew a touch of their own medicine and sprayed the place with bullets. Once or twice he tried to achieve his object with gas shells.

Through it all we sat with the lamp, sending an occasional flash and straining our eyes for the answer.

" Very likely they suspect there's a big dug-out somewhere about here as well as a machine-gun post, and kept trying to blow it in," said Maxwell. " There's supposed to be no walking about in the day-time, but there's always somebody coming and going. We have to be back and forward all the time."

" If he got the machine-guns it wouldn't be so bad," I said. " One of those big shells he keeps sending over would wreck that nest for good if it fell right. Then they'd have to go somewhere else."

Neither of us had candles. When off duty there was nothing to do but lie on the bunk, smoking, scratching or sleeping, but mostly sleeping. It was beautifully safe in the big dug-out and the darkness, and discomfort of lying with wet feet, were incidentals. I would no sooner drop off to sleep each time than Maxwell would be at my side tugging and calling. The two hours dragged until it seemed they would never come to an end. The two hours off went like lightning. We could easily have changed the shift to four hours each way, but four hours beside the lamp would have been too much, especially at night, and I took care not to suggest a change. Maxwell probably thought so too, for he never broached the subject. For that matter we hardly spoke to each other. From being a quiet fellow at best he became morose, and his face appeared to become bonier.

For my part I was a bundle of nerves. I hated the lamp as I had never hated anything before.

An amazing sight on the fourth day showed us what might happen. I had just had my skimpy breakfast and relieved Maxwell. The sun was shining and for once there was a complete absence of shells and bullets. The tidy trenches up in front with their regularly spaced bays had a peaceful deserted air, almost as if they were practice trenches miles from the line. A drowsy rumble from some far-off sector hardly broke the stillness. Suddenly there was a sound as if a heavily laden train were passing overhead and a heavy shell sent up a great column of earth and smoke five hundred yards to the rear. There was a moment's pause. As if the big shell had been the signal, the air suddenly became filled with the screaming of dozens of shells which plunged into an area of less than an acre round about where the first one had fallen. The solid ground heaved and boiled under the impacts. A dense cloud of smoke, edged and shot with stabbing flames, gathered over the spot.

In spite of the order about keeping under cover in the day-time the side of the dug-out trench nearest the scene became lined with awed faces.

It was a striking exhibition of good shooting, against nothing in particular. A little change in direction would have meant the end of the big dug-out and all in it. The enemy would find out their mistake and try again, sometime soon.

For ten minutes the rain of shells gouged and mauled the little stretch of bare ground with blind ferocity, and stopped as suddenly as it had begun, and with as little reason, leaving an enormous smoking hole as a souvenir of misguided effort.

The mysterious strafe had heartened Maxwell up wonderfully I found when my tour was up.

" They'll think they've caught the dug-out so we'll be left alone for a while," he said, and added meditatively, " Wonder would it have held out ? "

THE OLD SOLDIER

WE were relieved by signallers from another company, and departed to join our own station in the line.

The trenches we had been looking down at from battalion headquarters proved to be as neat and tidy at close quarters as they had looked at a distance. They were broad, well-made affairs, with sandbagged parapets, and everything in its place. They were well drained and laid with clean duckboards. Little shelters were let into the side and there was plenty of barbed wire in front. The only drawback to my mind was that they were just a trifle too broad and not more than six feet deep. Compared with the massive trenches at St. Quentin they were as cardboard is to wood.

" Here comes the bloated Staff wallahs," greeted Hopkins with his little friendly grimace. " Where did you leave your brass hats, eh ? Sitting back like nobs at your ease and leaving us poor fellows to keep the war going on our own."

Maxwell, tongue-tied as usual, grunted something and flushed.

" You don't know you're living here, you," I protested and proceeded to give an account of ourselves, taking care while emphasising the danger to hide that I had been nearly frightened to death a dozen times.

" I tell you we had the breeze up about proper," I ended, giving the words the necessary touch of casualness to make them appear to exaggerate slightly and yet speaking sufficiently earnestly to carry conviction. That was the old soldier way of talking.

" I suppose you're glad to get back then ? " said Beck with round eyes.

It was dry and warm in the trench and safe enough so long as we kept our heads down—a thing we were all most careful to do. I had not the slightest curiosity now as to what the German lines looked like, or where they were. Up to date I had not set eyes on any of our men trying to snipe Jerries. The one thing that was not heard up the line was the report of a rifle. Before going in we went through the rigmarole of filling our magazines and pushing down the safety-catch, but that was as far as we got. My ammunition pouches were badly made and as a result I was generally short of half the proper number of clips. The only time I missed them was at the kit inspections out at rest.

Rifles in 1918 were a joke.

Any sniping required was done much more satisfactorily with Lewis-guns. They were the real guardians of the trench. Occasionally the gunners sent a burst or two hissing over the edge of the enemy parapet just to keep their hand in and let the occupants know they were still there. At night they swept the ground methodically and drew occasional shells for their pains. Across the way the same rule held good. If a Tommy exposed himself he either got away with it or else got machine-gunned. There were no half measures. Periodically their machine-gunners sent a burst thudding into our parapet or humming harmlessly over our heads to the rear. It was an unwritten law.

Curiously enough the German infantry was never mentioned amongst us otherwise than in a friendly, rather admiring way. Sometimes we railed at them after the fashion of old cronies pouring abuse on each other, but mostly the talk had a familiar, and yet intangible, quality in which the German filled in turn the role of elder brother who had been able to show us some new trick, of a schoolmaster who had inflicted chastisement when it was due and against whom no great ill feeling was harboured, and of a sly acquaintance whose dodges needed constant watching, but who nevertheless was not a bad sort. It was their artillery we feared most.

If the rumour reached us that our side had caught him napping somewhere, it was received with casual, often sceptical, interest.

" Old Jerry got it in the neck that time, all right, eh ? He must have been asleep."

" They shouted ' Kamerad ' because they knew damn well they'd had enough."

It was all good humoured, without animus. Jerry had only done what our side would have done in like circumstances.

At times his vagaries were discussed impersonally as if he were a thousand miles away instead of a few dozen yards. The pros and cons of his actions were examined and praised or blamed impartially.

There was never any attempt to gloss over a defeat. On the contrary everyone seemed eager to give the Germans their full share of praise when they had succeeded in putting something over on either ourselves or our Allies. When the unfortunate Portuguese were ignominiously chased for their lives the men sneered at them contemptuously for a collection of washouts, no use for anything but breaking stones behind the line. The Germans were warmly commended for showing what they could do when a lot of Pork-and-beaners were shoved into the line. The Australians, who had been rushed in to fill the gap, were credited with shooting and bayoneting far more Portuguese than Germans, and lauded accordingly.

But over all this idle talk of the men loomed the threat, huge and terrible, of being involved in another big show—whether initiated by British or Germans mattered little—and I think that was why we kept low and looked upon our rifles in much the same way as we did our entrenching tools—useless lumber that had to be hawked about wherever we went, but which it was just possible would be of some use some day. To me the threat was strong enough to spoil the quietest day up the line. There was nothing doing! How did we know but what Jerries were massing for another 21st March when our line would crumple up like tissue-paper and not one in a dozen would live to tell the tale? Nobody knew—not even the airmen.

It was as if we shared a bedroom with a maniac, who was liable to wake up at the slightest noise and come at us with clawing hands and slavering jaws. The tension kept me on edge. I knew, subconsciously, that the other survivors of the retreat suffered in the same way, although, perhaps, to a lesser extent. The young troops that had been rushed out since then had listened to many a garbled tale of our vicissitudes. They shared our fears at second hand.

Our artillery was as windy as could be. Any untoward incident, however small, sent them thundering into action. In a minute a full-dress strafe would be in progress over a mile of front—exacting its toll of skulking, helpless infantry before giving way to the quietness which precluded the next scare.

The men manned the line and did what they were ordered to do without question and without heart. Disobedience meant quick vengeance by way of court martial and the firing squad. It took more courage to baulk than it did to obey. The only way out was stupid acquiescence or an S.I.W. Strange tales were told by men returning to the battalion after recovering from slight wounds, of hundreds of men at Boulogne, Le Havre and Etaples, who were penned behind barbed wire like prisoners of war while they recovered from wounds for which the enemy was not responsible.

" Boulogne's lousy with them," a man told me. " They're running about, half-starved, and sentries march up and down with order to shoot if they try to escape. I slipped one kid a fag one day and he nearly gave the game away by starting to cry. You never saw the like of them. The Jerry prisoners in hospital were well away compared with them."

There had been another stunt in favour with the troops of waiting until a machine-gun was sweeping the trench and then holding up a hand to catch a bullet. This had been knocked on the head by an order which stated that any man going down the line with a bullet wound through the hand would be court martialled.

Even then men " worked their ticket." A bullet made a distinctive wound. So did a shell splinter. The rest was easy enough to a determined man and only needed opportunity. First, collect shell splinters until a suitable one was found. Then extract the bullet from a cartridge and replace it with the splinter, hammering the sides of the cartridge case to make it a good fit. A wait until a strafe was on and a fellow was by himself or had his mates squared.

Down the line and the best of luck !

There were not a few industrious collectors of shell splinters. More than once men with whom I was on speaking terms unobtrusively showed me a home-made cartridge. A strict search from pocket to pocket as well as a kit inspection would have landed many a lad in the soup. Wiser ones, not to be caught napping, kept a suitable splinter loose, a souvenir, and a cartridge with a loose bullet in it, ready to effect the necessary change if opportunity offered.

On the other hand plenty bragged about what they would do, showing their " splinter-bullet " as proof, but without the courage to use it. Oddly enough, it required a lot of courage.

From time to time underground rumours circulated amongst us. So-and-so and his mate had worked the oracle, and got away with it. Through the foot. They were suspected, but seldom caught. If they got away with it they were envied. So far as I could make out no stigma attached to them either way. They had failed or succeeded. Ninety-nine out of a hundred would have changed places with the lucky ones without a second's thought. Love of country was there, but not in the patriotic sense—that kind of talk would have been so much Greek. Logically enough, it was transmuted into love of " a Blighty one," no matter how come by.

Two men had arrived back with the company a few days before. I had been on duty when the Company Officer was told of their arrival. They were back from a Base hospital and were suspected of being S.I.W. cases, but nothing had had been proved. Their Platoon Officer had been instructed to keep a careful watch on them in case they would try it again. They were two harum-scarum chaps, rather shame-faced at having bungled the Blighty one.

" We're going to have another try," they passed the word, " and if we're not hobbling along on nice comfortable crutches for the duration we'll deserve all we get."

There was one pukka old soldier in the company. He had been serving at the outbreak of war and had lived through everything ever since. He hadn't even been wounded, and had only his chevrons to show for it. He was short and bony, and easily the ugliest man in the battalion. His small red-rimmed eyes were widely separated. He had an abnormally long upper lip, and his small, sharp chin beneath a wide slit of a mouth gave the impression that his face was unfinished or that his mouth was in the wrong place. He suffered from a perpetual thirst for strong liquor. Booze or the years of exposure, or both, had turned his complexion to an unnatural blue colour, tinged here and there with red. His favourite drink was methylated spirits, and he nearly always succeeded in going into the line well soaked.

It was a standing mystery where he came by it. He was an outstanding example of the luck attendant on drunkards, as otherwise there was no plausible reason why he had lived so long. When sober he spoke little. When drunk, apart from swear-words, he was almost inarticulate. Like all real old soldiers he was a full Private.

I was hanging about the trench in the afternoon when to my surprise he came sidling up. He was sober, but full of glad tidings.

" Like a slug of whisky, Corp ? "

" Too true, where is it ? "

He jerked his thumb in the direction of the next traverse and, putting his finger to his lips to indicate caution, led the way. I followed, mystified, but interested, to the Company Officer's place, half shelter and half dug-out, let into the parapet. There was no sign of its occupant. A water-bottle stood invitingly just inside the low doorway.

" Keep your eye skinned," said the old soldier.

" But how do you know that there's anything in it ? He would hardly leave it lying about spare like that if it was full of spirits, would he ? We might get caught on, all over nothing."

" God, Corp, are you long out ? Didn't I shake it a minute ago when I spotted it. It's full. We'll pinch the half of it and he won't know."

Satisfied, I posted myself at the corner of the traverse where I could see both ways at once. My confederate got out his water bottle and slipped over to the shelter. If the officer caught us we would be for it about proper. I didn't know the penalty for robbing O.C. Company of his own liquor in the front line, but it wouldn't be light.

I turned my back on the funk-hole, the better to spot anyone coming. The little stretch of trench was deserted. I was still staring and listening when he came up behind. I turned to congratulate him on the success of our enterprise, but stopped when I saw his disgruntled face.

" Full—hell ! Full of lime juice. Rotten lime juice. What d'ye think of that ? Blasted luck. Me gasping with drouth."

" Oh, well," I said, swallowing my disappointment at sight of his woebegone look. He was uglier than ever in a rage. " Better luck next time, and we're no worse off."

He went off mumbling curses.

That same evening I doubted whether the old soldier had waited for better luck next time. One of the Lewis-gunners was speaking.

" Where the devil does he get hold of it, that's the thing ? As drunk as a coot to-night there, and a couple of hours ago he was as sober as you are. He'll be shot some day if he's not careful."

" Old soldiers never die, they just fade away," ran one saying. " Old soldier, old ——," ran another.

I had my pick.

We were in little shelters lining a road. Opposite us in a field was a big farmhouse. We were under front-line conditions and restrictions. We had to keep in touch with H.Q. by telephone, wherever they were, and keep under cover during the daytime. As a makeweight we had no stupid drills or fatigues, and were quite satisfied. As well, we were provided with a little war-time entertainment free of charge. Many a stay-at-home would have paid good money to see it.

It started with a shell plumping down near the road where we were, and quite naturally we got the wind up. Another came and then another. We had begun to think there was something seriously the matter when the next burst nearer the house, and we guessed what the Jerry gunners were aiming at.

For a long while they had the most amazing bad luck. They dropped their heavy stuff short. Then for a while the shells whined over and burst beyond. They rectified this error at last and commenced digging up the ground to the left at varying distances from the target. When they had narrowed the range of improbability down to one of possibility the other fellows were beginning to feel bored. I didn't. It was very pleasant to hear the long-drawn-out whine and watch the sudden eruption a bare three or four hundred years away, knowing that all the time I was perfectly safe on the road. It was the nearest I ever came to despising shell-fire.

At long last a red dust-cloud and a clattering of bricks signalled a direct hit. We smiled at this belated success. Having got the range with their usual thoroughness, they wasted no more time. Before our eyes a substantial dwelling-house became first a wreck and then a ruin as it went on fire. Hardly a brick remained in its original setting, but the field was much the same as ever and the house, what was left of it, looked out of place. A little time ago it had been fit to withstand the centuries and now it was only mounds of rubble.

Later that night we were warned off for a bathing parade and with the exception of Maxwell, who was on duty, set off. None of us wanted to go. The usual nightly strafe had set in in earnest, and it was bad enough as it was in the shelters, but there was nothing else for it. Three times we came on horses lying with smoking entrails and their feet in the air at the side of the road. Where horses had been killed men had probably been done in as well. Shells roared down, the twilight intensifying the terror they inspired. The bath-house became a haven. To reach it alive became our aim in life. When we did arrive we weren't reassured. Shells were going up nearby. We accepted quite literally the saying that cleanliness was next to godliness. Cleanliness didn't seem worth the risk. We undressed unwillingly, filled with the soldier's senseless fear of being caught naked under shell-fire, and stood shivering under the thin streams of water falling from the roof. It was then that Hopkins' months of mysterious efforts were rewarded. He was drying his half-raw body gingerly when an attendant caught sight of him. He came hurrying over and hardly gave Nigger time to collect his clothes before leading him away. He was under the delusion that it was some peculiar brand of skin disease.

Beck and I looked at each other, strangely disconsolate. He was out of it all. We had to make our way back to the shelter over roads which were being sprayed with shells. Beyond, was the dismal round of in and out of the trenches.

Nigger had won free, if only for a time. Perhaps for good, for he would take good care to keep on torturing himself.

THE SHELL TO HIMSELF

A YOUNG fellow named Cummins joined us from hospital to bring the station up to strength. He had a pale handsome face, with regular features except for a slight twist at the bridge of his nose. His eyes were grey-green and very alert. In spite of his frank, casual manner there was a touch of furtiveness about him as if he kept trying to give the impression that all his thoughts were on the surface while all the time there were others constantly occupying his attention which he did his best to conceal. He appeared to be continually weighing things up, no matter how trivial they were, with a view to his own advantage or safety as the case might be. He had joined the battalion six months before the Retreat and got slightly wounded before it came off. He was about the same age as the rest of us, or a little older. He made a point of speaking of everything off-handedly. The war was an old story to him with shells, bombs, bullets and gas all in the day's work. Generally he tried to give the impression—all in a careless way—that he had been born and reared on the Western Front. At first I was impressed. Anybody who was self-confident or had some personality or who even was just a bragger, impressed me. Filled with futile hatred of the war, with its senseless slaughter, and too conscious of myself to brag, I looked upon those who could make pretence to take the war casually as men to be admired. They at least had a standard of conduct to which they paid lip-service, if nothing else. I had none, except the poor knowledge that I had to hide my terror and yield up igno-minious acceptance of war's bestiality as best I could.

Within his limits Cummins was decent enough. Because I was the Lance-Corporal in charge of the station it seemed to be part of his code to assume tacitly that I was well-experienced and knew a thing or two. For a time I forced myself to try and live up to this good opinion and even took a certain pride in it. But soon I grew tired. I had enough poses to keep up without that. The first shell dropping near might let me down. We soon grew to make allowances for his anything-you-don't-know-ask-me air and carried on as usual. In our hearts we would much rather have had Nigger Hopkins back. Nigger had never attempted to give anybody any impression—good, bad or indifferent. He had had a wise, little womanish smile for most things which, in its way, was far more impressive.

Still, it might have been worse. And what did we care ?

We set off one evening as soon as it got dark and went in away to the right of Ypres. It was a stiff march, and the usual nightly shelling of the road didn't make it any easier. The silence among the men when going into the line seemed natural now. Once it had struck me as being unnatural. I knew the reason for it, and was silent too. Every man jack of us was asking the same question : " Will I come through this time ? " Their preoccupation as we marched along showed how searching and cankerous the question was. It was a long slanting march. As we progressed, life became at once cheaper and dearer. Never knowing where we were bound for exactly until we arrived, we always knew when the end of the journey drew near. In front the Verey lights grew brighter and more individual as they rose and fell, their beauty lost sight of in their significance.

Plodding footsteps resounded dully on the hard road. Our shoulders, freed for a few days from the weight of equipment, now bent forward, accustoming themselves to the backward drag of the packs.

The ground on either side was deserted and desolate except for the men, hidden from view, who were luckier than we. Unlike us, they hadn't to go any farther.

Over all, belittling the Verey lights, belitting us, was the flash of the guns and the lonely, menacing crash of shells as they fell on or about their invisible targets.

We slogged steadily towards the line—the relieving battalion—thinking of the moment, perhaps only a hundred yards ahead, when we should become the target—glad to escape if our luck held, yet sorry to arrive. I was only a late-comer to the war, but my heart misgave me. I thought of the journeys I had already made, and of the dark vista of similar journeys stretching away into a dim future— provided, that was, that the present one wouldn't be the last. The battalion was a battalion of boys, immature and unsure of themselves—deprived of the heritage of youth and love and finding out things. Instead of being carefree, as youth should be, we were careworn, obsessed with the fear of mutilation and death, knowing little of life and wondering what it was all about, and because of our vast, uncomprehending ignorance, not daring to question and rebel, as youth should do. To rebel meant certain death and we bowed our heads and dumbly, by default as it were, preferred the chances of life the shells offered. The shells were blind. The great trouble was we had no incentive to fight. The war was there, and we had been drawn into it, like weak swimmers into a whirlpool. If there had been an ideal dear to us to fight for we would have gone willingly into the trenches— something to quicken us and make us despise death, a new " Marseillaise." But the war was evil and old, its whys and wherefores lost in obscurity. There were no ideals in 1918. I kept quiet because I felt very lonely and helpless.

We fell out at the side of the road for a last halt. I searched around me in the gloom for a friendly face. Those of the men around me were strained and downcast, each man grappling with the premonition of senseless extinction.

It was forbidden to smoke, but some stealthily disregarded the order. To inhale was to enjoy the passing moment. The safety of the whole went for little. The majority lay spreadeagled on the road with their packs as pillows, like men already dead.

A few sat with their rifles upright between their knees. They talked in dull half-whispers about little things, with not a mention of what lay nearest their hearts : " Will I live to be relieved ? "

" What's this sector going to be like ? " was the nearest they got to it.

We had been resting only a couple of minutes when an altercation broke out down the indistinct line of resting men. Curses and counter-curses followed each other like the snarling of dogs.

We looked round, astonished at the idea of anyone having the energy or desire for a private quarrel. It seemed very silly.

The wranglers stopped abruptly as someone cursed with more authority.

By and by the reason for the quarrel came travelling from mouth to mouth, all disjointedly, but intelligible enough.

" Where does he get hold of it ? " " Full up again."

" Is it that old soldier merchant ? " I asked.

" Ay, wish we had his load. He's as drunk as a lord. Where does he scrounge it ? " Others muttered assent with a mixture of anger and admiration.

" He would drink through a dirty rag."

We sat silent again until the whistle came, followed by low-voiced exhortations from the N.C.O.s to hurry. Forgetting the old soldier, we went on, the question only time could answer dogging our footsteps. Each marching man seemed to imagine the question was peculiar to himself. Taxed with it he would possibly have denied with much profanity that such a thing had ever occurred to him. But denials were not worth the breath wasted in uttering them. The question would only have returned with an added touch of superstition at having denied its existence. Some men went so far as to believe they would be all right just so long as they could believe they would be. The moment they allowed a little doubt to raise its head their number was up. It was to bolster up the delusion that pocket Testaments—never by any chance read—were carried over the heart. Pagan charms. Ten years of life was all I asked for. If God had guaranteed that much we would have been content. But God was only a meaningless exclamation for most of us, a curseword interchangeable with any other of our limited range of cursewords. Lord God or God Almighty was used to lend emphasis, the same as putting Mr. before a man's name or Esq. after it. Men said : " For God's sake," or " For . . . sake."

Religion was a poor joke, a chestnut that had outgrown laughter.

"Who died to save our sins," a padre had told us at a drumhead service back at rest. We had gone to the service for the same reason that we went into the front line.

We had formed three sides of a square and listened to the snatches of sermon that came our way—it was a breezy day— or watched the preacher's billowing white surplice, which persisted in showing the officer's uniform underneath.

The padre had talked on, returning at appropriate moments to the words of his text. The men had shuffled their feet and scratched surreptitiously. They had no sins that they knew of. The chances of committing adultery were rare and Heaven-sent. Stealing, which was called scrounging, was good. A good scrounger was an asset to his squad, and generally the best soldier in it. Blasphemy was a blessing instead of a sin. Like blowing one's nose, it offered relief. Covetousness didn't apply. One man's possessions were common to all. Most of my neighbours hadn't had time to think of getting married and those of them who were married were too busy coveting their own wives to think of anyone else's.

As for killing. There was little likelihood of us having to kill anything, except lice. The guns did whatever killing had to be done.

Company headquarters were in a stretch of trench. It wasn't a very deep trench. For some reason or other a broad sloping ledge had been cut out of the parapet about half-way up instead of the usual firestep. A man could have lain full length on the ledge and fired over what was left of the parapet Perhaps that was the explanation.

We took stock. The hole where the phone was installed was so small that only the man on duty was able to squeeze in, and there was nothing for the rest of us but the trench. It struck us as being an unhealthy place if we were shelled. The Company Officers' quarters were a few yards away round the traverse.

We kept very low. Heavy shells rumbled overhead and crashes near at hand kept our nerves on edge. Both sides seemed uneasy. There were always fresh star-shells to take the place of descending ones. Machine-guns clattered unendingly, sweeping methodically over No Man's Land.

Taking over a new sector was bad enough, the first night particularly. The Jerries seemed to know that the relief was taking place and shelled heavier than ever. The Verey lights went up all round us, serving to emphasise our utter ignorance of where our line ended and Jerry's began. It seemed a bad place to be in for five minutes, let alone the usual tour of days.

There was a rumour that we were in for a longer period this time.

"Jerry must be in a salient here," Maxwell told us out of his larger experience, "and it looks as if we're at one corner of it. That's why he seems to be on either side as well as in front. I'd sooner be somewhere else, for with a bite out of the line like this, you never know where you are. It's a bit of bad luck."

"We're always in some sort of trouble," complained Beck. "Either in a salient or round about one, or up to the eyes in mud, or stuck in elephant huts when we should be in dug-outs."

"Well, you see, you can't expect jam on it all the time. Somebody has to hold this part," said Maxwell. "There are worse places, if you only knew it."

"Those Verey lights. If they'd stop sending them up all the time it wouldn't be so bad. But they put the breeze up a fellow, the way they're going up behind as well as in front."

I agreed with Beck, although I didn't like to say so in front of Maxwell and Cummins. Besides, I always wanted to keep silent when shelling was going on. A chap could listen better when his mouth was shut, and there was less chance of giving himself away. Talking was a distraction and therefore dangerous. "Listen hard and keep your eyes open," was my motto, even when it was dark. A man with his eyes open can hear better. I was still deaf in one ear and didn't like to handicap myself further by lack of concentration.

In the morning things were quieter. The sun came out and we were happy after a fashion. We sat warming ourselves. I held my face up and stared at the sun until my eyes were dazzled. Little fleecy clouds were in the sky and I looked at them with liking and satisfaction. They seemed very innocent and childish as they moved lazily along, sometimes catching up on one another and joining. The earth was a dirty, stupid place.

When the sun disappeared behind some clouds it wasn't

so nice in the trench. The ground was damp from a recent shower and the air was cold. The others were bored and moved restlessly, but I was never bored up the line, or down it for that matter. I was never bored when there was danger about. Down the line I enjoyed being alive too much.

The sector was a popular place with airmen. Our side went over in droves, apparently very sure of themselves. Occasionally battles were fought over our heads and we stared open-mouthed. The planes whirled in and out, their guns firing bursts which were our only indication that the quick dives and spirals were being done in earnest.

The encounters seemed to end without any great harm being done on either side, although, of course, it was difficult to tell. The planes would fade out of sight, generally behind the Jerry lines, and the sound become fainter and fainter until we lost interest. Sometimes when a plane made off in a hurry, flying low, we drew each other's attention.

" There's a Jerry down."

" There goes one of our lot."

But for all we knew they all landed alive and well.

Except for the fact that it took place in the air, air fighting didn't seem much more exciting than being on the ground. Airmen went up and exchanged shots or had a fight or two. If they were lucky they went back miles behind the line, where they were out of harm's way, until the next time. If they were unlucky they were killed or wounded, just as if a shell had caught them.

The infantry at once admired and despised them. Airmen had to be brave individually. We hadn't. The very fact that they had to fly through the air marked them out as a kind of supermen. It seemed much safer on the ground. On the other hand air duels were only side shows. It was as if two sparrows were chasing and pecking at each other while beneath them a dog-fight was in progress.

The Air Force was an officers' corps. Down the line they

had a good time, with plenty of wine and women. They did themselves well and cut a dash. We didn't.

With the phone shelter so cramped, off duty we had to lie in the open trench, with the result that I couldn't sleep. A roof of any kind, no matter how thin, gave a sense of security. Under a sheet of corrugated iron I could have dozed over, but to sleep in the open was beyond me. There was the chance of being taken unawares.

When the desire for sleep came I fought it off without much difficulty. The others didn't spend much time sleeping either. At night sleep was out of the question, whether on duty or not. There were frequent gas alarms, and no man has yet succeeded in sleeping with a mask on.

Three or four hundred yards behind us there was a couple of heavily sandbagged huts in a hollow surrounded by some stunted trees and undergrowth. At night a working party came up and remained until nearly dawn. They were digging a trench or making a dug-out, and now and then the clink of shovels and picks came to us. Once, repairing a break in our wire, I saw shadowy forms, but that was as near as I got to them. It was an eerie place at night.

Jerry must have taped them, for the second night he suddenly sent a dozen shells screaming over and we heard the working party no more. The rumour that a lot of them had got knocked out drifted up to us along with the rations.

It was to these huts we went when we left the trench. They had a damp, earthy smell and were infested with rats, attracted by the working party's blood perhaps. We crept silently into the one allotted to us and set up the phone, praying that the Germans would let us alone, and only too conscious of the atmosphere of tragedy that hung about the place.

Tiers of bunks occupied most of the floor space, but for a while we disregarded them and sat round a lighted candle talking in low voices. Outside the shells boomed. It was four days since I had slept and the bunks looked more and more inviting.

" Waken me when my turn comes," I said at last, getting into one of the bottom ones and was asleep before my head touched the pillow.

When I woke up I felt curiously refreshed. For a time I lay motionless and then, fishing out a cigarette-end, lit up. I felt very hungry. Everything was quiet.

" Hey, there, what's the time ? " I called out, and put my feet on the ground.

" He's awake at last," said a voice—Cummins'.

" Why, what's the matter ? " I asked in surprise as he and Beck appeared in the narrow passage-way between the bunks.

" Do you know the time ? " said Cummins.

" No, what about it ? "

" It's three o'clock, and you've been sound asleep for about fourteen hours. You're for it, all right."

" The officer wanted you last night," burst out Beck with round eyes. " He sent for you. We tried to waken you up, but couldn't."

" Then he arrived himself," said Cummins. " He was raging. He punched you and slapped you and we threw water over you, but it was all no bon. You were snoring like a pig."

" Right enough, Corporal," said Beck. " We thought there was something the matter with you. You were like a dead man."

I listened, flabbergasted.

" What did he want ? "

" Something about some message or other," said Cummins. " He didn't say exactly."

A feeling of anger and shame came over me. He would

know damned well that I hadn't been able to sleep in the
front line. So would the others. Maybe he had suspected I
was windy and had just wanted to make sure.

" You should have heard what he called you," said
Cummins laughing.

" Well, two can play at that game," I said.

After a couple of days in the hut we moved half a mile
farther back. Battalion headquarters were in a deep dug-out
and we were in an old shaft, the floor of which was under
water. We envied the headquarter lot until huge shells
began falling near and they had to evacuate. The shells
came from a 16-inch gun which rumour had it came up
the German line on a train. They sounded as if they were
coming over on a train too. They searched for the dug-out
and put the breeze up its inhabitants.

Eventually one lit just beside it, blocking up the dug-out
entrance.

We went along to see the craters. They were great round
holes and could easily have accommodated a horse and wagon
below ground level. We stood looking into the one that had
made the dug-out uninhabitable and argued gravely on just
what would have happened if it had scored a direct hit, citing
precedent after precedent, like young lawyers making the
most of a brief, only ours were based more on imagination
than fact.

We lived for a few days under front-line conditions as
regards shells and then moved back into the line. Instead
of going back to the same place we went in farther to the
left, but in the same sector. As before, the Verey lights went
up all round. We had taken over the opposite corner of the
salient.

It was a bad change. There was no trench at all in the
new place. A series of tumbledown shelters were partly
scooped out of and partly built into a little ridge overlooking
the German line. They were covered with sheets of

2 B

corrugated iron laid on planks and camouflaged with a thin layer of rotting sand-bags. Behind the shelters, the ground fell into a little valley which ended in a bank a few hundred yards away. The bank was under observation and Jerry had a machine-gun trained on it so that it was prohibited to cross it in daylight. At night the machine-gun fired irregular bursts, making the bank a place to steer clear of either by day or by night. It was the only way to battalion headquarters.

The lie of the land was rather peculiar. Jerry was in a salient. On his side of No Man's Land the ground rose to a fair-sized hill. What happened over the hill was hidden from our view, but the front line and the ground behind it to the top was spread out invitingly before our eyes. Opposite us, half-way up the hill, was a big farmhouse. For some reason or other our guns never bothered with it although its cellars were believed to hold a lot of men. It was strange to see the intact house with its mellowed red brick standing up bravely almost in the firing-line.

On the other hand the Germans had an equally good view of our lines—better, for our gunners had no hill to hide behind. The only place he couldn't see into was the little valley behind the ridge where we lay, so that on both sides it was a case of lying very low. No Man's Land ran in a semicircle round the base of the hill to the other side of the salient, three or four thousand yards away.

It was the first time I had ever got a glimpse into actual German territory. On odd occasions when things were quiet I peered over the ridge at the big house and the bare slope. They drew my eyes almost against my will, but never by any chance did I see a single German, although they must often have spotted our fellows moving about. The British had not yet learned the art of keeping still, although it wasn't the men's fault. Some crank at battalion, brigade or divisional H.Q. was always wanting something done that wouldn't wait for night. Runners kept coming and going.

Our telephone wire ran back through the valley and across Machine-gun Bank to battalion headquarters somewhere behind. The floor of the valley was covered with long tangled grass and weeds except where shells had excavated crumbly craters. At some time or other the hollow must have been part of No Man's Land, for there were dense patches of rusty barbed wire and old stakes, almost hidden now by the grass. A narrow path wound across from where we were to the bank.

Because it was the only place they couldn't observe, the German gunners never tired of sending shells into the hollow. The first night, when they came screeching over our heads to burst a little way behind, we thought the mob we had relieved had been acting the fool somehow and that Jerry was going to blow us out of our holes as a reprisal. We hugged the ground, waiting for him to give the exact range and cursing our predecessors. Our chances of coming out alive looked slim.

" To be killed after all on a bit of dirty ground," I thought. " It would have been better if it had happened away at the first when there was a big show on. There would have been some reason to it then."

There was no sign of the shells coming nearer, and after a while we took heart.

" They are only wasting ammunition," said Cummins, lighting a cigarette-end in his cupped hands.

The real trouble started towards morning. I was sending through a message when the phone went dead. The officer who was sitting beside me with a silver flask in one hand and a thin, triangular sandwich in the other, looked up peevishly when I reported.

" It's very likely just down in that valley behind us," he said.

" Yes, sir."

" Well, damn it all, have it repaired at once then, Corporal. That message should have been there by now."

I crept out and looked about me, shivering in the sharp air. Dawn was just breaking, but the valley was dark. I stood, half bent, for a moment and then ducked as a shell burst below me, sending the earth spouting.

" Poor old Beck's unlucky this time," I thought. " It's his turn as linesman."

Making my way carefully to our shelter I pulled back the sandbag flap. Beck was sitting just inside the entrance, holding a dirty dixie of water over a trench cooker. An opened matchbox containing tea, sugar and dirt in about equal proportions was beside him on a spread-out khaki handkerchief to catch the grains. The handkerchief was drawn into little dry puckers, which showed that it had been often in use in a more legitimate way. The heat of the cooker had swollen the little globules of sweat about his nose until they were ready to run.

" Hello, Corp. I'm just drumming up. I was just going to slip along and give you a drop to warm you up. It'll be ready in a minute."

Maxwell, whom I had relieved half an hour before, was sitting, his head resting on his knees, sound asleep. The new fellow, Cummins, was hunched up against the earth wall at the back—the safest place, I noticed—with a message tablet in one hand and a pencil end in the other.

" Just writing to one of my harem," he volunteered, catching my eye. " Picked her up the last time I was home."

" The line is gone, boys," I said.

Another shell burst behind. I made a quick decision. I liked Beck, and Cummins had groused the last time we were in the line about helping Beck out with a message. Beck often required help on account of being slow at the Morse.

" You go along, Cummins," I said, " and let Beck here finish drumming up. He can go the next time."

Cummins froze.

" Why the hell should I have to go first any more than him ? "

" Why the hell not ? " I said.

" Aw, let him go," replied Cummins with a look at once defiant and appealing. " It's his turn, isn't it ? "

" Somebody has to go and it's the same going first as second."

" I'll go if you like, Corporal," put in Beck stupidly.

Another shell roared down into the valley. The explosion seemed worse in the shelter with a candle guttering than outside in the grey air of the morning.

" It's all because I'm new to your station," said Cummins bitterly. " You think you can pick on me. All filthy favouritism. I'll not stir a foot. Let Beck here go when he has volunteered for it. It's not my turn."

I was secretly at a loss.

" Oh, well, you can't say I didn't warn you. The officer in there says he has a message that has to go through. For all the importance of it I don't care a damn if it never goes. But you know what he is as well as I do."

" As far as I can see we'll all have to do our whack at linesman this tour," broke in Maxwell, awakened by the argument. " So you might as well go, Cummins, when you're told to go. The Corporal says it and you have to obey an order."

" Away with yourself you, and go to sleep. Who asked you to shove your ugly snout in ? " snarled Cummins, raging as the inevitable closed in about him. " A pack of twisters, that's what you are."

Beck put down the dixie and made to wriggle up. " Let me go, Corp'l. I'll go all right."

" You sit there and do what you're told," I said angrily.

Cummins sat glowering, his back pressed against the earth wall.

" If I can't get him to go now when I've told him he'll do what he likes ever afterwards and laugh at me," I thought. " Have a bit of sense, man, or I'll have to report you. I tell you he'll go next time," I went on aloud.

" All right, I'll go. And I'll take good care he goes next and you after him, Corporal or no Corporal," said Cummins.

" For goodness sake go and stop grousing. You could have been there and back by now," said Maxwell crossly. " Waking a fellow up all for nothing."

I went back to the phone.

" Well, is it fixed yet ? " demanded the officer.

" There's a man gone out to repair it. It'll be all right in a couple of minutes, sir."

I backed out hurriedly to make sure that Cummins was going out. He came along with a pair of nippers and an insulation tape in his hand and a thin coil of wire over one shoulder. Without speaking he caught up the line from the phone and started off, letting it run through his fingers. A shell burst at the far end of the valley just as he got down. He ducked, hesitated, and went on at a scrambling trot, stumbling as the rusty barbs caught at his feet.

His luck was out, for instead of the break being at our side of the valley the wire held until he was within fifty yards of Machine-Gun Bank, where the smoke still rose in spirals from the last burst. Then, finding the break, he began questing round in a little circle for the other end of the wire. The tangled grass and wire cost him valuable seconds. I strained my eyes.

Again a shell screamed. I held my breath as a great black column sprang up right in the centre of the valley, hiding Cummins from view. A minute later I spotted him through the drifting smoke down on his knees engrossed in the task of baring and insulating the broken ends.

There was a sound behind me. Looking round I saw Beck.

" It's a darned funny business," he said apologetically. " Here we are as safe as houses and there's Cummins just over there. I bet the splinters were whistling round his ears from that last one, eh ? "

" He's not out of the wood yet," I returned. " He'll need to get a move on before the next one comes."

Cummins, to give him his due, wasted no time. As if he heard my warning he got to his feet and started running back, with bent knees, his head between his hunched shoulders, his whole attitude plainly advertising his readiness to drop at the slightest alarm. He came on quickly, skirting the craters, until, happening to glance up, he saw us watching. He slowed down to a walking pace and straightened his head.

" The silly ass ! Look at him showing off now that the job's done," I muttered to Beck.

" He let himself down a bit, you see, about going out, Corporal."

Cummins seemed to read my thoughts again. He came sauntering along, kicking the grass. Coming to a halt almost in the lee of the bank he fished out a cigarette from his pocket and proceeded to light up.

When he was a bare score yards away there was a sudden shriek—nearer and more vicious than any that had gone before. Beck and I dropped like stones as the shell exploded deafeningly. Fragments of steel tore through the air above our bowed heads, followed, after an appreciable interval, by heavy clods of earth.

We lay motionless until the echoes of the explosion had died away and the blessed quiet came. Then, raising my head, I glanced down fearfully to see how Cummins had fared. There was no Cummins to be seen. Rubbing my smarting eyes I looked again. The smoke lingered a moment and then began drifting and thinning, leaving a shallow, evil-looking crater where he had stood a minute before. Wisps of loathsome oily smoke rose from it.

Maxwell came running up with an anxious look on his face. He became mystified when in reply to his excited question we pointed stupidly to the crater.

" Where ? Where is he ? "

" The shell-hole," said Beck, half-crying. " It must have lit right on top of him."

Without a word Maxwell ran down the slope. He stopped, staring about him. Something on the ground caught his eye. He bent down and put his hand out uncertainly. Straightening up he came slowly back.

" It's right enough," he said looking away. " He got it to himself. There's a boot down there and one or two bits of things, but that's about all."

" And I wanted to go, Corp'l," said Beck beginning to shake.

THE OLD MOTTO

I REPORTED to the Company Officer.

"And what about the line ? Is it fixed yet ? " he asked sharply when I had finished.

I had forgotten about the line and stammered stupidly under his cold grey eyes.

"Corporal, I'll have to report you if you waste any more time. Get a move on, to please me."

I went over to the telephone. To my surprise it was once more in working order. In a moment the message, a trivial affair, was through.

The Jerry gunners continued to plaster the valley with shells. Before nightfall we had each paid hurried visits into it, past Cummins' shell-hole, to repair the line. It began to rain, and the shacks were like sieves.

That night I was on duty when the Signal Officer and the Acting-Adjutant, young, pale-faced and rather fat, arrived, breathless from dodging shells in the valley. I had to go outside to make room for them. When they had departed a runner was sent off to one of the platoons with a chit. In a few minutes a Second Lieutenant made his appeareance. He was a fine-looking young fellow, easily six feet tall with broad shoulders and slim hips.

"Wanting me, sir ? " he said cheerfully. " Filthy night, isn't it ? "

"You are to take charge of a raiding party to-night," said the Company Officer without preamble. " The Colonel suggested your name himself, so I've nothing to do with it."

The young officer swallowed and his cheerful grin disappeared. His eyes narrowed and little hard lumps stood out at the angle of his jaws.

" Righto, sir," he said. " When is it to happen ? "

" Zero hour will be at two ack emma," replied the O.C. " Gas cylinders are being sent over and when they go up that will be your cue. Division want to know how strongly the line's held, it seems."

" I suppose one prisoner will be enough ? "

" If you can lay hands on one it'll be tophole. But it's believed that the Bosche deserts his front line during the day, leaving our artillery to waste good ammunition, and then comes along and patrols it strongly at night. So you mightn't get hold of one at all, and on the other hand you'll have to watch your step both going and coming, see ? "

The O.C. opened up a trench map and drew a candle nearer. I sat staring at the Platoon Officer as he followed his pointing finger and nodded silent agreement to his disposals. In a little while he would be out in No Man's Land, taking a poor chance of his life. Despite the rain dribbling through the crazy roof the shack seemed a very comfortable, desirable place.

" Well, now, we come to the question of men. How do you stand there ? "

" We-e-ll, sir, I have three or four stout fellows in the platoon, ones that I know can be depended upon, but that's hardly——"

" Good enough. I'll make you up to strength from the other platoons. I'll do the best I can for you, and ten will be enough along with a good N.C.O. By the way, you haven't got your M.C. yet ? "

" No, sir, not yet."

" Well, this is your chance to get it. No reason why you shouldn't if you do a good show. You may rely upon me so far as that is concerned, old chap."

" Thanks very much indeed. Too decent of you."

" That's all right. But I say. It's only a formality you know, but, just in case, I think you had better leave all your jewellery, etc., with me till you amble in again. What do you think ? "

The young officer appeared embarrassed as he twisted his big body in the confined space to reach his pockets, but at length the transfer was completed, and he went away, laughing rather strainedly after a hand-shake and an exchange of airy, false-sounding au revoirs.

Maxwell relieved me shortly afterwards, but I was unable to sleep and sat waiting timidly for the raid to commence. The Jerry guns would retaliate and whether the raid succeeded or failed we were due for a rough night.

When the gas cylinders went off like a thunderclap I crouched down along with Beck as the front came to life. For a minute or two there was no response from the other side and then shells began bursting near. Our wretched shelter shook and driblets of earth fell on our bowed heads. A cross plank gave way and fell across our shoulders, bringing some sodden sandbags with it, and for a long moment I thought it was a hit. Getting to my knees I yelled to Beck and we managed between us to put the beam back in its place. Where the sandbags had been we saw the sky lit by great flashes and hid our faces. In between the bursts came the rattle of machine-guns going full blast.

After a time the fire slackened. We patched up the roof as best we could from the inside. The rain stopped and the machine-gunners contented themselves with their usual roving night fire. When Maxwell's tour was over things were almost normal.

" It was a success as far as it went," he told me. " They got a prisoner, but he was done in by a shell on the way back along with a couple of the party."

" What about the officer ? "

" Oh, he came in all right. Hard luck he didn't get the Jerry in. But all he could bring was his papers. Said he had enough to do getting them, too. It must have been pretty hot out there, eh ? "

" Old Jerry must have got it hot by the way he was trying to get his own back," said Beck as a fresh flurry of shells burst viciously round our crest. " He'll smash that cursed wire again if he's not careful."

Next day the little valley behind us continued to act in the capacity of waking nightmare. Shells tore into it with sickening regularity. Off duty at the phone we eyed them as they burst, our ears keyed to hearing the call that we grew to hate from the man on duty. " Line gone again." The fate of Cummins preyed on our minds—not so much out of sympathy, but because it was a signpost pointing to our own fate. The wire was our taskmaster and the shells were God.

Always, when my turn came to chance my arm, the thought came to me that I should trade on my Lance-Corporal's stripe to get out of going. " Protection stripes," they were called anyway, and what was there to hinder me shoving it on to Beck and brazening it out with Maxwell ?

Then the old feeling—not fatalism, or submission, or fear of what they would think, but a mixture of all three —came to my aid as I picked up the linesman's tools. After all, why not me as well as all the others ? How much longer would we have to stick it ? How much longer would our luck hold out ? Every few minutes the valley resounded to a shell-burst and smoke wreathed lazily on the still air.

Late in the afternoon a message came for me to report at once at battalion headquarters. It was something fairly urgent or else they would have waited till dark. The other two looked blue.

" You've clicked for some cushy job somewhere or they wouldn't be in such a hurry," said Maxwell, and I thrilled at the thought.

" Remind them there's only two of us up here now," said Beck.

None of us knew exactly where battalion headquarters was, so taking the line in my hand I started off—waiting first, with the caution of experience, until a shell fell before running down. Then a nervous pause in the valley-bottom for the next one and a wild run up and over Machine-Gun Bank to the accompaniment of a few bullets, which spurted harmlessly into the ground a couple of yards behind. Beyond the bank Jerry was blind or indifferent and the going good.

The line brought me to an imposing château. It suffered more from general dilapidation than shell-fire, although it was in full view from the rising ground behind the Jerry front line, just as the house half-way up there was in full view from our line and still intact. A gentleman's agreement, perhaps. In a room at the rear I found the Signal Officer.

" Oh, here you are, Corporal. I've a very special job for you," he said, leading me out of earshot of the man at the phone. " And remember, you are to keep it under your hat."

" Yes, sir," I answered automatically, wondering what on earth the job was. Were Maxwell and Beck right after all ? Rosy visions of a job at battalion headquarters or perhaps as orderly-room clerk down in the wagon lines floated before me. They might have heard that I knew clerking. Clerks were rare birds in our battalion. Or could it be that the officer had taken a fancy to me and had nominated me for another course.

" He always did strike me as being a decent chap," I thought with a little surge of gratitude. No more scrambling into the valley to repair breaks or cowering down in the shelters on the ridge.

" Now then," said the Signal Officer. Pulling a trench map from his pocket he opened it out and spread it against the wall.

My hopes faded as quickly as they had come. A man going down the line didn't need a map. He trusted to instinct and his ears and followed his nose. After a few days up the line a blind man could have found his way down without stopping.

But the officer was speaking.

"—going to be a little stunt here to-morrow morning early. A fresh crowd is coming in to do it, thank goodness. The idea is to straighten out the line and push the Bosche out of his little salient. There have been so many telephone wires cut lately that when a real strafe starts the whole caboodle of them wouldn't last five minutes. Our ground is too exposed, you see ? "

" Yes, sir."

" So it has been decided to steal a march on the Bosche and lay a line through No Man's Land. There'll be less chance of it being smashed there while the ' do ' is in progress. Understand ? Anyhow, it gives us an extra circuit."

Running his finger over the map he began to explain where exactly the wire was to be laid. I listened dumbly and stared at the meaningless marks. It was my first look at a trench map.

" If you cut straight across here from your station until you strike our own line again at the far side here where it begins to bend forward, you'll be just about right. It's a goodish distance, but fairly straight going, allowing for the bend in the line. Don't forget, by the way, to do almost a half right at where you start off from our wire. Then carry straight on for a while before doing a half turn to the left to bring yourself at the other end of the salient, because it's there the boys are going over. It's believed, although we're not sure, that the Bosche patrols his line at night, so you'll need to keep your eye skinned. Is it all clear ? " I didn't like saying it wasn't a bit clear, and nodded.

" What men have you up there in the station now ? "

" Just Maxwell and Beck, sir, since the other man got knocked out."

" Oh, yes, I remember now. Well, I'm sending you up a new chap to bring you up to strength. I was thinking of sending another Lance-Corporal from one of the other company stations along with you on this job, but isn't Maxwell a pretty reliable, conscientious sort of man ? You could take him along instead, perhaps. What do you think ? "

It was pleasant to be asked for an opinion on another man by an officer as if I myself was above reproach.

" Yes, sir. He's very conscientious," I replied.

" Too conscientious altogether sometimes," I thought.

" That will do nicely, then. Another thing. Your company will be moving round to help consolidate the position, so you will be bringing the wire right into your own company headquarters. They'll be in a dug-out just about here, and, that reminds me, I mustn't forget to send word to them to be watching out for the pair of you in case they would take you for Huns."

The officer pointed to another spot on the map where the company dug-out was to be, but I might as well have been looking at the bedraggled wallpaper of the room for all the sense I could make out of it. My head was in a whirl as tiny yet insistent questions assailed me. Maxwell and I were to leave our own lines and wander across No Man's Land for a couple of kilometres or so until we blundered on to our own line again.

" When we get to the other side," I thought, " it'll be time enough to find out what to do with the wire."

" You had better start out fairly early, before midnight, say, so as to leave plenty of time for getting in before the show starts."

" Yes, sir," I said again, and the officer went off, leaving me wondering would it all come out according to plan as he seemed to think. To my knowledge I had never been in No Man's Land in my life before.

There was no sense in risking the return journey to the company in daylight. The crest in itself appeared a very dangerous place to have to go back to compared to the big château with its complement of officers and orderlies on the ground floor.

For a couple of hours I hung about, uncomfortably aware that I didn't belong. Then, accompanied by a dark, sullen-looking young fellow named Watson—Cummins' successor —I returned to the company. Between us we carried a heavy reel of thin, black-enamelled wire for the stunt.

Maxwell thought I was pulling his leg at first when I told him what was before us. He became quiet when he realised I was in earnest, the heavy drum of otherwise useless wire helping to convince him. He didn't seem very grateful either for the high opinion the officer and I entertained of him.

" It's a job for two Lance-Corporals he protested.

As the time for departure drew near Beck fussed round me, desirous of showing his good wishes for the success of the venture.

" You're sure you know exactly where to make for ? " he asked anxiously, pressing a cigarette on me from his small, crumpled store.

I thought less of the question, which I could only answer vaguely, than of the way he pressed the fag on me and a few minutes later refused sturdily to accept one in return, although, as it happened, I had twice as big a stock as he.

" So long, Corp," he said anxiously. " Be sure and don't wander into the Jerry lines or fool about till the bombardment starts. I'll be watching out for you," he called out as we snaked through our own wire.

I didn't bother to reply. Once over the top I forgot Beck

and everything else in the queer realisation that I had left the company, the battalion behind. I was surprised to find myself imbued with a feeling of adventure and daring such as I had never known in the trenches, or the holes that passed for trenches. Our lives depended on ourselves to a greater extent, in my case, at any rate, than ever before. It was a new feeling after months of senseless shell-fire which killed men indiscriminately, whether standing watchful on the fire-step or sitting doubled up on a field latrine. We had our eyes to depend on to pierce the darkness and our straining ears to catch the slightest sound. Most of all we had our animal wariness to warn us of danger and help evade it.

My nerves were keyed up, but not shaky. I was cool and picked my steps over old shell-holes, sensing rather than seeing them. It was very odd that I wasn't afraid, but there it was.

One after another complications set in, setting problems that had to be solved, or let slide with the luck.

The heavy drum had to be carried singly, we discovered. The wire was sticky and refused to unroll of itself, or perhaps it was owing to our slow progress. I took first turn and Maxwell followed close behind, keeping up a steady pull. It was dud wire, almost brittle, and was continually going into kinks which had to be straightened out before we could proceed. Kinked wire snapped easily, so unless we attended to each one as we went along all our trouble would go for nothing.

The constant winding around shell-holes was confusing, and after a few hundred yards we lost direction. It was hard to tell whether we were going too much to the right where our line was, or to the left, which was towards Jerry's.

We halted at intervals and argued in whispers about who the Verey lights belonged to. They seemed to meet in a circle far in front.

Carrying the drums was an awkward job. It had to be

2 C

held free from the body to let the wire run and we were each soon tired of the ungainly burden, necessitating numerous rests in convenient shell-holes.

Worst of all, and what he hadn't bargained for, was the rhythmic creaking of the revolving drum. At first it had been hardly noticeable, but before we had gone far it was loud enough to drown all sounds about us. The whole German Army could have come goose-stepping within a dozen yards of us without our being a whit the wiser. All we could do to counteract the noise was stop every few yards, crouch down and listen. We whispered encouragement to each other.

Once I could have sworn I saw dark shapes moving towards us. We stopped, scarcely daring to breathe.

Maxwell, in turn, grasped my arm, squeezing hard to indicate caution. After several such false-alarms I felt reckless and cursed aloud. It was a useless thing to do, but it restored my self-confidence.

Then Maxwell, carrying the drum, tripped and went headlong into an old crater. As he got to his knees something squelched and sighed with a curious sucking sound.

" It's—only—a—stiff. Smell—the—stink," he whispered taking a breath for each word.

Far away a lone machine-gun began to stutter, and gradually others took up the tale. Bullets hissed softly overhead —lost spirits seeking the haven of a warm human body. We lay flat.

The machine-guns stopped and we went on, but soon they were rattling away as if the first burst had only whetted their appetites. Again we lay low as they hummed past. Distant machine-guns joined in and swept methodically over No Man's Land—not so much with the hope of finding a billet as with the desire of discouraging anyone from taking the risk.

We lay for long minutes, our eyes cocked upward like a

man looking over his glasses. An odd feeling that we were neutrals obsessed me.

The machine-guns seemed to have come to stay. We progressed at times on hands and knees, stopping when the bullets came very near, and getting to our feet when they faded away in front or behind. Shells whined past over in sympathy, but we paid little attention to them. Neither side, we knew, wanted to waste ammunition on where we were. No Man's Land had its advantages.

Another stumble. The wire parted. We lost anxious minutes groping for the lost end to repair the break. The drum was half-way down now. Our halts became more frequent and the starts more hesitating. There was only the darkness and the shell-holes.

" Where are we ? "

I didn't know, but we had gone too far for sitting still, and retreat was out of the question.

" How much longer will the wire last, d'ye think ? "

The machine-guns died down, but the shells carried on a half-hearted strafe. We heard them leaving the gun and rumble overhead, and far away the melancholy boom of the explosions. The drum was easy to hole now, but the creaking came loudly.

" The wire'll soon be all gone, Corporal," whispered Maxwell anxiously. " We don't seem to be any nearer, either, to our line, and yet it must be somewhere about if we came in the right direction. What'll we do ? "

" We'll go on, anyway," I said."

We went on doggedly, trusting to luck. There was no such thing as using judgment, except to keep bearing to the left according to the officer's instructions.

A half right, straight on, and a half left, he had said, but it wasn't so simple as that. We mightn't have gone straight and now we might be bearing too much to the left, into the German lines.

Suddenly, out of the darkness, came a roaring, clattering staccato. In front of us a great red mouth took instant shape. Streamers of fire leapt at us, searing the air, snarling and hissing with appalling pent-up viciousness, hammering the fear of instant death into our dazed brains, paralysing our limbs.

We had walked into the teeth of a machine-gun.

My machine-gun luck held, even though I had actually seen the fiery tracers coming at us from the muzzle a few yards away. Diving down I landed in a shallow crater and lay pressing into the earth while bullets screamed past.

The noise stopped as abruptly as it had begun and silence fell with almost as great a shock. The darkness descended, blacker than ever.

An excited voice reached us from in front. Although I understood what it said it was several moments before the realisation came that it was an English voice.

" I'll take my bleeding oath there was somebody there," it said.

There was a confused murmur.

" Don't fire. Don't fire. Friend. Friend." I shouted, raising my head.

For answer the machine-gun restarted. Again the red mouth appeared spitting bullets. They were lower and sent trickles and tiny avalanches of earth about my face.

There was a final burst, and the voices came, obviously debating this time what to do. I shouted again, but in a different key, as I realised that I was safe after all.

" Hey, there. You windy bastards, what do you think you're on, firing like that. We are only signallers, God damn it."

" How many ? " came a voice—more authoritative this time.

" Two of us, laying a line."

" Only two. Are you sure ? Come up to the wire, one at a time, and no tricks, remember, or we'll fire."

I turned to Maxwell, surprised that he had kept silent so long.

" Maxwell. Where are you ? It's all right now, man."

No answer came. Getting stiffly to my knees I leant forward and resting one hand on the ground reached out gropingly.

" What's the matter, Maxwell. Are you hit ? Where are you ? "

My left hand moving hesitantly over the crumbly earth encountered first a warm puddle and then torn, slippy flesh. It was his face.

" For God's sake give me a hand, mates," I shouted, panic-stricken. " The other chap's hit and I've a big reel of wire here."

My hand was sticky with blood, and dread of the unknown seized me.

" Maxwell, Maxwell," I whispered distractedly, hoping against hope that he would answer and that all would be well. Then I crouched down in the shell-hole as far from him as I could.

" Whereabouts are you ? " came the voice.

" Here. Over here. Don't shoot."

" Hang on for a minute."

There was a twang of wire and stealthy rustling. Dark figures, blobs of deeper darkness, squirmed towards us. Catching hold of Maxwell's inert body they trailed it slowly under a thick belt of wire, mumbling curses as the barbs and stakes retarded them. I followed close behind, paying out the line as I went, and sprawled head foremost into a trench crowded with silent men.

The ones who had pulled Maxwell in bent over him. " Stretcher-bearers, stretcher-bearers," went the call.

I stood vacantly until a touch on my arm attracted my attention. The men had straightened up.

" Hard luck, sonny. Your mate has gone west, I'm afraid," said the voice—an officer's voice. " He stopped half a dozen if he stopped one."

I shook off his arm, without replying, and got hold of the drum. A Verey light went up, outlining the men standing shoulder to shoulder. The nearest man looked round fleetingly to see what the rumpus had been about, and then resumed their steady stare to the front. They were fresh troops, each man dressed as if for a general inspection, with new uniforms and every strap in place. It occurred to me that this was an assembly trench and that they were due to go over the top soon. Their almost complete lack of curiosity in anything else became understandable. They were probably blaming Maxwell and me inwardly for causing their Lewis-gunners to let fly and chance a few shells in return.

I started to make my way along behind them, but happening to glance up to the parapet as the Verey light fell I saw the Lewis-gun team. Disregarding the officer—he was still at my side—I spoke up to them, raising my voice a little to make sure they heard.

" That was a dirty trick, boys."

" Sorry, mate," came the answer after a pause, " but it's not our fault. We weren't warned to look out for you or it wouldn't have happened. And you know the old motto."

THE COMRADES-IN-ARMS

THE dug-out was deep. Thirty steps or more led into the earth. The air inside was warm and heavy.

The attack had commenced and for all its depth the ceiling shook. Little showers of earth fell. The phone was in the corner farthest from the stairway and the heat from half a dozen candles and a trench cooker, over which the company officer's batman knelt, was strangely pleasant after many nights and days in the open.

Besides being beautifully warm it was beautifully safe. I relaxed. The constant heavy rumbling overhead told of danger and death up on top, and I felt content. Quite a number of people seemed to have business in the dug-out and their breath added appreciably to the thickness of the atmosphere. I felt sleepy.

The Signal Sergeant of the attacking battalion came in with a couple of men, one of whom had a wire with him. The Sergeant asked permission to connect the wire temporarily to my phone.

" My signallers went over in the second wave with a line, Corporal," he said to me, " and we're anxious to find out how the attack's going."

" Right you are, Sarge," I said and surrendered the headpiece. The Sergeant put it on, and commenced tapping anxiously.

There was nothing for me to do. My eyelids began to droop.

By rights I shouldn't have been at the phone at all. My job had been, along with Maxwell, to bring the wire across No Man's Land, and after that let Beck or the new fellow carry on. But I wanted to stay on in the dug-out. It didn't seem right that after doing the dirty work I should go up on top again, leaving the warmth and safety of the dug-out to them. Heavy crashes that made the candles flicker warned me what it was like up there. And I had had very little sleep for several days.

I leaned back against the dug-out wall, watching the Sergeant trying to get through to his own crowd. Waves of desire beat down on me. My eyelids became weighed with lead. I dozed, only to wake up with a sharp voice in my ear. It was the company officer speaking as much to me as at me.

" If my Signal Corporal doesn't keep awake I'll crime him," he said with a coldly impersonal inflexion.

For a moment I was wide awake. Then, uncontrollably, my eyelids drooped. " Sleep, sleep," whispered my relaxed body. The warm heavy air, and, above all, the safety, murmured slumber.

My eyes closed again. I struggled to keep them open, but they seemed glued together.

The Sergeant jogged my elbow.

" Hey, Corporal, better keep awake," he muttered. " Your officer's watching you like a hawk."

I lapsed into unconsciousness, only to wake up again with a vague superficial awareness that something was happening that concerned me, while all the time three-quarters of me was stupid.

" Take the Corporal's name, Sergeant-Major. The charge is asleep on duty."

" But, but—the Sergeant here is on duty, sir. He has taken over the phone," I said, still half-bemused.

" It's your phone, and your station. You are responsible for it, and nobody else. Go up on top and send someone down that at least knows enough to keep awake."

Under the strange Sergeant's commiserating look I got

slowly to my feet, feeling very foolish and discredited and, at bottom, with a great hatred for all authority.

To reach the stairway I had to step carefully over the company officer's recumbent form.

The steps leading to the dug-out mouth were jammed with cowering men seeking shelter from the bombardment. They had no business there, but like first-nighters in a queue they clung obstinately to their places. It took me all my time getting past.

" Any of the company signallers here ? " I kept calling as I forced my way up. Near the top Watson, the new fellow, answered and I sent him down.

He obeyed with alacrity, and a scramble ensued for his place.

Once on top all desire for sleep left me so completely that I wondered, shivering in the raw air, where the drowsiness had come from. I was as wide awake as before I had been sleepy.

Shells crashed down among a grove of trees covering the entrance to the dug-out, their red glare dimming the pale gun-flashes trooping across the night sky. The heavy explosions momentarily eclipsed the general uproar, and I bent down.

The officer's threat seemed suddenly a very small affair, and I promptly forgot all about it. On top it was a matter of living or being killed.

Once out of the stairway there was no hope of obtaining a foothold on it. I prowled about, changing uneasily from one side to the other according to where the last shell had fallen, longing for the already distant heat and safety of down below.

The dug-out had been built by the Germans, so that the entrance faced towards their line. Even so, a niche on the steps was very desirable. Only a direct hit could have done any damage.

One or two other unlucky ones kept me company. One was Beck, who, although probably among the first to arrive, had been too soft to take advantage of it. We pressed close together, without speaking more than a muttered word or two as the shells roared down. I felt comforted by his simple company.

For a long time there was no lessening of the wild clamour. Great bursts sent the trees crashing. The sky glowed and waned, showing trailing, ragged clouds one minute and impenetrable darkness the next.

Towards morning the shelling eased off, and men who had no right to be near the dug-out at all went unwillingly about their business. None of them was concerned about the fate of the attack. It had nothing to do with them, and they had enough to think about minding their own skins.

When they had gone, we ensconced ourselves safely a dozen steps down. I told about Maxwell, speaking as if I had heard of it at second hand. A bombardment dulls all feelings but the desire to live.

" It's funny, too," I said after a pause. " There he was, always ready to do exactly what he was told—conscientious and all that. And at the end of all he hadn't even the satisfaction of being done in by the Germans."

" What does it matter to him now ? " said Beck, picking his nose.

" And dodging shells for month after month," I went on, speaking half to myself.

" But he might have thought it was a Jerry machine-gun that caught him and then he died happy enough," Beck said.

" You might be right, God knows. And anyway, what does it matter. He's as dead as a doornail. That's the main thing and the rest doesn't matter much. Very likely our Signal Officer forgot to let that crowd know to expect us. Yes, that'll be it, for he said at the time : ' I mustn't forget,' instead of : ' I must remember.' "

" But it's the same thing, isn't it, Corp'l ? "

" It is and it isn't. If you had a good memory you wouldn't say : ' I mustn't forget,' would you ? "

" I dunno. I dunno what kind of memory I have. But I wish to God I was only remembering about the war. I bet I wouldn't forget for a long time. Would you, Corporal ? It wouldn't seem too bad if you were only looking back on it."

" There he was. Didn't smoke, didn't drink, didn't swear. Even the Signal Officer had him tarred. Always down on grousing, too, and ready to do his whack. D'ye remember how he told off Cummins that time ? I couldn't understand him. He seemed to think we was fighting for something—his country, or some such bloody rubbish—or ' Little Belgium.' And at the end of all he was the best man of the lot of us for this job, for all his crankiness."

" I was never very struck on him myself—though, as you say, Corporal, he was all right."

" And look where he ended up ? ' Shoot first, mate, and inquire afterwards,' said the Lewis-gunner that shot him."

" There you are," said Beck, wiping his nose on his sleeve. " Maybe the gunner was another of them conscientious bastards."

A last heavy shell fell near the dug-out entrance and we were silent for a while, forgetting Maxwell.

" What's the war all about, anyway ? " said Beck, as if the question had just occurred to him for the first time. " Everybody fights away like they was hoeing potatoes or digging turnips for a living and didn't know any better."

" How should I know ? Why do fellows like dig turnips ? "

" Oh, but that's different. You see, you can eat turnips and you can't eat up the war, can you ? "

Beck seemed a little astonished at my obtuseness about so common or garden a thing.

" It's all the same," I said patiently, " only you're too damned stupid. You can eat turnips, and the war can eat you. You might be the bloody turnip for all you know, man."

" But what is it all about ? " persisted Beck.

" But that doesn't matter. Does a turnip know what it's all about ? You grow it and then eat it, don't you. You might as well say what does the ground know about it that it grows on. Nobody knows, but it's there just the same. And you're here."

" Ay, that's maybe all right, but it's not what I mean. What made everybody fight. Not everybody, of course, but us perishers ? "

" We don't fight, donkey, we're signallers."

Beck shuffled uneasily and stammered.

Things were quiet again, and pulling out a packet of issue we both lit up, shielding the glow from the cigarettes in our cupped hands.

" You know . . . but Corporal . . . what I mean . . ." went on Beck seriously. " Nobody here really fights—the same as a gang of fellows in a row at home. That's fighting, isn't it ? They have a row and give each other a dunt, and it's over. When will the war be over ? "

" Will you for God's sake stop asking so many questions. What do I know ? Maxwell must have been fighting or he wouldn't have been killed."

" Y-e-s, but I don't see the sense of it ; and what is it all about ? "

We learned next day that the do had been a great success. The new mob had taken the German trench with less than a dozen casualties, and there were no counter-attacks. For this we, who were left to consolidate, were duly thankful. The enemy showed his bad temper by heavy shelling and showers of gas. Our nerves were on edge. A counter-attack might come yet.

There was much grousing about lucky units that had only

to come up and do a little stunt and then beat it, leaving men who should have been relieved long ago to hang on.

As it turned out the lucky ones didn't get off quite so lucky. Rumour reached us that on their way down the line the German artillery, whether by good luck or good guidance, had caught them and inflicted heavy casualties. Nearly a hundred of them had been hit.

It was Mundy who told me the news. " Isn't it like it, something would happen ? " he said. " A good stunt, well thought out, goes off like clockwork, and then when it's all over and done with and the boys are smiling all over their face, Jerry drops a few shells in amongst them on the road back, miles away from the line, and knocks them. A bit thick I call it. It doesn't even do old Jerry any good, for he hasn't got the satisfaction of knowing that he did get his own back on them."

Mundy swore and went about his business.

Day followed day and still we remained in the line, almost giving up hope of ever getting away. The men became sullen. The officers, fed up also, sympathised, buoying us up with false promises. Wherever we went we were harried with eternal shell-fire, and our telephone wires had to be constantly repaired.

We didn't blame the Germans so much as we did our own artillery. They seemed to have gone mad and banged away all the time so that it was only a case of retaliating. We abused our own side accordingly.

" They don't care a damn. They're camouflaged, and if it gets too hot they stop firing and run into deep dug-outs. Trust the gunners for that. Here we haven't even got decent trenches."

There was still the chance, too, that Jerry would come over on us. It would have been a bad day for our side if he had. The battalion and the whole Division were inexperienced and yet war weary. Young, half-trained and untried

troops would have crumpled up in no time before a determined attack by experienced men.

The company had a good many casualties. It was a war
of artillery, but the infantry suffered most. If enough
shells came over so many men were bound to be killed and
wounded. It was a matter of arithmetic.

The battalion served the same purpose as a flag stuck in a
map. It was there to show that that particular piece of ground
was in British hands, and for little else. If the Germans
had seriously wanted the ground they had only to open up
on it in real earnest and come over in sufficient numbers.

After a full month up the line we were relieved. We
marched away, hardly daring to breathe until we were clear
of the shell zone—hardly aware that the desire for rest
and sleep and old half-forgotten things had taken the place
of fear.

The village was far enough back to be inhabited by a few
civilians. It was a pretty place off the main road. The
rumble of the guns in front was softened and almost blended
with its peacefulness. The inhabitants were openly out to
make money and nearly all of them had something to sell.
They knew as well as we did that soldiers down from the
line had a pay parade.

Our meagre pay didn't give us much scope, but while it
lasted we drank wine and watery beer. Each time we came
" out " things seemed to cost more. If Australians or
Canadians had been in the neighbourhood we got a poor
show. They threw money about like lords, and prices
went up accordingly. With them rest was a jolly affair and
worth looking forward to. Their officers thought little of
drinking with their men in the estaminets, to the despair of
the Red Caps. Our Sergeants would have thought that
beneath their dignity, let alone our officers.

The battalion was run on the caste system. For the
officers the men were a lower order of humanity. They

accentuated the difference both in and out of the line. " In " they drank whisky, ate the best food obtainable and had their batmen to look after them. " Out " they looked on the men as nuisances who had to be kept occupied. The mess provided good wine and good food and they had whatever comfort that was going in the way of billets. From their point of view it was all very natural and right. It almost seemed right from our point of view for that matter.

Of all the armies in France the B.E.F. was the most ridden by discipline, a cast-iron discipline that killed initiative. Instead of being relaxed when we were out " resting " it was made stricter. The men, especially the young ones, were cowed, and because of it the Colonial troops despised us for having no backbone.

Australians and Canadians made a point of refusing to salute our officers. Not that the officers in the battalion were really to blame, perhaps. The majority of them had come to us from Service mobs and accordingly looked down on " regulars " as being so much ragtail and bobtail. When they got talking together up the line they cursed their luck and spoke longingly of their own crowds which they had been separated from or which had been washed out. They took little interest in us. The war was too old for that, and life was too short.

The signallers were billeted in an empty two-roomed cottage outside the village. At first we thought it was better than the barns and outhouses where the companies had their quarters, but the first night soon disabused us of that idea. There was no straw and no blankets and we had to do the best we could with our greatcoats. It was a frosty night and we huddled together on the flagged floor. We slept and shivered by turns, the only change from front-line conditions being that we could take our boots off and lap our puttees around our feet. Bereft of their usual tight covering my legs felt naked and itchy as the cold air, and the lice, circulated.

It became unbearable in the hour before dawn. In desperation I got up and walked about outside swinging my arms and stamping in a last effort to generate enough heat for another short, uneasy sleep. I had plenty of leeway to make up.

The cold kept some of the men running to make water. They had to pick their way over closely packed forms to reach the door. It was impossible to avoid tramping on their mates, so there was more trouble. In the morning there was bitter grousing but nothing to be done to improve matters.

" I can't make bleeding blankets," the Signal Sergeant expostulated, " so you'll just have to put up with it. There are none in the store and there's no straw."

The Sergeants had their own billet, of course.

Still, after we had washed in a ditch on the other side of the road from the cottage, the night's doings didn't seem so important. A slice of fried bacon, a round of loaf and half a dixie of scalding tea and what more could a man want ?

Then there was the peculiar joy of resurrecting our caps and polishing up our cap badges. A little dent in the cloth above the treasured badge made us feel like real soldiers. We stared disdainfully at occasional R.E.s and A.S.C. and other behind-the-line wallahs. It was something, after all, to belong to a regular battalion of an infantry regiment. The colours on our shoulder looked smart and distinctive —distinguished, we thought.

The line-dodgers bore up wonderfully under our contemptuous glances.

According to custom the first day of the rest was devoted to getting cleaned and outfitted, if required, with new uniforms. Second-hand, patchy stuff seldom came our way. If a man didn't like the fit of his tunic or cap he ripped a seam here or put a hole there and paraded for a fresh issue. " A regular unit must be spick-and-span," was the order, " Spit and polish," our lot.

A kit inspection followed, and this was always a touch-and-go affair.

We paraded in two lines, each man with his possessions spread neatly before him on the grass in the prescribed order, and each man generally short of iron ration, knife, fork, pull-through, oil-bottle, field dressing, mess-tin lid or such-like. Detection meant being crimed. Being crimed meant fines, pack drill and extra fatigues.

Naturally we had a well-developed system of evading detection. Before the inspecting officer—generally the Signal or Intelligence Officer—arrived on the scene the wants of those in the front rank were made up by the men in the rear. The officer would appear, consult with the Sergeant and begin, anxious to find something missing, should it be only a housewife, to show that he knew what he was about. As soon as he had passed three or four yards down the line those who had survived his eagle eye surreptitiously brought the depleted kits of the rear rank men up to strength. The only fly in the ointment was that the men at the end of the lines had to rely on themselves as the rear rank had no chance of getting stuff back in time before the officer was upon them. This defect in an otherwise excellent system was not so bad as it might appear. The officer was generally fed up looking for missing links long before he reached the end of the first row. The inspection became a cursory affair, as he hurried along the rear rank in order to get back to his mess or billet.

Next morning I was put under arrest, charged with being asleep on duty in the line. I was taken aback, but believing that I had a fairly good case I didn't worry overmuch until I was taken before the Captain of the company to which I nominally belonged. He met us on the street as we were on

2 D

the way to his quarters. I went through the formality of
being remanded to the C.O.

" This is a very serious affair for you, Corporal," he said.
" I can do nothing but send the case to the C.O. You'll
probably be court martialled."

I felt suddenly afraid.

The escort brought me farther along the street to where
Battalion Orderly Room had been established in a little
house. The second-in-command was acting C.O. The old-
stagers said he had been second-in-command of the battalion
when the war started and for some reason or other had never
been promoted. He had some job at Divisional headquarters
and was only seen with the battalion when it was temporarily
shy a Colonel which was every other month.

After half an hour's uneasy wait I was brought in and
stood stiffly to attention while the officer gave his version,
making it as black as he could by not mentioning about the
Signal Sergeant of the attacking battalion.

The Major listened attentively to him, and paid scant
attention to me when I told mine.

" Perfectly disgraceful," he rasped, " and an N.C.O., too,
who should know better. You should be shot for this. Only
that I don't want to get the battalion a bad reputation you
would be. You, in charge of the company signal station,
going off to sleep ! The very man on whom the safety of
the company or the attack might depend ! The very fact
that an attack was taking place should have made you doubly
keen. Many a man has been shot on the spot with far less
cause. Do you prefer being dealt with by me or do you want
a court martial ? "

I still believed that, technically, I had some right on my
side. A feeling of recklessness came over me. They
couldn't shoot me. No and damn them. The Sergeant
had taken over the phone with the officer's permission.

The Signal Officer, who was standing along with other

officers behind the C.O.'s chair, and who should have stuck up for one of his own men, caught my eye. He nodded vigorously.

For a moment I looked at him stupidly, and then understood. The sea-lawyer mood passed.

" By you, sir," I answered.

The C.O. mumbled something which I didn't catch. In a moment I found myself outside.

The R.S.M.—a rare bird only to be met with out of the line—followed me out. Still under escort I was marched down the village street. When a halt was called he obligingly loosened the solitary stripe on each arm for the Provost Sergeant, another rare bird.

The Provost Sergeant jerked the stripes off contemptuously, at the same time doing his best to impart some dignity to the proceedings for the edification of a little circle of women and children, who looked on with puzzled, friendly smiles.

THE ADVANCE

THE Germans were retreating when we started back for the line. It was early in the evening, so we knew we had a long way to go.

Away in front great wavering columns of smoke marked where villages, dumps and farm-houses were going up in flames. There was something desolate and savage about the columns that made our own puny fate hardly worth recording, providing that a Recording Angel was on the job.

At intervals the distant boom of heavy guns came to us, but nothing came our way. We marched on, bewildered at this strange turn of events, wondering just what it all portended. Did it mean more danger or less danger?

A feeling of vague expectancy, strongly tinged with uncertainty, possessed us. There had been yarns like that before.

We halted for the night in our old front line. There was no question of doing anything but kip down. There were no phones to mind and no shell-fire.

We were advancing, but we distrusted what the morrow would bring. Most of us but would have felt somehow safer and better off if we had arrived in the line in the ordinary course.

In the morning early the Signal Officer harangued us before we moved off.

" It's open warfare from now on," he said, making an effort to sound jubilant. " The enemy are beaten. They are evacuating the whole country and making for the Rhine as fast as their legs can carry them. It's all over, almost, bar the shouting. We must ram our victory home, and at all costs we are to keep in touch with them. It is the last great battle of the war, and we are sure of success. It is up to the signallers to show what they are made of. When the battalion goes over the top, as they will any time now, the signallers will follow in the second wave, and they must keep in touch with battalion headquarters. It is essential that headquarters should know just how everything is going on so that there shall be no delay. It is victory at last, and the Bosche is demoralised."

The officer did his best to make his words as weighty as possible, and we did our best to fall in with his words. But the guns boomed sullenly in front. The faint rattle of machine-guns was carried to us on a cold wind.

When the officer's back was turned we looked at each other. His efforts to infuse some enthusiasm into us had fallen flat.

They had been half-hearted efforts at best. The officer knew as well as we did that it was just as easy to get killed in the last battle as in the first, and a damned sight more unlucky. Jerry was retreating. He had retreated before. He might even be beaten, although we didn't really believe that, but he was still fighting. That was the main thing.

If the Germans were demoralised there was one thing certain. The British weren't far behind. Only for the Yanks he probably would have been after us.

Before moving off great strips of white canvas from six to twelve feet long were served out—" For signalling to our airmen, if we go forward too fast for laying down telephone wires," the officer told us.

" More lousy stuff to carry. Do they think we haven't enough as it is ? " we grumbled, eyeing the childish-looking things in disgust.

They were to be used for making letters spread out on the ground. Little books were handed out giving the code letters, in series of three, for different messages as necessity might arise.

For victorious troops chasing a defeated enemy some of the messages were not reassuring. They would have come in handy enough back in March.

" We are surrounded."

" We are in need of reinforcements."

" We are short of food."

" Short of ammunition."

" Require immediate assistance."

" Require artillery support, water, information, or what not," they went on, and so on through all kinds of desperate situations.

" But what happens if there is no airman flying about to see the message ? " asked Beck with the awkward, yet determined air of one who has discovered a serious flaw in an otherwise perfect system, and naïvely surprised that nobody else had noticed it.

The same thought had occurred to me a moment before, but I had said nothing, afraid of showing ignorance. I looked expectantly at Corporal Mundy, who was superintending the issue.

Some of the others were evidently struck, too.

" What happens if there isn't an airman to fly back with· the message ! " repeated Mundy suavely.

" Ay, that's it," said Beck, more confidently.

" Why, fly back with it yourself, donkey. It wouldn't be you perishers, if you didn't want jam on it. What happens, indeed ! Don't you know damned fine that there won't be an airman within a hundred miles of us. And if there was, d'ye think he'd bother his backside with the likes of you ? Who the hell do you think you are, anyway ? Haig ! "

Poor Beck was crushed, but good humour was restored. The unwieldy canvases were stored away on top of our packs.

We were still apparently a goodish bit in the rear and marched off by companies with the Signal Section and runners as the headquarters unit. It was a cold, early September morning with a touch of mist at first, and then a uniform greyness—all right for marching, but cold hanging about.

After progressing a couple of miles we had a solemn lecture about the dangers of drinking any but our own water issue, going into strange dug-outs until they had been certified free from booby-traps by the Engineers, and poking about in general. The Germans, it seemed, had dropped all kinds of poisonous germs, from typhus to tetanus, into the wells, and planted bombs where they thought they would do most good. According to rumour all the cross-roads were mined.

I determined to touch nothing and go nowhere unless actually ordered to, but some of the others had already an eye out for loot.

Once inside the old Jerry line we had convincing evidence of the havoc wrought by our artillery. I almost felt sorry for the enemy. I had never given much thought to the fact that our guns sent as much, or more, " dirt " over as came over to us. Shell-fire, for me, naturally meant the shells that came our way and nothing else. I had never been able to tell very clearly whose shells were passing overhead. I couldn't even distinguish between the various calibres, although the few more experienced men were never at a loss, and at night could pick out the enemy machine-guns' fire from ours by some slight difference in the rattle, or said they could.

The only thing I could distinguish was the innocent-sounding plop of the gas-shells, and as they didn't make much noise I didn't mind them overmuch compared with ordinary shells. I made up for my ignorance by according a wholehearted respect to all shells of no matter what brand. Their nearness was my only guide, and the best at the end of all. The drawback was that where the experienced soldier would say to himself, " There's Jerry shelling that bit of trench in front, that battery or dug-out or road behind," I could only say to myself, " There's a shell a couple of hundred yards away. There's another nearer," and wait uneasily and silently for the next. " Where will the next one alight ? " was the principal question up the line, providing you had survived the one before it.

Now I was filled with tardy respect for our gunners. A feeling almost of confidence possessed me. I felt elated, for the time being at any rate, at our having such allies. The Artilleryman was a big brother who had been doing his best to make things easy for us. Always before that he had been a big bastard who was always letting us in for trouble not of our seeking.

We stared about us at the grey earth, churned by count-less thousands of shells. The narrow road we were walking on was almost impassable for marching men let alone limbers. Although we had it to ourselves we made slow progress past a constant succession of craters. What it must have been for the Germans crawling up and down the line at night was hard even for us to imagine.

Tattered corpses in field grey, with blackened, emaciated faces, lay at the roadside, the curious aloofness that dead men have of giving their stark, uncouth attitudes a certain dignity.

We halted for a time at a place where the road on one side was lined with ramshackle shelters. A few hours before the Germans had skulked in them, ekeing out a miserable hour-to-hour existence. Everything about them, from the battered sheet of corrugated iron roofing to the odds and ends of equipment, had a makeshift, synthetic air as if all was made of grey paper. The crumbly, caked-mud earth seemed unnatural too—like the ugly soil of a refuse tip.

I stared at the shacks for a long while, fascinated. When the officers went off somewhere we went over. Disregarding orders and caution we poked about inquisitively.

A little farther along in the centre of the road was a big shallow crater. The bottom of it was covered with some slimy greenish stuff, and in the middle, half embedded, lay the body of a German officer. He had on a smart, tight-fitting tunic and riding-breeches, with a broad black stripe down the outside seams. The clothes looked perfectly new and fresh, and his long boots were polished, but his face was quite black.

" How does it come that their faces are black ? " wondered Beck.

I wondered too, but couldn't think of an answer. How did it happen that an otherwise fresh-looking corpse had a perfectly black face ?

" Would he be a nigger, d'ye think ? " asked Beck.

" The Jerries don't have niggers, for God's sake, man," said Watson. " He's no more nigger than you are, though you have a filthy dirty neck. It's the bad food. They say old Jerry gets all kinds of rotten stuff to eat nowadays."

" How is it our fellows don't turn black, then ? "

" We don't get bad grub, not really stinking, I mean. We just don't get enough," explained Watson patiently. " Our alleged Army Service Corps pinch the rest."

" That's very likely the way of it," agreed Beck, still at a loss.

" That's all bunkum," chimed in Jenkins. He had lounged up in time to hear what the talk was about. " It's not the food at all. If it doesn't turn them into niggers when they're alive it stands to sense it couldn't do it when they are dead. It's our gas that does it on them. They always turn black after catching a dose and kicking out. This lad here got a few mouthfuls all right."

For a moment Jenkins stood looking at the dead officer with casual appraisement. Lighting a cigarette he turned his back, smiling.

" Old Jerry must be in a bad way right enough when

he doesn't bother burying the stiffs—the officers, anyway," he said, and walked off leisurely, as if that was the only moral to be drawn from the crumpled cadaver lying in the slime.

By the afternoon we had covered a good few kilometres. The sounds of the pursuit were always a little ahead of us, which suited us down to the ground. We moved erratically, sometimes stepping out briskly and sometimes halting for an hour.

We were advancing on the leap-frog system, the Signal Officer told us when another halt was called later on. "One battalion keeps in touch with the enemy rearguard for so long and then another battalion goes through them and carries on until their turn comes to be relieved."

It began to get cold, and we stumped about, swinging our arms. We were on a patch of high ground which sloped down in front to a wood. There were no dug-outs or shelters to squat in, and we felt curiously at a loss without them. We were hungry, but there was no sign of rations.

Shells began to fall at regular intervals just ahead of us. They were big ones, and went up with an ear-splitting roar, sending the trees crashing. They came over every three or four minutes, always lighting in a different place, as if searching for us. Their heavy, malignant roar got on our nerves badly, and I found myself listening intently. Each time one burst I felt a little shiver of satisfaction that we had escaped that one, anyhow.

In spite of our scepticism about the war being nearly over the officer's yarn earlier in the day had made me think hazily that perhaps we had finished with shells. I had felt happy all day without knowing exactly why. Now reaction came. I felt in my bones that I was going to be killed.

The shells came closer, and others began to get wind-up. The Germans, like ourselves, seemed to have called a halt.

Our own artillery opened up, and both sides had the prospect of an uncomfortable night ahead.

A big hole with shelving sides which we had noticed earlier began to look inviting, although it was too open to offer much protection. Still, it had possibilities. A dozen of us got to work. We scrounged round collecting branches of trees, stray planks and brushwood. Then, getting out our entrenching tools we scooped out the parapet side, using the excavated earth to strengthen the other parts.

Our industry didn't pass unnoticed. We had hardly settled ourselves when the Runner Sergeant ordered us out sharply.

" What do you louts think you're on, eh ? Digging yourselves in and the Colonel and the rest of the officers having to walk about outside. Clear off to hell."

We obeyed unwillingly. We had the doubtful satisfaction a few minutes later of seeing the officers take our place in the hole.

It got quickly dark and steadily colder. We hung about, asking each other peevish questions without expecting answers. A shell fell quite close, and the cry " Stretcher-bearer ! Stretcher-bearer ! " came with mournful insistence.

" Who's hit ? " we inquired, with the aimless curiosity of men who don't really care a damn, so long as it isn't themselves, but stirred for all that because it so easily might have been.

" Jenkins, the Corporal runner," came the reply after a pause.

" Jenkins ! " I repeated astonished, and afraid. I could hardly have told why, except that he was about the last man I would have dreamt of being hit. He was always so capable and self-confident, so very much a soldier and so cynical withal, ready to jeer at anything and everything, but decent and comradely, equally ready to share a cigarette. Even yet I found it hard to understand that the shells blindly killed off real fighting men with the same ease and casualness as they did others, like myself, for instance.

The wounded man was carried past us. He must have seen us, for he made an effort to sit up. The stretcher tilted dangerously.

" It's a soldier's farewell for me, boys," he called out thickly and fell back, his arm swinging helplessly.

The bearers chided him gently and went on at their steady, swaying pace.

" Good luck, good luck. It's a Blighty one," we called after him, but there was no response. The dangling arm told its own tale.

" He was a rare good plucked un," said Beck.

" I wonder is he done for ? " I said, more to cover my own thoughts.

One of the runners came up, and we gathered round him.

" It was damned funny the way it happened," he said. " He was in the latrine when the shell burst and blew a hole in him. He had a letter from his girl in his hand."

The runner chuckled.

" How do you know it was a letter from his girl ? " demanded Mundy, joining our little group. Jenkins and he had been pally when out of the line, and he seemed to dislike the other's tone.

" I knew all right, because they're the only letters he ever gets," said the runner. " But I put it back in his pocket again, Corporal, so if he does go west she'll get it back."

" That was right, mate," said Mundy and turned away as somebody told him the Signal Officer was looking for him.

" And it's a damned good job the shell didn't get him a minute later, or his girl would have been all annoyed if she had got it returned to her," added the runner significantly, and went off in his turn.

The shelling died down. The rations came up. We made a poor meal of rabbit and boiled rice and plum and apple jam.

The sand-bags the rabbits came in were wet and muddy, having met with a mishap on the way up. One or two men got out their jack-knives. They made a show of scraping the muck off their share of the meat, but the majority of us were not so fastidious and swallowed it greedily, mud and all.

About midnight the order came to fall in. Soon we were moving forward again. It was our turn to play leapfrog.

" The officers didn't get stopping long in the hole we dug," said one.

Watson, who had done more than his share of the digging and had been correspondingly angry at the trick played on us, gave his pack a vicious jerk.

" Hell slap it up them."

After half an hour's slow progress we halted and the Signal Sergeant warned us off to our stations. The companies prepared to make their jump.

" I'm putting you in battalion H.Q. this time on account of the other affair. Take Beck with you," he told me.

" I wish I had lost that cursed protection stripe long ago," I said jubilantly as by and by we found ourselves in a rather draughty but otherwise comfortable hut which boasted a couple of feet of sand-bag roof. The crowd we had relieved had already laid wires down, so the phones had only to be connected up.

We discovered a nasty snag, however, when the pair of us were given the job of linesmen. It wasn't so easy getting a job on the switchboard at battalion H.Q.

" Still, it's a lot better than being stuck away in front somewhere with the company," I opined.

Beck agreed wholeheartedly.

Shelling was going on in earnest outside. I looked enviously at the man on duty. He, at any rate, was in no danger of being sent outside to repair breaks.

" We might have to go out soon if it keeps on," said Beck in my ear, but I put the thought as far from me as I could.

In a few minutes a heavy strafe was in progress. Things began to look ugly for the lot of us. The hut shook and showers of dirt came from the roof.

Beck and I crouched down in a corner. We kept very still, hoping earnestly that the lines would hold out, and, like ostriches with their head in the sand, that our presence would go unnoticed if they didn't.

The hut was useless as cover if a shell came. Its sides were built of old rotted sand-bags—the sand keeping the shape although the bags were decayed—but it had a roof, and that was the main thing. Not a man in it would have gone outside willingly. The possibility for Beck and I of remaining inside made the idea of our having to go out doubly repugnant.

Then, somewhere near by, a klaxon horn sounded. We dived for our masks. The H.E. slackened and stopped. Instead, there came a succession of gas shells.

They came thicker—plop, plop, plop. The grotesque heads about me moved uneasily as each man sought to reassure himself that he was not alone, or was seized with an obscure, panicky desire to pierce the masks around him and find out what the men behind them were thinking.

Long minutes passed. The little elfin noises, with their incongruous suggestion of softly popping corks, crept timidly into the strained silence of the room as if anxious to protest their innocence of any evil intent.

It got heavier. A whitish vapour seemed to fill the hut. The figures around me became more and more indistinct and shadowy. Like worms emerging from the earth they made little, rhythmic movements from side to side, groping blindly and instinctively for self-preservation.

Fearful of what was going to happen I put my hand out and encountered Beck's shoulder. He pressed closer.

We were no longer a signal station—the nerve centre of the battalion. We were only a few individuals, shut off the one from the other—dumb men, without a sign language—each one thinking only of his own safety.

It was the heaviest gas bombardment I had ever been in. I wondered stupidly what the Germans meant by it when they were retreating anyway, and of their own accord.

" Plop, plop," came the shells, and the tension grew in the hut. There was something ghostly about the sound, and something disarming and seductive that only served to increase the menace. The hut was draughty, but it was a haven. Outside death walked. Spittle dribbled from the corners of my mouth and down my chin. It ran down the mouthpiece, and, afraid of the tube becoming clogged, I sucked it back and forced myself to swallow it. It was cold and slimy, flavoured with the rubber, and tasted like somebody else's spittle.

Gradually the shelling dropped off. The men moved restlessly, and tentatively fingered their masks, waiting nervously for the " All Clear."

Beck released his nose clip, and, taking the tube from his mouth, sniffed venturesomely. His face was dripping with sweat.

" It's all right now, Corp.," he mumbled, forgetting that I was no longer a Corporal, and nudged me with his elbow.

I took a deep breath, and pulling out the mouthpiece, half raised my mask.

" Keep it on, you hopeless fool you. Don't you know there are officers here. You'll get crimed," I whispered urgently. He obeyed reluctantly.

I knew from experience that Beck hated nothing so much as wearing a mask. He was always the first to take it off. Many a time Maxwell and I had remonstrated with him.

" But I can't stand it, it makes me sweat," he always returned, as if that was sufficient reason.

There were many like him among the later comers to the battalion, though their reasons were different.

" The young blighters keep sniffing it as if poison gas was a joke, just because they can't see it," a Sergeant had complained to me bitterly before we came out of the line the last time. Three or four in his platoon had been choked to death before they could be got to the first-aid post.

I hated the mask, too, but put up with the sensation of slow suffocation which it induced, knowing that there was nothing else for it. My first experience on the St. Quentin road, so long ago, had been the worst and since then there had been an unconscious lessening of the horror each time. I knew little or nothing about gas and its effects, but had a wholesome fear of it.

THE CASUALTIES

A T last the "All Clear" signal sounded. We folded up
the masks and replaced them hastily, anxious to get
rid of the taste of them with the aid of cigarettes.

" You'll get caught working that trick yet," I said angrily.
" You'd have been properly in the muck if any of the officers
had seen you."

" I was half-choked, honest, and I can't stand the thing
when it gets all slobbery. I sweat, y'know, and with that
old rubber round me face I get all tickly. It's very hard,
Corp'l, after it's been on a while, isn't it ? "

" I wish to God you would stop calling me a Corporal,"
I said huffily.

" Ah, well, you know what I mean. You're a smarter
bloke than me, you're eddicated."

" Educated my foot. None of us would be here if we
were even half educated in the right way."

" The old mask half sickens me, but——"

" You'll be far sicker if you get a dose of gas down your
neck some day, you young idiot," I retorted, disarmed, as
usual, by the fellow's simplicity, and was about to carry
on with the lecture when the Signal Officer called my
name.

· Jumping to my feet I went over to where he stood at the
switchboard.

" The line to brigade has gone completely," he said
apologetically. " There is a pretty important message to go
down, and I'm afraid it will have to go by hand. Take the
message first and you can repair the line on the way back
when things are a bit quieter. Better the pair of you go.

2 E   433

Brigade is straight down the road for about five or six kilometres. You can't miss it. It's right on the roadside.
Here's the message, and try your best to get it through."

The mist seemed to fill the room again, obscuring everything but the slip of paper held out to me. I stared blankly
for a moment and then mechanically reached out and took it.
The man at the phone looked at us commiserating.

" It's an important message, so try and get through as
quickly as you can," said the officer.

" Yes, sir," I said, and saluted. They were strict on
saluting in the battalion.

The old hut seemed a very desirable place as we crawled
out and made our way slowly over fresh craters on to the
road. There was a strong smell of gas in the air and we put
on our masks, still wet and slimy from the last time. A few
yards away I glimpsed the dead bodies of two young lads,
lying side by side.

We had barely reached the road when the gas shells
started again unevenly. Nothing moved except ourselves.
We felt very lonely.

We went along cautiously, the warmth and companionship
of the hut already forgotten, ready to drop to the ground or
run as circumstancs dictated. Sometimes the shells sounded
startlingly close. We stared about us apprehensively, but
there was nothing but the dim greyness of the rutty, uneven
road and the darkness at either side.

We kept to the left-hand side, although, for that matter,
we might as well have kept to the right or in the centre. The
shells were invisible.

It got worse as we went along, until the road must have
been drenched with gas. The Germans had it well taped.
We met nobody, which was a bad sign, in its way, with a
brigade headquarters down the road.

I tried to look all ways at once to spot where the last shell
had landed, but the misty goggles negatived my efforts.

They were futile efforts at best. We had to go on in spite of them.

They came in gusts. One minute the ghostly plops were almost on top of each other and we huddled down together, knowing each other's fears, and trying, always without success, to see where they lit, though that would have done us no good either. Next minute they would cease abruptly, and we hurried on, the drooling mouthpieces acting as a brake if we tried to go too fast and got out of breath. We stumbled on like blind men wandering amidst pitfalls, with nothing but blind luck to guide us, and the shells for company. We were very near extinction, and my breath came painfully. Our labouring lungs, from much stooping, running and sudden halting, longed for a free deep breath, instead of the awkward, dripping, wheezing mouthpiece which had to be held tight between the teeth.

The way in front became lined with tall, dark houses. We drew each other's attention and hurried on thankfully, thinking ourselves at the end of the journey, only to be disappointed. The houses were derelict and mostly without roofs. Gloom encompassed us as we breasted the first of them and went on down the narrow street of a village, only to halt undecided as a new sound reached us.

From the far end of the street came a great empty crash as a heavy burst among the houses. In the comparative silence that followed bricks cascaded noisily and raggedly. Another screamed over our heads and burst up the street—the part we had to pass. We halted in painful indecision and then shrank down on a big, inviting doorstep. The lintel of the door above us gave an appearance of safety, and we hugged the feeling to us, like children anxious to be deluded. We sat with our heads near our knees, cocking our ears as monster shells screeched down, wondering how we would get through.

" Pretty important," the Signal Officer had said.

We seemed safe enough where we were for a few minutes. After a little while Beck signalled that he wanted to urinate. Stupidly enough, he got up from where he was sitting and went through the open doorway and along the inside of the wall for a few paces, for all the world as if the women of the village had returned and were congregated in the street or peeping from the dark window-spaces opposite.

When he returned we crouched side by side on the door-step listening. The gas-shells had either stopped or were drowned in the noise of the heavy shells.

Beck pulled his mask down and jogged my elbow. I leant close, wondering what was up now. He took a deep breath through the mouthpiece, and put his head close to my ear.

" It's a bloomin' church inside there," he said, in naïve astonishment at what he had done.

I didn't reply, but motioned imperatively for him to put on the mask. Instead he began sniffing the air inquisitively, like a dog.

" I say, Corporal, it's nearly all away. What about a fag ? " he said hurriedly, feeling in his pockets. Without waiting for me to reply he lit a cigarette, and commenced sucking in huge mouthfuls of smoke.

I signed to him again, but he took no notice.

" It can't be so very bad," I thought, watching him covertly to see if the gas had any effect. He seemed to have forgotten about the gas in his enjoyment of the cigarette.

The cold spittle dribbled down my chin. I couldn't force myself to swallow it.

" It must be nearly all gone right enough," I thought again. My resolution wavered. Taking a last safe breath through the tube I discarded the mask and lit up too. The air seemed fairly clear, and we sat listening to the crashes, wondering how we were going to get by. Still, we could afford to wait a while. When we had come so far safely there was no reason why we shouldn't deliver the message. From battalion headquarters to the village was probably the worst part of the journey. I sat pressing against the side of the doorway ready to sprawl down into the street or backwards into the ruined church, according to where a shell would alight if it came our way. A few stars shone down from where the roof should have been, but the wall would be a protection provided we were on the right side of it, and it didn't collapse on top of us.

There were a few puffs left in my cigarette, but a curious prickly sensation on the skin of my face warned me to be quick. Taking a last mouthful of smoke I threw the butt away and put on the mask again. Not that it was an unpleasant sensation. My face felt firm and tingly and the skin slightly stretched, as if I had just had a good shave.

Beck looked round at me. I felt rather foolish and windy compared with him.

The shelling slackened. We got to our feet and went forward cautiously, waiting until one had burst ahead before taking to our heels. Our luck held and we left the village behind, but we had only gone a few yards when the cursed plop plop started all over again. Beck hurriedly put on his mask, and we went on as before, keeping to the left of the road. Sometimes we broke into a shambling trot when the plops came from behind, and sometimes we crouched down in terror as a flurry of bursts came from in front.

Always we strained our eyes, but the shells remained invisible, with not even a flash to show where they had actually fallen. It was amazing that one didn't fall right on top of us. Sometimes we were yards apart and at others we kept close together, our hand on each other's arm to signify caution.

We had almost forgotten what we were on the road for when a line of shelters appeared indistinctly on the right.

They were in darkness and seemingly unoccupied. We blundered about, at a loss what to do.

" This is bound to be the place," I argued.

" They might have chased off on account of the strafe," said Beck.

I tapped tentatively with my knuckles at a couple of the shacks, but without response.

" You might knock up some General and he'll chew the gills off you for waking him up," said Beck, standing a little apart from me.

Going up to another shack I hammered the door with the butt of my rifle. It opened and an R.E. Signal Sergeant appeared. He looked at us curiously when he learned where we had come from.

" There's no sense in you two lads chancing your arm going back to your mob to-night. You're very lucky as it is, with all that gas and stuff flying about. Hang round for a bit till I see to this message, and I'll fix you up for the rest of the night and get hold of some grub for you."

The Sergeant was as good as his word. We were soon installed in a tiny shelter all to ourselves, with half a loaf and a wedge of cheese. We felt well rewarded. The shelling went on outside, but we paid scant attention to it, and presently went off to sleep, happy, first seeing to the sacking over the door.

When we awoke it was full daylight. Everything was quiet, and we made shift to get out into the fresh air. The shelter had a close, sour smell, and I had a headache. The smell was reminiscent of the gas the previous night. It occurred to me that there might have been some of it in our sweaty clothes.

There was no sign of the decent Sergeant, or we might have begged a breakfast, and we set off for the battalion. The sun was shining, and I liked the clear, sharp air. The road, now that we could see it, was pleasantly level and dusty, and went through green fields which showed few signs of war. It was hard to believe that it was the same road we had travelled a few hours ago.

It was pleasant, too, to be on our own, and we didn't hurry.

" I'll bet they think we never got through with the message," smiled Beck.

" So long as the other fellows haven't scoffed our breakfast."

Beck stopped and I strolled on ahead. The sun didn't seem so warm somehow. I felt sickish and, wondering what was the matter, stopped, and turned to tell Beck about it. Beck was on his knees at the roadside staring at the ground with his mouth open. As I looked at him in amazement his shoulders jerked forward convulsively. He vomited.

" What the hell's the matter ? " I started to exclaim, and then stopped. Nausea seized me. After one or two false alarms I vomited too.

" Maybe the cheese was rotten," I thought, looking in disgust at the watery, green stuff I had got rid of as it sank into the thirsty road.

We compared notes and found that the symptoms were the same.

" It must have been the grub, the bread or the cheese, though it tasted good enough," I said at last.

" Ay, I wondered at that bastard Sergeant being so free with it," agreed Beck.

We went on slowly, stopping now and then to vomit the same evil-looking stuff. Beck was worse than I was, and staggered like a drunken man.

After a few more spasms we felt better, and laughed at the idea of being sick with our stomachs—" like civvies at home " as Beck put it.

" All the same, if we come across a first-aid post we should call in and get a pill or something. There was bound to be something the matter or we wouldn't have been sick," I said, as we made better progress.

"What would be the use of doing that. We'd only get chased."

"But, damn it all, man, it won't cost them anything to give us a dose of medicine, will it. It's not that there's anything really the matter, so we're not swinging the lead."

"All right, then," said Beck, dubiously.

We came to a gate at the left of the road. A weedy path ran from it across a pleasant field to a farmhouse half hidden by a clump of trees. There was a notice "Aid Post" stuck on the gate. We went through hesitantly.

"Wait till you see what'll happen," prophesied Beck, hanging back.

His face, I noticed, had a yellowish tinge now, and was oddly pinched-looking. There's something the matter, I thought.

"Come on. For all you know it was that gas last night."

"It couldn't be. We can breathe all right. It's a pity it wasn't, isn't it ? "

We walked slowly along towards the house. I felt nearly all right again, but didn't want to turn tail at the last minute.

We went round a bend and found ourselves at a half-ruined house. An R.A.M.C. orderly was doing something in a barn, the doors of which were missing. Beck stood uncomfortably where he was while I went over and accosted the orderly. He listened while I explained haltingly what had brought us.

" 'Arf a mo, mates," he said quickly, and disappeared into the house.

I crossed over to Beck. We stood waiting.

The orderly returned, followed by an officer, and we came to attention.

The officer gave one look at us, and pointed to a couple of stretchers lying on the ground a dozen yards away at the side of the house. Without speaking a word he turned and re-entered the house.

We looked at the orderly nonplussed.

" One at a time now, mates," he said. Going over to Beck he put his arm tenderly round his shoulder and helped him over to a stretcher. He lowered him on to it, and fixed his helmet underneath his head for a pillow. Returning, he did the same for me. Then running into the barn he brought us a blanket apiece, tucking us in carefully before going away.

Beck and I looked at each other in blank astonishment.

" The man's mad," he whispered.

" There's a mistake somewhere," I whispered back. " They'll catch themselves on in a minute and chase us for our damn life."

" God Almighty, did you see the way he helped me over ? "

" And me, too."

" You must have told him an awful pack of damned lies. What did you tell him ? "

I sat up in the stretcher to fish out a butt and Beck half raised himself with the same object in view, but the orderly must have had an eye on us. He came hurrying over.

" Hi, mateys ! You're not to move. Lie down and keep still."

" But, my God, chum, what's the matter with us ? " I said, mystified.

" Why, you've been gassed and you mustn't move. It's a dose of mustard you've got and that stuff's bad for the heart. If you move about the old ticker might stop on you altogether, so don't say I didn't warn you. There was a good few casualties last night from the bleeding strafe."

" Will we go away in an ambulance ? " asked Beck eagerly.

We both waited breathlessly.

" You'll go in the very next one—if you keep still, that is, mateys," promised the orderly. " If you don't you'll go into a blanket and it'll be charged up to you. I'll bring you something to drink in a minute to pass the time."

We lay back and kept quiet. It was nice to lie comfortably on a stretcher, with the beautiful prospect of going away from the line. Not a shell fell. Probably Jerry was continuing his retreat and was already miles away, with the battalion at his heels.

Already in imagination the front was fading.

" I'm out of it—out of it—out of it," ran a little happy refrain through my head. I blessed the gas for delivering me. No blood, or muck, or pain—just a little pain, hardly noticeable where my lungs were. Gas was kinder.

And then hospital—if we got beyond the C.C.S., that was. A little doubt gnawed at me. But the orderly had said we hadn't to move, so perhaps we were sufficiently bad. Unless he was making a mistake or kidding us on.

What would hospital be like ? How lovely and strange ! There might even be a nurse like Yvonne. Not really like her, of course, but one who would like me. And away from the shells and fear.

I couldn't see Beck from where I lay, and wondered how he was getting on and what his thoughts were. I debated whether I should speak to him or not, and then decided not to. He was lying perfectly quiet.

Gradually a feeling of lassitude came over me. The pain in my chest came and went, and my eyes began to feel hot and watery. I felt thirsty again, but didn't bother asking for anything. There was still time to be bunged back up the line if we made a nuisance of ourselves.

When the ambulance came up smoothly and silently, however, I felt no elation as I was hoisted on to a narrow shelf. A couple of bandaged men were carried out of the house and put in along with us. One was unconscious, but the other—he was on the shelf below me—kept asking questions which I didn't attempt to answer.

" What was our crush ? Where had we copped it ? Was it a Blighty one ? "

Beck was silent, too.

The ambulance sped on with hardly a bump, but the air seemed to get very stuffy and warm. There was a strong smell of iodine. It was odd to be lying down and yet at the same time to be getting carried along so swiftly and surely. It was the wheels going round that did it.

The ambulance stopped at last and we were carried into a tent. A man in a white overall came along with a syringe and stuck the needle into my chest, dabbing the place with iodine first.

" Against tetanus," he said.

In a little while I was carried into a big marquee, the bearers stepping carefully in the half-darkness along narrow passages formed by rows of wounded. A place was found for me against the canvas wall in a dark corner, and an orderly brought me a bowl of milk. Beck had disappeared.

I looked about me curiously. I was almost surrounded by long, shapeless bundles. In spite of their number each man was very quiet and alone-looking. They lay curled up as well as the stretcher would permit and the brown blanket around each one made them all equally mysterious, as if the blanket was there to cover a secret rather than a man. Sometimes a bundle made a little convulsive movement and from another a smothered groan came, but the majority lay still.

" Some of them might be dead," I thought, uneasily aware of their remoteness.

I lay low, feeling like a new boy at a strange school. It was odd to be lying on a stretcher on the grass in the corner of a marquee instead of squatting in a funk-hole up the line. It came to me that it was the silence that was strange.

A little glow pervaded me as I realised afresh that I was a casualty although I had nothing, as yet, to show for it in the line of bandages or medicine.

" Maybe it would have been better after all if I had been hit somewhere," I thought as an occasional orderly made his appearance and passed by, shooting little darting glances to right and left.

Gradually the glow grew and spread in some unaccountable way. My stomach, hips and thighs tingled and then began to burn, slightly at first, and then as if they were being inexorably forced nearer and nearer a blazing fire. I turned and twisted on the narrow stretcher, only to stop and lie motionless as stabbing pains ran through my chest. I breathed as lightly as I could to get rid of them, but after a time they came no matter whether I moved or not.

But my eyes were the worst. They were no longer eyes, but red-hot cinders burning their way into my brain. Scalding tears streamed down my cheeks and bit into the flesh like acid.

" If I could only get an orderly," I thought distractedly, but the blurred immobile forms about me deterred me. I lay writhing and tossing, torn between desire for some relief and dread of my neighbours seeing me give way to pain.

At last I gave up and shouted for the orderly. I tried to shout, that is, but no sound came until the breath had almost been expended. Then odd little mumbling noises, grotesque caricatures of what I had wanted to say, came like an echo. I thought my ears had deceived me and tried again, but the result was the same. When I shouted there was no sound, and when I had stopped the noises came, broken and hoarse.

I had only a hazy notion of the effects of gas when I found myself going blind, and dumb despair seized me. I clawed at my eyes, almost ready to sink my nails in them and come to grips with the pain. When reaction came I caressed them with helpless, clumsy fingers.

When the air raid came I was in a stupor. My ears registered the roar of bursting bombs, the hoarse bass of the klaxons and the futile barking of archies, but I paid no attention. I had no fear of death any more.

Even when a fiercer roar came I was uncaring. I heard the screams of twice-wounded men, but the fact that we were already casualties didn't seem to matter very much. It was only too natural to be assailed by rushing, screaming explosions. The big marquee bellied and loose canvas settled over my head. I could still breathe and made no attempt to leave the stretcher.

A curious kind of pandemonium reigned. From a great distance excited cries reached me. Panic-stricken voices called out. The wounded cursed and pleaded and groaned.

Where I was everything was comparatively still. The fallen sides of the marquee pressed down protectingly, limiting my little world of pain to the stretcher where I lay. Bombs roared down, but my semi-consciousness defied them.

The raiders passed on. Searching men found me. There was a short, jolting journey. I found myself in a slow-moving train.

Dull satisfaction possessed me. I was out of the war at last. Passing troop trains would look at the ambulance train with mingled envy and fear as it rumbled along towards the base and safety—perhaps Blighty. I lay on the floor in the centre of the gangway. Blurred tiers of stretchers rose on either side. The matter poured from my eyes in an unending stream, searing my cheeks. I wasn't quite sure where my eyes were now. They seemed to have grown bigger and bigger until they occupied most of my face. Flames licked at the soft parts of my body.

The knowledge that I was on a train heartened me, but soon the swaying lost its novelty and I was back in the old stupor. Bright lights glared down and I turned and twisted in a vain effort to avoid them.

And then a strange vision came to me. It was a very hazy vision, but I knew it was all in white. It was a woman, her voice pure and detached, speaking the language I had been brought up to, but with altogether different intonation to what I had become accustomed to. I had forgotten that somewhere in the world were such women. Here was one bending over me, stroking my forehead, touching my tortured eyes with cool, impersonal fingers. Dislike and fear of her calm, condescending accent possessed me.

" Why, you are only another boy ! " she said. I was struck with the surprise in her voice.

" What did she think I was—an old man ? "

" Do you want anything ? " came the voice.

" The pain. The pain in my eyes," I said, trying to rise, but I only heard a croak.

The nurse disappeared, and I fell back baffled. In a moment she was back with a bitter drink, holding my head up while I swallowed. With deft fingers she fixed a bandage round my eyes.

The bandage was cool and soft. I tried to thank her, as she bent over me, but I was glad when she went away. She was a being from an alien world, a world in which cool, matter-of-fact efficiency and unexpressed superiority took the place of the cynical, blaspheming, harsh-disciplined and yet simple world I knew and belonged to.

The train rolled on monotonously, but whether for hours or days I didn't know. I lay on my back silent and motionless. The bandage became hotter and hotter, as if it too had been mustard gassed. I let it remain and was glad that it covered me from all the other men in the train, and particularly from the nurse. I didn't want to attract any more attention to myself whether the pain got worse or not.

When the train stopped I was still in the same position. The stiffened cloth was sticking to my eyes. In a dream I was lifted and borne along by stretcher-bearers.

THE GURGLE

IT was pleasant to lie between cool sheets in a little world of one's own. A strange world, where quietness reigned as of right. Occasionally subdued noises—a groan, the broken mutter of a man talking in his sleep, a bed creaking as its occupant turned over—emphasised the unknown world of the ward.

There had been a hurried bath on arrival—a cold affair of lukewarm water in a too-small tub, a half-hearted rub down by a harassed orderly, a hot drink, and then to bed. For the first time in my life I wore pyjamas. A fresh bandage was round my eyes. I lay docilely at full length, the way I had been placed.

The bed had been cold at first, but gradually it became warm and I moved restlessly. The last time I had made water was back at the battalion somewhere, but it was only now that I wanted relief. I didn't know what to do.

Long hours passed and the ward remained quiet.

When the ward came to life I knew that morning had come. I prayed feverishly that someone would guess what I wanted. The idea of soiling the beautiful clean bed horrified me. I sweated with the effort of holding myself in.

When the nurse came round to make the bed I was too shy to tell her what the trouble was, even if I had been able. I had never been in a hospital in my life before, or even ill in bed at home, and was completely at a loss.

" There must be some way," I thought desperately when the nurse departed. " Maybe an orderly comes round later to find out who wants to do anything."

The morning dragged on minute by minute. I became weak with the unnatural, long-drawn-out strain. I forgot my other ills. Every breath, no matter how light I tried to make it, pressed cruelly.

I could stick it no longer. Sitting up carefully in the bed I commenced groping my way out on to the floor. I had no idea of where to go or how I would get there, but I had to go. It was that or burst.

" Here, hey, stop ! What's the matter, mate ? " cried a startled voice beside me.

" I'm bursting. Where do I go for——" I started to explain, and stopped as no sound came. I had forgotten about my voice. It was gone completely now.

" Do you want a bottle ? " asked the man encouragingly.

I shook my head in despair and tried again, essaying a single word this time, but without success.

He must have read the movement of my lips.

" That's it," he laughed. " You want a bottle. Get back into bed, there, and I'll fix you up in a tick." He raised his voice :

" Hey, there. Nurse, nurse. This bed wants a bottle."

There was a rustle of skirts and something fell on the bed at my knees. I groped and held the thing up uncertainly.

" You're a green 'un all right. Stick it under the clothes and go ahead. The nurses are used to all that, matey. Just shout for a bottle whenever you want one."

The ward was a closed book.

Every morning the doctor came his rounds. Every morning my eyes were swabbed and the bandage changed. Sores which the mustard had brought out on the sweaty parts of my body were treated. Some kind of an electrical contrivance was put to my throat and sent pins and needles through it. Several times a day a thing shaped like a big kettle was brought to me and I breathed in strongly-flavoured steam from the spout. For the rest, I lay in vast, silent content, never tiring of the luxury of the bed.

The hurried bath I had got on admission to the hospital hadn't rid me of the lice. I was ashamed of them now and stealthily explored my body, particularly at night when no one could see. Lice were all right in their proper place, but not in a good clean bed.

Dressing time was the time of tribulation for the men in the ward. The groaning began at the bottom from where I was and rose in a ragged crescendo on the opposite side. Then the doctor crossed over and soon it was my turn. The groans grew weaker until all was over for another day.

Halfway down the ward on the other side was a man who always started groaning before his turn came. When it did he screamed and shrieked heartrendingly, imploring the doctor for mercy. When it was all over he continued moaning and crying with pain.

At first I felt a kind of shamed sorrow for him. I knew by his deep voice that he was a grown man. It was a very terrible thing that a man should be reduced to behaving like a child.

Often, as soon as the doctor and sister had gone, disgusted curses would be directed at him. The ward was ashamed of him.

" Shut up, you white-livered bastard ! "

" Put a sock in it ! "

" Pull yourself together, man."

When eventually the bandage did come off my eyes, I was surprised to see that he had a long, dark, virile face with strongly marked features and a blue cleft chin. I had expected to see some milk-and-water creature. The mystery was somehow explained when he got out of bed, one morning when the nurse came round to make it. He was only a mannikin, with narrow, sloping shoulders and sickly, skinny legs, half-covered with coarse black hair.

2 F

They were all gas casualties in the ward, I learned, with the exception of a canny Jock, who was swinging the lead with running eczema on his scalp. Most of them had been burned with mustard gas. Their lungs weren't affected, but they had sat down in shell-holes that had been drenched with the stuff, or on the ground. The result was that they had a great saucer-sized hole in each hip. In the centre of the burn was a solid yellow core of suppuration. Cleaning the wounds was a long-drawn-out affair. They had to lie on their face in bed most of the time.

The little man had them—two great festering sores sunk deep in his narrow, bloodless hips, so he had some excuse for kicking up a row.

My skin must have been specially receptive to the gas. A few days after my arrival the doctor brought several other medicos round to have a look at me.

" Here he is," I heard him say. " Look at his face. He's done to a turn."

Stripping the bedclothes off me, he drew attention to my armpits, stomach and thighs in a pleased voice and went off into technicalities.

At first I was windy, wondering what he was getting at, but it seemed to be only a demonstration of what Jerry's mustard gas could do, so I didn't worry.

I loved listening to our doctor's voice, and waited for it every morning. It was rich and syrupy. The words seemed to drip from his lips without requiring a breath to set them going.

" He must have just finished a good feed, with plenty of meat and wine," I always thought when I heard him on his rounds, and hugged a vicarious satisfaction to me. Without seeing him I knew he was fat and pinky. When he spoke to the sister or to me there was casual condension in his voice.

" Does he take a deep breath and then close his throat and

speak, or does he blow the air all out first,'' I wondered, enchanted.

But of all the sounds made by the pain-racked men in the ward there was one sound more terrible than the rest. It came from a man just opposite me. He was being slowly suffocated by gas. Every few minutes, when he tried to cough, it came—a deep gurgle. It was as if, on the point of drowning, he had given up all hope of rescue and opened his throat to the water. Every few minutes, day and night, the gurgle came monotonously. It had a sad futility worse than pain. In the day time, when it came, the other men broke off their aimless talk and waited as if in some obscure way their silence helped to make things easier for him. When it was more long-drawn-out than usual the nurse came hurrying up and scolded gently, playing a one-sided game of make-believe.

'' You really must stop that now How often am I to tell you ? If you don't be good I'll tell the doctor of you, and then you'll catch it, bad boy, you.''

At night, when the ward was still, the gurgle sounded inexpressibly lonely and remote. The man uttering it was a lost child wandering in a dark forest thousands of miles away from the rest of humanity. Sometimes, lying awake, the horrid hopeless sound got on my nerves badly. I pulled the warm blankets around my head to shut it out, but there was no escaping it.

The gurgle. A little silence. The gurgle. Silence.

Night and day it went on, animal, relentless, purposeless— a British soldier dying hard through no fault of his own.

When he succeeded in getting a mouthful of phlegm up we heard his feeble, pitiful attempts to spit it into a mug.

'' That poor bastard isn't going to do,'' my generally cheerful neighbour whispered over softly more than once. '' His lungs are full of it. They're just filling with water, a little more every hour and every day, until at last he'll drown just the same as if he was actually drowning. That's the way it takes you when you've got it bad. He's on brandy and eggs all the time, and you are in a hell of a bad way when they give you that here. Only a kid, too. Damned hard lines.''

The thought came to me of how easily I could have been in the same case. A few more minutes sitting on the door-step of the wrecked église in the village. A few more puffs at the cigarette. A little more aimless conversation with the heedless Beck and I would have been in——

Beck !

I had forgotten about Beck completely. Where, and how, was he ? I felt suddenly cold. The words of the fellow in the next bed came to me.

'' Only a kid.''

Beck was only a kid, and a damn stupid one at that. But likeable.

I listened intently after that when the gurgle came. There was nothing about it, however, to suggest that Beck was the victim. There was nothing human about it at all.

One night we had an air raid.

We were near Boulogne, it appeared, and already there had been three or four night visits there. Nobody paid much attention to the dull rumbling of bombs and the barking of the anti-aircraft, except that each time a battery of heavy guns right beside the hospital, judging from the row they kicked up, had tried conclusions with the raiders.

'' They have a battery of big ones—great howitzers —only a few hundred yards away between our hospital and the next one,'' I was told.

'' Ay, they have them planted right amongst the hospitals because they think old Jerry won't notice them away up here on the heights above the town," said another angrily. " They have a hard neck putting them here at all."

" Th-a-t's right. A damned dirty trick, no matter how you look at it."

This particular night the Jerry airmen must have caught the game on. The alarm had hardly sounded for all lights to go out when they were right overhead, sending heavy bombs thundering and crashing down near the huts. I still had the bandages on my eyes and lay helpless, unable to move, even if I had wanted to. But I was curiously unafraid. It didn't seem possible that anything could happen to me lying stretched out in a nice, clean, white bed, all complete, in so civilised a place as a hospital.

Tremendous explosions sounded outside, making the bed shake. Some medicine bottles and crockery down the ward fell and smashed. Crash after crash came until the whole ward trembled. I lay perfectly still as if in some degree safety depended on listening intently.

In the midst of it all the door at our end of the hut flew open. I became aware of a scuffling noise underneath my bed. Next I heard a confused shouting. It came from the man in the next bed. I wondered had he lost his nerve. Then, in between the exploding bombs I heard him distinctly.

" Get to blazes out of here, you windy devils. Allez. D'ye hear."

" There must be men under the beds," I thought in astonishment, hardly able to realise that I was acting as a living screen.

For a couple of long minutes the raid continued. Suddenly everything became quiet. A sound came from underneath me again. There was the hurried breathing of a man and then hurrying footsteps. The door of the hut banged.

The klaxons sounded the " All clear," and the nurse came round to see that everybody was all right.

" What do you think of that ? " asked my neighbour, disgustedly. " Three or four lazy orderlies were hiding under our beds. That's what these base-wallahs think of us. We're the mugs, even in hospital, and they're the smart Alecs so long as the dirt isn't scared out of them, and then they stink. Our orderlies—blinking heroes, I don't think."

The doctor decided that the bandages could come off my eyes. I was glad because it meant that soon I would be able to go to the ward latrine. I didn't like having to call the nurse, although they did think nothing of it, or pretended to. But the thing I most wanted to know was denied me. When I looked the bed opposite was vacant, and the gurgling cough was no more. When Jock came along I pointed questioningly to the empty bed.

He shrugged his shoulders. Later the day nurse came along, and I heard the others asking her the same question.

" He was taken away early this morning," she scolded. " The Sister said this ward was far too noisy for him, and he'd have to go to a quieter ward. I'm always telling you boys that you should keep quiet, but you don't seem to pay any heed."

When she had gone the others looked wise.

" They don't talk, not even in their sleep, in the place he's bound for. She's a decent sort, our nurse, and thinks we'd be upset. A pity, too."

I made a strong effort, and after a couple of failures managed to ask a question. It had been trembling on my lips for a long time.

" What—was—he—like ? "

" Just a kid, you know," said Jock. " Very likely he hadn't enough wit to know what he was in for. Looked as if he didn't understand what had happened to him. What it was all about, like. Puzzled up, poor chap."

" I'll swear he wasn't nineteen. He got younger and more youngsterlike-looking every day," said another softly. " He came in about the same time as you. The very same night, I think, although I'm not sure. You might have known him !"

Rightly or wrongly I took silent farewell of Beck. I felt sad. I had been fond of him for all his simplicity—or because of it. My mind went back to the night he had followed Maxwell and me out to the wire.

"He wanted to go too," I thought. "He knew me, and liked me." And sometimes I had written his letters to the "old woman." Just stupid and simple.

And yet I was glad it was him instead of me.

The ward was strange to my freed eyes, still misty and incomprehensible. From being hardly separate sounds the patients were suddenly separate human beings, the face of each one showing that he was a single personality imbued with his own hopes and fears and likes and dislikes, some crotchety, some uncomplaining and some impenetrable. Feeling rickety on my unaccustomed legs, I got out of bed and made for the lavatory at the other end of the ward, as much on a tour of inspection as anything else. Outside of my own immediate circle, whose voices I knew, I was amongst strangers, and felt timid accordingly. Strange men with strange ills hidden by the bedclothes stared at me impassively.

On the way back to bed I noticed a mirror hanging on the wall and went over and had a look at myself. I didn't recognise the face that stared back. It was blackened and scorched-looking. A broad furrow ran down each cheek, changing the contour of my face, making it look bleary and old. It was astonishing that I could see at all. Instead of being smooth and shiny the whites of my eyes were spongy and oozed blood. The eyelids were shrivelled and split and without eyelashes. A thin, straggly growth, about half an inch long, completed my ugliness. I stared aghast. Was that the face that the doctor and nurses had to look at every day ? Secret

panic came over me. What would they think with such a
being to attend to ? And the other chaps in the ward ?
Creeping back to bed I covered my face up with the blankets,
hoping nobody had seen me—forgetting that they were used
to it.

A little later I got a Channel Islander, who belonged to
some funny rifle crush of his own, to give me a shave. He
was a dark, pale-faced, refined-looking fellow, and eyed me
cheerfully and sympathetically when I asked him.

" Saw you admiring yourself," he said, showing his white
teeth in a grin, as he perched on my bed and lathered my
face.

He was an odd character in his way. He had a French
name starting with Le, and the quick, sensitive look of some
Frenchmen. He was a merry fellow, and for my benefit
sometimes broke into a rapid patter of " the bat." Although
I had been in France a good while now I hadn't heard French
spoken half a dozen times. One day someone called him a
half-caste Froggie. He went up to the offender and demon-
strated his complete Englishness by threatening to " knock
his block off."

" Me a half-caste," he exclaimed furiously. " It's you
lousy gang who are the mongrels if you only knew it. I'm a
pure Norman. Same as William the Conqueror, when he
chased your great-great-grandfathers for their lives."

The majority of the troops detested the French and refused
point-blank to believe anything good of them. The longer
they had been in France the more bitter they were. " Old
Jerry isn't a bad sort," they said. " He's the best soldier of
the lot, and if we'd both been fighting against the French
the war would soon have been over, you bet."

The " Norman " had a way with him. He used to get
hold of a gramophone for an hour from somewhere, along
with half a dozen records. One record he never tired of
playing. It was a simple thing. The tune came clear and

sweet, and inevitable, like water welling from a spring in the rocks, each note a crystal drop.

" What is it ? " I asked him diffidently.

" It's from the shirt-tails of Hoffman—a barbarous Hun," he replied laughing slyly.

" Shirt-tails ? Hun ? What the devil is he talking about ? " I thought, as once more he wound up the gramophone and sat back dreamily, his black eyes sparkling under their half-closed lids.

I listened greedily, surrendering myself to new, strange sensations and half-formed thoughts and desires that crowded in on me and turned the ward into a mysterious, enchanting place into which I was peeping for the first time. I determined to make the acquaintance of such Huns should ever the opportunity present itself.

It was nice to get into a suit of hospital blue and potter about the ward. I was an old habitué now, and felt at home. Breakfast, the doctor, dinner, tea and supper were the chief events of our existence.

Every morning Jock led me out to the wash-house where I bathed my eyes until they became unstuck. There were a few shoddy books in the ward, and I recovered my lost love of reading, even though the print had a habit of becoming dim. The only treatment I went under now was medicine —strychnine, Jock said—and sucking vapour from a kettle for the heavy cough which seemed to have come to stay. For it, also, I had a spitting mug which I used conscientiously. Every day the doctor put his stethescope to my chest and marked something on the chart above my bed. When he had finished his rounds and gone off I always had a look to see what he had put, but his writing was crabbed, and all I could make out was something that looked like " rates," whatever they stood for.

Ours was a big hospital I discovered when I was allowed to wander outside. It was divided into three sections—British,

Germans, and S.I.W. The last two were only to be viewed through barbed wire, and of the two the S.I.W.s were the more miserable looking. They were in tents and guards paced up and down. Sometimes I caught a glimpse of the patients, and wondered what kind of life theirs was with a court martial waiting for them when they were cured. Did they shoot them ? When a nurse broke some rule or other in our section and was caught out—letting us smoke at night generally if we couldn't sleep—she was sent to the German wards for punishment, but no farther. The S.I.W.s were considered beneath the dignity of nurses in disgrace, and had only orderlies to look after them. Whether or not the same system of punishment applied to doctors was not known. Perhaps they never made mistakes. According to popular rumour the Germans had amputations on the slightest pretext—as a reprisal, the yarn went, for what the Jerry doctors did on our men—so God knows what happened to the S.I.W.s.

THE TENT

THE days passed into weeks. I became accustomed to hospital life, with no desire for any other. I had no knowledge of any other. I had a curious facility for forgetting things—although that was not the right word—as soon as they were past. The soft-footed nurses, with their gleaming white head-dress, the syrupy doctor with his fleshy, pinky face, which just escaped being fat, were real, along with the quietness and the long double row of white beds, and regular meals. Behind me was the dim, drab life of the trenches, ever present, yet faded and unreal. Away at the back of my mind was the thought that the boys I had left behind were still stuck into it.

" I wonder would he bleed much if he got a packet," I thought, staring surreptitiously at the doctor as he went his rounds. His cheeks and lips were nearly the same colour and his neck filled the collar of his tunic. He was like a pink pin-cushion.

Just to be out of range of the shell-fire was enough. Except for it I could have stuck the war all right. Bullets, gas, machine-guns, bombs—all these were bad enough, but endurable. The shells were the worst. Men were either brave or cowardly, but what did that matter ? Bravery went for nothing if sufficient shells fell.

Generals and so on visited the line, were under shell-fire for an hour or two, and went away, satisfied. Shelling was then only an incidental thing. The rank and file had exactly the same opinion—for an hour or two. But they didn't get away. They stayed on and learned that no matter how many shells missed them the very next one might get them. That was the lesson of shell-fire. It was that that destroyed men's nerve.

" What has made you so thin ? " the Doctor asked me.

I was astonished. Was I thin ?

" Don't know, sir, the route-marching."

" Give him a bottle of Guinness every night," he directed the Sister, who took a note of it.

The first time I sipped the stuff gingerly. It was in a mug and seemed all froth and bubbles. Underneath it was like treacle toffee.

" It's a bit high," said Jock, who brought it round, " but gulp it down for it's the stuff to give 'em."

He seemed to know its condition very well.

One morning the doctor drew me to one side.

" Of course, you're not due to go out for a long while yet," he said. " Not until that cough of yours mends, and you put some flesh on your bones. Still, you are coming on, and if you think you are fit enough to give Jock and the nurse a hand at tidying the ward and cleaning up—well, I think you could be here for another month or so. What do you think ? "

I felt very grateful, and eagerly agreed to do what he asked.

" He's not a bad fellow, quite decent," I thought, and went off to find Jock.

Jock wasn't too enthusiastic. Perhaps he saw in me not only an assistant, but a successor. He scratched his head. He had a habit of picking at his sores when the nurse wasn't looking. It helped to keep the eczema running.

" The floor needs a bit of a polish," he said reflectively, " an' it's a good while since it was scrubbed. A good scrub first and a polish over afterwards wouldn't do it any harm."

It seemed a fairly tall order, but I got a pail of water, soap and a scrubbing-brush and set to work. The floor seemed to get larger as I proceeded, and I developed housemaid's knee. When I had nearly done one side I had to give up.

" Ah, well, that'll do us for one day," said Jock. " We can do the rest of it to-morrow, and get some of the other geezers to do the polishing."

But when the morrow came he had something else to do, and I was left to carry on myself. I struggled on manfully, sweating, coughing and short of breath.

It was the Continental *Daily Mail* and an American paper printed in Paris that first brought the news, if I had had the wit to know it, that my chances of a soft billet were a washout. One morning they appeared with double-column headings in heavy type, one on the main news page, and the other on the magazine page. One report went into rhapsodies about our side crossing the canal at St. Quentin, capturing a whole system of trenches and thousands of prisoners and guns. The other had much the same tale of overwhelming victory. In both the troops had advanced with even more than the usual lightheartedness and élan, and much less than the usual toll of casualties.

" Victory in Sight," screamed the headlines, but as victory had been in sight or just around the corner ever since the war started we read the news with more than one grain of salt. I remembered what the papers had said about the March Retreat. Nevertheless, they made thrilling reading. War is a very interesting thing to read about from a safe distance, even when you have an inkling of what the reality is like. I felt damned glad that I was in hospital. I tried to imagine the boys of the Bat going forward eagerly to the attack and sweeping all before them, but failed. All I could imagine was men going forward because there was nothing else for it.

The first part of the reports about successes was probably right enough. We were quickly disillusioned about the casualty part of it. A rumour came from nowhere that all except actual bed cases were going to be sent to the con.

camps. At first we put it down to " only a yarn " because of its manifest absurdity, but we soon had official confirmation of its accuracy.

" I'm sorry, but you'll have to go with the rest," said the doctor to me. " There's an extra large convoy coming and we simply have to make room for it, nothing else for it. You will have to take care of yourself for a while until you get strong again, remember."

" Yes, sir," I said.

" I suppose you thought you were going to peg out when you arrived at first," he went on jovially.

" Why, no, sir. I never thought of that," I answered honestly, filled with belated apprehension.

" Oh, well. I wouldn't have blamed you if you had," he concluded, clapping me on the back.

We drew our uniforms from the store, packed kitbags, and departed.

The camp we went to first was just below the hospital. It was more of a clearing house, and meals and parades and sleeping accommodation were makeshift affairs.

It was one of those uncomfortable places where a man didn't know whether he would be there for an hour or a week. I was in it for two days. A score of different regiments were represented in each marquee, and I was alone in a crowd. The rest were in the same case, but they seemed to hang together after a fashion. The ones who had been slightly wounded and were now all right physically were less self-centred. They made up to each other and swopped yarns and were in the van when the " Cookhouse door " blew. Others, pale and weak from hospital, were quieter and sat disconsolately on their kitbag or lay most of the time on the single blanket served out as bedding between them and the floor. I felt very unsure of myself and shy, like a newly joined recruit. Parades were frequent, but they resolved themselves into interminable roll-calls, which ended nowhere. One time I was put into one squad and then after another taking of names would find myself in another one.

My thoughts were continually straying back to the hospital, the ward, and what they would be doing there now. If it was morning they would be tidying up for the doctor on his rounds. Afternoon, and we would be sitting on our beds reading or gossiping. Evening, and the ward would be still, the nurse flitting about giving medicine or seeing to little things. There would be a newcomer in my bed.

I heard some of the others talking of a nearby estaminet, and went along to it and sipped wine until my money was done. I had only a couple of francs and they were soon spent. It was strange to sit in a café again, and the thin wine sent a little glow through me. I sat in a corner and made it last as long as I could. If I had had more money and some company I would have got drunk. Very few in the camp had money. A fellow in the marquee I was in went round offering to sell a German revolver for ten francs, and then for five. It was a good souvenir, but there were no takers. For some reason it was forbidden to have revolvers as souvenirs. They were much lighter than our Lewis-gunners' revolvers, and made a different wound perhaps. Anyone caught with one was severely punished, so the would-be seller was doubly handicapped in his search for money.

Lorries arrived and we departed for the convalescent camp.

It was on the dunes near a place called Wimereux. It consisted of a collection of drab, smoke-grimed huts built around a big, bleak square. It was a cold, desolate place. The billowing sand banked against the huts was like stained snow.

I was hungry when I arrived, and remained hungry all the time I was there. At meal times men crowded into the dining huts, sunk in the sand, and ate like wolves, hardly savouring the rough food before gulping it down. Those who missed the " first house " had to hang about outside until the luckier ones were finished. N.C.O.s were posted to see that nobody worked the double.

At the other end of the square from where I was a canteen catered for those with money—mostly Colonials and N.C.O.s—who eked out the rations with biscuits, tinned meats and tea. The canteen was run by some Church crowd, but it was a strictly commercial concern. No money no grub.

Those without money hung about watching the others eat. There was the usual concert party, complete with principal " girl " and stock jokes. I wandered about by myself, taking a curious, almost unconscious, pleasure in being alone. More and more I disliked having to mix with others. Why, I didn't know, except that once away from the trenches I seemed to lose touch with the ordinary simplicity of talk and outlook of my neighbours. Up the line I wouldn't have cared tuppence about them, knowing that everybody had the same thoughts. Now I felt like a fish out of water.

In the morning after breakfast we lined up and went down the dunes towards the shore for games, and the same in the afternoon. Constant exercise was necessary to keep warm in the cold October wind and we needed little urging. The " games " started with handball. Each squad made a ring and the ball was thrown about jerkily, the man that muffed a catch being laughed at. Tactful instructors sedulously fostered the fun. I enjoyed it, but when we progressed on to physical jerks and football and leapfrog I didn't get on so well.

The instructor sent me to the camp doctor, who after the usual rigmarole with a stethoscope gave me the usual kettle of steam to suck. I had the rest of the day off. When I went back to him next day he told me not to bother doing any more parades.

" It's not much good your stopping here, my lad," he

said gruffly. " This isn't the right place for you. How long were you in hospital ? "

" Since the beginning of September, sir."

" Humph. All right. Run along now, and I'll see about you."

I went off obediently, wondering what he meant.

" I'll do damned well if he lets me off parades for a few days until I get properly on my feet," I thought, vaguely comforted, as I lay down in the hut. There were worse places than Wimereux, and I would be all right if I was left alone. I put the trouble down to the sudden change from the soft hospital life.

That same night after " Lights Out " the fellow next to me spoke to me for the first time. He was a Canadian, nearly six feet in height and big boned, but only a youngster.

He wasn't nineteen yet, he said, and I believed him. He had a big unformed face. His husky voice, with its broad a's, trembled slightly as he spoke of his home in Alberta. He was the first one I had wanted to talk to in the camp, and I plied him with questions about his beloved Canada. He replied slowly, taking time to think out the answers as if afraid of giving me a wrong impression. I liked him for that—no shove on.

" It's a great country so long as you have a proper home in it, or were born in it, of course, like me. It's tough on the new settlers at first.

" I would be glad if this war was over and I was back home," he went on wistfully, " but you see I've only been out three or four months, so there isn't much hope. What do you think ? "

He was the only Canadian I had met, and all he said was interesting.

A loud conversation started in the hut and we had to stop whispering. One fellow, a Jock, launched into a tale of the doings of his Division in some push, for the benefit of a

2 G

Guardsman on the opposite side. When the Guardsman, a rather undersized individual with a moustache, interrupted to recount in an off-hand voice some feat of the Guards' Division, the Jock accorded him a respectful, brother-in-arms hearing, although obviously impatient to get on with the tale of his own crowd's doings under a terrible one-armed Major, who, like Gordon before him, had gone armed with a cane.

" We went over kicking a football—you should have seen us," said the Jock. He had a pale freckled face and a lose down-drawn mouth.

" When the Guards came up Jerry damned soon chased off," went on the Guardsman negligently. " He knew when he was up against it."

" We took no prisoners," said the Jock excitedly, " just went through them like a dose of salts. One put up his hands to me and shouted ' Kamerad.' I stuck my bayonet in his guts and ripped him open. You should have seen his face."

" I know," said the Guardsman, " like a stuck pig."

" That's it. Just like that."

The other men in the hut maintained a stolid silence. By and by the two heroes noticed that they had the conversation to themselves, and stopped.

Next day I was ordered to parade with my kitbag. I hadn't the slightest idea what for, but was rather surprised when presently I found myself, along with half a dozen others, in a slow-moving train in charge of a taciturn Sergeant. It was a change, and it was the habit of infantry to pin their hopes to change, on the principle that things couldn't be worse and might be better. The con. camp was the place where unwilling men were made ready again for the slaughter.

Rain was falling when we arrived at a bare little station. I had been in it once before and knew at once where we were bound for. It was the station where I had entrained from Le Havre for the line with the draft.

It was late in the afternoon, and we were glad to stretch our legs. We had been cooped in a third-class carriage. We went along a muddy road for a few kilometres and reached the Base. There were no troops to be seen and everything had a dingy miserable air in keeping with the cold raw day. The rain came down in a heavy drizzle. We walked on and on, getting wetter with every step. The clusters of huts and dining-rooms forming the different Divisional bases were left behind and I wondered where we were bound for.

It was a long walk for the likes of us. My kitbag, though it was barely quarter full, began to feel unconscionably heavy. It was a long time now since I had carried a pack or done any route marching. We sweated and ached in our damp clothes. The others groused, but I slogged on silently. "It's a rotten business, but there are no shells falling and I can stick the rain surely," I thought, finding a peculiar happiness in the discomfort. Somewhere in front shelter was awaiting us, and the false heat of the march kept me warm.

At length we halted. It was getting dark, but we made out a long galvanised iron hut—a combined orderly room, store and corée house. A sentry paced to and fro along the covered verandah. The taciturn Sergeant went up the wooden steps and disappeared through one of the doors. We stood fatalistically, looking at the smart sheltered sentry. He took no notice of us, pacing up and down like an automaton, clicking his heels sharply at the turnabout and looking straight to his front. One of the men asked him for a match, but he didn't stop.

"Look at the lousy base-wallah," growled the others deep in their throats.

"Knows as much about soldiering as a W.A.A.C."

A strange Sergeant appeared, drawing a waterproof sheet over his shoulders as if rain was something to be carefully guarded against. He was followed by a nondescript, bare-headed private carrying a big bundle. Without a word the orderly handed each of us a skimpy blanket and went indoors hurriedly.

"This way, boys," said the Sergeant encouragingly, hunching his shoulders, and we followed obediently as he led us along the dark road. A few yards past the orderly room he turned to the left and led the way down a rocky path, streaming with water, to where lines of bell-tents stood. Even in the bad light I could see that they were much the worse for wear. The sides of each one were patched and torn, and the canvas shrunken and discoloured. The guy ropes stood out like ribs on an old corpse. When we had reached the first of the double row lining the sloping path the Sergeant waved his hand in a wide, sweeping gesture.

"Pick any one you fancy, boys. They're all half empty," he called out, and departed the way he had come.

Poking my head inside the flap of the nearest I looked round. A couple of men were lying on the ground wrapped in their blankets, their knees drawn up to their chin.

"Any room, mates?" I asked perfunctorily, more by way of advertising my presence, and fumbled with the laced flaps, tight and slippy with the rain, preparatory to entering. One of the men looked up.

"There's plenty of room, mate," he said, with emphasis on the "room," "but the place is waterlogged, you needn't come in here."

Looking closer I saw he was right. The only near dry spot was where he and his companion lay. The rest of the ground space was taken up by a channel of muddy water, which wandered in under the canvas at one end and across and out at the other, being joined with numerous little tributaries as it went.

" Right you are," I said, and withdrew hastily.

The other men who had arrived with me had gone off, and I found myself on my own.

I tried the next tent in the row. There was half a dozen men in it, lying bunched together to the left of the pole.

" Full up, mate," said the end one nearest the entrance without looking up, in reply to my question. The same stream, or possibly a different one, zig-zagged along beside him.

" No room at all ? " I asked shyly.

" No, mate, not an inch."

I wandered listlessly down the line. The rain beat down, but I was wet through now and didn't care overmuch. There was a certain satisfaction in being able to defy it to do its worst. I came to the last tent in the row. There was nobody in it for the good and sufficient reason that the floor was mostly under water. Little bumpy patches here and there rose clear. I was dog-tired now. The blanket I had got served out with was wet too.

I pulled open the flap and went in. It was a job getting it laced up again, but I succeeded in a sort of way, and selected what appeared to be the driest part by feeling the ground. Doubling the blanket I lay down between the fold with the overcoat on top and my rolled-up kitbag for a pillow. The damp crept into my bones, but I felt content. I was alone, and I knew that that was what I wanted more than anything else. I could cough and spit, and talk to myself, or I could mumble strings of curses. I smiled at the thought. The rain had become heavier, but it had a friendly sound as it drummed down. I had it to thank for being on my own instead of jammed in among a crowd of strangers.

THE FINISH

THERE was a routine about our little camp. In the morning there was roll-call, after which we went down the road to a big dining hall and had breakfast. As soon as we got back the Sergeant paraded us and warned off fatigue parties. Some returned to the dining-room and washed up the hundreds of dirty dishes used for the meal. Others went here, there and everywhere scrubbing, cleaning and carrying. The same process was repeated after dinner, and after tea the dishwashers went back another time. I was generally on dining-hall fatigue. At first I thought I was on to a good thing in the way of getting more grub, but there was nothing doing. The food served up was hopelessly inadequate and vilely cooked. After each meal there wasn't so much as a crust or a spoonful of stew left on the plates. Still, the dish-water was pleasantly hot.

The evenings were free, and I wandered about. There was a score of different regiments represented in our camp, but as it happened I was the only representative of mine, which made for solitariness.

I was in a crowded Y.M.C.A. canteen a couple of nights later out of the rain when I ran into Watson, who had been the latest recruit to the company station back in the battalion. I caught his arm, surprised at seeing a face I knew. He looked me up and down doubtfully at first, his attention partly distracted by trying to keep a cup of " char " he was carrying from being spilled.

" Why, we all thought you were done in that night you left with the message for Brigade, you and that other young skitter, what's his name. What happened to him ? "

" Beck. He kicked the bucket in hospital, I think."

" Ay, young Beck. We heard about it afterwards. What, were you hit ? "

" No, gassed."

" Well, by the look of you you won't be far behind him if you're not careful. Why, man, you're like a scarecrow."

There was a derisive frankness in the way he looked me up and down, taking in the tunic that hung on me like a sack—it was a bad fit anyway.

" And what are you doing here ? " I asked, to turn the talk. There didn't seem to be anything the matter with him.

" Oh, I was out mending the line one morning and clicked for a bullet through the arm. It was through the fleshy part, and didn't hit a bone, worse luck, or it would have been a Blighty one."

There was nothing more to be said.

We exchanged perfunctory " Good lucks " and he left me to elbow his way to a table.

A loud rumble of conversation filled the hut. Men jostled their way to the counter and came away from it holding plates of pastry and steaming cups of tea and coffee in the air. The smell of damp uniforms mingled with cigarette smoke. From groups at the tables excited oaths came as yarns were swapped of the doing of this or that mob or division. Faces were sweaty in the heated air.

I had no money. There had been no need for it in hospital, and I had been afraid to send home for some when I came out in case I should be shifted about and never receive it. Even if I had had money I wouldn't have stayed.

" Like a scarecrow."

I hadn't given a thought lately to what I looked like, and there were no looking-glasses to show me. But the men about me were red-faced and healthily carefree. Again a belated apprehensiveness seized me. I left the canteen and stood in the dimly-lighted hall-way for a minute, nerving myself to go out into the rain, feeling like an outcast. A bareheaded man in a smooth, olive-tinted uniform, who had been standing at the door came over. Putting his hand familiarly on my arm he reached something towards me.

"It's very wet outside, and you might as well stay," he said persuasively.

I stared at him without replying, wondering what he was getting at. The raw night air caught at my throat after the close atmosphere of the canteen.

"That's right, my boy," said the man softly, taking silence for consent.

He pressed a slim, limp-backed book into my hand.

"Stay for what?" I asked.

"Why, for the praise service. Christ Jesus died for us all on Calvary's Cross. There will be some hymns. That is the hymn-book. Then there will be a few minutes' talk and prayer. We want all you dear lads to attend and give thanks."

A fit of coughing occupied my attention for a moment.

"Good. You'll stop then. The service will commence in a few minutes," he said, patting me on the back.

Hysterical rage flooded me. This was the last of a long list of insults and indignities. Throwing off his arm, I flung the book violently from me. "Go to blazes, you and your rotten service," I cried, and blundering through the door ran out quickly into the rain and darkness in case he might try to get me into trouble.

Once well clear of the hut I stopped. I felt exultant, and repeated slowly what I had said, savouring each word, and thinking of how many other things I could have said when I was at it, each more brutal, cynical and blasphemous than the last. But the pelting rain warned me at length to get a move on. I tramped back to the hut, stopping now and then to live over the scene and curse afresh at the bare idea of attending a praise service or any other service.

"The Bible-thumper didn't know what he was raving about," I decided, but in some obscure way I felt that at last I had had the opportunity of asserting long dormant feelings of hatred and disgust at the hypocrisy of a religion which went blandly hand in hand with ferocious cruelty, slaughter and savagery.

The reason why I had been discharged from the camp became clear. Instead of going on dining-room fatigue I was warned off, along with a dozen others, to appear before a medical board. They were all crocks in our camp. We paraded by ourselves and marched off to another part of the base which I had never been in before. After spending most of the morning waiting our turn I went into a hut and was put through a stiff examination by a couple of suspicious doctors. One was a Colonel and the other a Major. They were elderly, dried-up men who had long since lost their bedside manner. They gave sharp orders, and when they asked sharp questions pretended to take no notice of the answers.

On the afternoon parade the Sergeant gave the results of the Board. Three or four men were told to pack up then and there and clear off to their regimental bases. They obeyed unwillingly. They were for it again. The rest of us had been made " category " men, B.1., B.2., B.3.

I was B.3., which I understood to mean " Fit for garrison duty only," but the others weren't so sure.

" We'll be sent up the line just the same, wait till y'see," they prophesied gloomily.

" B.1 men might have to go, but not B.3 surely ? "

" It makes little odds. There's whole divisions of B. men in the line. All the hopeless wrecks that could hobble along. The only way you can be sure you're out now is when you've lost a leg or an arm or got blinded. Anything does to stop a shell nowadays. They've discovered that there'll be no cushy jobs for the likes of us."

" Come along. Come along. Stop that gabbling there," broke in the Sergeant. " You, you and you go along to the dining-room fatigue, and you, you and you come along with me. The orderly room and guard-room have to be scrubbed out."

The talk about divisions of B. men shocked me. The Army was hard up for men when it fell back on them, but I knew in my heart that I would never see the line again.

I went to a Y.M.C.A. hut, a different one, and wrote a letter home. There was a certain comfort in doing that now. " Dear mother, I am all right again, but I think I will be kept here at the base, so you needn't worry about me any more. The doctor at the convalescent camp said there was no need for me to stop there. I wash dishes most of the time now, so I'll be able to show you a thing or two when I come home." I also sent a note to my brother.

He came up to see me a couple of nights later. He had some money and stood a supper in the canteen. It was very odd to be sitting amongst a crowd of strangers talking to a strange Engineer who was also my brother. He had been around Dunkirk all summer, and had only returned to Le Havre in September. According to him the conditions in both places had been worse than in the line. He broke into an account of his adventures since I had seen him last. His voice seemed to have taken on a new accent and I listened more to the sound of it than to what he was saying. It was becoming increasingly difficult to take an interest in anything. He was talking more by rote anyhow, and looked away hastily when I caught his eyes fixed on me. On the way back to my tent he wanted to know if I had written home since leaving the hospital.

" Mother says you write very seldom and only a few lines at a time. What did you tell her ? "

" Just that I was back at the Base and in no danger of going up the line. That's the main thing, isn't it ? "

" I'll be writing home one of these days myself—to-night, when I get back, probably. I'll tell them I saw you. But you're not looking well. You've got a cold, too. If mother knew, she might want to send out a parcel with some kind of tonic in it and some warm underwear. I tell you what. I'll give you what I have on. It's not very clean, but it's dry and I only put the socks on this morning."

" Not at all, man. I'm all right," I said, perturbed by his kindness.

He persisted and, stripping off his uniform, gave me his underclothes.

" I'll hardly catch the cold on the way back, so I'll not take yours. But you should try and get into another tent. This one's very damp."

" San fairy Ann, man. They're all the same."

My brother departed. I felt glad when he had gone. It was better to be on one's own. Still, it was decent of him. going back with only his uniform on, in a cold night. And he might be crimed for being short one shirt, one pair of drawers and one pair of socks. It was a mistake, though, for when I lay down I would soon be as badly off as before. Our ramshackle tents, which had probably been put up when the Base was first started, were worse than useless when it rained.

We kept on grousing half-heartedly, but there was nobody to pay any heed. No officers came near us. We were a little community on our own and only useful for dirty fatigues—men whom it was nobody's business to care for.

When the Armistice came I heard the news almost apathetically. My armistice had already arrived. A dull anger rose in me. I had been cheated.

" Cough."

" Say ninety-nine."

" Mark time at the double."

" Again."

And all for nothing. The whole British Army had suddenly become category men without the formality of first becoming casualties. I had pitied the unlucky ones as they packed their kits and departed with downcast faces for their regimental depots. They had been considered well enough to go back and do another bit for King and Country. All the time they had been the lucky ones.

According to the papers the Germans had been on their last legs for months past. It didn't seem to have occurred to anybody that the British Army, with the possible exception of Australians and Canadians, had been on their last legs too. It wasn't the British infantry that had beaten the German infantry, and we knew it. In our hearts we had known ourselves for what we were—slave men, without sufficient courage to break the bonds.

I stood outside a canteen listening to the cheers and hearty choruses of men who a few short hours ago had had nothing to look forward to but a cynical half-contemptuous, " Up the line and the best of luck." The Armistice meant something to them, so they gave vent to their relief.

The men who had been dug in in soft jobs about the Base weren't just quite so enthusiastic.

Amidst all the excitement a disturbing feeling crept over me that I, like many another, was one of the mugs. Already —miraculously—the war was receding.

Armistice !

We didn't know how to pronounce the word even, but with every passing minute its meaning and implications became clearer.

Peace !

Home !

Back to work !

Soon everybody would be out of uniform. Civilians.

Men whom the war had left unscathed—who had jobs to

go back to, or who were good tradesmen and knew their worth—drew a little apart from the rest. Visualising peace, they totted up their chances.

The false comradeship of war would become a thing of the past, to be forgotten as soon as possible—to be ashamed of, even. There would be the same old distinctions of tinker, tailor, soldier, sailor, rich man, beggar man, thief. Perhaps more so. Another sort of war, in a different setting.

From the town below the sound of bells came faintly, continuously. I wandered down past the tents to where a little rustic bridge spanned the stream forming the Base boundary. A small crowd of infantry stood staring longingly at the bridge, and at two military policemen barring the way.

" Every man must have a pass to get into Le Havre," said one M.P. flatly, and turned his back.

" But all our officers have gone off and there's nobody to dish passes out."

" But, Corporal, it's the Armistice. What do passes matter for once ? "

The M.P.s took no notice.

The men cursed beneath their breath and then out loud, calling the police filthy names. Urging each other on they pressed forward threateningly, but helpless.

The pair had their revolvers and the men were unarmed.

In another week or two the hated Red Caps would be lying low while half-starved mutinous men set fire to dining halls and assaulted Colonels who tried to placate them with promises. Such things were undreamt of as yet.

The police held the bridge, fingering their weapons ostentatiously.

" God damn it," said a man bitterly. " The Froggies have gone mad in the town. They say the streets are running with booze." The speaker had up four wound stripes.

Others took up the tale, glaring with hate-filled eyes at the policemen, big and healthy.

" That's right. Oceans of the stuff. And all buckshee."

" Vin blanc, rum and cognac, and even champagne—all for the taking——"

" They say the women are throwing themselves at the boys. All mad, and all for love."

" And the lousy base-wallahs are clicking for it all ; ones that never saw a shot fired, while we——"

For a while I hung about the outskirts of the angry crowd, listening and sympathising, but for myself I felt no desire to share in the rejoicings down in the town.

All I was conscious of was an uneasy dread such as I had often felt up the line when shelling was going on. An overwhelming desire to escape, if only for a little while, from all this topsy-turvydom possessed me. Almost unconsciously I directed my steps to the camp.

There at any rate things were the same. The damp blanket that I wrapped about me. The damp overcoat. The particular remembered stones beneath that I had to fit my body to and the kitbag with its bundle of damp underclothing for pillow.

" This is a damned funny place for a fellow just out of hospital, Armistice or no Armistice," I thought, hugging loneliness to me. " And I might be here for months to come, for all winter."

It was almost dark in the tent. I lay staring at the discoloured canvas. Then lighting the butt of a cigarette I watched the smoke as it curled lazily upwards, and how it eddied and scattered when it tickled my throat.

A few deep mouthfuls always brought ease, and I lay quiet again, listening to far-away pealing of bells in the town. There was something unsettling about the sound. For a while I took no notice. Then, obeying a sudden impulse, I turned over on to my right side, leaving my dud ear uppermost. The sound of the bells, with their tale of glad tidings, ceased.

To occupy my thoughts I started puzzling out what day it was, so that I should always remember. Then the date— 10th, 11th, 12th ? When had I left the camp ? What date was the medical board ? That was it. The 11th. The 11th day of November.

But there was something familiar about that date ? Didn't it recall something ? I puzzled my brains. The 11th of November ! What could it be ?

Quite easily recollection came. It was my birthday and I was nineteen years of age that day. For a time I played with this surprising discovery. It was almost as if there was something mystical about it or something.

How did it come that I had fallen into the habit of thinking of my father and mother as very old people ? Whenever I thought of them at all, that was. Each time, in imagination, they had been more stooped and grey and wrinkled.

And it was only a year—less than a year—since I had bade good-bye to them at the railway station. Why, they were the same age, for what did a few months here or there mean to people on the wrong side of fifty ? Nothing. A mere bagatelle.

For that matter, what were a few months more or less to a chap in his teens, to whom one day was much the same as the next ? But this business about ages seemed less important the more I pondered it. I felt drowsy and turned and twisted, seeking greater ease.

Once more the sound of the bells came, a faint epitome of victory and peace—of a sad people rejoicing. What had I to do with peace, who was only a relic of the war ?

An ugly question.

By way of answer a little thought came. I smiled, wryly at first, and then with a curious, inexplicable satisfaction.

There was the first night in the trenches—the raid—the 21st of March and the forgotten rearguard actions—the Colonel and the mad Adjutant—Butcher Brown. Afterwards the holes in the mud and the trenches—No Man's Land—Jenkins on the stretcher—the message to brigade—Beck and the gurgle.

What, after all, had I to do with war ? I searched my memory again. And again the answer came, softly mocking. Nothing.

I had never fired a shot. I had never wanted to fire a shot. I had never been a soldier.

THE END